BASIC
**An Introduction to
Computer Programming
with the Apple**

Brooks/Cole Series in Computer Science

Program Design with Pseudocode
T. E. Bailey and K. A. Lundgaard

BASIC: An Introduction to Computer Programming with the Apple
Robert J. Bent and George C. Sethares

BASIC: An Introduction to Computer Programming, Second Edition
Robert J. Bent and George C. Sethares

Business BASIC
Robert J. Bent and George C. Sethares

FORTRAN with Problem Solving: A Structured Approach
Robert J. Bent and George C. Sethares

Beginning BASIC
Keith Carver

Beginning Structured COBOL
Keith Carver

Structured COBOL for Microcomputers
Keith Carver

Learning BASIC Programming: A Systematic Approach
Howard Dachslager, Masato Hayashi, and Richard Zucker

Problem Solving and Structured Programming with ForTran 77
Martin O. Holoien and Ali Behforooz

Basic Business BASIC: Using Microcomputers
Peter Mears and Louis Raho

Brooks/Cole Series in Computer Education

An Apple for the Teacher: Fundamentals of Instructional Computing
George Culp and Herbert Nickles

RUN: Computer Education
Dennis O. Harper and James H. Stewart

BASIC

An Introduction to Computer Programming with the Apple

Robert J. Bent
George C. Sethares

Bridgewater State College

Brooks/Cole Publishing Company

Monterey, California

Dedicated to Eleanor T. Keane
and to the memory of
John F. Rogan
Marjorie L. Southwick
Howard R. Sample

Brooks/Cole Publishing Company
A Division of Wadsworth, Inc.

© 1983 by Wadsworth, Inc., Belmont, California 94002.

Printed in the United States of America
10 9 8 7 6 5 4

Library of Congress Cataloging in Publication Data

Bent, Robert J. (date)
    BASIC: an introduction to computer programming
with the Apple.

    Includes index.
    1. Apple computer—Programming. 2. Basic (Computer
program language) I. Sethares, George C. (date)
II. Title.
QA76.8.A66B46 1983   001.64'24   82-20572
ISBN 0-534-01370-8

Subject Editor: *James Leisy, Jr.*
Production Editor: *Marlene Thom*
Manuscript Editor: *Don Yoder*
Interior and Cover Design: *Victoria A. Van Deventer*
Illustrations: *Tim Keenan*
Typesetting: *Graphic Typesetting Service, Los Angeles, California*

□ □ □ □ □ □ □ □ □ □ □ □ □ □

Preface

This book is intended to serve as an introduction to computer programming in the environment of an Apple computer system. The programming language used is an extended version of BASIC for Apple computers called Applesoft BASIC. No prior experience with computers or computer programming languages is assumed. Included are descriptions of the computer equipment you will encounter and procedures for using this equipment. The programming language Applesoft BASIC is described in detail and illustrated in numerous examples. Most of the material is semitutorial and intended to be studied with an Apple close at hand. For beginning programmers, hands-on experience with a real computer is the most effective way to learn about computers.

We wrote this book with two principal goals in mind. First, we felt it important to present the elements of Applesoft BASIC so that meaningful computer programs could be written at the earliest possible time. We adhere to the notion that one learns by doing. As a result, problem solving is emphasized from the beginning, and the various aspects of Applesoft BASIC are introduced only as needed. Our second goal was to write a book that would serve as a general introduction to computer programming, not just to a programming language. Simply describing a variety of computer applications and ways to go about writing BASIC programs for these applications does not constitute an introduction to programming. What is required is a consideration of the entire programming process.

The approach we have taken toward this objective is to introduce programming principles only as they can be understood and appreciated in the context of the applications being considered. For example, a beginning programmer can easily appreciate the necessity of choosing variable names and determining how they are related. Hence, this step is introduced and discussed very early. On the other hand, the value of modularization—that is, breaking down a long and possibly complex task into more manageable subtasks—is not so easily grasped in the context of the straightforward programming problems first encountered. As natural as modularization may appear to an experienced programmer, a beginner must "see" its usefulness before being convinced of its value. Therefore, this programming principle, although illustrated in the early examples, is not discussed as a programming principle until later in the book.

A few remarks are appropriate concerning the order in which we have introduced the elements of Applesoft BASIC. The INPUT statement (Chapter 5) is introduced early and before the READ and DATA statements to emphasize the interactive nature of BASIC. The GOTO statement is presented with the INPUT statement so that the nature of the computer as a fast and sophisticated calculator can be shown early. The IF statement is introduced in the very next chapter so that certain difficulties arising from the use of GOTO statements can quickly be resolved. Chapters 7 through 9 (more on the PRINT statement, FOR/NEXT loops, and the READ/DATA statements) complete what is often called Elementary BASIC. Selecting an order in which to present the remaining BASIC statements was not so simple. So that a person using the text will not be tied down to the order we have chosen, the introductory material for the remaining BASIC statements is presented in such a way that these statements can be easily taken in any order after Chapter 9.

Following are several special features of this book.

An early introduction of string variables. String variables are introduced with the numerical variables, and their use is illustrated throughout the text.

An introductory chapter on problem solving. In Chapter 2, the terms *algorithm* and *variable* are defined, and the sense in which computer programs and algorithms are equivalent is explained. Also, the steps leading to the discovery of algorithms to carry out specified tasks (that is, the steps involved in problem solving) are discussed and illustrated by example.

An early introduction to top-down programming. The method of top-down programming is used from the very beginning. It is introduced in Chapter 2 (without giving the method a name) and illustrated in many of the worked-out examples throughout the text. In addition, a separate chapter (Chapter 10) summarizes the method of top-down programming.

A separate section (Section 6.9) on structured programming. The flowchart constructs used in structured programming are described, and the terms *structured algorithm* and *structured program* are defined. A sequence of short examples shows how the structured programming constructs are easily coded in the BASIC language. Also, the benefits to be gained by writing structured programs are discussed.

A complete chapter on data files. Both sequential-access files (Section 14.1) and random-access files (Section 14.5) are described together with programming techniques used in file processing. A separate section on file maintenance is included.

Graphics. Complete descriptions of the Apple's low-resolution graphics (Section 17.1) and high-resolution graphics (Section 17.5) are given. Examples include, among others, a kaleidoscope program and a video-game illustration.

We wish to take this opportunity to acknowledge the helpful comments and criticisms of our reviewers: Allen Holbert, Cabrillo College; Mary K. Keller, Clarke College; and Rebecca H. Montgomery, Edmonds Community College. We feel that their many thoughtful suggestions have led to a greatly improved book.

A very special thanks goes to Patricia Shea, our typist, proofreader, debugger, and general assistant. Her six years of cheerful cooperation are greatly appreciated. Finally, we are happy to acknowledge the fine cooperation of the staff at Brooks/Cole Publishing Company.

Robert J. Bent
George C. Sethares

Contents

4

First Session at the Apple Keyboard   33

5

Interacting with the Computer   47

6

The Computer as a Decision Maker   61

7

More on the PRINT Statement   97

13 More on Processing String Data   207

14 Data Files   225

15 Subroutines   259

16 Random Numbers and Their Application   271

17 Graphics   291

1

□ □ □ □ □ □ □ □ □ □ □ □ □ □ □

Apple Computer Systems

Any device that can receive, store, process, and transmit data (information)—and can also receive and store the instructions to process these data—is called a **computer.** Figure 1.1 shows an Apple® personal computer.* The *main board* shown in the figure contains many miniaturized electronic and magnetic devices together with circuitry interconnecting them. The main board is the computer component that can receive, store, process, and transmit data. The case that houses it also contains a keyboard at which you can type any data and instructions that are to be transmitted to the computer.

A **computer system** is any group of interrelated components that includes a computer as one of its principal elements. Figure 1.2 shows an Apple computer system that includes an Apple computer, video display screen, two disk units, and a printer for producing printed documents.

A computer system has the ability to store large quantities of data, to process these data at very fast rates, and to present the results of this processing in ways that are meaningful to the task at hand. If the task is to prepare a payroll, for example, employee data will be transmitted to the computer, the computer will process these data to calculate relevant wage statistics, and the results will be presented in printed form, possibly including paychecks. This payroll example illustrates the three principal tasks involved in every computer application: data must be presented to the computer **(INPUT),** data must be processed **(PROCESS),** and results must be presented in a useful way **(OUTPUT).** (See Figure 1.3.)

The purpose of this chapter is not to convince you that a computer can do many things, nor even to indicate the computer applications you will be able to carry out after completing this book. Rather, our objectives are to acquaint you with the types of computer equipment you may encounter as part of your Apple system, to describe what a computer program is, and to introduce certain terminology that is helpful when talking about computers.

*Apple is a registered trademark of Apple Computer, Inc.

Figure 1.1
Apple II computer with
cover removed. *(Apple and
the Apple logo are registered
trademarks of Apple Computer,
Inc.)*

Figure 1.2
An Apple computer
system. *(Courtesy of Apple
Computer, Inc. Apple and the
Apple logo are registered
trademarks of Apple Computer,
Inc.)*

Figure 1.3
An INPUT-PROCESS-
OUTPUT diagram.

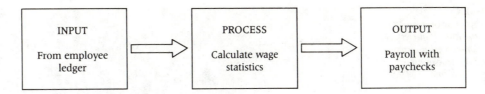

1.1 Computer hardware

The principal function of a computer is to process data. The computer component that does this is called the **central processing unit (CPU).** The Apple's CPU is called a **microprocessor** because of its microminiaturized circuitry. It is an *integrated circuit* about the size of a fingernail and is housed in a container labeled 6502 (see Figure 1.4.).* The 6502 microprocessor can perform more than 50 different operations and can carry out over 500,000 of these in a single second. Computers, such as the Apple, whose CPUs are microprocessors are called **microcomputers.**

In addition to the CPU, every computer has a **memory unit** that can store data for processing. This memory unit consists of thousands of memory locations, each with its own address. The term **random access memory (RAM)** is used when referring to a computer's memory. This term indicates that any memory location can be referenced directly by specifying its address. The Apple's RAM consists of ICs placed on the main board as shown in Figure 1.4. It is *volatile* memory—that is, when you turn the power off, everything stored in RAM is lost. Fortunately, you need not understand how your Apple stores and processes data to make it work for you. The circuitry in a computer is not unlike that in an ordinary pocket calculator, and anyone who has used a calculator knows that you don't have to understand its circuitry to use it.

Data must be transmitted to the computer (*input*), and results of the processing must be returned (*output*). Devices that transfer data to and from a computer are called **input and output (I/O) devices.** As you learn computer programming on the Apple you are likely to encounter the following I/O devices, which serve as the principal means of communication between you and the Apple:

Keyboard and *video display screen* (Figure 1.2): You transmit information to the computer simply by typing it at the keyboard and the computer transmits the results back to you by displaying them on the video screen.

Printers: A printer, such as the Silentype shown in Figure 1.2, serves only as an output device. Figure 1.5 shows a *line printer* capable of printing an entire line of output simultaneously. A single line printer can be used as the output device for many Apple computers.

Most modern computer systems are equipped with memory storage devices other than the main memory unit. They are called *external* (or *secondary*) storage devices because, unlike the memory unit, they are not part of the computer. The following external storage devices are used with the Apple computer:

Cassette-tape units: Information is stored on magnetic tapes (cassettes) as sequences of magnetized "spots" by using an ordinary cassette tape recorder. Data are "read" from a tape sequentially until the desired data are found. For this reason, tape units are called *sequential-access devices.*

---

*An integrated circuit (IC) is an electronic circuit that has been etched into a small thin wafer of a glasslike substance such as silicon. A single IC less than a square inch in area can contain several thousand distinct but interconnected electronic components such as transistors and diodes.

Figure 1.4
The Apple's processor and memory unit. *(Courtesy of Apple Computer, Inc. Apple and the Apple logo are registered trademarks of Apple Computer, Inc.)*

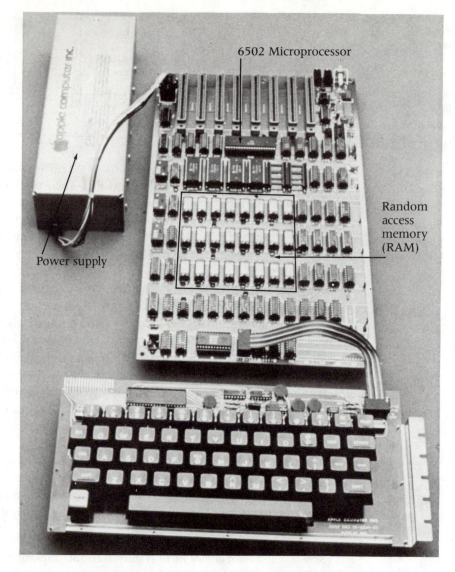

Disk-storage units: Information is stored on rotating *diskettes* that resemble phonograph records. The diskettes have no grooves, however; the data are stored as sequences of magnetized spots appearing on concentric circles. Disk units are called *random-access devices.* The term *random access* indicates that data stored on any part of a disk can be accessed directly without having to read through the entire disk to find the desired data. Figure 1.6 shows an Apple Disk II unit together with a 5¼-inch diskette.

Video display units, printers, tape units, disk units, and all other mechanical and electrical devices other than the computer itself are referred to as **computer peripherals.** The computer and all peripherals constitute the **hardware** of the computer system. Figure 1.7 illustrates the flow of information between a computer and its peripherals.

1.2 Computer software

The physical components, or hardware, of a computer system are inanimate objects. They cannot prepare a payroll or perform any other task, however simple, without human assistance. This assistance is given in the form of instructions to the computer. A sequence of such

Figure 1.5
Dataproducts' B-series band printer. *(Courtesy of Dataproducts Corporation.)*

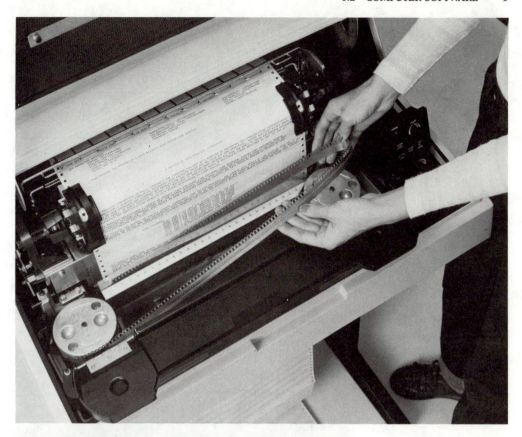

Figure 1.6
Apple Disk II unit with 5¼-inch diskette. *(Apple and the Apple logo are registered trademarks of Apple Computer, Inc.)*

instructions is called a **computer program,** and a person who composes these instructions is called a **programmer.**

The precise form that instructions to a computer must take depends on the computer system being used. **BASIC** (Beginner's All-purpose Symbolic Instruction Code) is a carefully constructed English-like language used for writing computer programs.* **Applesoft BASIC**

*BASIC was developed at Dartmouth College under the direction of John G. Kemeny and Thomas E. Kurtz.

Figure 1.7
Flow of information through
a computer system.

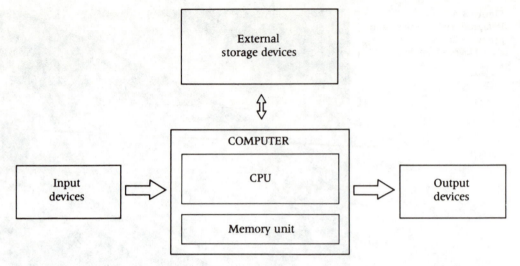

is an extended version of BASIC for Apple computers. Instructions in the BASIC language are designed to be understood by people as well as by the computer. Even the uninitiated will understand the meaning of this simple BASIC program:

```
1 LET A=3
2 LET B=A+5
3 PRINT B
4 END
```

A computer is an electronic device and understands an instruction such as LET A = 3 in a very special way. An electronic device can distinguish between two distinct electrical or magnetic states. Consider, for instance, an ordinary on/off switch for a light fixture. When the switch is in the "on" position, current is allowed to flow and the light bulb glows. If we denote the "on" position by the number 1 and the "off" position by the number 0, we can say that the instruction 1 causes the bulb to glow and the instruction 0 causes it not to glow. In like manner, we could envision a machine with two switches whose positions are denoted by the four codes 00, 01, 10, and 11 such that each of these four codes causes a different event to occur. It is this ability to distinguish between two distinct states that has led to the development of modern computers. Indeed, modern computers are still based on this principle. For example, each memory location in the Apple's RAM can store a sequence of eight 0s and 1s, and one or more such sequences, called *bytes,* can be used to represent either data (in coded form) or instructions to the Apple's processing unit.

As mentioned in Section 1.1, there are more than 50 different instructions that the Apple's 6502 microprocessor can carry out. Together these instructions are called the *machine language* for the Apple. Although the Apple's hardware understands only these machine instructions, you will not be required to write programs in machine language. Your Apple system comes with a **translator** which automatically translates your BASIC instructions into equivalent machine language instructions that are then executed by the computer. There are two essentially different types of BASIC translators, called **interpreters** and **compilers.** An *interpreter* translates a BASIC instruction into machine code each time it is to be carried out; a *compiler* translates an entire program into machine code only once. For this reason, a BASIC program will execute much more rapidly on computers that use compilers than on computers that use interpreters. The difference can be significant! Because of their limited memory capacity, most microcomputers, including the Apple, use interpreters.

BASIC interpreters and compilers are themselves computer programs. They are called **systems programs** because they are an integral part of the computer system itself. The BASIC programs in this book, as well as the programs you will write, are called **applications programs.** They are not an integral part of the computer system, so they are not called systems programs. All computer programs, both systems programs and applications programs, are called **computer software.**

In addition to the Applesoft interpreter, your system contains other systems programs. Perhaps the most important of these are programs that allow you to use a disk unit as an external storage device. These include programs to store information on diskettes, to retrieve any information previously stored on a diskette, and to perform several other useful tasks

Figure 1.8
Apple system in an office setting. *(Courtesy of Apple Computer, Inc. Apple and the Apple logo are registered trademarks of Apple Computer, Inc.)*

Figure 1.9
Apple system in an
educational
setting. *(Courtesy of Apple
Computer, Inc. Apple and the
Apple logo are registered
trademarks of Apple Computer,
Inc.)*

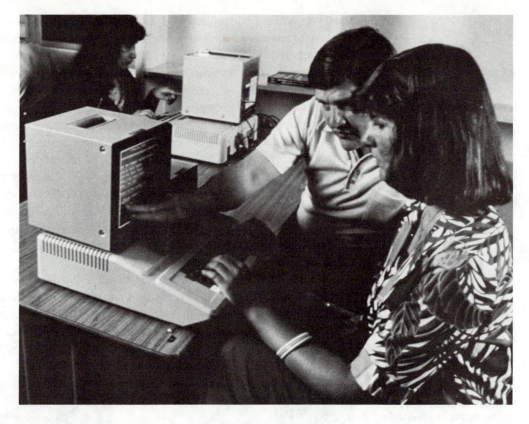

involving disk units. Together, all systems programs designed to carry out disk operations are called the **disk operating system (DOS).**

The emergence of computer science as a new discipline has been accompanied by a proliferation of new words and expressions. Although they are useful for talking about computers, they are for the most part absolutely unnecessary if your objective is to learn a computer language such as BASIC to help you solve problems. In our discussion of computer hardware and software, we have introduced only fundamental concepts and basic terminology. Even so, if this is your first exposure to computers, you may feel lost in this terminology. Don't be disheartened: much of the new vocabulary has already been introduced. You will become more familiar with it and recognize its usefulness as you study the subsequent chapters. You will also find it helpful to reread this chapter after you have written a few computer programs.

1.3 Review true-or-false quiz

1. Any electronic device that can process data is called a computer.   T   F
2. Input/output devices, external storage devices, and the central processing unit
   are called computer peripherals.   T   F
3. Any computer whose central processing unit is a microprocessor is called a
   microcomputer.   T   F
4. The terms *microprocessor* and *integrated circuit* are used synonymously.   T   F
5. An automobile that uses a microprocessor to control the gas and air mixture is
   correctly referred to as a computer system.   T   F
6. Whatever information is stored in the Apple's RAM is lost when power to the
   Apple is cut off.   T   F
7. The terms *compiler* and *interpreter* are used synonymously.   T   F

8. A BASIC program written to solve a particular problem is called a systems program.   T   F
9. A computer system must contain at least one printer.   T   F
10. Disk storage units are called *random-access devices* because information stored on a diskette is accessed by randomly searching portions of the diskette until the desired data are found.   T   F
11. The Apple's disk operating system (DOS) is a computer system.   T   F

2

□ □ □ □ □ □ □ □ □ □ □ □ □ □

Problem Solving

A computer program consists of a sequence of instructions to the computer. These instructions describe a step-by-step process for carrying out a specified task. Such a process is called an **algorithm.** Algorithms have been with us since antiquity: the familiar division algorithm was known and used in ancient Greece; the activities of bookkeepers have always been guided by algorithms (an algorithm to determine a tax assessment, an algorithm to calculate a depletion allowance, and so on); even the instructions for assembling a child's new toy are often given as an algorithm.

Since a computer program describes an algorithm, the process of writing computer programs can be equated to the process of discovering algorithms. For this reason, an understanding of what is, and what is not, an algorithm is indispensable to a programmer.

2.1 Algorithms

An algorithm is a prescribed set of well-defined rules and processes for solving a problem in a finite number of steps. Here is an algorithm giving instructions for completing a financial transaction at a drive-in teller port:

    a. Press the call button.
    b. Remove the carrier from the tray.
    c. Place your transaction inside the carrier.
    d. Replace the carrier.
    e. When the carrier returns, remove the transaction.
    f. Replace the carrier.

To see that these six steps describe an algorithm, we must verify that each step is well defined and that the process stops in a finite number of steps. For example, step (a) requires that there be only one call button, and step (b) requires that there be but one tray containing a single carrier. Having verified that each step is well defined, and noting that the process is obviously finite, we are assured that the process does indeed describe an algorithm. Moreover, it should be clear that the algorithm "does" what is claimed.

The previous example illustrates the following three properties of an algorithm:

1. Each step must be well defined—that is, unambiguous.
2. The process must halt in a finite number of steps.
3. The process must do what is claimed.

The following two examples should help you understand what an algorithm is and gain some practice with the process of discovering algorithms.

EXAMPLE 1. Let's find an algorithm to calculate the year-end bonus for all salaried employees in a firm. Employees are to be paid 3% of their annual salary or $400, whichever is larger.

To carry out this task, a payroll clerk might proceed as follows:

a. Open the employee ledger.
b. Turn to the next employee's account.
c. Determine the employee's bonus.
d. Write the employee's name and bonus amount on the bonus sheet.
e. If all bonuses have not been determined, return to step (b).
f. Close the ledger.

It is not difficult to see that these six instructions constitute an algorithm. Each step is well defined, and, since a business can employ only a finite number of people, the algorithm will terminate in a finite number of steps. Moreover, if this algorithm is followed, all employee bonuses will be determined as specified.

Although the algorithm does what was asked, the process could be made more specific by including more detail in step (c). Recalling the method specified for calculating bonus amounts, we can substitute the following for step (c):

c1. Multiply the employee's salary by 0.03 to obtain a tentative bonus.
c2. If the tentative bonus is at least $400, go to step (d).
c3. Set the bonus to $400.

Making this change, or *refinement*, we obtain the following more detailed algorithm:

a. Open the employee ledger.
b. Turn to the next employee's account.
c1. Multiply the employee's salary by 0.03 to obtain a tentative bonus.
c2. If the tentative bonus is at least $400, go to step (d).
c3. Set the bonus to $400.
d. Write the employee's name and bonus amount on the bonus sheet.
e. If all bonuses have not been determined, return to step (b).
f. Close the ledger.

Remark 1   The first algorithm is more general than the second. It describes a process you might follow to determine employee bonuses, however they are to be calculated. The second algorithm can be used only if bonuses are calculated as specified in the problem statement.

Remark 2   Since the first algorithm contains fewer specifics than the second, it is somewhat easier to verify that it does what was asked. Having verified that the first algorithm is correct, to verify that the second algorithm is also correct we need only check that steps (c1), (c2), and (c3) describe the same task as step (c) of the first algorithm.

EXAMPLE 2. Let's find an algorithm to determine the largest number in a list of numbers.

One way to determine the largest number in a list of numbers is to read them one at a time, remembering only the largest of those already read. To help us give a precise description of this process, let's use two symbols:

L   to denote the largest of the numbers already read
N   to denote the number currently being read

The following algorithm can now be written:

a. Read the first number and denote it by L.
b. Read the next number and denote it by N.
c. If L is at least as large as N, skip the next step.
d. Assign the number N to L.
e. If all numbers have not been read, go to step (b).
f. Print the value of L and stop.

To verify this algorithm for the list of numbers

4, 5, 3, 6, 6, 2, 1, 8, 7, 3

we simply proceed step by step through the algorithm, always keeping track of the latest values of L and N. An orderly way to do this is to complete an assignment table as follows:

Algorithm step	L	N
a	4	
b		5
d	5	
b		3
b		6
d	6	
b		6
b		2
b		1
b		8
d	8	
b		7
b		3

Note that after all numbers have been processed, the largest number in the list is the last value of L.

Remark   If the ten numbers were written on a sheet of paper, you could simply look them over and select the largest. This process is heuristic, however, and does not constitute an algorithm.* To see that this is so, imagine many hundreds of numbers written on a large sheet of paper. In this case, selecting the largest simply by looking over the numbers could easily result in an error. What we need is an orderly process that will ensure that the largest number is selected. Examining numbers one at a time, as in this algorithm, is such an orderly process.

2.2 Variables

Algorithms can often be stated clearly if symbols are used to denote certain quantities. Symbols are especially helpful when used to denote quantities that may change during the process of performing the steps in an algorithm. The symbols L and N used in Example 2 are illustrations of this practice.

A quantity that can change during a process is called a **variable quantity,** or simply a **variable.** A symbol used to denote such a variable quantity is the name of the variable. Thus L and N, in Example 2, are names of variables. It is common practice, however, to refer to the *symbol* as being the variable itself, rather than just its name. For instance, step (f) of the algorithm for Example 2 says to print the value of L. Certainly this is less confusing than saying "Print the value of the variable whose name is L."

Each of the examples in Section 2.1 concerns an algorithm describing a process to be carried out by people. A computer programmer must be concerned with algorithms describing processes to be carried out by a computer. This means that each step must describe an action that a computer can perform. This constraint is not so restrictive as it may appear. Computer languages, such as BASIC, contain instructions to assign numerical values to variables, to perform arithmetic operations, to compare numerical quantities and transfer control to different instructions depending on the result of this comparison, and to print numerical values. Each step in the algorithm of Example 2 represents one of these four types of action, which means that the algorithm does indeed describe a process that can be carried out by a computer.

Even instructions that appear to have nothing at all to do with computers can sometimes describe meaningful computer operations. As you progress through your study of BASIC, you will find that statements such as "Open the employee ledger," as found in the algorithm of Example 1, can indeed correspond to actions a computer can carry out.

The problems at the end of this chapter are designed to give you practice with the process of discovering algorithms. At this point it is not important that the individual steps in an algorithm correspond to actions that a computer can perform. A knowledge of what constitutes an admissible instruction to a computer will come as you gain experience in working with the BASIC language. What is important is that the individual steps are easy to understand and that the process described is an algorithm that, when carried out, does what is asked. We conclude this chapter with a third example illustrating the process of discovering algorithms.

---

*A **heuristic process** is one involving exploratory methods. Solutions to problems are discovered by a continual evaluation of the progress made toward the final result. For instance, suppose you come upon an old map indicating that a treasure is buried in the Black Hills. You may be able to work out a plan that you know will lead to the location shown on the map. *That's an algorithm.* However, suppose you can find no such plan. Determined to find the location, or to verify that the map is a fake, you decide upon a first step in your search, with no idea of what the next step will be. *That's exploratory.* Carrying out this first step may suggest a second step, or it may lead you nowhere, in which case you would try something else. Continuing in this manner, you may eventually find the location, or you may determine that the map is a fake. But it is also possible that the search will end only when you quit. Whatever the outcome, the process is heuristic. Someone else using this process will undoubtedly carry out entirely different steps and perhaps reach a different conclusion.

EXAMPLE 3. Find an algorithm to prepare a depreciation schedule for a delivery van whose cost is $10,000, whose salvage value is $2000, and whose useful life is 5 years. Use the straight-line method. (The straight-line method assumes that the value of the van will decrease by one-fifth of $8000 (cost − salvage value) during each of the 5 years.)

For each year, let's agree to write one line showing the year, the depreciation allowance for that year, the cumulative depreciation (sum of yearly depreciations to that point), and the book value (cost − cumulative depreciation) at the end of the year. A person carrying out this task might proceed as follows:

a. Look up the cost ($10,000), the salvage value ($2000), and the useful life (5 years).
b. Determine the depreciation allowance for 1 year.
c. Subtract the depreciation allowance from the book value (initially the cost).
d. Add the depreciation amount to the cumulative depreciation (initially zero).
e. Write one line showing the year, the depreciation allowance for that year, the cumulative depreciation, and the book value at the end of the year.
f. If the schedule is not complete, go to step (c).
g. Stop.

Let's modify this algorithm to apply to any capital item whose cost, salvage value, and useful life are known but are not necessarily equal to those given in the problem statement. To describe this more general algorithm, let's first choose variable names to denote the various quantities of interest:

B = book value (The initial book value is the cost.)
S = salvage value
Y = useful life in years
D = depreciation allowance for 1 year (D = (B − S)/Y)
C = cumulative depreciation (initially zero)

The following algorithm describes one way to carry out the specified task:

a. Assign values to B, S, and Y.
b. Assign the value $0.00 to C.
c. Calculate D = (B − S)/Y.
d. Subtract D from B.
e. Add D to C.
f. Write one line showing the year and the values D, C, and B.
g. If the schedule is not complete, go to step (d).
h. Stop.

This algorithm leads to the following depreciation schedule:

Year	Depreciation allowance	Cumulative depreciation	Book value
1	$1600	$1600	$8400
2	1600	3200	6800
3	1600	4800	5200
4	1600	6400	3600
5	1600	8000	2000

Remark   It is not often that a problem statement exactly describes the problem to be resolved. Problem statements are usually written in a natural language, such as English, and thus are subject to the ambiguities inherent in natural languages. Moreover, they are written by people, which means that they are subject to human oversight and error. Since an algorithm describes a precise, unambiguous process for carrying out a task, the task to be performed must be clearly understood. If it appears ambiguous, the ambiguities must be resolved. If it appears that one thing is being asked but another is actually desired, the difference must be resolved. For instance, the problem statement in the present example asks for only a very limited algorithm (a book value of $10,000, a salvage value of $2000, and a useful life of 5 years) when what is really desired is the more general algorithm that has a wider application.

Skill in discovering algorithms must be developed by practice. The problem-solving methods begun in this chapter will be emphasized throughout the book. If you study the examples carefully and work a good selection of the problems at the end of each section, you will have ample opportunity to improve your problem-solving ability.

2.3 Problems

Problems 1–4 refer to the following algorithm for completing an invoice:

a. Let AMOUNT = 0.
b. Read QUANTITY and PRICE of an item.
c. Add the product QUANTITY × PRICE to AMOUNT.
d. If there is another item, go to step (b). Otherwise, continue with step (e).
e. If AMOUNT is not greater than $500, go to step (h). Otherwise, continue with step (f).
f. Evaluate the product 0.05 × AMOUNT.
g. Subtract this product from AMOUNT.
h. Record the value AMOUNT and stop.

1. What interpretation could be given to the product appearing in step (f)?
2. What purpose would you say is served by step (e)?
3. If the values (10, $3), (50, $8), and (25, $12) are read by step (b), what value will be recorded by step (h)?
4. If the values (100, $2) and (50, $1) are read by step (b), what value will be recorded by step (h)?

Problems 5–8 refer to the following algorithm, which is intended for use by a payroll clerk as a preliminary step in the preparation of a payroll:

a. Read the next time card.
b. Let H = number of hours worked.
c. If H is not greater than 32, let G = B = 0 and go to step (f). Otherwise, continue with the next step.
d. Evaluate 6 × (H − 32) and assign this value to both G and B.
e. Let H = 32.
f. Evaluate 4 × H and add this value to G.
g. Write the values G and B on the time card.
h. If there is another time card, go to step (a). Otherwise, stop.

5. If the numbers of hours shown on the first four time cards are 20, 32, 40, and 45, respectively, what amounts will be written on these cards?
6. What is the base hourly rate for each employee?
7. What is the overtime rate?
8. Explain step (c).

In Problems 9–12, what will be printed when each algorithm is carried out?

9. a. Let SUM = 0 and N = 1.
   b. Add N to SUM.
   c. If N < 6, increase N by 1 and return to step (b). Otherwise, continue with step (d).
   d. Print the value SUM and stop.
10. a. Let PROD = 1 and N = 1.
   b. Print the values N and PROD on one line.
   c. Increase N by 1.
   d. If N exceeds 6, stop. Otherwise, continue with the next step.
   e. Multiply PROD by N and go to step (b).
11. a. Let A = 1, B = 1, and NUM = 3.
   b. Evaluate A + B and assign this value to F.
   c. If NUM does not exceed 9, increase NUM by 1 and proceed to step (d). Otherwise, print the value F and stop.
   d. Assign the values of B and F to A and B, respectively, and go to step (b).
12. a. Let NUM = 56, SUM = 1, and D = 2.
   b. If D is a factor of NUM, add D to SUM and print D.
   c. If D ≥ NUM/2, print SUM and stop.
   d. Increase D by 1, and go on to step (b).

In Problems 13–19, write an algorithm to carry out each task specified.

13. A retail store's monthly sales report shows, for each item, the fixed cost, the sale price, and the number sold. Prepare a three-column report with the column headings ITEM, GROSS SALES, and INCOME.
14. Each of several three-by-five cards contains an employee's name, Social Security number, job classification, and date hired. Prepare a report showing the names, job classifications, and complete years of service for employees who have been with the company for more than 10 years.
15. A summary sheet of an investor's stock portfolio shows, for each stock, the corporation name, the number of shares owned, the current price, and the earnings as reported for the most recent year. Prepare a six-column report with the column headings CORP. NAME, NO. OF SHARES, PRICE, EARNINGS, EQUITY, and PRICE/EARNINGS. Use this formula:

$$\text{Equity} = \text{number of shares} \times \text{price}$$

16. Each of several cards contains a single number. Determine the sum and the average of all the numbers. (Use a variable N to count how many cards are read and a variable SUM to keep track of the sum of numbers already read.)
17. Each of several cards contains a single number. On each card, write the letter G if the number is greater than the average of all the numbers. Otherwise, write the letter L on the card. (You must read through the cards twice: once to find the average and again to determine whether to write the letter G or the letter L on the cards.)
18. A local supermarket has installed a check validation machine. To use this service, a customer must have previously obtained an identification card containing a magnetic strip and also a four-digit code. Instructions showing how to insert the identification card into a special magnetic-strip reader appear on the front panel. To validate a check, a customer must present the identification card to the machine, enter the four-digit code, enter the amount of the check, and place the check, blank side toward the customer, in a special clearly labeled punch unit. To begin this process, the CLEAR key must be pressed, and, after each of the two entries has been made, the ENTER key must be pressed. Prepare an algorithm giving instructions for validating a check.
19. Write an algorithm describing the steps to be taken to cast a ballot in a national election. Assume that a person using this algorithm is a registered voter and has just entered the building in which voting is to take place. While in the voting booth, the voter should simply be instructed to vote. No instructions concerning the actual filling out of a ballot are to be given.

2.4 Review true-or-false quiz

1. The terms *algorithm* and *process* are synonymous.   T   F
2. The following steps describe an algorithm:
   a. Let N = 0.
   b. Increase N by 10.
   c. Divide N by 2.
   d. If N < 10, go to step (b).
   e. Stop.   T   F
3. A computer program should describe an algorithm.   T   F
4. Every algorithm can be translated into a computer program.   T   F
5. The expression *heuristic process* refers to an algorithm.   T   F
6. It is always easier to verify the correctness of an algorithm that describes a specific
   task than the correctness of a more general algorithm.   T   F
7. The expressions *variable quantity* and *variable* are used synonymously. Both refer
   to a quantity that can change during a process.   T   F

3

□ □ □ □ □ □ □ □ □ □ □ □ □ □

A First Look
at Applesoft BASIC

We must communicate with a computer before it will perform any service for us. The medium for this communication is the computer program—for our purposes, a sequence of commands to the computer in the English-like language BASIC. Here is a BASIC program whose purpose is described in the first line:

```
1ØØ REM PROGRAM TO AVERAGE 3 NUMBERS
11Ø REM   X,Y,AND Z DENOTE THE NUMBERS.
12Ø REM    A DENOTES THE AVERAGE.
13Ø LET X=43
14Ø LET Y=27
15Ø LET Z=23
16Ø LET A=(X+Y+Z)/3
17Ø PRINT "AVERAGE IS",A
18Ø END
```

If a computer carries out the commands appearing in this program, it will produce the following output:

```
AVERAGE IS    31
```

The lines in this program are labeled with line numbers that determine the order in which the commands are carried out by the computer. (Note that the digit zero is denoted by Ø to distinguish it from the letter *O*.) The program uses four words, called **keywords,** from the BASIC language: REM, to include remarks or comments as part of the program; LET, to associate certain numerical values with certain symbols (for example, line 13Ø associates 43 with the symbol X); PRINT, to print the results; and END, to terminate the program.

Unlike a natural language, such as English, a programming language must not allow ambiguities. The computer must do precisely what it is instructed to do. For this reason, great care must be taken to write BASIC commands precisely according to the BASIC **syntax** (BASIC rules of grammar). The following sections describe how the keywords REM, LET, PRINT, and END can be used to form admissible BASIC programs. A complete treatment of these topics is not intended at this time; our immediate goal is to provide you with the essential information you need to understand and write some BASIC programs.

3.1 Numerical constants and variables

Three types of numerical constants are allowed in BASIC:

Type	Examples				
Integer	726	99234	-726 $+423$	-16023	0
Decimal	726.	-133.50	$+10.001$ .201	0.201	
Floating-point (exponential)	1E4	$-13.6E-2$	.12345E03	$+2.345E-01$	

Integers are numbers with no decimal point, and decimals are numbers in which a decimal point appears. The use of commas and dollar signs in numbers is not allowed; using 99,234 to represent 99234 will result in an error. The third type of numerical constant may be new to you. The general form for a floating-point constant, together with its meaning, is

$$n\text{E}m = n \times 10^m$$

Here n may be any integer or decimal, but m must be an integer. E stands for "exponent" and is read "times 10 to the power." Thus 1E4 is read "1 times 10 to the power 4." The values of the four floating-point numbers shown above are

$$
\begin{aligned}
1\text{E}4 &= 1 \times 10^4 &&= 1 \times 10000 &&= 10000 \\
-13.6\text{E}-2 &= -13.6 \times 10^{-2} &&= -13.6 \times .01 &&= -0.136 \\
.12345\text{E}03 &= .12345 \times 10^3 &&= .12345 \times 1000 &&= 123.45 \\
+2.345\text{E}-01 &= 2.345 \times 10^{-1} &&= 2.345 \times .1 &&= 0.2345
\end{aligned}
$$

Although in some programming languages the programmer must be cautious about representing numbers in these three forms, the BASIC programmer is free to use any form desired.

As numerical variable names, Applesoft BASIC allows sequences of alphanumeric characters (letters A–Z and digits 0–9) beginning with a letter. In choosing variable names, you must observe two restrictions:

1. In distinguishing one variable name from another, Applesoft recognizes only the first two characters in each name. Thus A1 and A2 are names of distinct variables whereas SUM1 and SUM2 refer to the same variable.
2. Applesoft uses certain words (such as LET, PRINT, and REM) for special purposes. These are called **reserved words** and cannot be used as variable names or parts of variable names. A complete list of the Applesoft reserved words is given in Appendix D.

Admissible variable names	Inadmissible variable names	
X	3RD	(Begins with a digit.)
SUM	S-200	(Contains a dash.)
AVERAGE	SSN.	(Period is not allowed.)
T3275	RATE	(AT is a reserved word.)
DEPT17	SCORE	(OR is a reserved word.)

The variables just described are called **real variables.** This name indicates that they can be used to store any of the numerical constants (real numbers) allowed in BASIC. In addition to *real variables*, Applesoft BASIC provides **integer variables** that can sometimes be helpful in applications that involve only the integers from −32767 to 32767. Integer variable names differ from real variable names in one way only: their last character must be the percent symbol (%). Integer values for such variables are obtained by truncation, if necessary. Thus, the command

```
LET A%=15.987
```

associates the integer 15 with A%. The fractional part (.987) is simply discarded. Other than pointing out situations in which integer variables might be useful, we will restrict ourselves to real numerical variables. They are adequate for essentially all programming applications. In keeping with the most common BASIC terminology, we will use the expressions *numerical variable* and *real variable* synonymously.

3.2 String constants and variables

A **string constant** is a sequence, or **string,** of BASIC characters enclosed in quotation marks. The following are string constants:

```
"INCOME"              "NANCY JONES"
"X="                  "567"
"19 APRIL 1775"       "*****"
```

The *value* of a string constant is the sequence of all BASIC characters, including blanks, appearing between the quotes. Thus the value of the string constant "NANCY JONES" is the string NANCY JONES. A string may contain up to 255 characters.

Variables whose values are strings are called **string variables.** Their names differ from numerical variable names in one way only: their last character must be a dollar sign ($). Thus B$, NAMES$, A45$, and SSN$ are admissible names of string variables and WORD$ is not—it contains the reserved word OR. Also, NAME1$ and NAME2$ refer to the same variable since variable names are distinguished only by their first two characters.

3.3 Arithmetic operations and expressions

BASIC uses the following symbols to denote arithmetic operations:

BASIC symbol	Meaning	Priority
−	Negation	1
∧	Exponentiation	2
*	Multiplication	3
/	Division	3
+	Addition	4
−	Subtraction	4

Any meaningful combination of BASIC constants, variable names, and operation symbols is called a BASIC **expression.** In a BASIC expression the order in which the operations are performed is determined first by the indicated priority and then, within the same priority class, from left to right.

EXAMPLE 1. In the following expressions the circled numbers indicate the order in which the operations will be performed by the computer:

$$\begin{array}{ccc} ① & ② \\ \text{a.} \quad 5 - 4 + 3 = \\ 1 \quad + 3 = \\ 4 \end{array}$$

Since addition and subtraction have the same priority, they are performed from left to right. Note that performing the + first gives the incorrect value −2.

$$\begin{array}{ccc} ③ & ① & ② \\ \text{b.} \quad 2 + 6/2 * 3 = \\ 2 + \quad 3 * 3 = \\ 2 + 9 = \\ 11 \end{array}$$

Since / and * have the same priority, they are performed from left to right. Note that performing the * first gives the incorrect value 3.

$$\begin{array}{ccccc} & ③ & ① & ④ & ② \\ \text{c.} & 5 * 2 ^\wedge 2 + 3 ^\wedge 2 \end{array}$$

Performing these operations one at a time, we obtain

$$\begin{array}{c} 5 * 2 ^\wedge 2 + 3 ^\wedge 2 = \\ 5 * \quad 4 + 3 ^\wedge 2 = \\ 5 * \quad 4 + 9 \quad = \\ 20 \quad + 9 \quad = \\ 29 \end{array}$$

$$\begin{array}{cc} ① & ② \\ \text{d.} \quad -5 ^\wedge 2 \end{array}$$

Since negation (−) has the highest priority, it is performed first. Thus this expression, the square of negative 5, results in the value 25. Note that performing the $^\wedge$ first gives the different value −25.

Parentheses are used in BASIC expressions just as in ordinary algebra. They may be used to override the normal order in which operations are performed. If you need the negation of the sum of A and B, for example, you can use the expression − (A + B). They may also be used to clarify the meaning of numerical expressions. For example, 5*2/3 and (5*2)/3 have the same meaning in BASIC, but the second form is less likely to be misinterpreted.

EXAMPLE 2. In the following table, A=3, B= −2, and C=4:

BASIC expression	Value of expression
A/(2*B)	−0.75
A/2*B	−3
−(A+C)	−7
−A+C	1
(B+C)/(C−A)	2
B+C/C−A	−4
(B+C)^(−2)	0.25
−(B^C)	−16
−B^C	16
B^C	16

Roots of numbers may be indicated in BASIC by using the exponentiation operator ^. Recall from algebra that

$$\sqrt{9} = 9^{1/2} = 3$$

In BASIC, we write this as

9 ^ (1/2)   or   9 ^ 0.5

EXAMPLE 3. In the following table, M = 4 and N = 5:

Algebraic expression	Equivalent BASIC expression	Value
$\sqrt{M}$	M^(1/2)	2
$\sqrt{M+N}$	(M+N)^0.5	3
$\sqrt[3]{2M}$	(2*M)^(1/3)	2
$\sqrt[3]{7+MN}$	(7 + M*N)^(1/3)	3
$6\sqrt{5+M-N}$	6*(5 + M − N)^0.5	12

Caution

BASIC systems are not designed to take roots of negative numbers. For example, the cube root of −8 is −2, but the BASIC expression (−8)^(1/3) will not give this value. BASIC expressions such as A^B will result in an error if A is negative and B is not an integer.

3.4 Problems

1. Evaluate the following.

a. 2+3*5
b. 5*7−2
c. −4+2
d. −(4+2)
e. −3*5
f. −3^2
g. 1+2^3*2
h. 6/2*3
i. 1/2/2
j. −2*3/2*3
k. 2^2^3
l. −3*(4+0.1)
m. −2^2*3
n. 1.23E7
o. 75E−5
p. 9^1/2
q. 9^0.5
r. (2+(3*4−5))^0.5

2. For A = 2, B = 3, and X = 2, evaluate each of the following.

a. A+B/X
b. (A+B)/2*X
c. B/A/X
d. B/(A*X)
e. A+X^3
f. (A+B)^X
g. B^A/X
h. B+A/B-A
i. A^B+X
j. B^(X/A)
k. -A^B
l. (-A)^B

3. Some of the following are not admissible BASIC expressions. Explain why.

a. (Y+Z)X
b. X2*36
c. A*(2.1-7B)
d. SUM*SUM
e. SCORE*7
f. -(A+2B)
g. 2X^2
h. X2^2
i. X-2^2
j. A12+B3
k. -9^∅.5
l. A2-(-A2)

4. Write BASIC expressions for these arithmetic expressions.

a. $0.06P$
b. $5x + 5y$
c. $a^2 + b^2$
d. $\dfrac{6}{5a}$
e. $\dfrac{a}{b} + \dfrac{c}{d}$
f. $\dfrac{a + b}{c + d}$
g. $ax^2 + bx + c$
h. $\sqrt{b^2 - 4ac}$
i. $(x^2 + 4xy)/(x + 2y)$

5. Write equivalent BASIC expressions without using parentheses.

a. ((X+1)+Y)
b. (A+B)*(A-B)
c. A*(A*(A+B)+1)
d. (A*B)/C
e. A/(B*C)
f. X*(X*(X*(X+D)+C)+B)+A
g. P^(Q*R)
h. 1/(A*B*C*D)

3.5 The LET statement: Assigning values to variables

In Section 3.3 you learned how to write arithmetic expressions in a form acceptable to the computer. Now we will show you how to instruct the computer to evaluate such expressions.

A BASIC **programming line** consists of a command to the computer preceded by an unsigned integer called the line number:*

> **line number**   BASIC **command**

For example,

>   1∅∅ LET A=2+5

has line number 1∅∅ and contains the BASIC command LET A = 2 + 5. This line will cause the computer to evaluate the sum 2 + 5 and then assign this value to the variable A.

A BASIC **program** is a collection of BASIC programming lines. The BASIC commands contained in these lines are executed by the computer in the order determined by increasing line numbers, unless one of the commands overrides this order. In this book we'll often use the expression BASIC **statement** to refer to either a BASIC command or a BASIC command with a line number. This practice is in keeping with current programming terminology.

The general form of our first BASIC statement, the LET statement, is

> **ln** LET **a**=**e**

or, more simply,

> **ln** **a**=**e**   (LET is optional.)

where **ln** stands for line number, **a** denotes a variable name, and **e** denotes a BASIC expression that may simply be a constant. This statement directs the computer to evaluate the expression

*Applesoft BASIC allows you to include more than one BASIC command in a programming line (see Section 3.8).

e and then assign this value to the variable **a**. Only numerical values may be assigned to numerical variables and only strings to string variables.

The next two examples contain BASIC programs ready to be typed at the Apple keyboard and executed. (The next chapter will show you how to do this.) The columns to the right of each program show how the values of variables are changed during program execution.

EXAMPLE 4. Assignment of numerical values:

The program	*After execution of each statement*	
	Value of P	*Value of Q*
1ØØ LET P = 12	12	0
11Ø LET Q = P/2 + 1	12	7
12Ø LET P = Q/2 + 1	4.5	7
13Ø LET Q = P/2 + 1	4.5	3.25
14Ø END	4.5	3.25

Remark 1

Note that a zero value is shown for Q following execution of line 1ØØ. Applesoft assigns a value of zero to all numerical variables at the time of program execution. This *initial* value is retained by each variable until the variable is reassigned a value by the program. Line 1ØØ assigns only the value 12 to P. Thus, at this point, Q still retains its initial value of zero.

Remark 2

The practice of increasing line numbers by increments other than 1 is a good one (10 is very popular). It allows you to insert additional statements, which may have been forgotten, in their proper place.

Remark 3

The END command causes program execution to terminate. Later, you may have need to include more than one END in a program. In Applesoft BASIC, this is allowed.

Remark 4

The END command in this example is optional—program execution will automatically halt whenever the Apple runs out of commands to execute. It is common practice, however, to write BASIC programs so that the last command carried out is an END command. The END command in this example serves this purpose.

Remark 5

Newly written programs seldom do what they were meant to do. The programmer must find and correct all errors. (The errors are called **bugs,** and making the corrections is referred to as **debugging** the program.) A useful debugging technique is to pretend that you are the computer and prepare a table of successive values of program variables as in this example.

EXAMPLE 5. Assignment of string values:

The program	*After execution of each statement*		
	Value of A$	*Value of B$*	*Value of C$*
2ØØ LET A$ = "AND"	AND		
21Ø LET B$ = "SO"	AND	SO	
22Ø LET C$ = B$	AND	SO	SO
23Ø LET B$ = A$	AND	AND	SO
24Ø LET A$ = C$	SO	AND	SO
25Ø END	SO	AND	SO

Remark 1   Strings appearing in LET statements *must* be quoted. Note, however, that it is the *string* and not the *quoted string* that is assigned to the variable.

Remark 2   Although no values are shown for B$ and C$ following execution of line 200, Applesoft does assign an initial **empty string** (written "") to each string variable.

The BASIC statement

```
4Ø LET N = N+1
```

does not mean that N is equal to N + 1 (since that is impossible). It means that the expression N + 1 is *evaluated* and this value is *assigned* to the variable N. For example, the effect of the two programming lines

```
3Ø LET N = 5
4Ø LET N = N+1
```

is that the value 6 is assigned to N. Similarly, the statement

```
7Ø LET S = S+Y
```

evaluates S + Y and then assigns this new value to S. Thus line 40 increases the value of N by 1 and line 70 increases the value of S by Y.

EXAMPLE 6. In the following table, S = 3, Y = −2, H = −4, Z = 6, and M = 10:

BASIC statement	After execution
35 LET S = S+Y	S has the value 1.
9Ø LET H = H+2*Z	H has the value 8.
4Ø LET M = 2*M−Z	M has the value 14.

3.6 The PRINT statement

Every computer language must be designed so that the results can be made available in a usable form. In BASIC, the PRINT statement meets this requirement. The simplest form of this statement is

ln PRINT **a**

where **ln** denotes a line number and **a** denotes any string or numerical expression. For example, the statements

```
1ØØ PRINT "THIS IS A MESSAGE."
11Ø PRINT 7*8+3
12Ø PRINT X
13Ø PRINT A$
```

are all admissible. When a PRINT statement is executed, the value of the expression is printed and then a carriage return is executed—on the Apple's display screen, this means that the cursor is positioned at the beginning of the next display line. Thus if X has the value 723.45 and A$ has the string value END OF MESSAGE, lines 100 to 130 will produce the following output:

```
THIS IS A MESSAGE.
59
723.45
END OF MESSAGE
```

As illustrated in the next example, BASIC allows you to print the values of more than one expression on a single line.

EXAMPLE 7. Printing labels for output values:

```
100 REM ** AUTOMOBILE SALES TAX
110 REM COMPUTATION PROGRAM **
120 REM
130 PRINT "TAXATION DEPARTMENT"
140 LET PRICE=7295
150 PRINT "PRICE:",PRICE
160 PRINT "SALES TAX:",.05*PRICE
170 END
```

When this program is executed, it will produce the following output:

```
TAXATION DEPARTMENT
PRICE:          7295
SALES TAX:      364.75
```

Both line 150 and line 160 print a numerical value preceded by a label identifying what this value represents.

Note that the two expressions in lines 150 and 160 are delimited (separated) by a comma. This comma instructs the Apple to space the two output values as shown. In particular, if the first value printed on a line uses fewer than 16 spaces, the comma instructs the Apple to begin printing the second value in the seventeenth print position counting from the left margin.*

Remark

In this program, string constants are included in PRINT statements to print a heading (TAXATION DEPARTMENT) and two labels (PRICE: and SALES TAX:) identifying the numerical output values. You can also use string *variables* for this purpose. For instance, if you add the line

```
90 LET P$="PRICE:"
```

to the program and change line 150 to

```
150 PRINT P$,PRICE
```

the program will produce exactly the same output as before.

---

*The forms of the PRINT statement described in this section are adequate for many programming tasks. Chapter 7 presents a more detailed description of how Applesoft BASIC allows you to format your output values.

3.7 The REM statement: Remarks as part of a program

In the program shown at the outset of this chapter, certain comments are included (lines 100 to 120) to indicate the program's purpose and identify the quantities represented by the variables X, Y, Z, and A. The BASIC statement that allows you to insert such comments is the REM (REMark) statement. The general form is

ln REM **comment**

where **comment** denotes any comment or remark you may wish to include.

EXAMPLE 8

```
100 REM ** DETERMINE THE RATE OF
110 REM RETURN GIVEN THE CURRENT PRICE
120 REM AND EARNINGS OF A SECURITY.**
130 REM   P DENOTES PRICE.
140 REM   E DENOTES EARNINGS.
150 REM   R DENOTES RATE OF RETURN.
160 LET P=80.00
170 LET E=6.00
180 REM ** CALCULATE RATE OF RETURN
190 REM AND PRINT SUMMARY RESULTS **
200 LET R=100*E/P
210 PRINT "PRICE",P
220 PRINT "EARNINGS",E
230 PRINT "RATE OF RETURN",R
240 END
```

If this program is executed, the output will be as follows:

```
PRICE           80
EARNINGS        6
RATE OF RETURN  7.5
```

Remark 1   In this program, REM statements are used for three different purposes: to give a brief description of the program (lines 100 to 120), to describe the quantities represented by the variables (lines 130 to 150), and to describe the action of certain groups of programming lines (lines 180 and 190). Using REM statements in this manner is an excellent programming practice. Your programs will be easier to read and understand, easier to modify at some later date (should that be required), and easier to debug.

Remark 2   Comments appearing in REM statements need not be enclosed in quotation marks.

Remark 3   Unlike quoted messages appearing in PRINT statements, comments included in REM statements cause nothing to be printed when the program is executed by a computer. Their sole purpose is to document a program.

3.8 Multiple commands in a programming line

To this point, each line of a BASIC program has contained only one BASIC command. Applesoft BASIC, however, allows you to include many commands in a single programming line—you simply separate the commands with colons. For example,

```
10 LET A=5 : LET B=7 : PRINT A+B
```

is an admissible Applesoft BASIC programming line that assigns 5 to A and 7 to B before printing the value of their sum. The general form of a multiple-command programming line is

ln *command* {: *command* }

where **ln** denotes a line number and *command* denotes a BASIC command (no line number).* The commands are executed from left to right unless one of them overrides this order. The number of commands allowed in a programming line is limited only by the 239 maximum number of characters per line.

If a multiple-command line contains a REM command, anything that follows the keyword REM is part of the remark. Thus the following two lines are admissible but not equivalent:

```
10 REM PRINT THE RESULT : PRINT X
10 PRINT X : REM PRINT THE RESULT
```

The first is simply a remark and will cause no action during program execution. The second will print the value of X.

Be cautious when using multiple-command lines. Overusing them tends to clutter a program and obscure its meaning. Their appropriate uses will be illustrated as we go along. The following program shows how REM commands in this context can clarify the action of the program.

EXAMPLE 9. Multiple-command lines:

```
10 LET N=130     : REM NUMBER SOLD
20 LET C=300     : REM COST OF EACH ITEM
30 LET S=1.2*C   : REM SELLING PRICE OF ITEM
40 LET G=N*S     : REM GROSS SALES
50 LET P=G-N*C   : REM PROFIT
60 PRINT "SALES",G
70 PRINT "PROFIT",P
80 END
```

3.9 Problems

1. Write LET statements to perform the indicated tasks.
   a. Assign the value 7 to M.
   b. Increase the value assigned to B by 7.
   c. Double the value assigned to H.
   d. Assign the value of the expression $(A - B)/2$ to C2.

*The notation {*item*} means that *item* may be repeated one or more times or omitted entirely. (In this instance, *item* refers to : *command*.)

    e. Assign the tenth power of 1 + R to A.
    f. Decrease the value assigned to X by twice the value assigned to Y.
    g. Assign the string COST to C$.
    h. Replace the value of A$ by the string DOE, JANE.
    i. Store the contents of P$ in Q$.
    j. Assign the string ***** to S$.

2. Which of these are incorrect LET statements? Explain. (Be sure to check the table of reserved words.)

a. 1∅ LET X=(A+B)C	b. 15 LET M=A1-A2
c. 2∅ LET A+B=S	d. 25 LET DEPT#5=17
e. 3∅ LET A3=A*A*A	f. 35 LET 5M=2+7*X
g. 4∅ LET X=1.23E5	h. 45 LET Y=2.19E-8
i. 5∅ LET Z=4E2.5	j. 55 LET AREA=LENGTH*WIDTH
k. 6∅ LET SUM=SUM+NEXT	l. 65 LET DIFF=FIRST-SECOND
m. 7∅ LET A$=SAMMY	n. 75 LET NAME$="JANE DOE"
o. 8∅ LET P$=Y$	p. 85 LET "DEPT#7"=D$
q. 9∅ LET M="MONTHLY RENT"	r. 95 LET D$="A+B+5"

3. Which of these are incorrect PRINT statements? Explain. (Be sure to check the table of reserved words.)
    a. 5 PRINT SO-AND-SO
    b. 1∅ PRINT "5+13=",5+13
    c. 15 PRINT COST$,COST
    d. 2∅ PRINT RATING
    e. 25 PRINT "RATE-OF-RETURN"
    f. 3∅ PRINT SEVEN$,7
    g. 35 PRINT SCORE
    h. 4∅ PRINT "FINAL RESULT",AVERAGE

4. Show the output when each program is run.

```
a. 1∅∅ LET A=5          b. 1∅ LET P=1∅∅
   11∅ LET B=A+2           2∅ LET R=8
   12∅ LET C=A+B           3∅ LET I=R/1∅∅
   13∅ PRINT C             4∅ LET A=P+I*P
   14∅ END                 5∅ PRINT "AMOUNT=",A
                           6∅ END


c. 5∅∅ LET X=∅          d. 1∅ LET A=2
   51∅ LET X=X-1           2∅ LET B=6
   52∅ LET Y=X^2+3*X       3∅ LET A=2*A
   53∅ PRINT Y             4∅ LET B=B/2
   54∅ END                 5∅ LET C=(A∧2+B∧2)∧(1/2)
                           6∅ PRINT C
                           7∅ END


e. 1∅ LET L=1∅ : REM LENGTH      f. 1∅ LET L$="LIST PRICE"
   2∅ LET W=5 : REM WIDTH           2∅ LET D$="DISCOUNT"
   3∅ LET H=4 : REM HEIGHT          3∅ LET S$="SELLING PRICE"
   4∅ LET V=L*W*H : REM VOLUME      4∅ LET L=45
   5∅ PRINT V                       5∅ LET D=(1∅/1∅∅)*L
   6∅ LET L=W : H=W                 6∅ LET S=L-D
   7∅ PRINT V                       7∅ PRINT L$,L
   8∅ END                           8∅ PRINT D$,D
                                    9∅ PRINT S$,S
                                    99 END


g. 1∅ PRINT "BOBBY LOVES"
   2∅ LET M$="MARY."
   3∅ LET B$="BARB."
   4∅ LET B$=M$
   5∅ LET M$=B$
   6∅ PRINT M$
   7∅ END
```

5. Complete the tables of values as in Examples 4 and 5.

a.
```
1Ø LET A=1 : B=2 : C=1
2Ø LET C=C+B
3Ø LET A=B^2
4Ø LET B=C-B+A
5Ø LET C=C-1 : B=A*B
6Ø LET A=A/C : C=B/A+1
7Ø END
```

A	B	C

b.
```
1Ø LET N=1 : PRINT N
2Ø LET N=N*(N+1) : PRINT N
3Ø LET N=N*(N+1) : PRINT N
4Ø LET N=N*(N+1) : PRINT N
5Ø END
```

N	Output

c.
```
1ØØ LET X = Ø
11Ø LET Y = X + 7
12Ø LET Z = Y+X^2
13Ø PRINT Z
14Ø LET X = Z
15Ø LET Y = X*Y*Z
16Ø PRINT Y
17Ø END
```

X	Y	Z	Output

6. Prepare tables showing the successive values of all variables and what will be printed.

a.
```
1Ø LET S=Ø : A=25
2Ø LET S=S+A : PRINT S
3Ø LET S=S+A : PRINT S
4Ø LET S=S/2: PRINT S
5Ø END
```

b.
```
1ØØ LET X=1.5
11Ø LET Y=3/(2*X+2)
12Ø PRINT Y
13Ø LET X=-X
14Ø PRINT X
15Ø PRINT Y
16Ø END
```

c.
```
1Ø LET N=13Ø : REM COUNT
2Ø LET C=3.ØØ : REM COST
3Ø LET S=1.2*C : REM PRICE
4Ø LET G=N*S : PRINT "SALES",G
5Ø LET P=G-N*C : PRINT "PROFIT",P
6Ø END
```

d.
```
1ØØ PRINT "NTH POWERS OF 7"
11Ø LET A=7
12Ø LET P=7
13Ø LET P=A*P
14Ø PRINT "FOR N=2",P
15Ø LET P=A*P
16Ø PRINT "FOR N=3",P
17Ø LET P=A*P
18Ø PRINT "FOR N=4",P
19Ø REM "END OF TABLE"
2ØØ END
```

3.10 Review true-or-false quiz

1. Parentheses may be used only to override the normal order in which numerical operations are performed by the computer.   T   F

2. A BASIC program is a collection of BASIC programming lines.   T   F

3. The terms BASIC *command*, BASIC *statement*, and BASIC *programming line* are used synonymously.   T   F

4. $(A+B)^{\wedge}\emptyset.5$ and $(A+B)^{\wedge}1/2$ have the same meaning.   T   F

5. 2/3 is a numerical constant in BASIC.   T   F

6. 1.ØE1 = 1Ø.   T   F

7. If A = 3, the statement 43 LET $1+A^{\wedge}2=B1$ assigns the value 1Ø to the variable B1.   T   F

8. 15Ø LET A3 = A3*A3 is a valid BASIC statement.   T   F

9. 3ØØ LET M = "1984" is a valid BASIC statement.   T   F

10. LET X = X + 1 is a valid BASIC command but will result in an error because there is no number X for which X = X + 1.   T   F

11. 400 PRINT HARRY is a valid BASIC statement, but it will not print the name
HARRY.   T   F

12. 5ØØ PRINT A+B : 51Ø PRINT A*B is a valid programming line.   T   F

13. 6ØØ SCORE=A+B : PRINT SCORE is a valid programming line.   T   F

14. REM statements can be used to print messages during program execution.   T   F

15. Comments appearing in REM statements must be enclosed in quotation marks.   T   F

4

□ □ □ □ □ □ □ □ □ □ □ □ □ □ □

First Session
at the Apple Keyboard

In Chapter 3 we presented examples of BASIC programs ready to be typed at the Apple keyboard. This keyboard (Figure 4.1) consists of keys for the 26 uppercase letters of the English alphabet, the digits Ø through 9, and certain other familiar characters, such as $\#,.;: = ()-/$. In addition, there is a space bar, a RETURN key, and several other keys whose functions will be explained as the need arises.

Before beginning to type a program, you must first have Applesoft BASIC up and running. Your Apple computer is supplied with this language in one of three versions—firmware, diskette, or cassette Applesoft. Firmware Applesoft is installed as part of your Apple's permanent *read-only memory* (*ROM*). Diskette (or cassette) Applesoft is provided as a program on a diskette (or cassette) supplied with your system.

Getting Applesoft BASIC up and running is not difficult. The steps you must take for each version of Applesoft are described in Appendix A. The purpose of this chapter is to show how BASIC programs are entered at the Apple keyboard and also to guide you in your first encounter with the computer. In what follows, we assume that Applesoft BASIC is operational. As described in Appendix A, this means that the screen displays the **Applesoft prompt]** fol-

Figure 4.1
The Apple keyboard.(*Apple and the Apple logo are registered trademarks of Apple Computer, Inc.*)

lowed immediately by a blinking square called the **cursor.** To get the most out of this chapter, you are urged to read through the material quickly to get a general idea of what is involved, and then to read it again, this time being sure to try all the examples on your computer.

4.1 Entering a programming line: The RETURN key

Here is a program ready to be entered at the Apple keyboard:

```
100 REM       FIRST SESSION AT
110 REM        APPLE COMPUTER
120 REM FIND SUM AND PRODUCT.
130 LET A=5
140 LET B=8
150 LET S=A+B
160 LET P=A*B
170 END
```

Before you begin typing this program, type

NEW   Ⓡ

where Ⓡ denotes the RETURN key on your keyboard. The Applesoft command NEW clears the part of the Apple's random-access memory (RAM) in which BASIC programs are stored. It is carried out as soon as you press the RETURN key. Now type the first line of the program and end the line by pressing Ⓡ. Your screen should now display

```
]NEW

]100 REM       FIRST SESSION AT

]□
```

The symbol □ denotes the cursor. When a line being typed begins with a number (100, in this case), pressing the RETURN key causes the line to be entered (stored in the computer's memory); it is not executed. You then continue typing:*

```
]110 REM        APPLE COMPUTER
]120 REM FIND SUM AND PRODUCT.
]130 LET A=5
]140 LET B=8
]150 LET S=A+B
]160 LET P=A*B
]170 END
]□
```

Remember you must press Ⓡ to enter each line. If you make a typing error, simply press Ⓡ and retype the entire line, including the line number.

Since this program contains no PRINT statement, there will be no output if it is executed. To rectify this situation, you could add PRINT lines simply by typing the following:

```
]155 PRINT "SUM IS",S
]165 PRINT "PRODUCT IS",P
]□
```

---

*On your video screen, these lines will appear on alternate display lines.

BASIC allows you to enter these lines out of their natural numerical order; the program will still be executed according to the sequence of line numbers from smallest to largest. Thus if you omit a line in typing a program, you can insert it at any time before execution simply by typing it in.

The Apple's video screen is limited to 24 horizontal display lines. As you undoubtedly have discovered, making an entry on the twenty-fourth line causes all lines to be moved up with the top line being scrolled off the screen. Scrolling a line off the screen in no way affects what has already been stored in memory. Indeed, you can even clear the entire screen without affecting your program. To do this, type

HOME (R)

The Applesoft command HOME clears the screen and moves the cursor to the upper left corner of the screen. Your program, although no longer visible, remains intact.

4.2 The commands LIST and RUN

The Applesoft command LIST is used to display some or all of the programming lines you have entered:

Command	Effect
LIST	Entire program is listed.
LIST ln	Only line ln is listed.
LIST ln$_1$, ln$_2$	Lines ln$_1$ through ln$_2$ are listed.

We illustrate the LIST command for the program entered in the previous section. Although not shown, the RETURN key must be pressed after each LIST command.

```
]LIST                                      (You type this.)

100    REM        FIRST SESSION AT         (Displayed by the Apple. Blanks separating lines are not
110    REM        APPLE COMPUTER           used when the Apple lists a program.)
120    REM FIND SUM AND PRODUCT.
130    LET A = 5
140    LET B = 8
150    LET S = A + B
155    PRINT "SUM IS",S
160    LET P = A * B
165    PRINT "PRODUCT IS",P
170    END

]LIST 155                                  (You type this.)

155    PRINT "SUM IS",S                     (Displayed by the Apple.)

]LIST 130,150                              (You type this.)

130    LET A = 5                            (Displayed by the Apple.)
140    LET B = 8
150    LET S = A + B

]□
```

Note that lines 155 and 165 have been inserted in their proper places even though they were actually typed after line 170. If at this time you should notice a typing error, simply retype the line containing the error.

When you are reasonably certain that you've typed the program correctly, you can cause it to be executed (run) by typing RUN⟨R⟩. The Applesoft command RUN causes the program statements to be executed according to the sequence of their line numbers. We illustrate for the program just entered:

```
]RUN                              (You type this.)
SUM IS           13               (Displayed by the Apple.)
PRODUCT IS       40

]□
```

If your Apple system includes a diskette or cassette unit (most do), you can save programs you write for use at a later time. Appendices B (diskette) and C (cassette) describe how this is done.

4.3 Spacing and length of a programming line

You will have noticed that the spacing in the listing of a program differs from that in the program as typed. The only spacing over which you have control in an Apple listing is that in the comments included in REM statements and strings enclosed by quotation marks. All other spacing is determined by the computer according to Applesoft's predefined format—the previous listing is a typical example.* It makes no difference to the Apple whether you type

```
15ØLETS=A+B
```

or

```
15Ø LET S = A + B
```

or

```
1   5   ØLET  S  =A   +  B
```

In all three cases this line will be listed as

```
15Ø    LET S = A + B
```

Each display line on the Apple's video screen has a maximum capacity of 40 characters (unless the Apple has been specially modified to display 80 characters per line). Should you need to enter a programming line that exceeds this 40-character maximum, just keep typing and the Apple will automatically continue onto the next display line. In all, you can type up to 239 keys while entering a single programming line. You must not press the RETURN key until the entire programming line has been typed, however. If you list a continuation line, Applesoft follows its own format in the listing. For example:

```
]1Ø PRINT "123456789Ø123456789Ø123456789Ø        (You type this.)
123456789Ø123456789Ø123456789Ø"
```

*Although some Apple systems give you more control over the spacing of a program line, they are at present the exception.

```
]LIST 1Ø
```

```
1Ø  PRINT "123456789Ø123456789Ø12          (Displayed by the Apple.)
        34567890123456789Ø123456789Ø
        123456789Ø"
```

```
]□
```

In program listings, Applesoft always indents continuation lines as shown.

4.4 Making corrections

During a session at the keyboard you are bound to make occasional typing errors. As noted previously, an incorrect keyboard entry can be corrected by retyping the entire line. If you wish to delete a line from your program, simply type its line number and immediately press the RETURN key. (In all subsequent examples, we will show the Applesoft prompt] only if doing so helps to clarify what is being illustrated.)

EXAMPLE 1. Changing and deleting program lines:

```
3Ø  LET Z=5                          (You type this.)
4Ø  PRINT X
5Ø  LET Z-7=X
6Ø  PRINT X
7Ø  END
4Ø
5Ø  LET X=Z-7
LIST
```

```
3Ø  LET Z = 5                        (Displayed by the Apple.)
5Ø  LET X = Z - 7
6Ø  PRINT X
7Ø  END
```

Another valuable editing feature requires the use of the **backspace key** (←) and allows you to correct errors *before* the line being typed has been entered—that is, before you press the RETURN key. Suppose you are typing the line

```
55 PRINT M
```

but notice that you have typed

```
55 PTIN
```

At this point you should type the backspace key (←) three times. This moves the cursor back three spaces so that it will be positioned over the incorrect character T:

```
55 P█IN
```

Then type the correct character R:

```
55 PR█N
```

You can now retype the remaining correct characters (IN) or you can press the **retype key**(→) until the cursor returns to the position at which you started making the correction:

```
55 PRIN□
```

Appendix E describes other Applesoft editing features that you may find helpful in correcting your BASIC programs.

4.5 Error messages

You may not always be fortunate enough to detect *syntax errors* (violations of BASIC rules of grammar) before attempting to run your program. Should you issue the RUN command for such an incorrect program, the Apple will display an error message indicating the line number at which the error occurs. The following example illustrates how these error messages can help you to correct a program.

EXAMPLE 2. Finding and correcting syntax errors:

```
10 LET X=7                    (You type this.)
20 LET X+9=Z
30 PRINT 'ANSWER IS',Z
40 END

RUN

?SYNTAX ERROR IN 20          (Displayed by the Apple.)

20 LET Z=X+9                  (You type this.)

RUN

?SYNTAX ERROR IN 30          (Displayed by the Apple.)

30 PRINT "ANSWER IS",Z       (You type this.)

RUN
ANSWER IS      16            (Displayed by the Apple.)
```

Remark   If you don't understand a particular error message, try listing the indicated line to see if that helps. For instance, if after obtaining the message

```
?SYNTAX ERROR IN 30
```

you did not recall that double quotes must be used for strings, you would list line 30:

```
]LIST 30

30  PRINT 'ANSWERIS',Z
```

The missing blank in the string ANSWER IS might then suggest to you that the string constant is incorrectly formed.

As illustrated in the following example, error messages are sometimes printed even though a program contains no syntax errors.

EXAMPLE 3. Here is a syntactically correct program with an error:

The following program is designed to compute the ratio

$$\frac{\text{Cost} + \text{Markup}}{\text{Cost} - \text{Markup}}$$

```
1Ø REM C DENOTES THE COST.
2Ø LET C=1ØØ
3Ø REM M DENOTES THE MARKUP.
4Ø LET M=1ØØ
5Ø LET R=(C+M)/(C-M)
6Ø PRINT "RATIO =",R
7Ø END
RUN  (R)

?DIVISION BY ZERO ERROR IN 5Ø
```

Each line in this program is an admissible BASIC statement, hence the program is syntactically correct. When run, the computer assigns 100 to C (line 2Ø), assigns 100 to M (line 4Ø), and then attempts to evaluate the expression in line 5Ø. The error message tells you that the computer does not "know" how to divide by zero.

Unfortunately, error messages are not always printed when incorrect programs are run. The following example shows a program with an error that the computer will not detect.

EXAMPLE 4

```
1Ø REM COMPUTE THE AVERAGE OF X AND Y.
2Ø REM THIS PROGRAM IS SYNTACTICALLY
3Ø REM CORRECT BUT PRODUCES
4Ø REM INCORRECT RESULTS.
5Ø LET X=1Ø
6Ø LET Y=5
7Ø LET A=X+Y/2
8Ø PRINT "AVERAGE IS",A
9Ø END
RUN
AVERAGE IS        12.5
```

The computer does precisely what you instruct it to do; it does not do what you *meant* it to do. The programming error in line 7Ø is not a syntax error but an error in the logic of the program. Such errors are often very difficult to find.

4.6 Immediate and deferred mode

You will recall that we have been typing each NEW, HOME, LIST, and RUN command without a line number, whereas each REM, PRINT, END, and LET command has been preceded by a line number. In Applesoft BASIC, each line whose first character is a digit (0–9) is entered as a programming line and is not executed until a RUN command is issued. This is called **deferred execution mode**—execution of the command (or commands) contained in the line is deferred until later. If a keyboard entry does not begin with a line number (that is, if the first character is not a digit), the Apple will understand the entry as a command to be carried out immediately. This is called **immediate execution mode.**

Each BASIC command described to this point can be issued in either deferred or immediate mode. Here is an illustration for the LET, PRINT, and LIST commands:

Display screen	Explanation
]PRINT 2+3*5 17	The PRINT command is executed as soon as (R) is pressed.
]LET A=24	The Apple reserves memory space for the variable A and assigns the value 24 to A.
]PRINT A+25 49	The PRINT command is executed as soon as (R) is pressed. Note that A has retained the value 24.
]B=A+2	The Apple reserves memory space for the variable B and assigns the value 26 to B. (Recall that the keyword LET is optional.)
]200 LIST	The LIST command is entered as line 200 of the BASIC program being typed. It will not be carried out until the program is executed.

Note: All characters following each prompt] are typed at the keyboard and entered by pressing the RETURN key (R).

Immediate execution mode can often be used effectively while you are debugging a program. After a program has been run, the Apple retains the final values of all variables. Thus if your program produces incorrect results, you can use PRINT commands to examine these final values. This information may be just what you need to locate the error. We illustrate with a short program that contains a single error.

EXAMPLE 5. Immediate mode and debugging.

```
10 REM INCREASE SALARY
20 REM BY 4 AND 1/2 PERCENT.
30 REM    S=OLD SALARY
40 REM    R=RAISE
50 REM    NS=NEW SALARY
60 LET S=24500
70 LET R=4.5*S
80 LET NS=S+R
90 PRINT "OLD SALARY:",S
95 PRINT "NEW SALARY:",NS
99 END
RUN
OLD SALARY:     24500
NEW SALARY:     134750
```

Clearly this program has a bug—the new salary amount is much too large. Let's examine the final values of the variables:

```
]PRINT S
24500
]PRINT R
110250
```

At this point we can see that S is correct (assigned in line 60), but R (assigned in line 70) is not. Thus the error must be in line 70. You would now type

```
70 LET R=.045*S
```

and run the program again to get the correct results.

Most, but not all, Applesoft BASIC commands can be used in either immediate or deferred mode. Although this information is given in Appendix F, you can always find out by experimenting. Nothing you type gently at the keyboard can harm the Apple. If you enter a command that is not an admissible Applesoft command, the computer will usually display the message

```
?SYNTAX ERROR
```

If at any time the Apple behaves in a way that you don't understand, you can try pressing the RESET key or you can refer to Appendix A, which explains other ways to recover the Applesoft prompt]. If nothing works, simply turn off your Apple and start over. No harm will have been done and, at worst, you will have to retype your program.

4.7 Directing output to the printer

Thus far in your work at the Apple, every character typed by you at the keyboard, or generated as the result of some action by the computer, has appeared only on the display screen. Often, though, you will want a printed copy of your program or its output. For this your Apple must be equipped with a printer, connected by cable to one of eight sockets inside the computer. These sockets, called slots, are numbered from 0 to 7. In this book we will assume that the printer is connected to slot 1, the conventional slot for printers.

To obtain a printed copy of your program, first type the command

```
PR#1 Ⓡ
```

This instructs the Apple to direct all further output through slot 1. If you now type

```
LIST Ⓡ
```

nothing will be displayed on the screen. Instead you will obtain printed copy containing the word LIST followed by a listing of your program. Any further entry you make at the keyboard will follow this printed listing. To redirect output back to the screen, type

```
PR#0 Ⓡ
```

Note: With some printers, keyboard entries made while the command PR#1 is in effect will not be printed as you type them. Rather, all characters typed will be stored until the RETURN key is pressed, at which time they will be printed. If your printer behaves in this way, it will seem as though nothing is happening while you are typing a line.

If you type the RUN command while PR#1 is in effect, your program will be executed and the output will be transmitted to the printer rather than to the display screen.

Generally, printers are not restricted to 40 characters per line as is the Apple display screen. Thus programming lines that must be continued to several display lines on the screen may appear on one line in a listing by the printer.

4.8 On writing your first program

You are now ready to write your first program. Even for very simple problems, certain steps should be followed. Experience has shown that the following approach to problem solving applies to both simple and complex problems:

1. Be sure you thoroughly understand what is being asked in the problem statement. A good way to do this is to identify the following items:
   Input: Data to be presented to the computer for processing.
   Output: The results called for in the problem statement. This may involve identifying both output values and the form in which they are to be printed.
2. Identify what, if any, mathematical equations will be needed. For example, to convert degrees Celsius to degrees Fahrenheit, you could use the equation $F = (9/5)C + 32$.
3. Devise a step-by-step process (algorithm) that will result in a correct solution. For simple programming tasks, this step is usually straightforward. For example, to convert degrees Celsius to degrees Fahrenheit you could use the following algorithm:
   a. Assign a value to C (degrees Celsius).
   b. Calculate $F = (9/5)C + 32$.
   c. Print the result F and stop.
4. Write the program statements to carry out the algorithm you have described. This is called *coding the program.* Be sure to include adequate and meaningful REM statements.
5. Debug the program. This means running it to test for syntax errors and also to ensure that the program produces correct results.

EXAMPLE 6. Write a program to calculate the simple interest and the amount due for a loan of P dollars, at an annual interest rate R, for a time of T years. Use the program to find the interest and amount due when P = $600, R = 0.1575, and T = 2.

A quick reading of this problem statement shows that the input and output values are as follows:

Input: P, R, and T
Output: Simple interest and the amount due

We should all recognize the familiar formulas that govern this situation:

Simple interest: $SI = P \times R \times T$
Amount due: $A = P + SI$

Knowing these formulas, we can write the following algorithm:

a. Assign values to P, R, and T.
b. Calculate the interest SI and the amount due A.
c. Print the results (SI and A) and stop.

The program

```
100 REM SIMPLE INTEREST PROGRAM
110 REM    P    AMOUNT OF LOAN
120 REM    R    ANNUAL INTEREST RATE
130 REM    T    TERM OF LOAN IN YEARS
140 REM ASSIGN VALUES TO P,R, AND T.
150 LET P=600
160 LET R=0.1575
170 LET T=2
180 REM FIND INTEREST AND AMOUNT DUE.
190 LET SI=P*R*T
200 LET A=P+SI
210 REM PRINT THE RESULTS.
220 PRINT "INTEREST",SI
230 PRINT "AMOUNT DUE",A
240 END
RUN
INTEREST         189
AMOUNT DUE       789
```

Remark 1

To find the interest and amount due for other loans, it is necessary only to retype the given conditions at lines 150, 160, and 170. (In Chapter 5 you will see how different values can be assigned to P, R, and T without having to retype programming lines.)

Remark 2

Notice that the REM statements in lines 140, 180, and 210 correspond to the three steps in the algorithm written for this example. Not only does this emphasize how the coding process follows from the algorithm, but it also suggests that each step in an algorithm should contain enough detail so that it can easily be coded. Writing your algorithms according to this principle and using the individual steps as REM statements are excellent programming practices.

The development of programming habits, both good and bad, begins with your first program. At the end of this chapter you will be asked to write some programs. To learn good habits from the start, you should follow the steps suggested in this section. *Coding should almost never be your first step.*

4.9 Problems

In Problems 1–4, assume that the lines shown are typed immediately after the Applesoft command NEW has been carried out. What will be printed (or displayed) if the LIST command is entered?

```
1. 100 LET A=14              2. 100 LET X=5
   110 LET B=20                 110 LET X=10
   120 LET S=A+B               120 LET Y=20
   130 PRINT "SUM IS S"        130 PRINT "X+Y"=S
   140 END                     110
   110 LET B=30                125 LET S=X+Y
   130 PRINT "SUM IS",S        130 PRINT "X+Y=",S
                               140 END
                               150 RUN
                               150
```

```
3. 100 PRINT "DISCOUNT CALCULATION"   4. 100 LET L$=AVERAGE
   100 REM DISCOUNT PROGRAM              110 LET A=5
   100                                   120 LET B=7
   110 LET P=120                         130 LET M=A+B/2
   120 LET D=0.1*P                       140 PRINT L$,M
   130 LET P=P-D                         150 END
   140 PRINT "DISCOUNT",D                110 LET A=9
   150 PRINT "COST",C                    130 LET M=(A+B)/2
   130 LET C=P-D                         100 LET L$="AVERAGE"
   160 END
```

In Problems 5–10, the programs contain one or more bugs—either syntax errors (violations in the BASIC rules of grammar) or programming errors (errors in the logic of a program). Find each bug, tell which type of error it is, correct the programs, and show the output that will be generated if the corrected programs are run.

```
5. 10 REM PROGRAM TO COMPUTE      6. 10 REM PROGRAM TO AVERAGE
   20 REM SIX PERCENT OF $23,000     20 REM TWO NUMBERS
   30 LET D=23,000                   30 LET N1=24
   40 LET R=6                        40 LET N2=15
   50 LET R*D=A                      50 LET A=N1+N2/2
   60 PRINT "ANSWER IS",A            60 PRINT AVERAGE IS,A
   70 END                           70 END
```

```
7. 10 REM SALES TAX PROGRAM       8. 10 REM PROGRAM TO FIND SOLUTION
   20 REM T=TAX RATE : T=5           20 REM TO THE FOLLOWING EQUATION
   30 REM P=PRICE : P=120            30 REM    35X+220=0
   40 LET S=P+(T/100)*P              40 LET A=35
   50 PRINT "TOTAL COST:",S          50 LET B=220
   60 END                           60 LET A*X+B=0
                                     70 PRINT "SOLUTION IS",X
                                     80 END
```

```
9. 100 REM PROGRAM TO SWAP THE    10. 100 REM PROGRAM TO COMPUTE THE
   110 REM VALUES OF A AND B          110 REM EXCISE TAX ON TWO CARS
   120 LET A=5                        120 REM IF THE TAX RATE IS
   130 LET B=8                        130 REM 66 DOLLARS PER 1000
   140 PRINT "A=",A                    140 LET V=4500
   150 PRINT "B=",B                    150 LET R=66/1000
   160 REM INTERCHANGE A AND B.        160 LET T=V*R
   170 LET A=B                         170 PRINT TAX ON FIRST CAR IS T
   180 LET B=A                         180 LET V=5700
   190 PRINT "A=",A                    190 PRINT TAX ON SECOND CAR IS T
   200 PRINT "B=",B                    200 END
   210 END
```

In Problems 11–34, write a BASIC program for each task specified. Be sure to follow the guidelines suggested in Section 4.8. Use PRINT statements to label all output values and be sure to include adequate REM statements.

11. Compute the selling price S for an article whose list price is L if the rate of discount is D%.

12. Compute the original price if an article is now selling at S dollars after a discount of D%.

13. Compute the state gasoline tax in dollars paid by a driver who travels M miles per year if the car averages G miles per gallon and the tax is T cents per gallon.

14. Find the commission C on sales of S dollars if the rate of commission is R%.

15. Find the principal P that, if invested at a rate of interest R for time T years, yields the simple interest SI. (Recall that $SI = P \times R \times T$.)

16. Compute the weekly salary, both gross G and net N, for a person who works H hours a week for D dollars an hour (no overtime). Deductions are S% for state taxes and F% for federal taxes.

17. Convert degrees Celsius C to degrees Fahrenheit F ($F = (9/5)C + 32$). Run the program for several values of C, including C = 0 and C = 100.

18. Convert degrees Fahrenheit F to degrees Celsius C. Run the program for several values of F, including F = 0, F = 32, and F = 212.

19. Convert pounds L to grams G (1 oz = 28.3495 g).

20. Convert grams G to pounds L.

21. Convert yards Y to meters M. Run for several values of Y, including 1760 (1 in. = 2.54 cm).

22. Convert meters M to yards Y. Run for several values of M, including 1 and 1000.

23. Compute the area of a triangle of base B and height H.

24. Compute both the circumference and the area of a circle given the radius. Use $\pi = 3.14159$.

25. Solve the equation $AX + B = 0$. Run the program for several values of A and B, including the case A = 0.

26. Compute the batting average A of a baseball player who has S singles, D doubles, T triples, and H home runs in B times at bat. (A = number of hits/B.)

27. Compute the slugging percentage P of the baseball player described in Problem 26. (P = total bases/B.)

28. Find the total cost C of four tires if the list price of each is L dollars, the federal excise tax is E dollars per tire, and the sales tax is S%.

29. Compute the total cost C of a table listed at L dollars selling at a discount of D% if the sales tax is S%.

30. Find the total taxes T on the McCormick property assessed at D dollars if the rate is R dollars per 1000. If the community uses X% of all taxes for schools, find how much of the McCormick tax is spent for schools.

31. The market value of a home is M dollars, the assessment rate is A% of the market value, and the tax rate is R dollars per 1000. Compute the property tax.

32. Compute the volume and surface area of a rectangular solid.

33. Compute the area of a triangle whose sides are *a*, *b*, and *c*. (Heron's formula for such a triangle is $A = \sqrt{s(s - a)(s - b)(s - c)}$, where $s = (a + b + c)/2$.)

34. A tin can is H inches high and the radius of its circular base is R inches. Calculate the volume and surface area. (Volume = area of base × height. Curved surface area = circumference of base × height.)

4.10 Review true-or-false quiz

1. The command NEW is used to clear the part of the Apple's random-access memory (RAM) in which BASIC programs are stored.　　T　　F

2. If you forget the line number while typing a BASIC statement, the Apple will respond by displaying an error message.　　T　　F

3. To correct an error committed while typing a program, you must retype the entire line.　　T　　F

4. A line may be deleted from a program simply by typing its line number and then pressing the RETURN key.　　T　　F

5. A program containing no syntax errors can cause error messages to be printed.　　T　　F

6. A BASIC programming line must contain exactly one BASIC command.　　T　　F

7. 300 LIST 300 is an admissible BASIC statement.　　T　　F

8. If a printer is connected to slot 1, the command PR#1 will cause subsequent output to be transmitted to the printer as well as being displayed on the video screen.　　T　　F

9. Coding a BASIC program involves determining the programming lines to carry out a known algorithm.　　T　　F

5

□ □ □ □ □ □ □ □ □ □ □ □ □ □ □

Interacting with the Computer

In this chapter we discuss two BASIC commands. The first is the INPUT command, which allows you to type values for variables during program execution and thus interact with the computer while your program is running. The second is the GOTO command, which allows you to override the normal sequential order in which programming lines are executed.

5.1 The INPUT command

The INPUT command is best illustrated by example.

EXAMPLE 1. **Here is a program to print the square of any number typed at the keyboard:**

```
1Ø PRINT "TYPE A NUMBER."
2Ø INPUT T
3Ø LET A=T^2
4Ø PRINT "SQUARE IS",A
5Ø END
```

When line 2Ø is executed, a question mark (the Apple's *input prompt*) will be displayed and nothing further will take place until you type a BASIC constant and enter it by pressing Ⓡ. This value will be assigned to T, and only then will program execution continue. Let's run this program:

```
]RUN                        (You type RUN Ⓡ.)
TYPE A NUMBER.              (Displayed by the Apple.)
?13                         (You type  13Ⓡ.)
SQUARE IS        169       (Displayed by the Apple.)

]□
```

More than one value may be assigned by an INPUT statement. The program statement

```
9Ø INPUT X,Y,Z
```

causes a question mark to be displayed, and three numerical constants, separated by commas, should be typed. If you type 5,3,24 after this question mark and then press (R), the value 5 will be assigned to X, 3 to Y, and 24 to Z. If you type fewer than three values, the Apple will display two more question marks and wait for you to complete the entry. Here are three equivalent ways to respond to this INPUT statement:

?5,3,24(R)   ?5,3(R)   ?5(R)
                    ??24(R)   ??3(R)
                                     ??24(R)

If you type more than three values, the Apple will assign the first three to X, Y, and Z, it will ignore any others that you typed, and before executing the next program statement it will display the message ?EXTRA IGNORED.

EXAMPLE 2. Here is a program to compute the cost C of renting a car for D days and driving it M miles. The rental rate is $12 per day and 11¢ per mile.

```
1Ø PRINT "ENTER NUMBER OF DAYS"
2Ø PRINT "AND NUMBER OF MILES,"
3Ø PRINT "SEPARATED BY A COMMA."
4Ø INPUT D,M
5Ø LET C=12*D+.11*M
6Ø PRINT "TOTAL COST IS",C
7Ø END
RUN

ENTER NUMBER OF DAYS          (Displayed by the Apple.)
AND NUMBER OF MILES,
SEPARATED BY A COMMA.
?
```

At this point you simply follow the instructions and type two numbers separated by a comma. Let's complete this run as follows:

```
?3,253                        (Underlined characters are typed by a user.)
TOTAL COST IS    63.83
```

Remark 1

Lines 1Ø to 3Ø display a message telling a user how to respond when the input prompt (?) is encountered. Without this explanation, a user would have no way of knowing what to type. It is a cardinal rule of programming that the person using a program should never be confronted with an unexplained input prompt.

Remark 2

The Apple begins displaying the output of a program on the line following the RUN command. We include a blank line for readability. If you want the Apple to skip this line, you can insert

```
5 PRINT
```

in the program. This statement will produce no output, but it will cause a RETURN to be executed. If you include

```
5 PRINT :  PRINT
```

two blank lines will appear after the word RUN.

EXAMPLE 3. This example shows that the INPUT command can be used to input string values for string variables.

```
1Ø PRINT "ENTER A NAME."
2Ø INPUT N$
3Ø PRINT "ENTER THE DATE."
4Ø INPUT D$
5Ø PRINT
6Ø PRINT N$
7Ø PRINT "INITIATION:",D$
8Ø END
RUN
```

```
ENTER A NAME.                    (Underlined characters are typed by a user.)
?STEVE MARTIN
ENTER THE DATE.
?MAY 1983
```

```
STEVE MARTIN
INITIATION:    MAY 1983
```

Note that the two input strings STEVE MARTIN and MAY 1983 were typed without quotation marks. Unlike strings in PRINT and LET statements (which must always be quoted), strings being typed in response to INPUT statements must be quoted only in two situations:

1. When significant blanks *begin* the input string. If such a string is not enclosed in quotation marks, the *leading* blanks are ignored.
2. When a comma is included in the input string. BASIC uses the comma as a delimiter of input values. If we had typed

```
MARTIN, STEVE
```

in response to the statement INPUT N$, the Apple would assign MARTIN to N$, ignore STEVE, and display the message ?EXTRA IGNORED before continuing program execution. However, typing

```
"MARTIN, STEVE"
```

instructs the Apple that all characters between the quotes, including the comma and the blank, constitute the string being input.

It is always correct to quote input strings, even when quotes are not required.

The readability of both screen and printer output can often be improved by having an input value appear on the same line as the message identifying this value. In Applesoft BASIC, this can be accomplished in two ways:

1. If you end a PRINT statement with a semicolon, the RETURN normally occurring after execution of the PRINT statement is suppressed. Thus if you type 358 in response to the programming lines

```
200 PRINT "WEEKLY INCOME";
210 INPUT I
```

your screen or printer will display

```
WEEKLY INCOME?358
```

If you want spaces to separate the input prompt (?) from the input value 358, simply press the space bar one or more times before typing 358.

2. You can include the message identifying what is to be input as part of the INPUT statement. Simply place the quoted string after the keyword INPUT and separate it from any variables whose values are to be input with a semicolon. For example, if you type 358 in response to the statement

```
200 INPUT "WEEKLY INCOME: $";I
```

your screen or printer will display

```
WEEKLY INCOME: $358
```

Note that the input prompt (?) is not displayed when you include a string constant in an INPUT statement as described.

Remark   If your printer has been specified as the output device as described in Section 4.7, you may find that the entire line

```
WEEKLY INCOME: $358
```

will be printed only after you type 358 and press the RETURN key. If this happens, you should use the first method of prompting the user; that is, if your program is to be executed with the printer selected as the output device, use PRINT statements to print instructions to the user.

EXAMPLE 4. Determine the yearly income and savings of a person whose weekly income and average monthly expenses are given. Two values must be specified (weekly income and monthly expenses) and two values must be determined (yearly income and savings). Let's agree to use the following variable names:

Input: I = weekly income
           E = monthly expenses
Output: Y = yearly income (note that $Y = 52 \times I$)
           S = yearly savings (note that $S = Y - 12 \times E$)

An algorithm for solving this problem can now be written:

a. Assign values to I and E.
b. Determine yearly income and savings.
c. Print results.

Before this algorithm can be coded, you must decide how to assign values to I and E. Available are the LET and INPUT statements. Since we may use this program for different weekly incomes and monthly expenses, the decision is easy: use an INPUT statement.

The program

```
100 REM PROGRAM TO FIND YEARLY INCOME AND SAVINGS
110 REM GIVEN THE WEEKLY INCOME AND MONTHLY EXPENSES
120 REM
130 INPUT "WEEKLY INCOME: ";I
140 INPUT "MONTHLY EXPENSES: ";E
150 REM
160 REM COMPUTE YEARLY INCOME AND SAVINGS.
170 LET Y=52*I
180 LET S=Y-12*E
190 PRINT "YEARLY INCOME:",Y
200 PRINT "YEARLY SAVINGS:",S
210 END
RUN
```

```
WEEKLY INCOME: 350
MONTHLY EXPENSES: 1325
YEARLY INCOME:  18200
YEARLY SAVINGS: 2300
```

(Underlined characters are typed by a user.)

Remark 1

The short discussion appearing just before the algorithm is called a **problem analysis.** It may simply describe the variables and show how they are interrelated, as is the case here, or it may include a thorough analysis of alternative approaches to a solution. In any case, a problem analysis is the process of discovering a suitable algorithm.

Remark 2

If you list this program, lines 100, 110, and 160 will each require two display lines on your 40-character screen. On most printers each will be printed on its own line.

The general forms of the Applesoft command INPUT are

    INPUT **input list**
    INPUT quoted string; **input list**

where **input list** denotes a list of variable names separated by commas. (Most often just one variable name will be included.) The semicolon in the second form is required. When executed, the first form displays the input prompt (?) and the second form displays the included string. In either case, you must respond by typing a value for each variable in the input list. The values you type must be separated by commas.

5.2 Problems

In Problems 1–14, complete the following partial program so that it will perform the tasks specified. Be sure that messages printed by line numbers 100 and 130 are appropriate for the problem being solved. No references to the variable names X and A should be made in these messages.

```
100 PRINT "              "
110 INPUT X
120 LET A =
130 PRINT "         ",A
140 END
```

1. Determine how much $100 earning 6% interest compounded annually will be worth in X years (value after X years is $100(1 + 0.06)^x$).
2. Determine the commission earned by a salesperson who sells a $625 television set if the rate of commission is X%.
3. Determine the total cost of an article whose selling price is X dollars if the sales tax is 4.5%.
4. Determine the weekly salary of a part-time employee working X hours at $4.47 per hour (no overtime).
5. Determine the cost per driving mile for a car that averages 19.2 mpg if gasoline costs X cents per gallon.
6. Determine the average of the four grades for a student who has received grades of 73, 91, 62, and X on four exams.
7. Determine the equivalent hourly salary, assuming a 40-hour week, for a worker whose annual salary is X dollars.
8. Determine the area of a circle given its diameter.
9. Determine the diameter of a circle given its area.
10. Convert inches to centimeters (1 in. = 2.54 cm).
11. Convert centimeters to inches.
12. Convert degrees to radians (1 degree = $\pi/180$ radians; use π = 3.14159).
13. Convert radians to degrees.
14. Determine the distance A to the horizon as viewed over a smooth ocean from a vantage point X feet above sea level. (Consider the right triangle in the following diagram.)

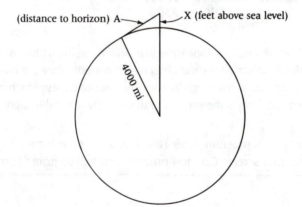

In Problems 15–21, write a program to perform each task specified. Use statements to instruct a user concerning input values and also to label any output values.

15. For any three input values A, B, and C, determine the three sums A + B, A + C, and B + C and find the average of these sums.
16. For any three input values P, Q, and R, determine the mean M and the three differences P − M, Q − M, and R − M.
17. Semester grades are based on three 1-hour tests and a 2-hour final examination. The 1-hour tests are weighted equally, but the final counts as two 1-hour tests. (All tests are graded from 0 to 100.) Determine the semester average for a student whose name N$ and grades G1, G2, G3, and F (F for final) are input.
18. Janet and Jim are bricklayers. In an hour Janet can lay J1 bricks and Jim can lay J2. Determine how long it will take both of them to complete the job if the total number N of bricks required is known. Values for J1, J2, and N are to be input.

19. A baseball player named N$ is to be paid P dollars the first year of a 3-year contract. Find the total dollar value of the contract over 3 years if the contract calls for an increase of I% the second year and J% the third year. Values for N$, P, I, and J are to be input.
20. Determine the yearly gross pay, net pay, combined tax deductions, and retirement deductions for a person whose monthly salary is given. The combined tax rate is R%, and 6% of the gross salary is withheld for retirement. Both R and the monthly salary are to be input.
21. A manufacturer produces three items that sell for $550, $620, and $1750. A profit of 10% is realized on items selling below $1000, and 15% is made on all other items. Determine the profit before and after taxes for a particular year, given the quantity of each item sold. The current tax rate on profits is R$.

5.3 The GOTO command: A first look at loops

As we mentioned at the beginning of this chapter, the GOTO command allows you to override the normal sequential order in which programming lines are executed. This means that you can direct the computer to execute sections of your program repeatedly and thus to perform hundreds of calculations with only a few programming lines. Using only the LET, INPUT, GOTO, and PRINT commands, the computer is transformed into a very fast and useful calculator.

The general form of the GOTO command is as follows:

GOTO **ln**

When executed, program control is immediately transferred to line number **ln.**

EXAMPLE 5. Here is a program containing a loop:

```
100 LET I=0
110 PRINT I
120 LET I=I+1
130 GOTO 110
```

This program will cause the numbers 0, 1, 2, 3, . . . to be printed one number per line. Each time line 130 is executed, control is transferred back to line 110. This is what is meant by a *loop*. The loop consists of the three program statements 110, 120, and 130.

If the program in Example 5 is run, it will not halt of its own accord. To stop it, you can issue the Applesoft command **ctrl C** (control C): hold down the key labeled CTRL while you type C.

This command transmits a single character to the Apple—the nonprinting character ctrl C. Program execution will terminate and the Apple will display the message

BREAK IN XX

where XX denotes the line number of the last command that was executed. Thus a run of the program in Example 5 might be displayed as follows:

```
]RUN
0
1
2
3

BREAK IN 110
]
```

EXAMPLE 6. Here is a program to do multiplication:

```
100 PRINT "AFTER EACH ? ENTER TWO NUMBERS."
110 INPUT A,B
120 LET P=A*B
130 PRINT "PRODUCT IS",P
140 PRINT
150 GOTO 110
RUN

AFTER EACH ? ENTER TWO NUMBERS.      (Underlined characters are typed by a user.)
? 5,3
PRODUCT IS   15

? 9,13.59
PRODUCT IS    122.31

?                                    (User types ctrl C command.)

BREAK IN 110
```

Remark 1

To interrupt an INPUT statement, ctrl C must be the first character you type. If you have already typed some of the input data, ctrl C will cause the Apple to display

```
?REENTER
?
```

At this point, type ctrl C again and program execution will terminate.

Remark 2

You will note that the programs shown in this section contain no END statements. Since each program is intended to be stopped manually by typing ctrl C, there is little reason for including a final END statement—it would never be executed.

Remark 3

Using ctrl C is not the customary way to stop a program that contains a loop. We use it here so that these early examples can be kept as simple as possible. In the next chapter, you will learn how to program an automatic exit from a loop so that a person using your programs will not be required to use ctrl C. The ctrl C command is included in Applesoft BASIC to assist you, the programmer; it is not intended for use by a user of your programs.

EXAMPLE 7. The program

```
100 LET X=0
110 LET X=X+1
120 GOTO 110
```

will cause the variable X to take on the successive values 0, 1, 2, 3, . . . but will not print or do anything else. Again you would use the ctrl C command to stop program execution.

Remark

If you run a program that seems to be doing nothing, simply type the ctrl C command and then look over your program listing for a possible loop containing no PRINT statements. To assist you in this search, you can use PRINT statements in immediate mode to examine the current values of any program variables. The Apple retains these values after a program is interrupted by a ctrl C command. Indeed, you can even cause program execution to continue from where it left off, with all variable values intact, by typing the Applesoft continue command CONT. We illustrate for the short program shown above:

```
]RUN
                              (ctrl C is typed.)
BREAK IN 120
]PRINT X                      (Examine current value of X.)
149

]CONT                         (Continue program execution.)
                              (ctrl C is typed again.)
BREAK IN 110

]PRINT X                      (Examine current value of X.)
743

]□
```

Programming tasks often call for output documents in tabular form. Normally these tables consist of one or more columns of data, each with a descriptive column heading. In the next example, we use a loop containing a PRINT statement of the form

PRINT *expression1, expression2*

to print the values in a two-column salary report. It is the comma in this PRINT command that causes the values of *expression1* and *expression2* to line up in columns. We also use PRINT statements of the same form to print the column headings. Forms of the PRINT statement that can be used to produce reports with more than two columns are described and illustrated in Chapter 7.

EXAMPLE 8. Prepare a table showing the equivalent annual salaries for persons working 40 hours a week if their hourly rates are $4.50, $4.60, $4.70, . . . , $5.50.

Problem analysis

The weekly pay W for a person working 40 hours a week at H dollars an hour is $W = 40 \times H$ dollars; the annual salary A for this person is $A = 52 \times W$ dollars. The hourly rates H = 4.50, 4.60, 4.70, and so on should not be input. Since successive H values differ by the same amount (0.10), you can start with H = 4.50 and simply keep adding 0.10 to H (LET H = H + 0.10) to get the other values.

Algorithm

The following algorithm shows one way to carry out the given task:

    a. Print the two column headings.
    b. Let H = 4.50.
    c. Evaluate $W = 40 \times H$ and then $A = 52 \times W$.
    d. Print H and A on one line.
    e. Add 0.10 to H and go to step (c).

The program

```
100 REM SALARY TABLE PROGRAM
110 PRINT
120 PRINT "HOURLY", "ANNUAL"
130 PRINT "RATE  ", "SALARY"
140 PRINT "------", "------"
150 LET H=4.50 : REM HOURLY RATE
160 LET W=40*H : REM WEEKLY SALARY
170 LET A=52*W : REM ANNUAL SALARY
180 PRINT H,A
190 LET H=H+0.10
200 GOTO 160
RUN
```

```
HOURLY              ANNUAL
RATE                SALARY
------              ------
4.5                 9360
4.6                 9568
4.7                 9776
4.8                 9984
4.9                 10192
5                   10400
5.1                 10608
5.2                 10816
5.3                 11024
5.4                 11232
5.5                 11440


BREAK IN 180
```

Lines 160 to 200 constitute the loop used to print the table values. Since the column headings must be printed first, and only once, the statements that do this (lines 120 to 140) must appear before the loop is entered.

Remark

The message BREAK IN 180 tells us that the ctrl C command was entered while the PRINT statement in line 180 was being executed. Not only does this BREAK message clutter the output, but having to stop a program in this manner means that you must be present to type ctrl C. This awkward situation can and should be avoided. As mentioned previously the BASIC command that allows you to do this is described in the next chapter.

___

We conclude this chapter with an example illustrating the programming practices we have been stressing:

1. To discover a correct algorithm for a given problem statement, carry out a complete problem analysis and record it in writing. The first step should be to determine precisely what is being asked. Determining the input and output values is a good way to begin.
2. Use PRINT statements (or INPUT statements containing strings) to tell the user what values are to be input during program execution. Also use PRINT statements to label

all output values. The precise form of these statements is usually determined during the coding process—that is, after the algorithm has been described.

3. Use REM statements to make your program more readable and to clarify what is being done at every point.

EXAMPLE 9

A man lives in a large house with many rooms. He wants to paint the walls and ceiling of each room, but before buying paint he naturally needs to know how much he needs. On the average, each window and door covers 20 sq ft. According to the label, each quart of paint covers 110 sq ft. Write a program that will allow the man to input the dimensions of each room and the number of doors and windows in each room and then determine how many quarts of wall paint and how many quarts of ceiling paint are needed for that room.

Problem analysis

Although this problem statement is somewhat lengthy, it should not be difficult to identify the input and output:

    Input: Name of each room
                Length, width, and height of each room
                Number of doors and windows in each room
    Output: Quarts of wall paint and quarts of ceiling paint needed for each room

To determine how many quarts of wall paint are needed for a particular room we must determine the wall area (in square feet) to be covered and divide this value by 110 since one quart of paint covers 110 sq ft. Similarly, the amount of ceiling paint is obtained by dividing the ceiling area by 110.

Before attempting to write down an algorithm for carrying out this task, let's choose variable names for the quantities of interest. Doing this will allow us to write a concise algorithm by using variable names, rather than verbal descriptions, for these quantities:

    ROOM\$ = name of the room in question
    L,W,H = length, width, and height of ROOM\$ (in feet)
       DW = total number of doors and windows in ROOM\$
       AW = area of all walls in ROOM\$ including door and window space
             $(AW = 2 \times (L + W) \times H)$
     ADW = area of the DW doors and windows $(ADW = 20 \times DW)$
       AC = area of a ceiling $(AC = L \times W)$
     QWP = quarts of wall paint needed $(QWP = (AW - ADW)/110)$
     QCP = quarts of ceiling paint needed $(QCP = AC/110)$

Using these variable names, we can write the following algorithm. Note that the order in which the steps are to be taken is just how you might carry out this task with tape measure, pencil, and paper:

    a. Enter values for ROOM\$, L, W, H, and DW.
    b. Determine the areas AW, ADW, AC.
    c. Determine the number of quarts of paint needed (QWP and QCP).
    d. Print the values of QWP and QCP.
    e. Go to step (a) and repeat the process for the next room.

The program

```
100 REM PAINT CALCULATION PROGRAM
110 REM
120 INPUT "ROOM: ";ROOM$
130 INPUT "LENGTH,WIDTH,HEIGHT: ";L,W,H
140 INPUT "NUMBER OF DOORS AND WINDOWS: ";DW
150 REM
160 REM CALCULATE AREAS.
170 LET AW=2*(L+W)*H : REM AREA OF WALLS
180 LET ADW=20*DW : REM AREA OF DOORS AND WINDOWS
190 LET AC=L*W : REM AREA OF CEILING
200 REM
210 REM PAINT CALCULATION
220 LET QWP=(AW-ADW)/110 : REM QUARTS OF WALL PAINT
230 LET QCP=AC/110 : REM QUARTS OF CEILING PAINT
240 REM
250 REM PRINT RESULTS FOR ROOM$.
260 PRINT "QUARTS OF PAINT NEEDED:"
270 PRINT "WALL PAINT",QWP
280 PRINT "CEILING PAINT",QCP
290 PRINT
300 GOTO 120
RUN

ROOM: KITCHEN
LENGTH,WIDTH,HEIGHT: 13,13,9
NUMBER OF DOORS AND WINDOWS: 5
QUARTS OF PAINT NEEDED:
WALL PAINT       3.34545455
CEILING PAINT    1.53636364

ROOM: FRONT BEDROOM
LENGTH,WIDTH,HEIGHT: 12,9,9
NUMBER OF DOORS AND WINDOWS: 4
QUARTS OF PAINT NEEDED:
WALL PAINT       2.70909091
CEILING PAINT     .981818182

ROOM:

BREAK IN 120
```

5.4 Problems

1. Show the output generated by each program.

a.
```
100 LET A=1
110 PRINT A
120 LET B=1
130 PRINT B
140 LET C=A+B
150 PRINT C
160 LET A=B
170 LET B=C
180 GOTO 140
```

b.
```
100 LET A$="A"
110 LET B$="B"
120 LET C$="C"
130 PRINT A$,B$,C$
140 LET T$=B$
150 LET B$=A$
160 LET A$=T$
170 PRINT A$,B$,C$
180 LET T$=C$
190 LET C$=A$
200 LET A$=T$
210 GOTO 130
```

```
c.  1Ø LET X=1              d.  1Ø LET S=Ø
    2Ø LET P=1                  2Ø LET A=5
    3Ø LET P=P*X                3Ø LET S=S+A
    4Ø PRINT X,P               4Ø PRINT S
    5Ø LET X=X+1               5Ø LET A=-(A+1)
    6Ø GOTO 3Ø                 6Ø GOTO 3Ø
```

2. Correct the following programs.

```
a.  1Ø REM PROGRAM TO PRINT THE    b.  1Ø REM PROGRAM TO DO SUBTRACTION
    2Ø REM ODD WHOLE NUMBERS           2Ø PRINT "TYPE TWO NUMBERS";
    3Ø LET N=1                        3Ø INPUT A,B
    4Ø PRINT N                        4Ø LET D=A-B
    5Ø LET N=N+2                      5Ø GOTO 2Ø
    6Ø GOTO 3Ø                        6Ø PRINT "SECOND - FIRST =",D
```

```
c.  1Ø REM PROGRAM TO PRINT AN     d.  1Ø REM PROGRAM TO PRINT A
    2Ø REM 8 PERCENT TAX TABLE         2Ø REM TABLE OF SQUARE ROOTS
    3Ø LET X=1ØØ                      3Ø LET N=2
    4Ø LET T=8*X                      4Ø PRINT "NUMBER","SQUARE ROOT"
    5Ø PRINT "PRICE","TAX"            5Ø LET R=N^1/2
    6Ø PRINT X,T                      6Ø PRINT N,R
    7Ø LET X=X+1                      7Ø LET N=N+1
    8Ø GOTO 4Ø                        8Ø GOTO 6Ø
```

In Problems 3–15, write a program to print each table described. Begin each program with a PRINT statement describing the table. If a table has more than one column, column headings should be printed.

3. The first column contains the number of miles (1, 2, 3, . . .); the second column gives the corresponding number of kilometers (1 mi = 1.6093 km).

4. The first column contains the temperature in degrees Celsius from −20 to 40 in increments of 2; the second column gives the corresponding temperature in degrees Fahrenheit ($F = (9/5)C + 32$).

5. A one-column table (list) contains the terms of the arithmetic progression $a, a + d, a + 2d, a + 3d, \ldots$. Values for a and d are to be assigned by the user.

6. A one-column table (list) contains the terms of the geometric progression $a, ar, ar^2, ar^3, \ldots$. Values for a and r are to be assigned by the user.

7. The first column gives the amount of sales (500, 1000, 1500, . . .); the second gives the commission at a rate of R%.

8. The first column contains the principal (50, 100, 150, . . .); the second gives the corresponding simple interest for 6 months at an annual rate of R%.

9. The first column contains the annual interest rate (7.0%, 7.25%, 7.5%, . . .); the second gives the simple interest on a principal of $1000 for 9 months.

10. The first column gives the list price of an article ($25, $50, $75, . . .); the second gives the corresponding selling price after a 15% discount.

11. Ucall Taxi charges 75¢ for a ride plus 13¢ for each tenth of a mile. The first column gives the number of miles (0.1, 0.2, 0.3, . . .); the second gives the total charges.

12. The first column contains the number of years ($n = 1, 2, 3, \ldots$); the second shows the amount to which an initial deposit of A dollars has grown after n years. The interest rate is R% compounded annually. (The value of A dollars after 1 year is $(1 + R/100) \times A$.)

13. The first column contains the radius of a circle in inches (1, 2, 3, . . .); the second gives the area of the circle.

14. The first column shows the radius in inches (1.0, 1.1, 1.2, . . .) of the circular bottom of a tin can; the second gives the volume of the can if its height is H inches. (H must be input.)

15. You require an accurate sketch of the graph of
$$y = \sqrt{1.09x^3} - \sqrt[3]{8.51x^2} + (1.314/1.426)x - 0.8$$
on the interval $1 \le x \le 3$. To make this task easier, produce a table of the y values where the x's are in increments of 0.1.

In Problems 16–19, write a program to perform each task specified.

16. A list of numbers is to be typed at the keyboard. After each number is typed, the program should cause two values to be printed: a count of how many numbers have been typed and the average of all numbers entered to that time.

17. A program should continually request two numbers of the user. After each pair of numbers is entered, the program should cause two values to be printed: the product of the two numbers just typed and the average of all products printed to that point.

18. A person wishes to determine the dollar amount of any collection of U.S. coins simply by specifying how many of each type of coin is included.

19. A manufacturer uses the following method to determine the selling price for an item. First the cost of materials is doubled to cover labor expenses. Then this figure is increased by 20% to cover overhead. The manufacturer uses this last figure to help decide on an additional percentage increase P to cover research and development (R & D) costs as well as profits. Only the manufacturer knows how P is determined. Write a program to assist with these calculations. Your program must contain two INPUT statements: one to obtain the cost of materials and a second to obtain a value for P. But remember: the manufacturer must be shown the total expense amount, including labor and overhead costs, before a value for P can be determined. (Use a GOTO statement to allow the manufacturer to determine the selling price for more than one item.)

5.5 Review true-or-false quiz

1. The statement INPUT A;B;N$ contains a syntax error.   T   F

2. BASIC allows you to type 3/4 in response to the statement INPUT X.   T   F

3. It is never correct to type THORPE,JIM in response to an INPUT statement.   T   F

4. The statement INPUT "COST",C contains a syntax error.   T   F

5. If the statements

```
149 PRINT "FIRST","SECOND"
150 PRINT A,B
```

appear in a loop, all A and B values will be printed in columns with the headings FIRST and SECOND.   T   F

6. If the statement 50 PRINT X,Y appears in a loop, the column of X values and the column of Y values will be aligned according to decimal points.   T   F

7. If a program contains the line 100 GOTO 130, the lines 110 and 120 will never be executed.   T   F

8. To halt an executing program, it is sufficient to hold down the CTRL key and type C.   T   F

9. The Applesoft command ctrl C halts program execution and resets all numerical variables to zero.   T   F

10. A *problem analysis* is the process of discovering a correct algorithm.   T   F

6

□ □ □ □ □ □ □ □ □ □ □ □ □

The Computer as a Decision Maker

BASIC contains several statements, called **control statements,** that allow you to control the order in which program statements are executed. The GOTO statement is an example. In this chapter we introduce the IF statement, whose purpose is to override the normal sequential operation of the statements in a program—but only if a certain condition, specified by the programmer, is satisfied. It is with this ability to make decisions that the full potential of the computer is realized.

6.1 The IF statement

The simplicity and usefulness of the IF statement are best illustrated by example.

EXAMPLE 1. Here is a program to print 6% of any input value, but only if the input value is positive:

```
1Ø INPUT "AMOUNT? ";A
2Ø IF A>Ø THEN PRINT "TAX IS",Ø.Ø6*A
3Ø END
RUN

AMOUNT? 43
TAX IS          2.58
```

After a value for A is input, the condition A>Ø in line 2Ø is tested. If it is true, the PRINT statement following the keyword THEN is executed. If it is false, the PRINT statement is not executed. In either case control passes to the next line, which in this example is an END statement.

EXAMPLE 2. Here is a program to print 6% of each of many positive input values and to stop when the number typed is not positive:

```
100 INPUT "AMOUNT? ";A
110 IF A<=0 THEN GOTO 160
120    PRINT "TAX IS",.06*A
130    PRINT
140    INPUT "NEXT AMOUNT? ";A
150 GOTO 110
160 PRINT "INVALID AMOUNT"
170 END
RUN

AMOUNT? 43
TAX IS              2.58

NEXT AMOUNT? 100
TAX IS              6

NEXT AMOUNT? 0
INVALID AMOUNT
]□
```

(Underlined characters are typed by a user.)

The condition $A<=0$ in line 110 is how you write the inequality $A \leq 0$ in BASIC. If this condition is true, the command GOTO 160 immediately following the keyword THEN is executed. The program then prints the message INVALID AMOUNT and halts. If the condition $A<=0$ is false, the command GOTO 160 is not executed and control passes to the line that follows the IF statement. The Apple then executes lines 120 to 140 as shown in the output and line 150 transfers control back to line 110. This looping is repeated until the condition $A<=0$ is true.

Remark 1

When the command following the keyword THEN is a GOTO command, Applesoft BASIC allows you to omit the keyword GOTO or the keyword THEN, but not both. Thus the following are equivalent ways of writing line 110:

```
110 IF A<=0 THEN 160
110 IF A<=0 GOTO 160
```

Remark 2

A word of caution is in order. When writing an IF statement you must not precede the keyword THEN by the letter A. Doing so introduces the reserved word AT into your program. For instance, the condition $0>=A$ is equivalent to $A<=0$, but you must not write line 110 as

```
110 IF 0>=A THEN GOTO 160
```

To see the problem, type the command LIST 110. The Apple will display this last line as

```
110 IF 0 >= AT HEN GOTO 160
```

This difficulty can always be avoided by enclosing the condition in parentheses.

Remark 3

In this program, the IF statement in line 110 and the GOTO statement in line 150 are used to set up a loop in which the group of statements

```
PRINT "TAX IS",.Ø6*A
PRINT
INPUT "NEXT AMOUNT? ";A
```

is executed repeatedly. We have indented these lines to improve the readability of the program. If your Apple system allows you to indent in this manner (unfortunately, many do not), we recommend that you do so. In this book we'll continue to indent groups of statements to improve program readability, fully aware that on many Apple systems they are listed without indentations.

These two examples illustrate the two very different uses of IF statements: *to construct loops* (Example 2) and *to make decisions* (Example 1). When the IF statement is used to construct loops, certain difficulties encountered with the GOTO statement are easily avoided. For example:

Loops using only the GOTO statement	Loops using the IF statement
1. The only way out of a loop is to stop the program manually (type ctrl C).	1. An exit from a loop can be made under program control.
2. Results obtained in a loop can be printed only using PRINT statements within the loop. This often results in the printing of unwanted intermediate results.	2. Results can be printed after completing a loop.
3. A program can execute only one loop.	3. More than one loop can be executed in a program.

When used to make *decisions*, the IF statement has many applications. As illustrated in Example 1, it can be used to examine a value typed at the terminal and then take a course of action that depends on this value.

In Applesoft BASIC, more than one BASIC command can follow the keyword THEN in an IF statement. For example:

IF statement	Effect
7Ø IF X>Ø THEN PRINT X : GOTO 3Ø	If X>Ø is true, X is output and control passes to line 30. If X>Ø is false, control passes immediately to the line following line 70.
5Ø IF A=Ø THEN PRINT "DONE" : END	If A is zero, DONE is output and program execution halts. If A is not zero, control passes immediately to the line following line 50.
65 IF X>6Ø THEN S=S+X : N=N+1	If X is greater than 60, X is added to S and N is increased by 1. If X is not greater than 60, these two assignment statements are skipped.

Although each of these IF statements contains only two commands, you can include as many as will fit on one programming line.

Note that these three programming lines are not multiple-command lines as described in Section 3.8. For example, line 70 is not the same as

```
7Ø IF X>Ø THEN PRINT X
71 GOTO 3Ø
```

This form transfers control to line 30 whatever the value of X, whereas

```
7Ø IF X>Ø THEᴺPRINT X: GOTO 3Ø
```

transfers control to line 30 only if X>0.

The preceding examples have illustrated three different forms of the IF statement:

```
IF condition THEN ln
IF condition GOTO ln
IF condition THEN command {: command}
```

Here **command** denotes any BASIC command (no line number). When executed, the *condition* is tested. If it is true, the first two forms transfer control to line **ln** and the third form causes the command or commands following the keyword THEN to be executed from left to right. If the *condition* is false, control passes immediately to the line following the IF statement. In the next section we'll discuss the precise form that the *condition* in an IF statement can take.

EXAMPLE 3. Here is a program to count how many of three input values are less than the average of all three:

```
1ØØ REM ***A COUNTING PROGRAM***
11Ø PRINT "TYPE THREE NUMBERS."
12Ø INPUT X,Y,Z
13Ø REM ***CALCULATE AVERAGE***
14Ø LET AV=(X+Y+Z)/3
15Ø REM ***BEGIN COUNTING***
16Ø LET N=Ø
17Ø IF X<AV THEN LET N=N+1
18Ø IF Y<AV THEN LET N=N+1
19Ø IF Z<AV THEN LET N=N+1
2ØØ PRINT "AVERAGE IS",AV
21Ø PRINT "BELOW AVERAGE:",N
22Ø END
RUN

TYPE THREE NUMBERS.
? 7Ø,9Ø,74
AVERAGE IS        78
BELOW AVERAGE:  2
```

Lines 110 to 160 accept input values for X, Y, and Z, assign their average to AV, and set the counter N to zero. For the input values shown, the condition X<AV in the first IF statement is true (70<78), so the statement LET N = N + 1 is executed and N becomes 1. The condition Y<AV is false, so the statement LET N = N + 1 in line 180 is skipped. The condition Z<AV is true, so line 190 increases N by 1 to give N = 2. Finally, the PRINT statements cause the output shown.

Remark

The first time the statement LET N = N + 1 is executed, it increases the value of N from 0 to 1; the second time, from 1 to 2. Thus the statement LET N = N + 1 actually does the counting. Such counting statements are used extensively in computer programming.

6.2 Relational expressions

The simplest form of the condition in an IF statement involves the comparison of two BASIC expressions. The BASIC symbols used to make such comparisons, together with their arithmetic counterparts, are shown in Table 6.1.

Any two BASIC expressions can be compared by using these symbols. Here are some examples of correctly written conditions:

```
X > 200          13 = B - C
M <> N           (A + B)/2 < A
17 <= 13         Y1 - Z1 >= 45
N$ = "YES"       A$ <> B$
```

TABLE 6.1 Relational Symbols Used in IF Statements

BASIC symbol	Arithmetic symbol	Meaning
=	=	Equal
<	<	Less than
>	>	Greater than
<>	≠	Not equal to
<=	≤	Less than or equal to
>=	≥	Greater than or equal to

Expressions such as these are called **relational expressions** and may be used as the condition in an IF statement. Their use is illustrated in the following examples.

EXAMPLE 4. In each part of this example we are given values for certain variables and an IF statement. We are to tell what happens when the IF statement is executed.

a. With X = 5000, consider

```
40 IF .07*X>300 THEN 70
```

Since .07*X has the value 350, the condition .07*X>300 is true. Transfer is made to line 70.

b. With A = 2, B = 3, and C = 1, consider

```
50 IF A-B<=C THEN LET C=A-B
```

Since A − B has the value −1 and C has the value 1, the relational expression A − B <= C is true. The LET statement is executed assigning the value −1 to C.

c. With M = 2 and N = 4, consider

```
120 IF N<>2*M THEN GOTO 200
```

Both N and 2*M have the value 4; hence the condition N<>2*M is false. No transfer is made to line 200, and control passes to the statement immediately following the IF statement.

EXAMPLE 5. Let's write a program to input two numbers A and B and print the message BOTH if both are negative and the message NOT BOTH otherwise.

Problem analysis   The logic of this problem is slightly complicated. First the number A must be tested to determine whether it is negative. If it is, then B must be tested. But as soon as a number being tested is not negative, the message NOT BOTH should be printed. Here's an algorithm for doing this:

a. Input values for A and B.
b. If A is not negative, print NOT BOTH and stop.
c. If B is not negative, print NOT BOTH and stop.
d. Print BOTH and stop.

The program

```
1Ø INPUT A,B
2Ø IF A>=Ø THEN 6Ø
3Ø IF B>=Ø THEN 6Ø
4Ø PRINT "BOTH"
5Ø GOTO 7Ø
6Ø PRINT "NOT BOTH"
7Ø END
RUN

? -5,-4
BOTH
```

Remark 1

The GOTO at line 50 simply serves to terminate this program. You can replace it with 50 END.

Remark 2

Beginning programmers are often tempted to begin coding a program without first describing an algorithm to be followed. If this practice were followed for the problem at hand, we could easily be led into making the tests $A < \emptyset$ and $B < \emptyset$ rather than the tests $A >= \emptyset$ and $B >= \emptyset$ as was done in lines 20 and 30. The result would be a program similar to the following:

```
1Ø INPUT A,B
2Ø IF A<Ø THEN 4Ø
3Ø GOTO 5Ø
4Ø IF B<Ø THEN 7Ø
5Ø PRINT "NOT BOTH"
6Ø GOTO 8Ø
7Ø PRINT "BOTH"
8Ø END
```

This is a correct but rather poor program. It contains an extra GOTO statement that makes it more difficult to follow than the first program. There are no hard and fast rules for choosing between the two tests $<$ and $>=$. The "best" choice will be dictated by a carefully prepared algorithm.

EXAMPLE 6. Here is a program segment that allows a user to instruct the computer to halt execution of a program:

```
3ØØ INPUT "ARE YOU FINISHED? ";C$
31Ø IF C$="NO" THEN 33Ø
32Ø PRINT "GOODBYE" : END
33Ø (Next statement to be executed)
```

Two strings are equal if they agree character by character. If you type NO for C$, the IF statement will transfer control to line 330. If you type YES, or anything other than NO, the string GOODBYE will be output and program execution will halt.

Remark 1   Strings appearing in relational expressions must always be enclosed in quotation marks. Failure to observe this rule will cause incorrect results or (if you are lucky) an error message.

Remark 2   If after typing NO you press the space bar and then the RETURN key, you will have assigned to C$ a three-character string containing NO and the nonprinting blank character. Thus the condition C$ = "NO" will be false. Remember: when input strings are not quoted, the Apple ignores leading blanks but not trailing blanks.

6.3 Compound logical expressions

A **logical expression** is an expression that is either *true* or *false*. Since the relational expressions encountered in the preceding section are either true or false, they are logical expressions. BASIC allows you to write *compound* logical expressions by using the logical operators AND, OR, and NOT. These are best illustrated by example.

EXAMPLE 7. Here is an illustration of the logical operators AND, OR, and NOT:

a. The logical expression

    (A<B) AND (B<C)

is true if both the relational expressions A<B and B<C are true; otherwise it is false. Thus the given expression is true only if A, B and C satisfy the double inequality A<B<C. Note that the expression A<B<C is not used in BASIC to compare A with B and B with C. A relational expression must contain only one of the relational operators =, <>, >, >=, <, and <=.

b. The logical expression

    (A<B) OR (A<C)

is true if either or both of the relational expressions are true. Thus the given expression is true if A is less than B, or C, or both; otherwise it is false. Note that this expression is false only if the expression

    (A>=B) AND (A>=C)

is true.

c. The logical expression

    NOT (A<B)

is true if the relational expression A<B is not true; otherwise it is false. Note that the given expression NOT (A<B) is equivalent to the relational expression A>=B. By equivalent, we mean that for any values of A and B, the expressions are both true or both false.

We now give precise definitions of the logical operators AND, OR, and NOT: If **le$_1$** and **le$_2$** are logical expressions, the truth values (*true or false*) of the three logical expressions (**le$_1$**) AND (**le$_2$**), (**le$_1$**) OR (**le$_2$**), and NOT (**le$_1$**) are shown in Tables 6.2, 6.3, and 6.4.

TABLE TABLE 6.2 The **AND** operator

le_1	le_2	(le_1) AND (le_2)
true	true	true
true	false	false
false	true	false
false	false	false

TABLE TABLE 6.3 The **OR** operator

le_1	le_2	(le_1) OR (le_2)
true	true	true
true	false	true
false	true	true
false	false	false

TABLE TABLE 6.4 The **NOT** operator

le_1	NOT (le_1)
true	false
false	true

EXAMPLE 8. The following illustrate typical uses of logical expressions containing the AND and OR operators:

a. The statement

    IF (A>Ø) AND (B>Ø) THEN 2ØØ

will transfer control to line 200 if both A and B are positive. Otherwise, control passes to the line following the IF statement.

b. The statement

    IF (G>=8Ø) AND (G<=89) THEN PRINT "B"

will cause the letter B to be printed only if the value of G is between 80 and 89, inclusive.

c. The statement

    IF (G<8Ø) OR (G>89) THEN 3ØØ

will cause a transfer to line 300 only if G is not between 80 and 89, inclusive.

A logical expression may contain more than one of the operators NOT, AND, and OR. An expression such as

    (M=0) OR (A<B) AND (A<C)

is admissible. The order in which the OR and AND operators are carried out does matter, however. In BASIC, the following priorities are used:

Logical operator	Priority
NOT	highest
AND	intermediate
OR	lowest

In every logical expression, the order in which the logical operators are performed is determined first by the indicated priority and then, within the same priority class, from left to right. As with arithmetic expressions, parentheses may be used to override this order or simply to clarify what order is intended. Thus the logical expression

```
(M=0) OR (A<B) AND (A<C)
```

is equivalent to the expression

```
(M=0) OR ((A<B) AND (A<C))
```

If you want the OR to be performed first, you must use parentheses and write

```
((M=0) OR (A<B)) AND (A<C)
```

EXAMPLE 9. Here is a program to input four numbers and print IN ORDER if they are in increasing order and NOT IN ORDER if they are not:

```
10 INPUT A,B,C,D
20 IF NOT ((A<B) AND (B<C) AND (C<D)) THEN PRINT "NOT ";
30 PRINT "IN ORDER"
40 END
```

We conclude this section by giving the rules governing the order in which the Apple carries out the operations in any logical, numerical, or string expression. As always, parentheses can be used to override this order. Moreover, it is an excellent programming practice to use parentheses consistently to clarify what is intended in an expression even when they are not required.

BASIC operators	Priority
− (negation), NOT	1 (highest)
∧	2
*, /	3
+, − (subtraction)	4
>, >=, <, <=, <>, =	5
AND	6
OR	7 (lowest)

In any expression, the operations are carried out from highest to lowest priority and operations having the same priority are carried out from left to right.

6.4 Problems

1. If A = 1, B = 2, and C = 3, which of the following logical expressions are true?
   a. A+B<=C
   b. A+B>=C
   c. 3<>C
   d. 7.0>=7
   e. A/C*B<=.5
   f. 3-(C/B)=3-C/B
   g. A/B/C>A
   h. -A-B-C<=-(A+B+C)*B
   i. (A<C) AND (A+B=C)
   j. NOT ((A>B) OR (C>A))
   k. ((A>B) OR (B>C)) AND (A-B+C<0)
   l. NOT (A>B) AND NOT (C>A)

2. Explain what is wrong with each statement. The problem may be a syntax error, or the statement may serve no purpose whatever.
   a. 90 IF 2<Y<4 THEN 27
   b. 60 IF M-N<27, THEN 13
   c. 30 IF X<ALPHA THEN 70
   d. 70 IF A<B THEN 70
   e. 50 IF X<X-B THEN 51
   f. 40 IF A1>A2 PRINT A1

3. Correct the following programs.
   a.
```
10 REM PROGRAM TO PRINT THE ODD
20 REM WHOLE NUMBERS THROUGH 15.
30 LET N=1
40 PRINT N
50 LET N=N+2
60 IF N<15 THEN 30
70 END
```
   b.
```
100 REM TELL WHETHER ANY NONZERO
110 REM INTEGER IS POSITIVE OR NEGATIVE.
120 INPUT N
130 IF N=0 THEN 120
140 IF N>0 THEN PRINT "POSITIVE"
150 END
160 IF N<0 THEN PRINT "NEGATIVE"
170 END
```

4. What will be printed when each of the following is run?
   a.
```
10 LET A=3
20 LET B=3
30 LET C=(A+B)/B
40 LET D=B/A-C
50 IF D>=0 THEN LET D=13
60 PRINT D
70 END
```
   b.
```
10 LET A=5
20 LET B=-A
30 IF A+B<>0 THEN 70
40 LET A=-B
50 PRINT A
60 GOTO 80
70 PRINT B
80 END
```
   c.
```
1 LET S=0
2 LET S=S+2
3 IF S<13 THEN 2
4 PRINT S
5 LET S=S/2
6 IF S>3.3 THEN 5
7 PRINT S
8 END
```
   d.
```
100 LET B=0
110 LET I=0
120 LET A=11
130 LET B=B+I+2
140 IF A<B THEN PRINT I : END
150 LET I=I+1
160 LET A=A-1
170 GOTO 130
```
   e.
```
10 LET L=22
20 IF NOT ((L<40) OR (L>60)) THEN 60
30 IF L<40 THEN LET L=L+50
40 IF L>60 THEN LET L=L-10
50 GOTO 20
60 PRINT L
70 END
```

5. Write programs that are equivalent to the following but contain no GOTO statements. (Use IF statements of the form IF *condition* THEN *line number* only if absolutely necessary.)

```
a. 1Ø LET S=1Ø              b. 1Ø INPUT N
   2Ø INPUT A                  2Ø IF N>=5Ø THEN 4Ø
   3Ø IF A>Ø THEN 5Ø           3Ø GOTO 5Ø
   4Ø GOTO 6Ø                  4Ø LET N=N/2
   5Ø LET S=2Ø                 5Ø IF N>=25 THEN 7Ø
   6Ø PRINT S                  6Ø LET N=N/2
   7Ø END                      7Ø PRINT N
                               8Ø END


c. 1Ø INPUT X,Y             d. 1Ø INPUT A,B
   2Ø IF X>Ø THEN 4Ø           2Ø IF A>B THEN 6Ø
   3Ø GOTO 1Ø                  3Ø PRINT "SMALLEST IS",A
   4Ø IF Y>Ø THEN 6Ø           4Ø PRINT "LARGEST IS",B
   5Ø GOTO 1Ø                  5Ø END
   6Ø LET S=X+Y                6Ø LET T=A
   7Ø PRINT S                  7Ø LET A=B
   8Ø END                      8Ø LET B=T
                               9Ø GOTO 3Ø
                               99 END
```

In problems 6–16, write a program to perform each task specified. Appropriate messages should be printed (keep them short) that give instructions to the user concerning values to be entered. (The operators NOT, AND, and OR are not required.)

6. Two numbers A and B are to be typed. If the first is larger, print LARGER; otherwise, print NOT LARGER.
7. Two numbers M and N are to be typed. If the sum equals 5, print 5; otherwise print NOT 5.
8. Two numbers X and Y are to be typed. If the product is less than or equal to the quotient, print PRODUCT; otherwise print QUOTIENT.
9. Three numbers are to be typed. If the second is less than the sum of the first and third, print LESS; otherwise print NOT LESS.
10. A person earns R dollars an hour with time-and-a-half for all hours over 32. Determine the gross pay for a T-hour week. (R and T are to be entered during program execution.)
11. The cost of sending a telegram is $1.35 for the first ten words and 9¢ for each additional word. Find the cost if the number of words is input.
12. If the wholesale cost of an item is under $100, the markup is 20%. Otherwise the markup is 30%. Determine the retail price for an item whose wholesale cost is entered during program execution.
13. Two numbers X and Y are to be typed. If the sum of X and Y is greater than 42, print 42. If not, increase X by 10 and Y by 3, print the next X and Y, and again check to see if the sum is greater than 42. Continue until the sum is greater than 42.
14. Input a positive integer N, and determine the first positive integer I whose cube is greater than N.
15. Division of one positive integer A by another positive integer B is often presented in elementary school as repeated subtraction. Write a program to input two positive integers A and B, and determine the quotient Q and the remainder R by this method.
16. Input two positive integers A and B, and compute A^B without using the exponential operator ^.

In Problems 17–21, write a program to perform each task. For these problems you may find the logical operators NOT, AND, and OR helpful.

17. For any two numbers M and N, print POSITIVE if both are positive and NEGATIVE if both are negative. Otherwise, print NEITHER.
18. One number is to be typed. If it is between 7 and 35, inclusive, print BETWEEN and stop. If it is less than 7, increase it by 5; if it is greater than 35, decrease it by 5. In either case, print the value obtained. The program should continue with this new value until it is between 7 and 35.
19. For any three numbers typed at the keyboard, print ALL if all three are negative; otherwise print NOT ALL.
20. For any three numbers input, print ALL NEGATIVE if all are negative, ALL POSITIVE if all are positive, and NEITHER in all other cases.
21. Find the first positive integer N for which $33N - 28 > 24N + 200$ and $5N - 63 \geq 2N + 21$.

6.5 Flowcharts and flowcharting

The following diagram is a pictorial representation of a simple algorithm to determine whether or not an input value is 5:

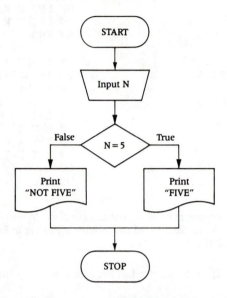

A pictorial representation of the sequence of steps in an algorithm or a program is called a **programming flowchart** or simply a **flowchart.** Flowcharts are useful for program documentation. Moreover, it is often easier to prepare a pictorial description of a process than to attempt a detailed description in words. The flowchart is an excellent way to do this. Some of the components used to construct flowcharts can be seen in the following examples.

EXAMPLE 10. Here are two equivalent flowcharts for a program to print the numbers 100, 110, 120, ..., 200:

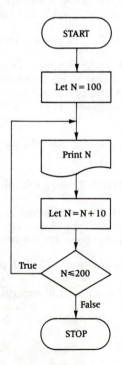

EXAMPLE 11. Here is a flowchart displaying the process of adding the integers from 1 to 10:

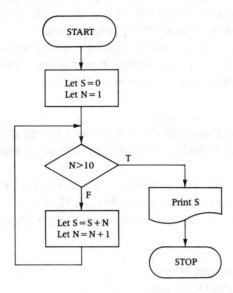

Remark 1   When two or more assignment statements are included in a single box they are evaluated from top to bottom.

Remark 2   Note that we have labeled the flow lines from the diamond-shaped decision symbol with the letters T and F for true and false, respectively.

In these examples, arrows connecting six different types of symbols are used to describe the sequence of steps in an algorithm. When possible, the flow should be directed from top to bottom or from left to right as in these examples. Although there are many flowchart symbols in use, the six presented here are adequate for displaying the flow of instructions for many BASIC programs.* Table 6.5 shows how these symbols are used.

TABLE 6.5   Flowchart Symbols

The symbol	Its use
	To designate the start and end of a program.
	To describe data to be input during program execution.
	To describe the output.
	To describe any processing of data.
	To designate a decision that is to be made.
	A connector—used so that flow from one segment of a flowchart to another can be displayed and also to avoid drawing long lines.

*The flowchart symbols proposed by the American National Standards Institute (ANSI) are described in "Flowcharting with the ANSI Standard: A Tutorial," by Ned Chapin, *Computing Surveys*, vol. 2, no. 2, June 1970.

The process of preparing a flowchart is called **flowcharting.** There are no fixed rules on how you should proceed in preparing a flowchart—flowcharting must be practiced. However, since a flowchart is simply another way to describe an algorithm, you should carry out a problem analysis just as you would for any programming task.

We conclude this section with two examples illustrating the process of flowcharting. Once a flowchart is prepared, the task of writing the program is reasonably straightforward; it consists only of coding the steps indicated in the flowchart.

EXAMPLE 12. Construct a flowchart to find the largest number in a list of input values. The special value 9999 is to be typed to indicate that all numbers in the list have been entered.

Problem analysis   One way to determine the largest number in a list is to read the numbers one at a time, remembering only the largest of those already read. (This method was discussed in Chapter 2, Example 2.) To help us give a precise description of this process, we'll use the following variable names:

L = largest number already read
N = number currently being read

It is not difficult to construct a flowchart describing an algorithm for this task. First we must input the first number and assign it to L. Thus we can begin with the following flowchart segment:

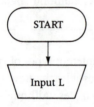

The next step is to input another value and compare it with 9999 to determine whether the end of the input list has been reached. To display this step, we can add the following segment to our flowchart:

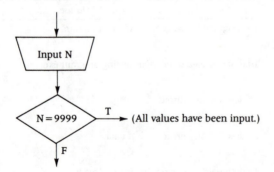

If N = 9999 (the *True* branch), we simply print L, the largest number, and stop. Thus we can complete the T (*True*) branch by adding the following segment to our flowchart:

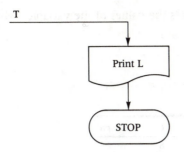

Note that while constructing the flowchart (that is, while discovering an algorithm), we always have a partial flowchart in front of us to help us decide what the next step should be. Continuing this process of construction, a flowchart such as the following will emerge:

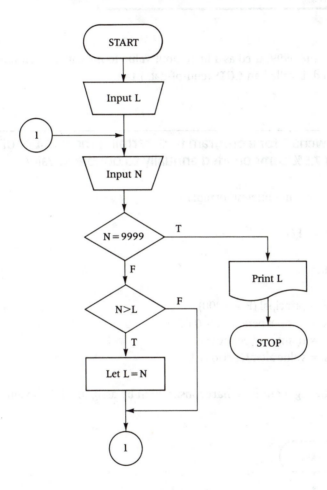

Here is one way to code this flowchart:

```
10Ø REM FIND LARGEST INPUT VALUE.
11Ø INPUT L
12Ø    INPUT N
13Ø    IF N=9999 THEN PRINT L : END
14Ø    IF N>L THEN LET L=N
15Ø GOTO 12Ø
```

The following table summarizes the values of the variables when this program is run with the input list

8, 3, 9, 2, 9999

Line number	N	L	Output
110	0	8	
120	3	8	
120	9	8	
140	9	9	
120	2	9	
120	9999	9	
130	9999	9	9

Remark

The value 9999, used as a final input value to indicate that all numbers in the list have been entered, is called an **EOD** (end-of-data) **tag.**

EXAMPLE 13. Construct a flowchart for a program to determine the number of years required for an investment of $1000 earning 7.5% compounded annually to double in value.

Problem analysis

The compound interest formula is

$$A = P(1 + R)^N$$

in which

P = principal (P = 1000)
R = rate per period (R = 0.075)
N = number of periods
A = value after N periods

We can begin our flowchart construction by assigning initial values to P, R, and N:

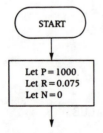

Next we must compare the value of A after 1 year with 2P. Since N denotes the number of years that have passed, we can add the following segment to our partial flowchart:

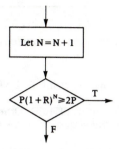

If the condition is true, we simply print N and stop. If it is false, we increase N by 1 and repeat the comparison. Adding these two steps to the partial flowchart, we obtain the following complete algorithm.

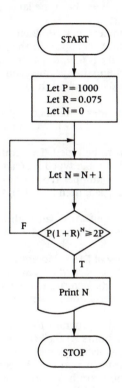

The flowchart

If this flowchart is coded, a GOTO statement will be needed following the IF statement. We can avoid this GOTO statement by using $<$ rather than $\geq$ in the decision box. The flowchart will have exactly the same structure, but the program will be easier to read.

The program

```
100 LET P=1000
110 LET R=0.075
120 LET N=0
130    LET N=N+1
140 IF P*(1+R)^N<2*P THEN 130
150 PRINT "YEARS TO DOUBLE",N
160 END
RUN

YEARS TO DOUBLE 8
```

6.6 Problems

In Problems 1–14, prepare a flowchart and then a program to accomplish each task specified. Try to avoid GOTO statements in your programs.

1. Input one number. If it is between 3 and 21, print BETWEEN. Otherwise, print NOT BETWEEN.
2. Input two numbers. If either one is positive, print EITHER. Otherwise, print NEITHER.
3. Input three distinct numbers. If the first is the largest, print LARGEST. Otherwise, print NOT LARGEST.
4. Input three distinct numbers. If the second is the largest, print LARGEST. If it is the smallest, print SMALLEST. Otherwise, print NEITHER.
5. Input two values A and B. Print the value 1 if A and B are both zero or both one. Print the value 0 in all other cases.
6. Input a list of numbers whose last value is 9999. Print the smallest and largest values in the list excluding the 9999.
7. Input a list of numbers whose last value is 9999. Print the largest number and also a count of how many numbers are included in the list.
8. (This is more difficult.) Input a list of numbers as in Problem 7. Print the largest number in the list and also a count of how many numbers appear in the list before the first occurrence of this largest number. For example, if the list is 6, 9, 6, 12, 10, 5, 12, 7, 5, the largest value is 12 and the count is three. (*Hint:* To determine the specified count you will need one variable to count the input values and another to keep track of the number of input values appearing before the current largest value.)
9. For any input list, determine how many times a number is strictly larger than the one just before it. For example, if the list is 17, 3, 19, 27, 23, 25, the answer will be three, because $19 > 3$, $27 > 19$, and $25 > 23$.
10. A list of numbers, terminated by 9999, is to be typed. Two counts, N and P, are required as follows. P is a count of how many times a number typed is greater than the number typed just before it; N is a count of how many times a number typed is less than the number typed just before it. (For example, if 1, 5, 3, 3, 7 are typed, then $P = 2$ and $N = 1$, whereas if 5, 4, 3, 4, 8, 9 are typed, then $P = 3$ and $N = 2$.)
11. Several pairs (X, Y) of numbers are to be input. Any pair with $X = Y$ serves as the EOD tag. Determine and print counts of how many pairs satisfy $X < Y$ and how many pairs satisfy $X > Y$.
12. Each salesperson earns a base weekly salary of $185. Moreover, if a salesperson's total weekly sales exceed $1000, a commission of 5.3% is earned on any amount up to $5000 and 7.8% is earned on any amount in excess of $5000. Determine the weekly pay, before deductions, for any salesperson whose total weekly sales amount is input. Use an EOD tag to terminate the program.
13. A company payroll clerk needs a computer program to help prepare the weekly payroll. For each employee the clerk is to enter the hours worked H, the hourly pay rate R, the federal tax rate F, the state tax rate S, and the Social Security rate T. The clerk needs to know the gross pay, the net pay, and the amount of each deduction. Employees receive time-and-a-half for each hour worked over 40 hours. (*Hint:* The algorithm should not be too detailed. For example, after H, R, F, S, and T have been called for, a single line might read "Determine the gross pay, the three deductions, and the net pay." The details for doing this would then be worked out as you construct the flowchart.)
14. A salesperson's monthly commission is determined according to the following schedule:

Net sales	Commission rate
Up to $10,000	6%
Next $4000	7%
Next $6000	8%
Additional amounts	10%

Determine the monthly commission given the total monthly sales.

6.7 Summing with the IF statement

As a programmer you will often encounter problems whose solutions require you to find the sum of many numbers. Since summing is a repetitive process, it can be accomplished efficiently with a loop. In this case it is important that an exit be made from the loop only after the required sum has been obtained. The examples in this section illustrate the following three ways to exit from a loop:

1. Before the loop is initiated, specify the exact number of terms to be added (Example 14).
2. Program the computer to terminate the loop upon recognition of a special value, such as 999 (Example 15).
3. Cause an exit from the loop when a certain condition has been satisfied (Example 16).

EXAMPLE 14. Construct a flowchart and write a program to evaluate the following sum where N is to be specified by the user. If the input value N is less than 1, the sum is zero.

$$S = 1^2 + 2^2 + 3^2 + \cdots + N^2$$

Problem analysis

Here's a simple algorithm for this task:

a. Input N.
b. Calculate the sum $S = 1^2 + 2^2 + \cdots + N^2$.
c. Print S and stop.

To carry out step (b), you can start with a sum S of zero and add the squares of the numbers 1, 2, 3, . . . , N to S, one at a time. The following flowchart describes this process:

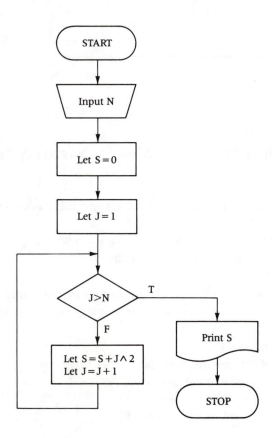

The program

```
1Ø INPUT N
2Ø LET S=Ø
3Ø LET J=1
4Ø IF J>N THEN 8Ø
5Ø    LET S=S+J^2
6Ø    LET J=J+1
7Ø GOTO 4Ø
8Ø PRINT "SUM IS",S
9Ø END
RUN

? 5
SUM IS            55
```

The following table traces the values of N, S, and J as this program is executed with the input value N = 5:

Line number	N	S	J	Output
1Ø	5	0	0	
2Ø	5	0	0	
30	5	0	1	
50	5	1	1	
60	5	1	2	
50	5	5	2	
60	5	5	3	
50	5	14	3	
60	5	14	4	
50	5	30	4	
60	5	30	5	
50	5	55	5	
60	5	55	6	
80	5	55	6	SUM IS 55

EXAMPLE 15. For any set of input values, find two averages: the average of those in the range 60 to 80 and the average of all the others.

Problem analysis

Input: A list of numbers typed at the keyboard. (Let's agree that 999 terminates this list.)

Output: A1 = average of numbers from 60 to 80.
       A2 = average of all other numbers.

To find the average of a collection of numbers, we must add them and divide by how many there are. This procedure suggests the following variables in addition to A1 and A2:

   X = current input value
   S1 = sum of numbers from 60 to 80
   S2 = sum of all other numbers (but not 999)
   N1 = count of numbers whose sum is S1
   N2 = count of numbers whose sum is S2

With these variable names, we can easily construct the following flowchart:

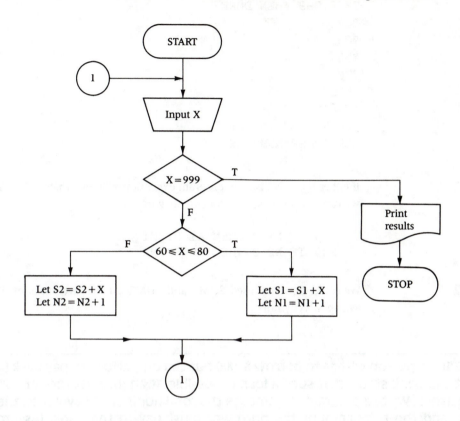

The double inequality in the second decision box suggests that we use an IF statement with
the condition $(60<=X)$ AND $(X<=80)$. This is done in line 150.

The program

```
100 PRINT "BEGIN DATA ENTRY-"
110 PRINT "TYPE 999 WHEN DONE."
120     INPUT X
130     IF X=999 THEN 220
140     REM***PROCESS X***
150     IF (60<=X) AND (X<=80) THEN 190
160     LET N2=N2+1
170     LET S2=S2+X
180 GOTO 120
190     LET N1=N1+1
200     LET S1=S1+X
210 GOTO 120
220 REM***PRINT RESULTS***
230 LET A1=S1/N1
240 LET A2=S2/N2
250 PRINT "AVERAGES:"
260 PRINT "NUMBERS 60 TO 80:",A1
270 PRINT "ALL OTHER NUMBERS:",A2
280 END
RUN
```

```
BEGIN DATA ENTRY—
TYPE 999 WHEN DONE.
?50
?80
?55
?70
?999
AVERAGES:
NUMBERS 60 TO 80:             75
ALL OTHER NUMBERS:            52.5
```

Remark 1   If either N1 or N2 is zero, program execution will terminate at line 230 or 240. To avoid this, we can replace these two statements with

```
230 IF N1>0 THEN A1=S1/N1
240 IF N2>0 THEN A2=S2/N2
```

Remark 2   We could not have used SUM1 and SUM2 for the two sums or AV1 and AV2 for the two averages. Why not?

EXAMPLE 16. A person wishes to borrow $1000 but can only afford to pay back $40 per month. A loan officer at the bank states that such a loan is possible at an interest rate of 1.2% per month on the unpaid balance. Write a program to compute the total number of payments, the amount of the final payment, and the total amount the borrower must pay to the bank. (Assume that the first $40 payment is to be made 1 month after the date of the loan.)

Problem analysis   So that the program will apply to any problem of this type, let's assign the variables as follows:

R = monthly rate of interest ($R = 0.012$)
P = monthly payment ($P = 40$)
B = balance still owed to bank at any time (initially 1000)
I = interest due for previous month ($I = B*R$)
N = number of payments made to date (initially zero)
T = total amount paid to date (initially zero)

Whenever a payment is made, the bank calculates the new balance as follows. The interest $I = B*R$ for the previous month is added to the old balance (LET $B = B + I$). If this balance B is not greater than P, a final payment of B dollars will be made. If B is greater than P, then the current payment of P dollars is subtracted from B (LET $B = B - P$) and this is the new balance. In either case the current payment must be added to the total amount T, and N, which counts the number of payments made, must be increased by 1.

The flowchart

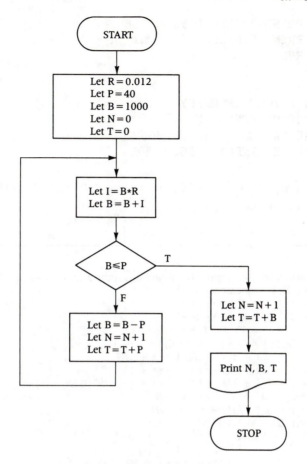

The program

```
100 REM INITIALIZE VARIABLES.
110 LET R=0.012
120 LET P=40
130 LET B=1000
140 LET T=0
150 LET N=0
160 REM CALCULATE INTEREST AND NEW BALANCE.
170    LET I=B*R
180    LET B=B+I
190    REM CHECK FOR LAST PAYMENT.
200    IF B<=P THEN 270
210    REM MAKE A PAYMENT OF P DOLLARS.
220    LET B=B-P
230    LET N=N+1
240    LET T=T+P
250 GOTO 170
260 REM MAKE FINAL PAYMENT AND PRINT RESULTS.
270 LET N=N+1
280 LET T=T+B
290 PRINT "LOAN PAYMENT SUMMARY:"
300 PRINT "NO. OF PAYMENTS",N
```

```
310 PRINT "FINAL PAYMENT",B
320 PRINT "TOTAL REPAYMENT",T
330 END
RUN

LOAN PAYMENT SUMMARY:
NO. OF PAYMENTS 30
FINAL PAYMENT   36.0570632
TOTAL REPAYMENT 1196.05706
```

Remark

So that the program can be used for other loans, R, P, and B should be input and not assigned values in LET statements.

6.8 Problems

1. Write programs to compute the following sums and products. N, if present, is to be assigned with an INPUT statement.
   a. $S = 1 + 2 + 3 + \cdots + N$
   b. $S = 5 + 7 + 9 + \cdots + 91$
   c. $S = 3 + 8 + 13 + 18 + \cdots + 93$
   d. $S = (-10)^7 + (-8)^5 + (-6)^3 + (-4)^1 + (-2)^{-1}$
   e. $S = 1 + 1/2 + 1/3 + 1/4 + \cdots + 1/N$
   f. $S = 1 - 1/2 + 1/3 - 1/4 + \cdots + (-1)^{N+1}/N$
   g. $S = 1 - 1/3 + 1/5 - 1/7 + \cdots + (-1)^{N+1}/(2N - 1)$
   h. $S = 2^2 + 4^2 + 6^2 + \cdots + (2N)^2$
   i. $S = 1 + 1/4 + 1/9 + \cdots + 1/N^2$
   j. $P = (1/2)(2/3)(3/4)(4/5) \cdots (N/(N + 1))$
   k. $P = (1 - 1/2)(1 - 1/3)(1 - 1/4) \cdots (1 - 1/N)$

In Problems 2–13, write a program to perform each task specified.

2. Calculate the sum and average of any 20 input values.
3. Input a list of numbers whose last value is 999. Calculate the sum and average of all input values excluding 999.
4. Many numbers are to be input. The number 0 is used as the EOD tag. Determine the sum of all positive numbers and the sum of all negative numbers. Both sums are to be printed.
5. A list of numbers is to be input as in Problem 4. Determine and print the average of all positive numbers and the average of all negative numbers.
6. Many scores from 0 to 100 are to be input. The number -1 is used as the EOD tag. Determine the average of all numbers less than 60, the average of those from 60 up to but not including 90, and the average of those 90 or more.
7. A young man agrees to begin working for a company at the very modest salary of a penny per week, with the stipulation that his salary will double each week. What is his weekly salary at the end of 6 months and how much has he earned?
8. Find the total amount credited to an account after 4 years if $25 is deposited each month at an annual interest rate of 5.5% compounded monthly.
9. Mary deposits $25 in a bank at the annual interest rate of 6% compounded monthly. After how many months will her account first exceed $27.50?
10. On the first of each month other than January, a person deposits $100 into an account earning 6% interest compounded monthly. The account is opened on February 1. How much will the account be worth in 5 years just prior to the February deposit?
11. Andrew's parents deposit $500 in a savings account on the day of his birth. The bank pays 6.5% compounded annually. Construct a table showing how this deposit grows in value from the date of deposit to his twenty-first birthday.
12. Sally receives a graduation present of $1000 and invests it in a long-term certificate that pays 8% compounded annually. Construct a table showing how this investment grows to a value of $1500.
13. Find the averages of several sets of numbers typed at the keyboard. The value 999, when typed, means that all entries for the set being typed have been made. The input value -999 means that all input sets have been processed.

6.9 Structured programming

The importance of preparing an algorithm before beginning the coding process cannot be overemphasized. But just as unreadable programs are often written by people who begin a programming task while seated at a computer, so too can unreadable algorithms be written if certain guidelines are not followed. The algorithms we have presented in this book take one of two forms:

1. An English-like step-by-step process describing how to carry out a specific task
2. A flowchart displaying the steps to be followed

When the first form is used, the individual steps often correspond to program segments rather than to single program statements. For instance, the following algorithm was written for the task given in Example 14 of Section 6.7:

a. Input N.
b. Calculate the sum $S = 1^2 + 2^2 + \cdots + N^2$.
c. Print S and stop.

If you can see how to code step (b), there is no need to include more detail in this algorithm. If it is not obvious to you how to code step (b), you can rewrite the step in more detail. Here is one way to do this:

b1. Let S = 0.
b2. For J = 1, 2, 3, . . . , N, add J ^ 2 to S.

This process of refining the steps in an algorithm is called the **method of stepwise refinement** and has been illustrated in several of the examples, beginning with those in Chapter 2. A more thorough discussion of this programming method is given in Chapter 10.

When using flowcharts to display the steps in an algorithm, you can use the same process of refinement. For the example cited, you could have begun by writing the following flowchart:

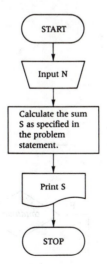

As before, if coding this flowchart is easy for you, there is no need to include more detail. If it is not clear how to code the box that calculates S, however, you should try to rewrite this step by including more detail. In Example 14, we displayed this detail by using the following flowchart segment:

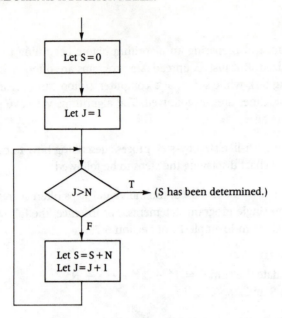

When writing an algorithm—whether in English, as a flowchart, or in BASIC—the following situations arise:

1. Two or more tasks are to be carried out in sequence (Figure 6.1).
2. One of two tasks is to be selected depending on a specified condition; one of the two tasks may be to do nothing (Figure 6.2).
3. A task is to be carried out repeatedly (Figure 6.3).

Figure 6.1
Sequence.

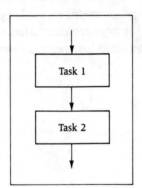

Figure 6.2
Selection.

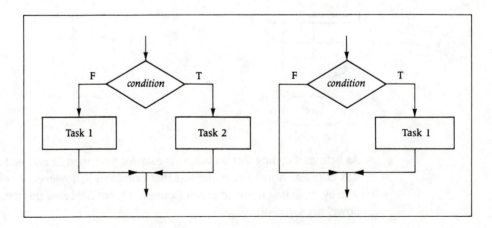

Figure 6.3
Repetition.

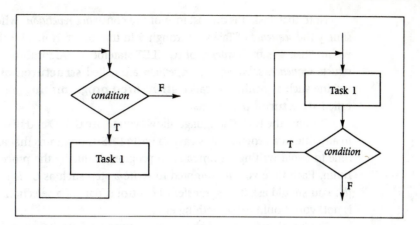

These three control structures are referred to as **structured programming constructs.** It has been shown that any algorithm can be written by using only these constructs.* The following diagram shows how two of these constructs (*sequence* and *repetition*) are used in the algorithm, shown in Example 14, to calculate the sum $S = 1^2 + 2^2 + 3^2 + \cdots + N^2$.

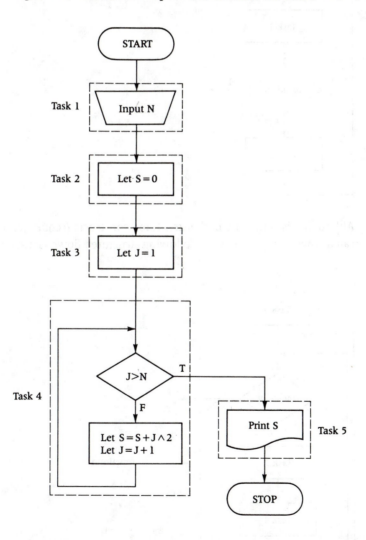

*See "Flow Diagrams, Turing Machines and Languages with only Two Formation Rules," by Corrado Bohm and Guiseppe Jacopini, *Communications of the A.C.M.*, vol. 9, May 1966, pp. 366–371.

Note that Task 4 is an instance of the construct *repetition*, whereas the entire program is simply the *sequence* of Tasks 1 through 5 in that order. Note also that the task being repeated within Task 4 is the *sequence* of two LET statements. Algorithms written with only the constructs *sequence, selection,* and *repetition* are called **structured algorithms.** The process of writing such algorithms is called **structured programming** and the resulting programs are called **structured programs.**

Because the BASIC language allows you to use GOTO and IF statements to transfer control to any line in a program, it is easy to write BASIC programs that are hard to understand. The time to avoid writing an unreadable program is during the process of discovering the algorithm. Each time you are tempted to write a step such as *Go to step (b),* or *If N<5, go to step (b),* you should ask if this transfer of control is part of a selection or repetition structure. If it is not, you should try something else.

Even with great care in algorithm construction, BASIC programmers often encounter the following control structure in their algorithms:

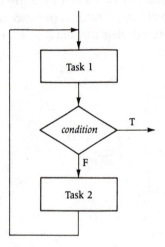

Although this is not one of the structured constructs (sequence, selection, and repetition), it can always be replaced by the following structured flowchart segment:

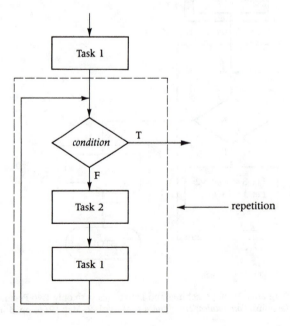

It is debatable, however, whether writing the BASIC code for Task 1 twice in the program is worth the effort. The usual practice among BASIC programmers is to allow this construct as one of the building blocks for programs. (It was used in Example 16 of Section 6.7.)

If you use only the programming constructs described in this section, your final product, the program, will have a simple structure and hence will be easy to read, to debug, and to modify, should that be required. For instance, note that each of the suggested constructs has exactly one entry point and exactly one exit point. This means that an entire program can be broken down into blocks of code, each block having but one entry point and one exit point. Since each of these blocks will perform a known task, the individual blocks can be debugged separately—greatly simplifying the task of verifying the correctness of the entire program. As you write larger and larger programs, you will find this method of debugging not only useful but essential.

Once you have written an algorithm using the suggested constructs, the task of coding it as a BASIC program is straightforward, as we now show.

EXAMPLE 17

To code the selection construct

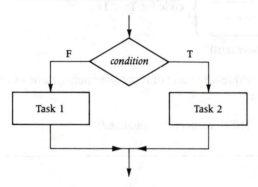

you can write (the line numbers are for illustration only):

500 IF *condition* THEN 600

$\left.\begin{array}{c}\rule{2cm}{0.4pt}\\\rule{2cm}{0.4pt}\\\rule{2cm}{0.4pt}\end{array}\right\}$ code for Task 1

590 GOTO 700

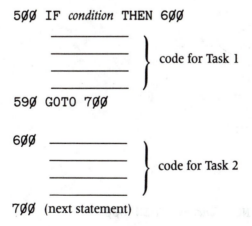

EXAMPLE 18

To code the selection construct

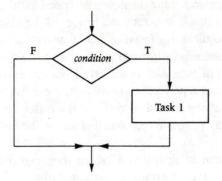

you can write

500 IF NOT *condition* THEN 600

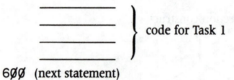

} code for Task 1

600 (next statement)

If Task 1 denotes a sequence of one or more statements, none of which is a control statement, you can use the form

IF *condition* THEN *command* {: *command*}

EXAMPLE 19

To code the repetition construct

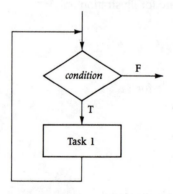

you can write

500 IF NOT *condition* THEN 600

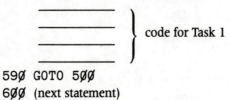

} code for Task 1

590 GOTO 500
600 (next statement)

Remark

Note that the code for Task 1 must contain a statement that changes some variable appearing in the condition. Indeed, the condition must eventually become false—otherwise you have an infinite loop.

EXAMPLE 20

To code the repetition construct

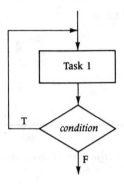

you can write

```
500  REM  (description of Task 1)
510  _____
     _____  } code for Task 1
     _____
     _____
600  IF condition THEN 510
610  (next statement)
```

EXAMPLE 21

To code the construct

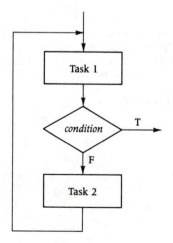

you can write

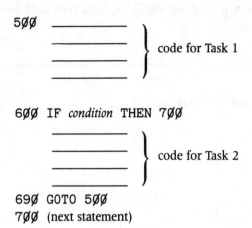

```
5ØØ  _____
     _____   } code for Task 1
     _____
     _____

6ØØ  IF condition THEN 7ØØ
     _____
     _____   } code for Task 2
     _____
     _____

69Ø  GOTO 5ØØ
7ØØ  (next statement)
```

6.10 Problems

In Problems 1–6, construct a flowchart for each algorithm shown. In each case use only the sequence, selection, and repetition constructs presented in Section 6.8.

1. a. Input values for N, R, and T.
   b. If N≤40, let S = N × R. Otherwise, let S = 40R + (N − 40)(1.5)R.
   c. Reduce S by the amount S × T.
   d. Print S and stop.
2. a. Input a value for N.
   b. If N = 0, print the message GOODBYE and stop.
   c. If N > 0, print the integers from 1 up to N. Otherwise, print the integers from 0 down to N.
   d. Input another value for N and repeat step (b).
3. a. Input values for A and B.
   b. If A and B have the same sign (the condition for this is A × B > 0), print POSITIVE or NEGATIVE according to whether A and B are positive or negative.
   c. If either A or B is zero, print FINI and stop. Otherwise, repeat step (a).
4. a. Input an integer N.
   b. If N = 0, stop.
   c. Print BETWEEN if N is between 70 and 80, exclusive; otherwise print NOT BETWEEN.
   d. Go to step (a).
5. a. Input values for X, Y, and Z.
   b. If X < Y, print Y − X and go to step (d).
   c. Print Z − X only if X < Z.
   d. Print X, Y, and Z.
   e. Stop.
6. a. Input a value for N.
   b. If N is less than or equal to zero, go to step (a).
   c. If N > 100, print VALUE IS TOO LARGE and go to step (g).
   d. If N > 50, calculate SUM = 50 + 51 + 52 + ••• + N and go to step (f).
   e. Calculate SUM = 1 + 2 + 3 + ••• + N.
   f. Print the value of SUM.
   g. Print the message GOODBYE and stop.

Reconstruct the flowcharts shown in Problems 7–10 by using only the sequence, selection, and repetition constructs shown in Figures 6.1, 6.2, and 6.3. In the given flowcharts, C1, C2, and C3 denote logical expressions and S1, S2, S3, and S4 denote single statements or groups of statements. To illustrate, the unstructured flowchart

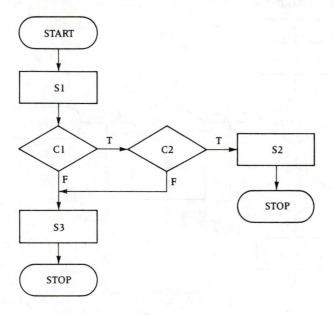

can be written in the equivalent form

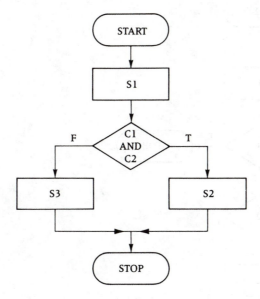

In this illustration, we had to combine two symbols. For the problems, you may also have to write a symbol more than once.

In this illustration, we had to combine two symbols. For the problems, you may also have to write a symbol more than once.

7.

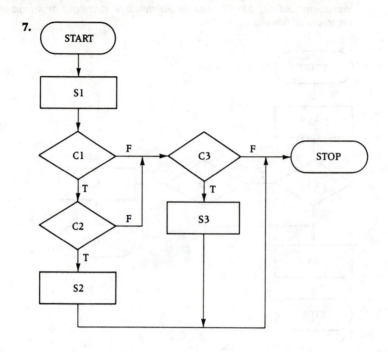

8.

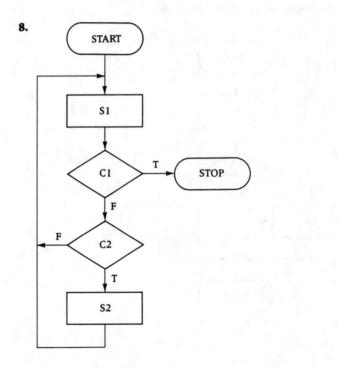

9.

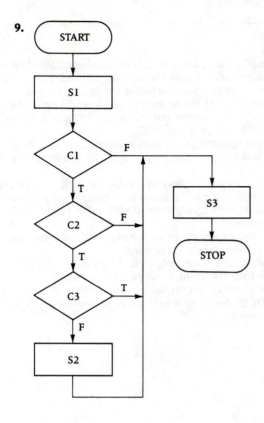

10.

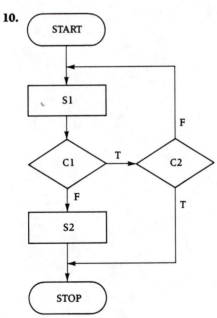

6.11 Review true-or-false quiz

1. In BASIC the IF statement is used for two fundamentally different purposes.   T   F
2. The IF statement makes it possible to write all BASIC programs so they will halt of their own accord after producing the desired output.   T   F
3. The IF statement should not be used to construct a loop within a loop.   T   F
4. If a program is to print results and stop when $P<Q$, it is always best to use an IF statement with the condition $P<Q$.   T   F
5. String constants appearing in relational expressions must be quoted.   T   F
6. A flowchart is a pictorial representation of the sequence of statements in an algorithm.   T   F
7. A flowchart is an excellent way to display the logic of a program, but flowcharting is of little value when it comes to writing the program.   T   F
8. The question asked in a decision box of a flowchart is the basis for the condition in an IF statement.   T   F
9. If the logical expression in an IF statement is false, the normal sequential execution of the program is interrupted.   T   F
10. A BASIC program containing only LET, PRINT, and INPUT statements, together with a proper END statement, is necessarily *structured*.   T   F
11. A program as described in (10), which also contains IF statements of the form IF *condition* THEN *statement*, where *statement* denotes a LET, PRINT, or INPUT statement, is structured.   T   F

7

□ □ □ □ □ □ □ □ □ □ □ □ □ □ □

More on the
PRINT Statement

Up to now we have been working with a very limited form of the PRINT statement. As a consequence, we have had little control over the format of the output generated by a program. In this chapter we'll show how many values can be output on a line (Sections 7.1–7.2), how the TAB and SPC spacing functions can be used to specify precise positions along a line for these values (Section 7.4), and how the HTAB and VTAB commands, which are used principally (but not exclusively) for screen output, can be used to specify both horizontal and vertical positions for any output values (Section 7.5).

7.1 Printing more values on a line

A line of output from an Applesoft program can be divided into units called **print zones** or **tab fields.** Each print zone, except possibly the last one on a line, contains 16 print positions; the last one contains however many remain. Accordingly, a line on the 40-character display screen can be visualized as

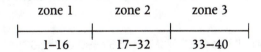

zone 1	zone 2	zone 3
1–16	17–32	33–40

and a line on an 80-column printer can be visualized as

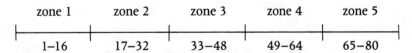

zone 1	zone 2	zone 3	zone 4	zone 5
1–16	17–32	33–48	49–64	65–80

A PRINT statement such as

```
25 PRINT A,B$,C$,D
```

which uses the comma to delimit the variables, will cause the values of the variables to be output, one item per zone, provided the item fits. If an item does not fit, it is continued into the next zone. If there are not enough zones on one line, Applesoft will continue to the next line until all items are output. Thus the comma is interpreted by the Apple as an instruction to move to the beginning of the next print zone. Indeed, the comma in the command

```
PRINT,A
```

instructs the Apple to skip the first zone and print the value of A in the second.

EXAMPLE 1

```
100 LET A=4.35
110 LET B=-3
120 LET C$="APPLE"
130 PRINT A,B,C$,C$,A,B
140 END
RUN
```

(40-column screen)

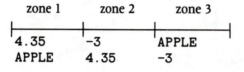

(80-column printer)

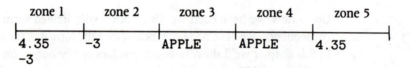

When an item is printed in a zone, printing always begins in the first position of that zone.

In Chapter 4 we cautioned against using the last position in a print zone. If a character is output in this position, the next zone on your display screen will be skipped and the next zone on a printer *may* be skipped. The next example gives another restriction when output is directed to a display screen.

EXAMPLE 2. A character displayed in positions 24 through 32 on the display screen causes the third zone of that line to be skipped.

```
10 PRINT "12345678901234567890l234567"
20 LET A=1 : B=3
30 PRINT B,A/B,A
40 END
RUN

12345678901234567890l234567
3               .333333333
1
```

Since characters are displayed in positions 24, 25, and 26 of the second line of output, zone 3 is skipped and the third output value (1) is displayed in the next zone as shown.

Remark If the output is directed to a printer, the three numbers are printed in zones 1, 2, and 3 of the same display line.

___

Many values can be output on a single line if semicolons instead of commas are used as delimiters in PRINT statements. When semicolons are used, print zones are ignored and output values are merged. Thus if line 130 of Example 1 is changed to

```
130 PRINT A;B;C$;C$;A;B
```

the output will be

```
4.35-3APPLEAPPLE4.35-3
```

which of course is meaningless. To preserve the identity of the output values you must provide for spaces in the PRINT statement. For example:

```
30 PRINT A;" ";B;" ";C$;" ";C$;" ";A;" ";B
```

will insert one space between each value, giving the output

```
4.35 -3 APPLE APPLE 4.35 -3
```

Similarly, if A$ = "TO", B$ = "GET", and C$ = "HER!!!", the two statements

```
100 PRINT A$;B$;C$
```

and

```
100 PRINT "TO";"GET";"HER!!!"
```

will both produce the same output:

```
TOGETHER!!!
```

If spaces are desired, they must be included as part of the strings. Or you can write

```
100 PRINT A$;" ";B$;" ";C$
```

A PRINT statement, whether it uses semicolons or commas as delimiters, may contain any combination of constants, variables, and expressions. In the next example, we use a PRINT statement to output the values of two numerical variables, a string constant, and a numerical expression.

EXAMPLE 3

```
10 INPUT "ENTER A NUMBER ";A
20 LET R=5
30    PRINT R;" PERCENT OF ";A;" IS ";A*R/100
40    LET R=R+1
50 IF R<9 THEN 30
60 END
RUN

ENTER A NUMBER 500
5 PERCENT OF 500 IS 25
6 PERCENT OF 500 IS 30
7 PERCENT OF 500 IS 35
8 PERCENT OF 500 IS 40
```

7.2 Suppressing the carriage return

It often happens that a program contains a loop in which a new output value is determined each time the loop is executed. If the print command is of the form

```
PRINT T
```

successive values of T will be output on separate lines (to the delight of paper manufacturers). If you terminate this print line with a comma or a semicolon, however, more than one value will be printed on each line—one in each print zone if a comma is used and as many as will fit on the line if a semicolon is used.

EXAMPLE 4

```
100 LET N=1
110    LET T=2*N-1
120    PRINT T;" ";
130    LET N=N+1
140 IF N<=10 THEN 110
150 PRINT
160 PRINT "THAT'S ALL FOLKS!"
170 END
RUN

1 3 5 7 9 11 13 15 17 19
THAT'S ALL FOLKS
```

Remark 1

After completing the loop, control passes to line 150, which causes a RETURN to be executed so that subsequent output will appear on a new line.

Remark 2

The blank (" ") must be included in line 120 to prevent the numbers from being printed with no intervening blanks.

EXAMPLE 5. Here is a program to print a row of N dashes:

```
100 INPUT "HOW MANY DASHES? ";N
110 LET K=0
120 IF K>=N THEN 160
130     PRINT "-";
140     LET K=K+1
150 GOTO 120
160 END
RUN


HOW MANY DASHES? 35
-----------------------------------
```

Note that the condition K>=N is tested before the loop is entered rather than after. This was done so that no dashes will be printed if zero is input for N.

7.3 Problems

1. Show the exact output of each program.

a.
```
10 PRINT "BASEBALL'S HALL OF FAME"
20 PRINT "COOPERSTOWN, N.Y.","U.S.A."
30 END
```

b.
```
100 LET N=0
110     PRINT N,
120     LET N=N+5
130 IF N<38 THEN 110
140 PRINT "FINI"
150 END
```

c.
```
10 LET X=5
20 LET Y=X+3
30 PRINT X;" TIMES ";Y;" = ";X*Y
40 END
```

d.
```
10 PRINT "HAPPY"
20 PRINT "         HAPPY"
30 PRINT ,"HOLIDAY"
40 END
```

e.
```
10 LET N=1
20     PRINT N; " ";
30     LET N=N+2
40 IF N<9 THEN 20
50 LET N=N-7
60 PRINT
70 IF N=2 THEN 20
80 END
```

f.
```
10 LET X=5
20     PRINT "IF A= ";
30     PRINT X;
40     PRINT " A+2= ";
50     PRINT X+2,
60     LET X=X+5
70     PRINT
80 IF X<=15 THEN 20
90 END
```

2. Assuming that X = 1 and Y = 2, write PRINT statements to print the following. No numbers are to appear in the PRINT statements.

a. 1/2=.5
b. X + Y = 3
c. X - 2 = -1
d. SCORE: 2 TO 1
e. DEPT.NO. 5
f. BLDG 4.25

3. The following programs do not do what is claimed. Correct them.

a.
```
100 REM A PROGRAM TO PRINT
101 REM     1 2 3
102 REM     4 5 6
110 LET X=1
120     PRINT X;
130     LET X=X+1
140 IF X<=3 THEN 120
150     LET X=X+1
160     PRINT X
170 IF X<=6 THEN 150
180 END
```

b.
```
100 REM A PROGRAM TO PRINT
101 REM     7A7A7A
110 LET X=1
120     PRINT 7;"A"
130     LET X=X+1
140 IF X<=3 THEN 120
150 END
```

In Problems 4–14, write a program to perform each task specified.

4. Fifteen years ago the population of Easton was 3571; it is currently 7827. Find the average increase in population per year. The output should be

```
FIFTEEN YEAR POPULATION INCREASE IS _____.
THIS REPRESENTS AN AVERAGE INCREASE OF _____ PER YEAR.
```

5. An item has a list price of L dollars but is on sale at a discount of D%. Find the selling price. The output should be

```
LIST PRICE $_____
DISCOUNT OF ____ PERCENT IS $_____
SELLING PRICE $_____
```

6. If the wholesale price of a car is under $4300, the markup is 22%; otherwise the markup is 27%. Determine the retail price if the wholesale price is input. The output should be

```
WHOLESALE PRICE IS _____ DOLLARS.
MARKUP IS ____ PERCENT.
RETAIL PRICE IS _____ DOLLARS.
```

7. A manufacturer produces an item at a cost of C dollars per unit and sells each unit for S dollars. Moreover, a fixed yearly cost of F dollars must be absorbed in the manufacture of this item. The number of units that must be sold in 1 year to break even (breakeven volume) is given by the formula

$$\text{Breakeven volume} = \frac{F}{S - C} \text{ units}$$

For any values of C, S, and F input, the output is to be

```
FIXED COST PER YEAR? _____
PRICE PER UNIT? _____
COST PER UNIT? _____
_____ UNITS MUST BE SOLD TO BREAK EVEN.
THIS REPRESENTS _____ DOLLARS IN SALES.
```

8. Print a row containing M dashes followed by the string THE END. M is to be input.
9. Print THE END beginning in column position N. N is to be input. (Use the statement PRINT " "; to print a space.)
10. Print a square array of asterisks with M rows and M columns. M is to be input.
11. Print a square array of # symbols with N rows and N columns. Printing is to begin in column position P. N and P are to be input.
12. Print a square array of asterisks with 12 rows and 12 columns. The design is to be centered on the screen (or page).
13. Print a rectangular array of + signs with R rows and C columns. The design is to be centered on the screen (or page). R and C are to be input.
14. Input four numbers for A, B, C, and D, and print the product (AX + B)(CX + D). If A = 2, B = 5, C = 3, and D = 4, for example, the output should be

```
(2X+5)(3X+4)=6X^2+23X+20
```

7.4 The TAB and SPC functions

By using the semicolon in PRINT statements, you can specify exact positions for your output values. However, as you probably found while writing the programs for the preceding problem set, this process can be cumbersome. To alleviate this difficulty, Applesoft BASIC provides the spacing functions TAB and SPC. Both of these functions must be included in PRINT statements. TAB(n) specifies that the next output value is to commence in column position n, and SPC(n) specifies that n spaces are to be skipped before printing the next item.

EXAMPLE 6

```
10 PRINT "12345678901234567890"
20 PRINT
30 PRINT TAB(7);"WET"
40 PRINT TAB(6);"PAINT"
50 PRINT
60 PRINT "BEWARE!";SPC(4);"ATTACK DOG"
70 END
RUN

12345678901234567890

      WET
     PAINT

BEWARE!    ATTACK DOG
```

Remark

Note the use of semicolons in the PRINT statements. Remember that a comma specifies that subsequent output is to commence at the beginning of the next print zone.

Several TAB and SPC functions may be included in a single PRINT statement. For example, if N = 3 and A = 1.234, the statement

```
PRINT A;SPC(N);10*A;SPC(N);100*A
```

will produce the output

```
 1.234    12.34    123.4
```

with exactly N = 3 spaces separating the three output values. Similarly, the lines

```
10 PRINT "12345678901234567890"
20 PRINT TAB(8);"ONE";SPC(4);"TWO"
```

will produce the output

```
12345678901234567890
       ONE    TWO
```

Note that SPC(4) says to skip four spaces; it does not say to move ahead four spaces.

Caution: With some printers, TAB(N) causes the next output value to be printed beginning N positions from the *current* print position. This will be column position N (the intended position) only if the printer happens to be positioned at the beginning of a new output line. To see how your printer works, type and run the following:

```
10 PR#1 : REM SELECT PRINTER.
20 PRINT "1234567890"
30 PRINT TAB(3);"A";TAB(5);"B"
```

You will obtain one of the following printouts.

(Printers for which TAB works correctly)	(Other printers)
1234567890	1234567890
A B	A B

If your printer is one of the "other" printers, you should use TAB only for output values that begin a new line. (Note that in the given illustration the first output value (A) is printed correctly in both cases.) To specify positions for other output values, you can use SPC. (In the next section we describe the HTAB command that can sometimes be used as an alternative to the TAB function should TAB not work correctly with your printer.)

The argument *n* in TAB(*n*) and SPC(*n*) can be any numerical expression. The Apple truncates the value of *n* to obtain an integer argument N. The following apply to both TAB(N) and SPC(N).

1. N must be in the range 0 to 255. If it is not, the error message
?ILLEGAL QUANTITY ERROR IN 1n is displayed and program execution halts.

2. If N is in the range 0 to 255, but TAB(N) or SPC(N) specify a position beyond the right margin allowed by the output device, continuation lines are used. *Remember:* In Applesoft BASIC a "line" can contain up to 255 characters. In most programming applications, however, N is kept small enough that all output generated by a single PRINT statement will appear on one line.

3. SPC(0) specifies that no space is to precede the next output value. TAB(0), however, is rarely used. It specifies the position just beyond the current 255-character output line. Recall that in Applesoft BASIC there is no position number 0 on a line.

The following three examples further illustrate the TAB and SPC functions.

EXAMPLE 7. Here is an illustration of the TAB function:

```
10 PRINT "12345678901234567890"
20 PRINT "--------------------"
30 LET K=1
40    PRINT TAB(K);3*K
50    LET K=K+1
60 IF K<6 THEN 40
70 END
RUN
```

```
1234567890123456789Ø
---------------------
3
  6
   9
     12
      15
```

Each time line 40 is executed, TAB(K) causes the value of 3*K to be output beginning in column position K.

EXAMPLE 8. Here is an illustration of the SPC function:

```
1Ø PRINT "12345678"
2Ø PRINT "--------"
3Ø LET K=Ø
4Ø    PRINT "N";SPC(K);"N";SPC(5-K);"N"
5Ø    LET K=K+1
6Ø IF K<6 THEN 4Ø
7Ø END
RUN

12345678
--------
NN      N
N N     N
N  N    N
N   N   N
N    N N
N      NN
```

EXAMPLE 9. Here we see TAB and SPC in one PRINT statement:

```
1ØØ PRINT "1234567890123456789Ø"
11Ø PRINT
12Ø LET T=8 : S=5
13Ø    PRINT TAB(T);"*";SPC(S);"*"
14Ø    LET T=T+1 : S=S-2
15Ø IF T<=1Ø THEN 13Ø
16Ø PRINT TAB(11);"*"
17Ø END
RUN

1234567890123456789Ø

       *     *
        *   *
         * *
          *
```

Each time line 130 is executed, TAB(T);"*" causes an asterisk to be output in column position T, and SPC(S);"*" causes a second asterisk to be output after skipping S positions.

Remark

This program can be simplified somewhat by replacing SPC(S) in line 13Ø by TAB(22-T) and deleting the variable S entirely. The simplified program will produce exactly the same output on any display screen, but only on certain printers (those for which TAB(N) always specifies that printing is to commence in column position N).

7.5 The HTAB and VTAB commands

The horizontal and vertical tab commands HTAB and VTAB allow you to move the cursor to any position on the Apple's display screen. For example, the three statements

```
1ØØ HTAB 5
11Ø VTAB 2Ø
12Ø PRINT "A"
```

will display the letter A in the fifth character position of display line 2Ø. The command HTAB 5 moves the cursor left or right, depending on the current cursor position, to position 5 of the current display line. The command VTAB 2Ø then moves the cursor up or down to display line 2Ø. Since the three commands shown are so closely related, it is natural to write the equivalent multiple statement line

```
1ØØ HTAB 5 : VTAB 2Ø : PRINT "A"
```

Any numerical expressions can be used to specify positions in HTAB and VTAB commands. For example, the program segment

```
1Ø LET N=1
2Ø    HTAB N : VTAB N : PRINT "APPLE"
3Ø    LET N=N+1
4Ø IF N<=4 THEN 2Ø
```

will display

```
APPLE
 APPLE
  APPLE
   APPLE
```

When N = 1, the PRINT command displays the string APPLE beginning in character position 1 of display line 1; when N = 2, the PRINT command displays APPLE beginning in position 2 of display line 2; and so on.

The HTAB and VTAB commands are most often used when output must be displayed at specific screen locations without affecting the rest of the screen in any way. This means that input values must not be entered on the last line (line 24) of the screen since each input line must be entered by pressing the RETURN key and this will cause everything on the screen to scroll up one line. For the same reason, PRINT statements that direct output to display line 24 should end with a semicolon (not with a comma, since a RETURN will be executed if anything is output in zone 3). To illustrate, consider the program lines

```
1ØØ HTAB 1 : VTAB 1 : PRINT "FIRST LINE"
11Ø HTAB 1 : VTAB 24 : PRINT "LAST LINE"
```

Line 100 displays the string FIRST LINE at the upper left corner of the screen and line 110 displays the string LAST LINE at the lower left corner. However, since the PRINT commands are not terminated by semicolons, each causes a RETURN to be executed. This presents no difficulty when line 100 is executed; however, after line 110 displays the string LAST LINE on display line 24, everything on the screen will scroll up one line leaving LAST LINE on display line 23 and causing the string FIRST LINE to be scrolled off the screen.

The general forms of the HTAB and VTAB commands are as follows.

HTAB **m** **m** denotes a numerical expression whose value is truncated, if necessary, to obtain an integer M. If M is in the range 1–40, the screen cursor is moved, left or right, to position M of the current display line.

Note 1: As with the TAB function, the Apple uses a 255-character line beginning in position 1 of the current display line and continuing through several of the screen's 40-character lines. If M is in the range 1–255, the cursor is moved to position M of this 255-character line. If M = 0, the cursor is moved just beyond this 255-character line. If M is not in the range 0–255, the error diagnostic ILLEGAL QUANTITY ERROR will be displayed and the program will terminate.

Note 2: If output is directed to a printer, HTAB will position the printer to one of the first 40 positions of a line, even if the printer allows 80-character lines. Moreover, HTAB will not reposition the printer to the left of its current position. Thus, when using a printer for output, HTAB serves only as a limited alternative to the TAB function.

VTAB **n** **n** denotes a numerical expression whose value is truncated, if necessary, to obtain an integer N. If N is in the range 1–24, the cursor is moved, up or down, to display line N. If N is not in the range 1–24, a fatal ILLEGAL QUANTITY ERROR will result.

Note: If output is directed to a printer, VTAB has no effect whatever.

The VTAB and HTAB statements will position the cursor at a location on the screen whether or not a character is already displayed at that location. Thus, the statements

```
100 VTAB 15 : HTAB 5 : PRINT "PINEAPPLE"
110 VTAB 15 : HTAB 5 : PRINT "APPLE"
```

will display the word PINEAPPLE beginning at the fifth position on display line 15, and then will display the word APPLE beginning at this same location. The effect is to display the characters APPLEPPLE. If the intent is to replace PINEAPPLE by APPLE, you can include the statement

```
105 VTAB 15 : HTAB 5 : PRINT "         "
```

to "erase" PINEAPPLE by displaying enough blank characters over it.

The following example illustrates a typical application of this ability to display new information over old information.

EXAMPLE 10. Selective modification of a screen display.

The program segment shown below consists of two parts. Lines 100–180 display the following table.

```
    ————————————————
    ITEM   PERCENT
     1.     1Ø.ØØ
     2.     1Ø.ØØ
     3.     1Ø.ØØ
     4.     1Ø.ØØ
     5.     1Ø.ØØ
    ————————————————
```

The second part (line 190 on) allows a user to enter different percent figures for one or more of the five items numbered 1 through 5.

```
1ØØ REM *****DISPLAY A SHORT TABLE*****
11Ø HOME : REM CLEAR THE SCREEN.
12Ø VTAB 5 : HTAB 15 : PRINT "————————————————"
13Ø VTAB 6 : HTAB 15 : PRINT " ITEM   PERCENT "
14Ø LET N=1
15Ø     VTAB 6+N : HTAB 17 : PRINT N;".    1Ø.ØØ"
16Ø     LET N=N+1
17Ø IF N<=5 THEN 15Ø
18Ø VTAB 12 : HTAB 15 : PRINT "————————————————"
19Ø REM *****UPDATE PERCENT FIGURES*****
2ØØ VTAB 2Ø : PRINT "TO CHANGE A PERCENT, TYPE THE"
21Ø VTAB 21 : PRINT "ITEM NUMBER. TYPE Ø WHEN DONE."
22Ø     VTAB 22 : INPUT "ENTER ITEM NUMBER: ";N
23Ø     IF N=Ø THEN 32Ø
24Ø     VTAB 23 : INPUT "ENTER NEW PERCENT: ";P
25Ø     REM CHANGE TABLE VALUE FOR ITEM N.
26Ø     VTAB 6+N : HTAB 23 : PRINT "        "
27Ø     VTAB 6+N : HTAB 23 : PRINT P
28Ø     REM ERASE OLD INPUT VALUES.
29Ø     VTAB 22 : HTAB 2Ø : PRINT "          "
3ØØ     VTAB 23 : HTAB 2Ø : PRINT "          "
31Ø GOTO 22Ø
32Ø (next program segment)
```

The action caused by the second part (lines 190 on) is as follows.

1. Lines 200 and 210 display the instructions

```
TO CHANGE A PERCENT, TYPE THE
ITEM NUMBER. TYPE Ø WHEN DONE.
```

on display lines 20 and 21. These instructions stay on the screen during the entire input session.

2. Line 220 displays the input prompt

```
ENTER ITEM NUMBER:
```

on display line 22 and if the user types a number other than 0, the following input prompt is displayed on line 23.

```
ENTER NEW PERCENT:
```

3. Lines 260 and 270 make the specified change in the table and then lines 290 and 300 erase the old input values from the screen so that another change can be made.

Remark 1   Many of the VTAB commands in this program segment are not actually needed. However, including them makes the program easier to understand, and certainly easier to modify, should that be required. (All of the HTAB commands are needed.)

Remark 2   Program lines 190–310 show but one of the many ways to update an existing table. For instance, after an item number, say 4, has been typed in response to the INPUT statement in line 220, you can immediately erase the percent currently in the table for item 4 and move the blinking cursor to the screen position where the new percent figure is to appear. The command INPUT "";P would then allow the user to type exactly what is to appear in the table. (As the program stands, typing 9.00 for P will result in the digit 9 being displayed in the table, and not 9.00.)

Remark 3   When the given program is run, the user will have to respond to the two input prompts

```
ENTER ITEM NUMBER:
ENTER NEW PERCENT:
```

The only thing that will draw the user's attention to either of these prompts is the blinking cursor. To direct the user's attention to a particular prompt, you can use the Applesoft commands FLASH and NORMAL.

FLASH   causes subsequent screen output to be alternately displayed in white on black and then black on white. To see the effect of FLASH, type the immediate mode commands

```
FLASH
PRINT "ANYTHING"
```

NORMAL   causes subsequent output to be displayed in the normal way—white characters on a black background. (Any flashing characters currently on the screen will continue to flash.)

To draw attention to the input prompt

```
ENTER ITEM NUMBER:
```

you can replace the statement

```
220 VTAB 22 : INPUT "ENTER ITEM NUMBER: ";N
```

with the following.

```
215 FLASH
220 VTAB 22 : INPUT "ENTER ITEM NUMBER: ";N
223 NORMAL
225 VTAB 22 : PRINT "ENTER ITEM NUMBER: "
```

Line 215 sets the flashing mode for screen output. (Strings included in INPUT commands represent computer output so they will flash. Values you type at the keyboard are not computer output so they will not flash.) After a value is typed for N, line 223 restores the normal white on black mode. At this point, the prompt ENTER ITEM NUMBER: is still flashing. Line 225 displays this prompt a second time, over the first, but this time in normal white characters on a black background. A similar change would be made for the input prompt ENTER NEW PERCENT:.

As mentioned in Section 7.4, the TAB function does not work as intended with some printers. Should this be so with your printer, you can use the HTAB command as a limited substitute for TAB. We illustrate with an example.

EXAMPLE 11. Here is a program to produce the table

```
NUMBER    1     2     3     4     5
CUBE      1     8    27    64    125
```

```
100 PRINT "NUMBER";
110 LET C=10 : N=1
120    HTAB C : PRINT N;
130    LET C=C+5 : N=N+1
140 IF N<=5 THEN 120
150 PRINT
160 PRINT "CUBE";
170 LET C=10 : N=1
180    HTAB C : PRINT N^3;
190    LET C=C+5 : N=N+1
200 IF N<=5 THEN 180
210 END
```

This program produces the indicated output on any display screen or printer, including printers for which TAB does not work as intended.

If TAB works as it should with your printer, you can replace lines 120 and 180 with

```
120 PRINT TAB(C); N;
180 PRINT TAB(C); N^3;
```

7.6 Problems

1. Show the exact output of each program.

```
a. 10 PRINT "1234567890"
   20 LET I=0
   30    PRINT TAB(2*I+1);-I
   40    LET I=I+1
   50 IF I<=4 THEN 30
   60 PRINT "THAT'S ENOUGH";
   70 END
```

b.
```
1Ø PRINT "7777777"
2Ø LET N=1 : S=6
3Ø    PRINT TAB(S);N+S
4Ø      LET N=N+1 : S=S-1
5Ø IF S>=1 THEN 3Ø
6Ø END
```

c.
```
1Ø PRINT "123456789Ø"
2Ø LET X=1
3Ø    PRINT SPC(2*X);"*"
4Ø      LET X=X+1
5Ø IF X<5 THEN 3Ø
6Ø END
```

d.
```
1Ø LET X=Ø
2Ø PRINT TAB(5);"X"; SPC(1Ø);"X^2"
3Ø    PRINT
4Ø      LET X=X+1
5Ø      PRINT TAB(5);X;SPC(11);X^2;
6Ø IF X<4 THEN 3Ø
7Ø END
```

2. Describe the screen display or displays produced by each program.

a.
```
1Ø HOME
2Ø LET B$="BASIC"
3Ø LET N=Ø
4Ø    HTAB 15-N : PRINT B$;
5Ø    HTAB 15+N : PRINT B$
6Ø      LET N=N+5
7Ø IF N<1Ø THEN 4Ø
8Ø END
```

b.
```
1Ø HOME
2Ø LET A$="APPLE"
3Ø LET N=1
4Ø    VTAB N : HTAB N : PRINT A$
5Ø    VTAB 6-N : HTAB N : PRINT A$
6Ø      LET N=N+1
7Ø IF N<=3 THEN 4Ø
8Ø END
```

c.
```
1Ø HOME
2Ø LET R=15 : C=8
3Ø LET N=Ø
4Ø    VTAB R+N : HTAB C : PRINT "H     H"
5Ø      LET N=N+1
6Ø IF N<7 THEN 4Ø
7Ø VTAB R+3 : HTAB C+1 : PRINT "HHH"
8Ø END
```

d.
```
1Ø LET TIME=Ø
15 HOME : LET N=1Ø
2Ø    VTAB N : HTAB 15 : PRINT "GOOD"
25      LET N=N+1
3Ø IF N<=15 THEN 2Ø
35 HOME : LET N=1Ø
4Ø    VTAB N : HTAB 2Ø : PRINT "GRIEF"
45      LET N=N+1
5Ø IF N<=15 THEN 4Ø
55 LET TIME=TIME+1
6Ø IF TIME<5ØØ THEN 15
65 HOME : END
```

3. Write a single PRINT command for each task.
   a. Print the letter B in print position 6 and the digit 3 in print position 10.
   b. Print the values of X, 2X, 3X, and 4X on one line about equally spaced. Do not use commas.
   c. Print six zeros on one line equally spaced along the entire line.
   d. Print your name centered on a line.

Write a program to perform each task specified in Problems 4–9. Use the TAB and SPC functions.

4. Print your name on one line, street and number on the next line, and city or town and state on the third line. Your name should be centered on a line and successive lines should be indented.
5. Print a row of 15 A's beginning in print position 21 and a row of 13 B's centered under the A's.
6. Print a rectangular array of asterisks with five rows and eight columns, centered on the page (screen).
7. Print a square array of # symbols with M rows and M columns, centered on the page (screen). M is to be input.
8. Print the numbers 1, 10, 100, 1000, 10000, 100000, and 1000000 in a column in the middle of the page so that they are "lined up" on the right.
9. Print the numbers .33333, 3.3333, 33.333, 333.33, and 3333.3 in a column so that the decimal points line up.

Write a program to produce each screen display described in Problems 10–15. Use the HTAB and VTAB commands.

10. Display the word APPLE at the four corners and at the approximate center of the screen. Be sure that the top line is not scrolled off the screen when the program halts.
11. Display X's along all four edges of the screen. Then display your name near the center of the screen. Be sure that the entire display remains when the program halts.
12. Display a square block containing thirty-six X's at the center of the screen.
13. Successively display the digits 0 through 9 in the 36-character block described in Problem 12. After repeating this process 500 times, the program should halt with a clear screen.
14. Display the following table approximately centered on the screen.

```
RANGE COUNT WEIGHT
_____ _____ _____
0 -10   0     1
11-20   0     1
21-30   0     1·
31-40   0     1
41-50   0     1
```

15. Display the table shown in Problem 14 and then allow a user to enter five counts in place of the five 0's, and five weights in place of the five 1's.

7.7 Review true-or-false quiz

1. The use of a semicolon in a PRINT statement always causes a separation of at least one space between the items being printed.	T	F
2. If you want to suppress the carriage return following execution of a PRINT statement, a semicolon must be used to terminate the PRINT command.	T	F
3. If commas are used to separate values to be printed, columns will "line up." However, this will generally not be the case when semicolons are used.	T	F
4. If a message is to be centered on a line, you must use either TAB, SPC, or HTAB.	T	F
5. The line 20 PRINT : PRINT TAB(20);"X" will display the letter X in print position 20.	T	F
6. If output is being directed to the Apple's screen, the program line 50 HTAB 5 : VTAB 5 : PRINT "X" will display X in position 5 of display line 5 regardless of the current position of the cursor.	T	F
7. HTAB and VTAB may be used in PRINT commands, just as the TAB and SPC functions are used.	T	F
8. The HTAB and VTAB commands are used almost exclusively for producing screen output.	T	F

8

Loops Made Easier

Loops occur in all but the most elementary computer programs. In addition to providing the IF and GOTO statements to construct loops, BASIC contains the FOR and NEXT statements, which in many situations can be used to simplify writing loops and also to produce more readable programs. In this chapter we describe the FOR and NEXT statements and explain when they should be used to construct loops.

8.1 FOR/NEXT loops

Here are two ways to print the integers from 1 to 5:

Program 1	*Program 2*
| ```
100 LET N=1
110    PRINT N;" ";
120      LET N=N+1
130 IF N<=5 THEN 110
140 END
RUN

1 2 3 4 5
``` | ```
100 LET N=1
110 IF N>5 THEN 150
120    PRINT N;" ";
130      LET N=N+1
140 GOTO 110
150 END
RUN

1 2 3 4 5
``` |

The same thing can be accomplished by the following program:

```
        Program 3
100 FOR N=1 TO 5
110    PRINT N;" ";
120 NEXT N
130 END
RUN

1 2 3 4 5
```

This program simply instructs the computer to execute line 110 five times, once for each integer N from 1 to 5. In Applesoft BASIC, program 3 is equivalent to program 1. Thus the action of program 3 can be described as follows:

1. Line 100 (the FOR statement) assigns an initial value of 1 to N.
2. Line 110 prints the current value of N.
3. Line 120 (the NEXT statement) increases N by 1 and then compares N with the terminal value 5. If N $\leq$ 5, control passes back to the line following the FOR statement (line 110); that is, step (2) is repeated. If N > 5, control passes to the line following the NEXT statement (line 130) and we say that the loop has been *satisfied*.

The following examples further illustrate the use of the FOR and NEXT statements to construct loops. To clarify the meaning of the FOR/NEXT loops, we have written each program in two equivalent ways—without and with the FOR and NEXT statements.

EXAMPLE 1. Here is a program to calculate and print the price of one, two, three, four, five, and six items selling at seven for $1.00:

```
100 REM U DENOTES THE         100 REM U DENOTES THE
105 REM UNIT PRICE.           105 REM UNIT PRICE.
110 LET U=1.00/7              110 LET U=1.00/7
120 LET K=1                   120 FOR K=1 TO 6
130     LET P=U*K             130     LET P=U*K
140     PRINT K,P             140     PRINT K,P
150     LET K=K+1             150 NEXT K
160 IF K<=6 THEN 130          160 END
170 END
```

The FOR/NEXT loop instructs the computer to execute the statements

```
LET P=U*K
PRINT K,P
```

six times—once for each integer K from 1 to 6. These two statements are called the **body** or **range** of the loop. We will indent the body of each FOR/NEXT loop to improve the program's readability.

EXAMPLE 2. Here is a loop to print the numbers −4, −2, 0, 2, 4, 6:

```
100 LET J=-4                  100 FOR J=-4 TO 6 STEP 2
110     PRINT J;" ";          110     PRINT J;" ";
120     LET J=J+2             120 NEXT J
130 IF J<=6 THEN 110          130 END
140 END                       RUN
RUN
                              -4 -2 0 2 4 6
-4 -2 0 2 4 6
```

The starting value for J is −4. Including STEP 2 in the statement

```
100 FOR J=-4 TO 6 STEP 2
```

specifies that J is to be increased by 2 each time NEXT J is encountered. Thus, the FOR/NEXT loop instructs the computer to execute the statement

```
11Ø PRINT J;" ";
```

for the successive J values -4, -2, 0, 2, 4, and 6.

EXAMPLE 3. Here is a loop to print 5, 4, 3, 2, 1:

```
1ØØ LET N=5              1ØØ FOR N=5 TO 1 STEP -1
11Ø    PRINT N;" ";      11Ø    PRINT N;" ";
12Ø    LET N=N-1         12Ø NEXT N
13Ø IF N>=1 THEN 11Ø     13Ø END
14Ø END                  RUN
RUN
                         5 4 3 2 1
  5 4 3 2 1
```

This example illustrates that negative increments are acceptable. The initial value of N is 5, and after each pass through the loop N is *decreased* by 1 (STEP -1). As soon as N attains a value less than 1 (as specified in the FOR statement), control passes out of the loop to the statement following the NEXT statement.

The general form of a FOR/NEXT loop is

> FOR **v** = **a** TO **b** STEP **c**
>
>   ⋮ (body of the loop)
>
> NEXT **v**

where **v** denotes a *simple* numerical variable name* and **a, b,** and **c** denote arithmetic expressions. (If STEP **c** is omitted, **c** is assumed to have the value 1.) The variable **v** is called the **control variable** and the values of **a, b,** and **c** are called the **initial, terminal,** and **step** values, respectively. These numbers can be any numbers, not just integers. The action of a FOR/NEXT loop is described by the following diagrams.

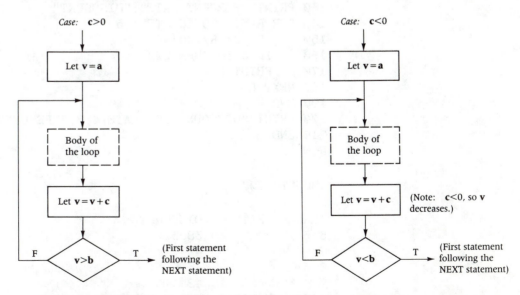

*The real numerical variables considered to this point are called *simple* to distinguish them from the integer variables described in Section 3.1 and the subscripted variables yet to be considered.

Note that the control variable **v** is compared with the terminal value **b** *after* the body of the loop has been executed. Thus executing a FOR statement in Applesoft BASIC causes at least one pass through the loop. This can cause unexpected results if you are not careful. For example, the program segment

```
5Ø REM PRINT N DASHES
6Ø FOR I=1 TO N
7Ø    PRINT "-";
8Ø NEXT N
9Ø (next statement)
```

will do what it claims if N is an integer 1 or greater. If N = 0, however, one pass will be made through the loop and cause an unwanted dash to be printed. You can always remedy such situations by preceding a FOR statement with a statement to skip the loop if certain conditions are not met. For instance, if you include the line

```
55 IF N<1 THEN 9Ø
```

the loop will be skipped entirely if N is not at least as large as 1.

This loop to print a row of dashes illustrates that the control variable in a FOR/NEXT loop does not have to appear within the loop. Indeed, the body of a loop can contain whatever BASIC commands you wish and as many as you need. The following example shows that you can even use a control statement to cause an exit from a FOR/NEXT loop before the loop has been satisfied.

EXAMPLE 4. Here is a program to print a table showing the 5.5, 6, 6.5, . . . , 10% discount on any amount typed at the keyboard. If for some percentage rate the discount exceeds $50, however, the printing is to terminate.

```
1ØØ REM DISCOUNT CALCULATIONS
11Ø INPUT "AMOUNT? ";A
12Ø PRINT
13Ø PRINT "PERCENT RATE","DISCOUNT"
14Ø FOR R=5.5 TO 1Ø STEP .5
15Ø    LET D=(R/1ØØ)*A
16Ø    IF D>5Ø THEN 2ØØ
17Ø    PRINT R,D
18Ø NEXT R
19Ø END
2ØØ PRINT "DISCOUNT FOR RATE ";R;" PERCENT IS ";D
21Ø END
RUN

AMOUNT? 7ØØ

PERCENT RATE    DISCOUNT
5.5             38.5
6               42
6.5             45.5
7               49
DISCOUNT FOR RATE 7.5 PERCENT IS 52.5
```

The FOR statement in line 140 specifies that the control variable R is to range from 5.5 to 10 with 0.5 as the increment. For R = 5.5, 6, 6.5, and 7, the discount values D (shown in the output) do not exceed 50. When R = 7.5, however, D is 52.5 and the IF statement in line 160 transfers control out of the loop to line 200, which produces the last line of output.

Remark

The FOR and NEXT statements are generally used to construct loops only if the number of times the loop is to be repeated is known before entering the loop. This is not the case here. However, since it is known that the loop is to be repeated at most for the values R = 5.5, 6, 6.5, . . . , 10, it makes sense to use a FOR/NEXT loop.

FOR/NEXT loops can be helpful in producing graphic displays on a video screen. In the following example, the control variable of a FOR/NEXT loop is used in HTAB and VTAB commands to specify exact screen positions for all output values.

EXAMPLE 5. Here is a program to produce alternating screen displays:

```
100 HOME : REM CLEAR SCREEN.
110 LET A$="APPLE"
120 REM ***DISPLAY A SCREEN GRAPHIC***
130 FOR L=1 TO 12
140    HTAB L : VTAB L : PRINT A$;
150    HTAB L : VTAB 24-L : PRINT A$;
160 NEXT L
170 REM ***PREPARE FOR NEXT GRAPHIC***
180 IF A$="BASIC" THEN 110
190 LET A$="BASIC" : GOTO 120
```

The FOR/NEXT loop in lines 130 to 160 alternates in displaying two screen graphics, one using the word APPLE and the other using the word BASIC. Moreover, each display erases the other. Before typing and running this program, it would be instructive to use pencil and paper to determine what it does.

Remark 1

When this program is run, the screen will alternate between the two displays very rapidly. The visual effect of this output can be enhanced significantly by including delays in the program. For instance, the line

```
155 FOR DLAY=1 TO 25 : NEXT DLAY
```

will cause each graphic to be displayed more deliberately, and the line

```
165 FOR DLAY=1 TO 100 : NEXT DLAY
```

will slow down the transition from one graphic to the next. (We chose the variable name DLAY rather than DELAY because DEL is a reserved word.)

Remark 2

The semicolons terminating the PRINT statements are not needed. However, if a value were output to line 24 of the screen, execution of a RETURN would cause the current display to scroll up one line and this would spoil (or at least change) the display. To see that this is so, change line 150 to

```
150 HTAB L : VTAB 25-L : PRINT A$
```

and run the program.

Remark 3   The graphics produced by this program consist entirely of letters chosen from the BASIC character set. Applesoft BASIC contains special graphics commands that allow you to produce enhanced graphics displays that are not restricted in this way. These commands are described in Chapter 17. Section 17.1 describes the so-called low-resolution graphics commands and Section 17.5 describes the Apple's high-resolution graphics commands. Both of these sections are written in such a way that the material can be taken up at this time, should that be desired.

Here are a few more key points concerning the use of FOR/NEXT loops:

1. The initial, terminal, and step values are determined once—when the FOR statement is executed—and cannot be altered within the body of the loop.
2. Although the control variable can be modified inside the loop, don't do it. The resulting program will be very difficult to read.
3. Entry into a loop should be made only by executing the FOR statement.
4. If an exit is made from a loop before its completion (an IF or GOTO statement), the current value of the control variable will be retained. (See Example 4.)
5. If an exit is made via the NEXT statement (that is, the loop is satisfied), the value of the control variable is the first value not used.
6. Although it is allowed, never transfer control out of a loop to perform some task and then return to the body so that looping can continue. Programs written in this way can be very hard to understand.
7. Loops may contain loops. (This is the subject of Section 8.4.)

8.2 Flowcharting FOR/NEXT loops

Since FOR/NEXT loops occur in many BASIC programs, special flowchart symbols have been designed for representing these loops. The diagram we'll use has found wide acceptance and can significantly improve the readability of flowcharts.

Using only the flowchart symbols given in Chapter 6, we can flowchart the loop

```
FOR I=1 TO N
    : (body of the loop)
    :
NEXT I
```

as follows:

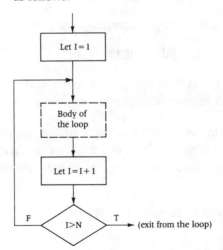

We'll represent this loop with the following diagram:

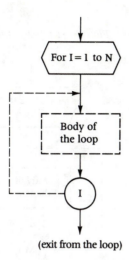

(exit from the loop)

EXAMPLE 6. Here is a flowchart for a program to input ten numbers and print their average:

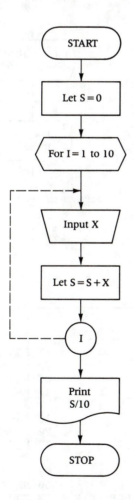

The flowchart symbol for a FOR statement is easily modified for loops with step values other than 1:

(FOR/NEXT loop)   *(Flowchart representation)*

```
FOR M=2 TO 9 STEP 3
    : (body of the loop)
    :
NEXT M
```

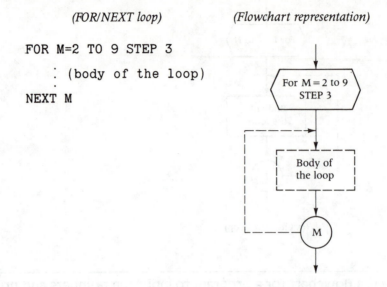

```
FOR X=10 TO 0 STEP -0.5
    : (body of the loop)
    :
NEXT X
```

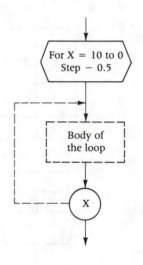

8.3 Problems

1. Show the output of each program.

a.
```
10 FOR J=2 TO 4
20     PRINT J+2
30 NEXT J
40 END
```

b.
```
10 FOR N=5 TO -3 STEP -4
20     PRINT N
30 NEXT N
40 END
```

c.
```
10 LET C=0
20 LET X=1
30 FOR Q=1 TO 4.9 STEP 2
40     LET C=C+1
50     LET X=X*Q
60 NEXT Q
70 PRINT "TIMES THROUGH LOOP= ";C
80 PRINT X
90 END
```

d.
```
10 FOR I=1 TO 3
20     PRINT "+";
30 NEXT I
40 FOR J=5 TO 7
50     PRINT "/";
60 NEXT J
70 END
```

```
e. 1Ø FOR J=2 TO 2          f. 1Ø FOR K=5 TO 1
   2Ø     PRINT "LOOP"          2Ø     PRINT "LOOP"
   3Ø NEXT J                    3Ø NEXT K
   4Ø END                      4Ø END
```

2. Each of the following programs contains an error—either a syntax error that will cause an error message to be printed or a programming error that the computer will not recognize but that will cause incorrect results. In each case find the error and tell which of the two types it is.

```
a. 1Ø REM 6% PROGRAM          b. 1Ø REM COUNT THE POSITIVE
   2Ø FOR N=1 TO 6               2Ø REM NUMBERS TYPED.
   3Ø     INPUT X                3Ø FOR I=1 TO 1Ø
   4Ø     PRINT X,Ø.Ø6*X         4Ø     LET C=Ø
   5Ø NEXT X                     5Ø     INPUT N
   6Ø END                        6Ø     IF N>Ø THEN C=C+1
                                 7Ø NEXT I
                                 8Ø PRINT C;" ARE POSITIVE."
                                 99 END
```

```
c. 1Ø REM SUMMING PROGRAM     d. 1Ø REM PRINT THE NUMBERS
   2Ø LET S=Ø                    2Ø REM 1 3 6 1Ø 15
   3Ø FOR X=1 TO 4               3Ø LET S=1
   4Ø     INPUT X                4Ø FOR N=1 TO 15 STEP S
   5Ø     LET S=S+X              5Ø     PRINT N
   6Ø NEXT X                     6Ø     LET S=S+1
   7Ø PRINT "SUM IS ";S          7Ø NEXT N
   8Ø END                        8Ø END
```

In Problems 3–10, write a program for each task specified. In each case a single FOR/NEXT loop is to be used.

3. Twenty numbers are to be entered at the keyboard. Determine how many of these numbers are negative, how many are positive, and how many are zero.

4. Print the integers from 1 to 72, eight to the line. Hint: Use a separate variable to count how many numbers have been printed on a line.

5. Print the integers from 1 to 72, eight to the line, equally spaced.

6. A program is needed to assist grade school students with their multiplication tables. After an initial greeting, the computer should ask the student to type a number from 2 to 12 so that products involving this number can be practiced. (Call this number N, but don't confuse the student with this information.) Next the student should be asked to answer the questions $2 \times N = ?, 3 \times N = ?, \ldots, 12 \times N = ?$ Of course, the *value* of N should be printed, not the letter N. If a question is answered correctly, the next question should be asked; if not, the question should be repeated. If the same question is answered incorrectly twice, however, the correct answer should be printed and then the next question should be asked. After all questions pertaining to N have been answered, the student should have the opportunity to try another multiplication table or stop.

7. Evaluate the following sums. If a value for N is required, it is to be input.
   a. $1 + 2 + 3 + \ldots + N$
   b. $1 + 3 + 5 + 7 + \ldots + 51$
   c. $1 + 3 + 5 + 7 + \ldots + (2N - 1)$
   d. $2 + 5 + 8 + 11 + \ldots + K$, where $N - 3 < K \leq N$
   e. $(.06) + (.06)^2 + (.06)^3 + \ldots + (.06)^N$
   f. $1 + 1/2 + 1/3 + 1/4 + \ldots + 1/N$
   g. $1 + 1/4 + 1/9 + 1/16 + \ldots + 1/N^2$
   h. $1 + 1/2 + 1/4 + 1/8 + \ldots + 1/2^N$
   i. $1 - 1/2 + 1/3 - 1/4 + \ldots - 1/100$
   j. $4[1 - 1/3 + 1/5 - 1/7 + \ldots + (-1)^{N + 1}/(2N - 1)]$

8. Produce a two-column table with column headings showing P% of the amounts $1, $2, $3, ..., $20. P is to be input.

9. Produce a two-column table with the headings N and $1 + 2 + 3 + \ldots + N$. The first column is to show the N values 1,2,3, ... ,20, and the second is to show the indicated sums. (Hint: The second column value for row N (N>1) is simply N plus the previous sum.)

10. For any positive integer N, the product $1 \times 2 \times 3 \times \ldots \times N$ is denoted by the symbol N! and is called N factorial. Also, zero factorial (0!) is defined to be 1. (Thus, 0! = 1! = 1.) Produce a two-column table with column headings showing the values of N and N! for N = 0, 1, 2, . . . , 10. (Hint: For N>0, N! = (N−1)! × N.)

Problems 11–16 describe tasks requiring screen output. Be sure to start each display with a clear screen.

11. Produce a changing screen display by repeatedly carrying out the following steps.
   a. Display a vertical column and a horizontal row of X's, each passing through the approximate center of the screen.
   b. Delay.
   c. Erase the display.
12. Modify Problem 11 so that a user can specify the length of the delay during program execution.
13. Alternately display the two "lines" of X's described in Problem 11. Include a delay to slow down the transition from one "line" to the next. (Be sure to erase the line on the screen before displaying the next one.)
14. Modify Problem 13 so that the user can specify the speed of transition from one display to the next during program execution.
15. Consider the following four "lines."
   Line 1: 12 X's from center of screen to the top.
   Line 2: 12 X's from center of screen to the right.
   Line 3: 12 X's from center of screen to the bottom.
   Line 4: 12 X's from center of screen to the left.
   Repeatedly display these four lines in the order given. Each line is to be erased before the next is displayed and a delay is to be used to slow down the transition from one line to the next. The user should be allowed to specify the speed of transition during program execution.
16. Consider four blocks B1, B2, B3, and B4 as in the following diagram.

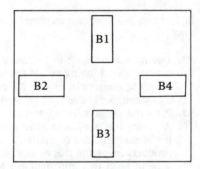

Produce a blinking-light display by repeatedly carrying out the following steps.
   a. Display *'s in blocks B1 and B3.
   b. Delay and then erase the screen.
   c. Display *'s in blocks B2 and B4.
   d. Delay and then erase the screen.
   A user should be allowed to specify the delay time during program execution.

8.4 Nested loops

It is permissible, and often desirable, to have one FOR/NEXT loop contained in another. When nesting loops in this manner, there is one rule that must be observed:

If the body of one FOR/NEXT loop contains either the FOR or the NEXT statement of another loop, it must contain both of them (see Figure 8.1).

Figure 8.1
Correctly and incorrectly
nested loops.

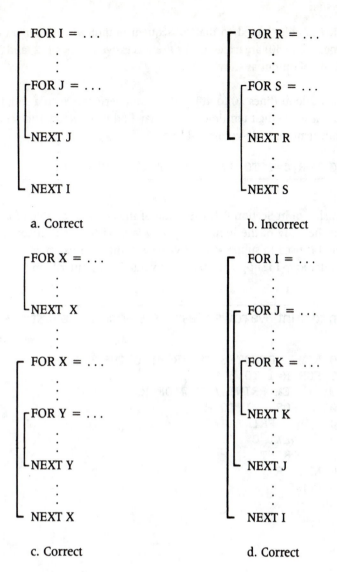

a. Correct

b. Incorrect

c. Correct

d. Correct

EXAMPLE 7. Here is an illustration of nested FOR/NEXT loops.

```
1Ø FOR I=1 TO 3
2Ø     FOR J=1 TO 1Ø
3Ø         PRINT I;
4Ø     NEXT J
5Ø     PRINT
6Ø NEXT I
7Ø END
RUN

1111111111
2222222222
3333333333
```

The FOR and NEXT statements in lines 1Ø and 6Ø cause the four lines between them to be executed three times. The first three of these lines (2Ø to 4Ø) output the value of I ten times on one line, leaving the cursor (printer) positioned at the end of this line. Line 5Ø causes a

RETURN to be executed so that subsequent output will appear on a new line. Since these four lines (20 to 50) are executed for the successive I values 1, 2, and 3, the program produces three lines of output as shown.

Remark

Since the J-loop (lines 20 to 40) is short and performs such a simple and well-defined task (displays a single digit ten times), you may find it convenient to replace these three lines by the equivalent multiple-command line

```
2Ø FOR J=1 TO 1Ø : PRINT I; : NEXT J
```

As shown in Section 8.1, the value of the control variable of a FOR/NEXT loop can be used in the body of the loop in any way you wish. In the preceding example, the control variable I is used to supply output values; in the next example, we use the control variable of an outer loop to supply the terminal value for an inner loop.

EXAMPLE 8. Here is a program to print five rows of asterisks—one in the first row, two in the second, and so on:

```
1Ø REM R DENOTES THE ROW; C THE COLUMN.
2Ø FOR R=1 TO 5
3Ø    REM PRINT A ROW OF R * 'S.
4Ø    FOR C=1 TO R
5Ø       PRINT "*";
6Ø    NEXT C
7Ø    PRINT
8Ø NEXT R
9Ø END
RUN

*
**
***
****
*****
```

To print this design nearer the center of the page (or screen) you can use the TAB function. To cause the output of each row to begin in column position 20, for example, simply include the statement

```
35 PRINT TAB(2Ø);
```

This statement causes the cursor (or printer) to move to print position 20 so that the loop in lines 40 to 60 will print R asterisks beginning in this print position.

Nested FOR/NEXT loops are especially useful when tables must be prepared in which the rows and columns each correspond to equally spaced data values. The following is an example illustrating one such application of nested loops.

EXAMPLE 9. Prepare a table showing the possible raises for salaried employees whose salaries are $10,000, $11,000, $12,000, . . . , $17,000. A raise is to consist of a flat across-the-board increase of F dollars and a percentage increase of either 2, 3, or 4%.

Problem analysis

Let's agree on the following variable names.

> S = present salary ($10,000, $11,000, . . . , $17,000)
> F = flat across-the-board increase (to be input)
> P = percentage increase (2, 3, 4%)
> R = amount of raise for a given S, F, and P

The formula governing this situation is

$$R=(P/1\emptyset\emptyset)*S+F$$

For each salary S, we must display three possible raises R—one for each of the indicated percentages P. Thus a four-column table is appropriate, the first showing the present salary S and the others showing the three possible raises. The following program segment can be used to print these values.

```
FOR S=1ØØØØ TO 17ØØØ STEP 1ØØØ
   PRINT S,
   FOR P=2 TO 4
      LET R=(P/1ØØ)*S+F
      PRINT R,
   NEXT P
   PRINT
NEXT S
```

All that remains is to include an INPUT statement, so that a value can be typed for F, and to add the PRINT statements needed to print a title for the table and appropriate column headings.

The program

```
1ØØ PRINT "                SALARY INCREASE SCHEDULE"
11Ø PRINT
12Ø INPUT "ACROSS THE BOARD INCREASE $";F
13Ø PRINT
14Ø PRINT ,"-----ADDITIONAL PERCENTAGE INCREASE-----"
15Ø PRINT "SALARY","2 PERCENT","3 PERCENT","4 PERCENT"
16Ø PRINT
17Ø FOR S=1ØØØØ TO 17ØØØ STEP 1ØØØ
18Ø    PRINT S,
19Ø    FOR P=2 TO 4
2ØØ       LET R=(P/1ØØ)*S+F
21Ø       PRINT R,
22Ø    NEXT P
23Ø    PRINT
24Ø NEXT S
999 END
RUN
```

SALARY INCREASE SCHEDULE

ACROSS THE BOARD INCREASE $55∅

	-----ADDITIONAL PERCENTAGE INCREASE-----		
SALARY	2 PERCENT	3 PERCENT	4 PERCENT
10∅∅∅	75∅	85∅	95∅
11∅∅∅	77∅	88∅	99∅
12∅∅∅	79∅	91∅	1∅3∅
13∅∅∅	81∅	94∅	1∅7∅
14∅∅∅	83∅	97∅	111∅
15∅∅∅	85∅	1∅∅∅	115∅
16∅∅∅	87∅	1∅3∅	119∅
17∅∅∅	89∅	1∅6∅	123∅

Remark 1

Note that commas are used in lines 18∅ and 21∅ so that the four values output to a line will appear in the first four print zones of the line. If the output is intended for a 40-character display screen, the TAB function or HTAB command should be used. For example, if you change the comma in line 18∅ to a semicolon, and replace line 21∅ by either

```
21∅ HTAB (P-1)*1∅ : PRINT R;
```

or

```
21∅ PRINT TAB((P-1)*1∅); R;
```

the four values on each line will be displayed beginning in positions 1, 10, 20, and 30.

Remark 2

It is a coincidence that all output values are whole dollar amounts. To ensure that only whole dollar amounts will be output, even when the calculated values are not integers, you can use the integer variable R% instead of the real variable R. This method of producing integer output has two limitations. First, integer variables such as R% can take on values only in the range −32767 to 32767. For the current application, this is adequate. Second, integer values for integer variables are obtained by discarding fractional parts of numbers. For instance, if the calculated raise (P/1∅∅)*S+F in line 2∅∅ is 873.95, the value 873 will be output even though the rounded value 874 may be desired. You may check that adding .5 to a number before discarding its fractional part will round the number to the nearest integer. (For instance, 873.95 + .5 = 874.45, and discarding .45 gives the rounded value 874.) Thus, changing lines 2∅∅ and 21∅ to

```
2∅∅ LET R%=(P/1∅∅)*S+F+.5
21∅ PRINT R%,
```

will cause all calculated raises to be rounded before being output. It should be emphasized that this method of rounding numbers can be used only for numbers in the range −32767 to 32767. A method for rounding any number, to any decimal position, is described in Section 11.4.

8.5 Problems

1. Show the output of each program.

a.
```
10 FOR I=1 TO 3
20    FOR J=2 TO 3
30       PRINT J
40    NEXT J
50 NEXT I
60 END
```

b.
```
10 FOR J=9 TO 7 STEP -2
20    FOR K=4 TO 9 STEP 3
30       PRINT J+K;" ";
40    NEXT K
50 NEXT J
60 END
```

c.
```
10 FOR X=1 TO 3
20    FOR Y=1 TO 5
30       PRINT X;
40    NEXT Y
50    PRINT
60 NEXT X
70 END
```

d.
```
10 FOR X=1 TO 4
20    FOR Y=X+1 TO 5
30       PRINT Y;" ";
40    NEXT Y
50    PRINT
60 NEXT X
70 END
```

e.
```
10 LET X=0
20 FOR P=1 TO 6
30    FOR Q=2 TO 7
40       FOR R=2 TO 4
50          LET X=X+1
60       NEXT R
70    NEXT Q
80 NEXT P
90 PRINT X
99 END
```

f.
```
10 FOR X=-2 TO 2
20    FOR Y=-2 TO 2
30       LET P=X*Y
40       IF P<0 THEN P=-P
50       IF P<1.5 THEN PRINT "*";
60       IF P>1.5 THEN PRINT " ";
70    NEXT Y
80    PRINT
90 NEXT X
99 END
```

2. Each of the following programs contains an error—either a syntax error that will cause an error message to be printed or a programming error that the computer will not recognize but that will cause incorrect results. In each case find the error and tell which of the two types it is.

a.
```
10 REM PRINT PRODUCTS.
20 FOR I=1 TO 3
30 FOR J=2 TO 4
40 PRINT I;" TIMES ";J;" = ";I*J
50 NEXT I
60 NEXT J
70 END
```

b.
```
10 REM PRINT SUMS.
20 FOR A=3 TO 1
30 FOR B=4 TO 1
40 PRINT A;" PLUS ";B;" = ";A+B
50 NEXT B
60 NEXT A
70 END
```

c. A program to print:
```
1  2
1  3
1  4
2  3
2  4
3  4
```
```
10 FOR I=1 TO 4
20 FOR J=2 TO 4
30 IF I=J THEN 50
40 PRINT I;" ";J
50 NEXT J
60 NEXT I
70 END
```

d. A program to print:
```
XXXXX
XXXX
XXX
XX
X
```
```
10 FOR R=1 TO 5
20 FOR C=1 TO 5
30 IF R>=C THEN PRINT "X";
40 IF R<C THEN PRINT " ";
50 NEXT C
60 NEXT R
70 END
```

In Problems 3–16, write a program to perform each task specified.

3. Produce M rows of output with each row consisting of N dashes. M and N are to be input.

4. Produce a tax rate schedule showing the 4, 5, 6, and 7% tax on the dollar amounts $1, $2, $3, . . . , $20.

5. Prepare a table showing the interest earned on a $100 deposit for the rates 0.05 to 0.08 in increments of 0.01 and for times 1, 2, . . . , 8 years. Interest is compounded annually $(I = P(1 + R)^N - P)$.

6. Prepare the table for Problem 5 except that rates are to be in increments of 0.005 instead of 0.01.

7. Present the information required in Problem 6 by producing seven short tables, one for each interest rate specified. Label each of these tables and also the information contained in the tables.

8. For each of the tax rates 5, 5⅛, 5¼, 5⅜, and 5½%, produce a table showing the tax on the dollar amounts $1, $2, $3, . . . , $20. Each of the five tables is to have an appropriate title and is to contain two labeled columns—the first showing the dollar amounts $1, $2, $3, . . . , $20 and the second showing the corresponding tax amounts.

9. Produce a square array of symbols centered on the screen (or page). The side length of the square and the symbol to be used are to be input.

10. Produce a listing of all three-digit numbers whose digits are 1, 2, or 3. (*Hint:* Use triple-nested loops with control variables I, J, and K ranging from 1 to 3.)

11. Produce a listing of all three-digit numbers as described in Problem 10. If no digit is repeated in a number, however, it is to be preceded by an asterisk. Thus a portion of your printout should be as follows:

```
        .
        .
        .
      121
      122
  *   123
      131
  *   132
      133
        .
        .
        .
```

12. Let's define an operation whose symbol is ⊙ on the set A = {0, 1, 2, 3, 4, 5} as follows. The "product" of two integers *i* and *j* is given by

$$i \odot j = \text{the remainder when } i \times j \text{ is divided by 6}$$

The remainder R when I∗J is divided by 6 can be obtained as follows.

```
LET Q%=I*J/6 (Q% gives number of times 6 goes into I*J.)
LET R=I*J-6*Q%
```

Write a program to print all possible "products" of numbers in the set A.

13. Determine the largest value the expression $XY^2 - X^2Y + X - Y$ can assume if X and Y can be any integers from 1 to 5, inclusive.

14. Find the maximum and minimum values of the expression $3X^2 - 2XY + Y^2$ if X and Y are subject to the following constraints.

$$X = -4, -3.5, -3, \ldots, 4$$
$$Y = -3, -2.5, -2, \ldots, 5$$

15. The expression $x^3 - 4xy + x^2 + 10x$ is to be examined for all integers *x* and *y* between 1 and 5 to determine those pairs (*x*, *y*) for which the expression is negative. All such pairs are to be printed, together with the corresponding negative value of the expression.

16. Find all pairs of integers (X, Y) that satisfy the following system of inequalities.

$$2X - Y < 3$$
$$X + 3Y \geqslant 1$$
$$-6 \leqslant X \leqslant 6$$
$$-10 \leqslant Y \leqslant 10$$

The solutions are to be printed as individual ordered pairs (X, Y). (*Hint:* The last two conditions give the initial and terminal values of FOR/NEXT loops.)

Problems 17–19 describe tasks requiring screen output. Be sure to start each display with a clear screen. Also, allow a user to specify lengths of any program delays during program execution.

17. Consider the display screen to be divided into four equal parts as in the following diagram.

P1	P2
P3	P4

Produce a changing screen display by repeatedly carrying out the following steps.
a. Fill P1 and P3 with asterisks.
b. Delay and then clear the screen.
c. Fill P2 and P4 with asterisks.
d. Delay and then clear the screen.

18. Produce a changing screen display as in Problem 17 except that the regions are to be filled with asterisks in the order P1, P2, P3, and then P4.

19. Produce changing screen displays by repeatedly filling the successive regions P1, P2, P3, and P4 with the digits 1, 2, 3, and 4, respectively.

8.6 Review true-or-false quiz

1. If a group of statements is to be executed several times in a program, it is always a good practice to use a FOR/NEXT loop.   T   F

2. The IF statement provides a convenient way to transfer control out of a FOR/NEXT loop.   T   F

3. If a loop begins with the statement FOR I = 1 TO 35, the variable I must occur in some statement before the NEXT I statement is encountered.   T   F

4. If an exit is made from a loop via an IF statement in the body of the loop, the current value of the control variable will be retained.   T   F

5. If an exit is made from a loop via the NEXT statement, the value of the control variable will be reset to zero.   T   F

6. The statement FOR J = X to 10 STEP 3 is valid even though X may have a value that is not an integer.   T   F

7. In the statement FOR N = 15 TO 200 STEP C, C must be a positive integer.   T   F

8. The initial, terminal, and step values in a FOR/NEXT loop cannot be modified in the body of the loop.   T   F

9. The control variable in a FOR/NEXT loop can be modified in the body of the loop; moreover, doing so represents a good programming practice.   T   F

10. The control variable of a loop containing a loop may be used as the initial, terminal, or step value of the inner loop.   T   F

9

□ □ □ □ □ □ □ □ □ □ □ □ □ □ □

Data as Part of a Program

To this point, values have been assigned to variables by using only LET and INPUT commands. BASIC provides alternative ways of presenting data to the computer. In this chapter, we describe three commands: the DATA command that allows you to include data as part of your programs; the READ command that is used to assign these data to variables; and the RESTORE command that allows you to "read" these data more than once during a single program run.

As you work through the examples in this chapter, you will see that these commands often provide a convenient, and sometimes necessary, alternative to the LET and INPUT commands.

9.1 The READ and DATA statements

These two statements are best illustrated by example.

EXAMPLE 1. Here is a program to "read" two numbers and print their sum:

```
100 READ A
110 READ B
120 PRINT A+B
130 DATA 17,8
140 END
RUN

25
```

Line 130 contains the numbers to be added. Line 100 assigns the first of these (17) to A, and line 110 assigns the next (8) to B. When line 130, the DATA line, is encountered, it is ignored and control passes to the next line, which in this program terminates the run.

The two READ statements in this program can be replaced by the single statement

```
READ A,B
```

as shown in the following equivalent program:

```
100 READ A,B
110 PRINT A+B
120 DATA 17,8
130 END
```

EXAMPLE 2. Here is a program to "read" and print a list of numbers:

```
100 READ X
110 PRINT X
120 GOTO 100
130 DATA 7,-123,40
140 END
RUN

7
-123
40
?OUT OF DATA ERROR IN 100
```

Line 130 contains the list of numbers. When line 100 is first executed, the first datum (7) is assigned to X and control passes to line 110, which prints this value. The GOTO statement transfers control back to line 100, which then assigns the next value (−123) to X. This process is repeated until the data list is exhausted. This will happen when the READ statement is executed a fourth time. Since only three values are supplied in the DATA line, this attempt to read a fourth value causes the error condition identified by the OUT OF DATA message and the program terminates.

EXAMPLE 3. Here is a program to "read" and print two strings:

```
100 READ A$,B$
110 PRINT B$;" ";A$
120 DATA FLIES,TIME
130 END
RUN

TIME FLIES
```

The READ statement assigns the first datum (FLIES) to A$ and the second (TIME) to B$. The PRINT statement then produces the output shown.

Note that the strings FLIES and TIME in the DATA line of Example 3 are not quoted. The same rules that apply to strings typed in response to INPUT statements apply to strings appearing in DATA lines. We'll repeat these rules:

1. Strings must be quoted only if:
    a. They contain significant leading blanks. (If not quoted, the leading blanks are ignored.)
    b. A comma appears in the string. (The comma is used to delimit the constants contained in DATA lines.)
2. A string must not contain the double quote character (").
3. It is always correct to enclose strings in quotation marks.

EXAMPLE 4. Here is a program to illustrate quoted and unquoted strings in DATA lines:

```
100 FOR I=1 TO 5
110    READ Z$
120    PRINT Z$
130 NEXT I
140 DATA VI;"  AL",1234,TO GO,"RICE,JIM"
150 END
RUN

VI
  AL
1234
TO GO
RICE,JIM
```

Quotes are needed for "   AL" because of the leading blanks; they are needed for "RICE,JIM" because of the comma. Note that it is the string 1234, and not the number 1234, that is assigned to Z$.

As illustrated in the next example, both string and numerical data can be included in a single DATA statement, and a single READ statement can be used to read values for both string and numerical variables.

EXAMPLE 5. Here is a program to produce a table summarizing the information contained in DATA statements:

```
100 REM *** PRINT COLUMN HEADINGS ***
110 PRINT "NAME"; TAB(15); "SCORE1";
120 PRINT TAB(24); "SCORE2"; TAB(33); "AVERAGE"
130 PRINT
140 REM *** PRINT TABLE VALUES ***
150 READ N : REM NUMBER OF STUDENTS
160 FOR I=1 TO N
170    READ NAME$, S1, S2
180    LET AV%=(S1+S2)/2+0.5 : REM ROUNDED AVERAGE
190    PRINT NAME$; TAB(17); S1;
200    PRINT TAB(26); S2; TAB(35); AV%
210 NEXT I
220 DATA 4
230 DATA CARL,71,79
240 DATA MARLENE,82,88
```

```
25Ø DATA SUZANNE,89,62
26Ø DATA WILLIAM,58,96
27Ø END
RUN
```

NAME	SCORE1	SCORE2	AVERAGE
CARL	71	79	75
MARLENE	82	88	85
SUZANNE	89	62	76
WILLIAM	58	96	77

The first READ statement (line 15Ø) assigns the first datum (4) to the variable N. This N is then used to ensure that exactly four names with their corresponding scores are read and processed. By using the first data value in this way, you can ensure that a READ command will not be executed after all data have been read.

Remark

If output is intended for a printer for which TAB does not work correctly (see Section 7.4) you can use the HTAB command. For instance, lines 11Ø and 12Ø, which print column headings, can be replaced by

```
11Ø PRINT "NAME";
115 HTAB 15 : PRINT "SCORE1";
12Ø HTAB 24 : PRINT "SCORE2";
125 HTAB 33 : PRINT "AVERAGE"
```

A similar change would be required for lines 19Ø and 2ØØ.

The general forms of the READ and DATA statements are as follows:

ln READ (list of variables separated by commas)
ln DATA (list of BASIC constants separated by commas)

The following rules govern the use of these two statements:

1. As many DATA lines as desired may be included in a program, and as many values as will fit may appear on each line. The values must be constants.

2. All values appearing in the DATA lines constitute a single list called the **data list.** The order in which data appear in this list is precisely the order in which they appear in the program—that is, from lowest to highest line numbers and, within a DATA line, from left to right.

3. When a READ statement is executed, the variables appearing are assigned successive values from the data list. You must write your READ and DATA statements so that only numerical values are assigned to numerical variables and only string values to string variables. The data appearing in DATA lines constitute a single data list; no special treatment is given to string constants. The execution of a READ statement will attempt to assign the next value in this list to the variable being assigned. If this next value is not of the same data type as the variable, either an error message will be displayed or your program will simply produce incorrect results.

4. It is not necessary that all data values be read. However, an attempt to read more data than appear in DATA lines will result in an error condition that causes the OUT OF DATA

message to be printed and program execution to terminate. Errors that stop program execution are called **fatal errors**.

5. If a DATA statement is encountered during program execution, the statement is ignored and control passes to the next line. Thus DATA lines may appear anywhere in the program, though you should position them to enhance the readability of your programs. Placing them just before the END statement is a common practice, especially if different data will be processed each time the program is run. If certain DATA lines will never be changed, it is sometimes better to place them just after the READ statements that read the data.

READ statements such as READ N and READ A, B, C would appear in a flowchart as follows:

A different symbol is needed for the READ statement, because the symbol for the INPUT statement is used to signify that data are to be input *manually* during program execution. The READ statement requires no such action on the part of the user.

The program shown in Example 5 includes the count 4 as the first value in DATA lines to indicate that scores for four students are included. In the following example we include a special value at the end of the data list to serve as an end-of-data marker (EOD tag). Doing this relieves us of the burden of counting the values in the data list.

EXAMPLE 6. Write a program to find the largest number in a data list and also to determine how many numbers are included in the list.

Problem analysis

Let's assign variable names as follows:

X = most recent number read from data list
N = a count of how many numbers have been read
L = largest number read

An algorithm for finding the largest number in a list is shown in Example 2 of Section 2.1. The following flowchart describes a slight modification of this algorithm that can be used in the present situation. Note that 9999 is used as the EOD tag.

The flowchart

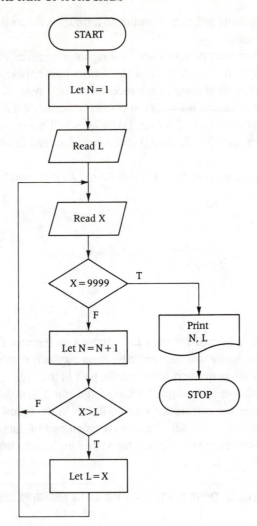

START

Let N = 1

Read L

Read X

X = 9999

T

Print
N, L

STOP

F

Let N = N + 1

X > L

F

T

Let L = X

The program

```
100 REM FIND THE LARGEST DATA VALUE.
110 REM    X=VALUE LAST READ
120 REM    N=NUMBER OF VALUES READ
130 REM    L=LARGEST OF ALL VALUES READ
140 REM
150 REM READ FIRST NUMBER INTO L AND SET COUNTER N TO 1.
160 READ L
170 LET N=1
180 REM READ AND PROCESS THE REMAINING NUMBERS.
190    READ X
200    IF X=9999 THEN 240
210    LET N=N+1
220    IF X>L THEN L=X
230 GOTO 190
240 PRINT "NUMBER OF DATA VALUES ";N
250 PRINT "LARGEST DATA VALUE ";L
900 DATA 88,72,64,89,93,72,65
910 DATA 84,92,69,73,91
```

```
998 DATA 9999
999 END
RUN

NUMBER OF DATA VALUES 12
LARGEST DATA VALUE 93
```

Remark 1   To run this program for a different list of numbers, only lines 900 and 910 need to be changed.

Remark 2   Note that there is no flowchart symbol for DATA statements. DATA statements simply provide a means of presenting data to the computer for processing. Since they cause nothing to happen during the actual execution of the program, they have no place in a flowchart whose purpose is to describe the flow of activity in a program.

9.2 Problems

1. Show the output of each program.

   a.
   ```
   10 FOR I=1 TO 4
   20     READ A,B,C
   30     IF A=7 THEN 50
   40     PRINT C
   50 NEXT I
   60 DATA 2,7,4,3,4,7,7
   70 DATA 6,9,12,7,1,6
   80 END
   ```

   b.
   ```
   10 READ N
   20 FOR J=1 TO N
   30     READ X
   40     LET Y=X+1
   50     PRINT Y
   60 NEXT J
   70 DATA 2,5,3,7,8,-4
   80 END
   ```

   c.
   ```
   10 READ A,B$,M$
   20 LET M$=B$
   30 PRINT M$;
   40 READ A,B$,M$
   50 LET M$=B$
   60 LET B$=M$
   70 PRINT B$
   80 DATA 6,CAT,MOUSE
   90 DATA 8,"WOMAN","MAN"
   99 END
   ```

   d.
   ```
   10 LET N=0
   20 READ X
   30 IF X=9999 THEN 80
   40     LET N=N+1
   50     PRINT X
   60     READ X
   70 GOTO 30
   80 PRINT N
   90 DATA 7,3,18,-5,9999
   99 END
   ```

2. Find and correct each error.

   a.
   ```
   10 READ X,X$
   20 PRINT X$;X
   30 DATA "1";A
   40 END
   ```

   b.
   ```
   10 READ Y;Z$
   20 PRINT Z$;" OF ";Y
   30 DATA 42,SUMMER
   40 END
   ```

   c.
   ```
   10 READ B$
   20 IF B$=HELLO THEN 10
   30 PRINT B$
   40 DATA HELLO,GOODBYE
   50 END
   ```

   d.
   ```
   10 READ N$
   20 READ A,B,C
   30 PRINT "NAME: ";N$
   40 PRINT "SCORES: ";A,B,C
   50 DATA DOOLEY,TOM
   60 DATA 85,81,76
   70 END
   ```

3. The following programs do not do what they claim. Find and correct all errors.

   a.
   ```
   100 REM SUM 5 NUMBERS.
   110 LET S=0
   120 FOR I=1 TO 5
   130     READ I
   140     LET S=S+I
   150 NEXT I
   160 PRINT S
   170 DATA 7,12,14,-3,6
   180 END
   ```

   b.
   ```
   100 REM PRINT SQUARES OF
   110 REM 12,37,21,96
   120 LET N=1
   130     READ A^2
   140     PRINT A^2
   150     LET N=N+1
   160 IF N<4 THEN 130
   170 DATA 12,37,21,96
   180 END
   ```

```
c. 100 REM AVERAGE N NUMBERS.      d. 100 REM SUM MANY SETS
   110 READ X                         105 REM OF NUMBERS.
   120 IF X=1E-30 THEN 160            110 REM 999 ENDS EACH SET.
   130    LET S=0                     120 REM 9999 ENDS THE RUN.
   140    LET S=S+X                   130 LET S=0
   150 GOTO 120                       140    READ X
   160 PRINT "AVERAGE IS",S/N         150    IF X=9999 THEN 999
   170 DATA 18,23,17,22               160    LET S=S+X
   180 DATA 1E-30                     170    IF X=999 THEN PRINT S
   190 END                           180 GOTO 140
                                     500 DATA 5,9,4,2,6,999
                                     510 DATA 41,16,18,2,999
                                     998 DATA 9999
                                     999 END
```

In Problems 4–13, write a program to perform each task specified.

4. Read values from DATA lines two at a time. Print each pair of values, their sum, and their average on one line. Run your program using the following DATA lines. The last two values (0,0) are to be used to detect the end of the data.

```
800 DATA 70,80,90,65,75,85
810 DATA 50,40,65,80,78,76
820 DATA 62,60,65,50,60,85
830 DATA 35,45,60,90,96,92
890 DATA 0,0
```

5. Read values three at a time from DATA lines and print them only if the third is greater than the average of the first two. Run your program using the data given in Problem 4. A slight modification of line 890 is needed.
6. Read values three at a time from DATA lines and print them only if they are in ascending order. Use the data shown in Problem 4. A slight modification of line 890 is needed.
7. Find how many of the numbers appearing in DATA lines lie between 40 and 60, inclusive, and also determine the average of these numbers. Use the data given in Problem 4.
8. A list of scores in the range 0 to 100 is to be examined to determine the following counts:

    $C1$ = number of scores less than 40
    $C2$ = number of scores between 40 and 60, inclusive
    $C3$ = number of scores greater than 60

Determine these counts for any list appearing in DATA lines. Use the data given in Problem 4.
9. A list of scores in the range 0 to 100 is to be examined to determine the following counts:

    $C1$ = number of scores less than 20
    $C2$ = number of scores less than 40 but at least 20
    $C3$ = number of scores less than 60 but at least 40
    $C4$ = number of scores less than 80 but at least 60
    $C5$ = number of scores not less than 80

Determine these counts for any list appearing in DATA lines. Use the data given in Problem 4.
10. A list of numbers is to be examined to determine how many times a number is strictly larger than the one just before it. For example, if the list is 17,3,19,27,23,25, the answer will be 3, since $19 > 3$, $27 > 19$, and $25 > 23$. Use the data given in Problem 4.
11. A candidate for political office conducted a preelection poll. Each voter polled was assigned a number from 1 to 3 as follows:

    1 = will vote for candidate
    2 = leans toward candidate but still undecided
    3 = all other cases

Tally the results of this poll. DATA lines are to be used to present the data to the computer.

12. Modify Problem 11 by assigning two values to each voter. The first is as stated; the second is to designate whether the voter is female (F) or male (M). There are now six counts to be determined. (Use READ A,S$ to read the two values, a number, and a string F or M, assigned to a voter.)

13. Values appearing in DATA lines are to be read three at a time to determine whether it is possible to construct a triangle using the three numbers as the lengths of the sides. If it is possible, print TRIANGLE POSSIBLE and the three values. If it is not possible, print TRIANGLE NOT POSSIBLE and the three values.

In Problems 14–17, write a program to produce a printed report as specified. Make sure that each report has a title, centered on the page, and that each column has an appropriate heading. All data are to be presented in DATA lines.

14. Given the following information, print a three-column report showing the employee number, monthly sales, and commission for each employee if the commission rate for each person is 6%.

Employee number	Monthly sales
6234	$4050
6551	6500
7321	3750
7718	3640
8049	7150

15. Given the following information, print a four-column report showing the employee name, the monthly sales, the commission rate, and the total commission for each employee.

Employee name	Monthly sales	Commission rate
Hart	$28,400	2%
Wilson	34,550	2.5%
Brown	19,600	3%
Ruiz	14,500	2%
Jensen	22,300	3.25%
Grogan	31,350	1.5%

16. Given the following information, print a four-column report showing the item number, quantity, unit value, and total value of each item. The total value of the entire inventory should be printed below the report.

Item number	Quantity	Unit value
3047	198	$ 2.43
3055	457	3.97
3068	237	1.96
3093	1047	5.47
3247	593	10.93
3346	1159	12.41
3469	243	.83
3947	2042	8.37

17. (Electric Bill Problem) Given the following information, print a report showing the customer number, total number of kilowatt hours (KWHs) used, and total monthly bill. The charges are computed according to the following schedule: $1.41 for the first 14 KWH, the next 85 KWH at $0.0389/KWH, the next 200 at $0.0214/KWH, the next 300 at $0.0134/KWH, and the

excess at $0.0099/KWH. In addition, there is a fuel-adjustment charge of $0.0322/KWH for all kilowatt hours used.

Customer number	Previous month's reading	Current reading
2516	25,346	25,973
2634	47,947	48,851
2917	21,342	21,652
2853	893,462	894,258
3576	347,643	348,748
3943	41,241	41,783
3465	887,531	888,165

9.3 The RESTORE statement

We have described a *data list* as the list of all data values appearing in all DATA lines in a program. Associated with a data list is a conceptual *pointer* indicating the value to be read by the next READ statement. The pointer is initially set to the first value in the list, and, each time a value is read, the pointer moves to the next value. The BASIC statement

ln RESTORE

positions this pointer back to the beginning of the data list so that the values can be read again. Following are three short examples illustrating the RESTORE command.

EXAMPLE 7. The program segment

```
1Ø READ A,B
2Ø RESTORE
3Ø READ C
4Ø RESTORE
5Ø READ D,E,F
6Ø DATA 1,2,3,4,5,6
```

assigns values to A, B, C, D, E, and F as follows.

Line 10 assigns the first two data values (1 and 2) to A and B, respectively.

Line 20 positions the pointer back to the first datum.

Line 30 assigns the first datum (1) to C.

Line 40 once again restores the pointer to the first datum.

Line 50 assigns the values 1, 2, and 3 to D, E, and F, respectively.

EXAMPLE 8. Here is a program to display two lists obtained from a single data list:

```
1ØØ PRINT "SCORES 7Ø OR MORE:";
11Ø FOR N=1 TO 1Ø
12Ø    READ X
13Ø    IF X>=7Ø THEN PRINT " ";X;
14Ø NEXT N
15Ø PRINT : RESTORE
16Ø PRINT "SCORES LESS THAN 7Ø:";
17Ø FOR N=1 TO 1Ø
18Ø    READ X
19Ø    IF X<7Ø THEN PRINT " ";X;
2ØØ NEXT N
```

```
210 DATA 78,84,65,32,93,58,88,76,68,83
220 END
RUN

SCORES 70 OR MORE: 78 84 93 88 76 83
SCORES LESS THAN 70: 65 32 58 68
```

The PRINT statements in lines 100 and 160 describe what this program does. Since all numbers 70 or greater must be displayed before any number less than 70 is, the data must be examined twice. The RESTORE command in line 150 allows this to happen.

Remark   Without the RESTORE command, ten variables would be needed for the ten numbers appearing in the DATA lines. With the RESTORE command, only one (X) is needed.

EXAMPLE 9. Here is a program to search a list for any value typed at the keyboard:

```
100 REM ------ON MIXING COLORS-----
110 PRINT
120 INPUT "NAME A COLOR: ";C$
130 REM ---SEARCH DATA LIST FOR C$---
140 FOR I=1 TO 11
150    READ X$,Y$
160    IF C$=X$ THEN 200
170 NEXT I
180 PRINT C$;" IS NOT IN MY LIST OF COLORS."
190 END
200 PRINT Y$
210 RESTORE : GOTO 110
500 DATA WHITE, USED FOR TINTING
510 DATA BLACK, USED FOR SHADING
520 DATA YELLOW, A PRIMARY COLOR
530 DATA RED, A PRIMARY COLOR
540 DATA BLUE, A PRIMARY COLOR
550 DATA ORANGE, MIX YELLOW AND RED.
560 DATA GREEN, MIX YELLOW AND BLUE.
570 DATA PURPLE, MIX RED AND BLUE.
580 DATA PINK, MIX RED AND WHITE.
590 DATA GRAY, MIX BLACK AND WHITE.
600 DATA MAGENTA, MIX RED WITH A SPECK OF BLACK.
RUN

NAME A COLOR: BLUE
A PRIMARY COLOR

NAME A COLOR: MAGENTA
MIX RED WITH A SPECK OF BLACK.

NAME A COLOR: AQUA
AQUA IS NOT IN MY LIST OF COLORS.
```

The list being searched in lines 140 to 170 consists of every other datum. The other values are read (Y$ in line 150) but are not used unless the corresponding color (X$ in line 150) is the color C$ input at line 120.

If the color C$ is one of the colors included in the DATA lines, line 160 transfers control out of the loop and the message Y$ is displayed. The RESTORE command in line 210 positions the pointer at the first datum so that the data can be examined *from the beginning* for the next color input for C$.

Remark

Note that the information contained in DATA lines does not represent input data in the usual sense. Rather, it represents more or less permanent data that the program uses while processing other information (values input at the keyboard). This represents a common usage of DATA commands.

Many applications require that the values given in DATA lines be used more than once. In Example 8, input data included in DATA lines had to be examined twice to produce the required output, and in Example 9, a table of colors and color-mixing instructions had to be examined from its beginning to process each input value typed at the keyboard. We conclude this chapter with a detailed analysis of another programming task that requires examining input data more than once.

EXAMPLE 10. The O'Halloran Shoe Company wants to know the average monthly income for its retail store and also the number of months in which the income exceeds this average. Write a program to carry out this task.

Problem analysis

The input and output values for this problem statement are as follows:

Input: Twelve monthly income figures
Output: Average monthly income for the year and a count of the number of months in which the income exceeds this average

To count the number of months in which the income exceeds the average, we must first find the average. This suggests the following algorithm:

a. Calculate the average monthly income for 1 year.
b. Count the number of months in which the income exceeds the average.
c. Print the results.

Before attempting to write the program segments that correspond to these three steps, we must decide how the 12 monthly income figures are to be presented to the computer for processing. If we use the INPUT statement, these 12 amounts must be typed *twice*, without error, during program execution. If a typing error is made, it may be necessary to begin over again. If we include these amounts in DATA lines, however, they can be read a second time by using a RESTORE statement. Moreover, a typing error can be corrected simply by retyping the line containing the error. Thus we will use DATA lines.

Next, let's choose variable names. Since exactly 12 values (the 12 income figures) must be read in both steps (a) and (b), we must keep a count of how many of these have been read. Let's use MTH (month) to denote this count and INC (income) for the monthly income figure last read. We'll use SUM for the sum of the monthly income figures, AVG for their average, and CNT for the count to be found in step (b). (This choice of variable names is summarized in lines 100 to 140 of the program.) Using these variable names, we can rewrite the algorithm as follows. Steps (a1) through (a3) describe step (a), and steps (b1) through (b3) describe step (b).

Algorithm (refined)

a1. Initialize the summer: SUM = 0.

a2. For MTH = 1 to 12 do the following.
     Read INC
     Add INC to SUM

a3. Let AVG = SUM/12.

b1. Restore the data pointer.

b2. Initialize the counter: CNT = 0.

b3. For MTH = 1 to 12 do the following.
     Read INC
     If INC > AVG, add 1 to CNT

c. Print the results.

Remark

In this problem analysis, we took considerable care to proceed in an orderly way toward an algorithm that would be easy to understand and whose correctness would be fairly obvious. We started by subdividing the task described in the problem statement into three simpler subtasks (steps (a), (b), and (c) in the first algorithm). Detailed algorithms for the first two of these subtasks were then written and inserted into the three-step algorithm to give us the final refined algorithm. This approach to problem solving is called the **method of stepwise refinement.** It represents an approach to problem solving that is applicable to both simple and complex problems. The method is discussed and further illustrated in Chapter 10.

The program

```
100 REM     MTH DENOTES THE MONTH (MTH=1,2,3,...,12).
110 REM     INC DENOTES INCOME FOR A SINGLE MONTH.
120 REM     SUM DENOTES THE CUMULATIVE INCOME.
130 REM     AVG DENOTES THE AVERAGE MONTHLY INCOME.
140 REM     CNT COUNTS THE NUMBER OF TIMES INC EXCEEDS AVG.
150 REM CALCULATE THE AVERAGE MONTHLY INCOME FOR ONE YEAR.
160 LET SUM=0
170 FOR MTH=1 TO 12
180     READ INC
190     LET SUM=SUM+INC
200 NEXT MTH
210 LET AVG=SUM/12
220 REM COUNT THE NUMBER OF MONTHS IN WHICH
230 REM THE INCOME EXCEEDS THE AVERAGE.
240 RESTORE
250 LET CNT=0
260 FOR MTH=1 TO 12
270     READ INC
280     IF INC>AVG THEN CNT=CNT+1
290 NEXT MTH
300 REM PRINT THE RESULTS.
310 PRINT "AVERAGE MONTHLY INCOME ";AVG
320 PRINT "NUMBER OF MONTHS INCOME EXCEEDS AVERAGE ";CNT
500 DATA 13200.57,11402.48,9248.23,9200.94
```

```
51Ø DATA 11825.5Ø,12158.Ø7,11Ø28.4Ø,228Ø4.22
52Ø DATA 18ØØ9.4Ø,126Ø7.25,19423.36,24922.5Ø
999 END
RUN

AVERAGE MONTHLY INCOME 14652.5767
NUMBER OF MONTHS INCOME EXCEEDS AVERAGE 4
```

Remark

Note that the REM statements in lines 150, 220–230, and 300 correspond exactly to the three steps of the original algorithm. Thus the program is *segmented* into three parts just as the original problem was segmented into three subtasks.

9.4 Problems

1. Show the output of each program.

a.
```
1Ø LET I=2
2Ø     READ Y
3Ø     PRINT Y
4Ø     LET I=I+2
5Ø IF I<=6 THEN 2Ø
6Ø RESTORE
7Ø DATA 9,3,5,8,12
8Ø END
```

b.
```
1ØØ FOR I=1 TO 4
11Ø     READ X
12Ø     IF X=5 THEN RESTORE
13Ø     PRINT X
14Ø NEXT I
15Ø DATA 3,5,8,9,6
16Ø END
```

c.
```
1Ø READ A$,B$,C$
2Ø RESTORE
3Ø READ D$
4Ø PRINT B$;C$;D$
5Ø DATA HEAD,ROB,IN,HOOD
6Ø END
```

d.
```
1Ø READ A1,A2,A3
2Ø PRINT A1,A2,A3
3Ø RESTORE
4Ø READ A3,A2,A1
5Ø PRINT A3,A2,A1
6Ø DATA 1Ø,2Ø,3Ø
7Ø END
```

e.
```
1ØØ FOR J=1 TO 4
11Ø     READ A$,S
12Ø     IF A$="BURNS" THEN RESTORE: GOTO 14Ø
13Ø     PRINT A$," ";S
14Ø NEXT J
15Ø DATA ALLEN,4Ø,BURNS,36
16Ø DATA CASH,38,DOOR,4Ø
17Ø END
```

In Problems 2–8, write a program to carry out each task described.

2. A user is to be allowed to input several numbers to determine whether they appear in the DATA lines. For each number input, the message IS IN THE LIST or IS NOT IN THE LIST, whichever is appropriate, is to be printed. The user should be able to terminate the run by typing 0. Try your program by using the following DATA statements:

```
5ØØ DATA 4Ø, 83, 8Ø, 65, 32, 91, 9Ø, 41, 92, 86, 8Ø, 7Ø, 55
998 DATA 9999
```

(*Note:* 9999 is an EOD tag.)

3. Several pairs of numbers are included in DATA lines. The first of each pair represents an item code number; the second represents the current selling price. Your program is to allow a user to type several code numbers to obtain the current selling prices. If an incorrect code is typed, an appropriate message should be printed. The user should be allowed to terminate the run by typing 0. Use the following data lines:

```
5ØØ DATA 1235, 12.39, 2865, 17.99, 4Ø2Ø, 23.ØØ, 364Ø, 2Ø.5Ø
51Ø DATA 493Ø, 43.5Ø, 5641, 88.2Ø, 66ØØ, 94.55, 5Ø2Ø, 16.79
998 DATA Ø,Ø
```

4. I. M. Good, a candidate for political office, conducted a preelection poll. Each voter polled was assigned a number from 1 to 5 as follows:

(1) Will vote for Good
(2) Leaning toward Good but still undecided
(3) Will vote for Shepherd, Good's only opponent
(4) Leaning toward Shepherd but still undecided
(5) All other cases

The results of the poll are included in DATA lines as follows:

```
5ØØ DATA 1, 1, 2, 5, 3, 5, 1, 2
51Ø DATA 5, 5, 2, . . .
   .
   .
   .
998 DATA 9999  :  REM EOD TAG
```

Your program is to print two tables as follows:

TABLE 1

	FOR	LEANING
GOOD	—	—
SHEPHERD	—	—

TABLE 2

	FOR OR LEANING	PERCENTAGE OF TOTAL NUMBER OF PEOPLE POLLED
GOOD	—	—
SHEPHERD	—	—
OTHERS	—	—

5. A list of words appears in DATA lines. A user should be allowed to type a word. If the word appears in the list, all words in the list up to but not including it should be printed. If the word doesn't appear, a message to that effect should be printed. In either case the user should be allowed to enter another word. If END is typed, the run should terminate.

6. Print all numbers appearing in a data list, in the order in which they appear, up to but not including the largest value in the list. Nothing else is to be printed. Test your program by using the data shown in Problem 2.

7. A wholesale firm has two warehouses, designated A and B. During a recent inventory, the following data were compiled:

Item	Warehouse	Quantity on hand	Average cost/unit
6625	A	52,000	$ 1.954
6204	A	40,000	3.126
3300	B	8,500	19.532
5925	A	22,000	6.884
2202	B	6,200	88.724
2100	B	4,350	43.612
4800	A	21,500	2.741
7923	A	15,000	1.605
1752	B	200	193.800

Prepare a separate inventory report for each warehouse. Each report is to contain the given information and is also to show the total cost represented by the inventory of each item.

8. Using the inventory data shown in Problem 7, prepare an inventory report for the warehouse whose entire stock represents the greatest cost to the company.

9.5 Review true-or-false quiz

1. The READ and DATA statements provide the means to present data to the computer without having to type them in during program execution.   T   F
2. DATA statements must follow the READ statements that read the data values.   T   F
3. The line 9Ø DATA 5,-3E2,7+3,12 is a valid BASIC statement.   T   F
4. A *pointer* is a special value appearing in a data list.   T   F
5. More than five variables may appear in a READ statement.   T   F
6. It is not necessary to read an entire data list before the first value can be read for a second time.   T   F
7. At most one RESTORE statement may be used in a BASIC program.   T   F
8. When large quantities of data are included in DATA lines, the first value must be a count of the number of values included.   T   F
9. The READ and DATA statements are often useful when no interaction between the computer and the user is required.   T   F
10. When we assign values to a string variable with the READ statement, quotation marks are sometimes necessary.   T   F
11. The EOD tag used in reading long lists of data must be a numerical constant, even though all other data values appearing in the DATA lines are string constants.   T   F
12. It is sometimes useful to assign values to both string variables and numerical variables using the same READ statement.   T   F

10

□ □ □ □ □ □ □ □ □ □ □ □ □ □ □

Top-Down Programming

In this chapter, no new programming techniques or BASIC commands are presented. Rather, we pause to review and summarize the approach to computer programming illustrated in the foregoing chapters.

Programming is essentially a three-step process.

1. Carefully read the problem statement so that it is completely understood. If necessary, rewrite the problem statement to clarify what is being asked.
2. Discover and describe an algorithm that, when followed, will lead to a solution to the problem.
3. Using the algorithm described in step (2), write and debug the program.

For lengthy problem statements or for tasks that are intrinsically difficult, step (2) can be troublesome. When you are confronted with such a situation, it is natural to segment the problem into simpler, more manageable tasks.

> We understand complex things by systematically breaking them down into successively simpler parts and understanding how these parts fit together locally.[*]

Each problem analysis in this book is essentially a description of how you might go about segmenting a task into simpler tasks; each algorithm displays these subtasks and shows the order in which they are to be carried out.

As natural as this approach to programming may appear, choosing subtasks that actually simplify matters may not be easy. Unfortunately, a formula for identifying appropriate subtasks

---

[*]"Structured Programming with **go to** Statements," by Donald E. Knuth, Computing Surveys, 6, No. 4 (December 1974).

is not known. Problem segmentation must be practiced. It is for this reason that we have carried out detailed problem analyses for several rather simple programming tasks. Programming tasks often are not simple, however, and discovering a correct algorithm whose steps are easily coded in BASIC may not be easy. Although a formula for identifying appropriate subtasks is not known, a method that will help in your attempts to find such subtasks is known. This method, the method of stepwise refinement, was illustrated in Example 10 of Section 9.3. The task to be performed in that example was as follows:

Problem statement Determine the average monthly income over a full year and the number of months in which the income exceeds this average.

We began with an algorithm containing as little detail as possible. Our objective, you may recall, was to describe an algorithm that would be easy to understand. This was the algorithm chosen:

a. Calculate the average monthly income for 1 year.
b. Count the number of months in which the income exceeds the average.
c. Print the results.

That this algorithm describes a process for carrying out the stated task should be evident—in spite of the detail omitted. For example, the algorithm contains no variable names (they were chosen later), and it does not tell how to find the average or how to determine the required count. Details should be introduced only as needed; each time a detail is introduced, the complexity of the algorithm increases. The algorithm was kept simple by considering *what* must be done, not *how* it should be done.

The next step was to introduce variable names and show how the steps in the algorithm could be carried out. The following variable names were chosen:

$$MTH \;=\; \text{month (MTH} = 1, 2, 3, \ldots, 12)$$
$$INC \;=\; \text{income for a single month}$$
$$SUM \;=\; \text{cumulative income}$$
$$AVG \;=\; \text{average monthly income}$$
$$CNT \;=\; \text{a count of the number of times INC exceeds AVG}$$

Using these variables, steps (a) and (b) were broken down into simpler steps to give the following more detailed algorithm.

a1. Initialize the summer: SUM = 0.
a2. For MTH = 1 to 12 do the following:
    Read INC
    Add INC to SUM
a3. Let AVG = SUM/12.
b1. Restore the data pointer.
b2. Initialize the counter: CNT = 0.
b3. For MTH = 1 to 12 do the following:
    Read INC
    If INC>AVG, add 1 to CNT
c. Print the results.

We then translated this algorithm into a BASIC program. Knowing that the original three-step algorithm was correct, and also that the refinements of steps (a) and (b) correctly carry out these two tasks, we can be sure that this final 7-step algorithm is also correct.

We illustrate this process of stepwise refinement with another example.

EXAMPLE 1

At the end of each month, a wholesale firm makes an inventory that shows, for each item in stock, the item code, the quantity on hand, and the average cost per unit. Here is a portion of the most recent inventory:

Item code	Units on hand	Average cost/unit
AA13	844	$1.63
MK21	182	5.93
⋮	⋮	⋮

We are asked to prepare an inventory report that contains the given information and also the total cost of the inventory by item. In addition, a second short report is to be printed identifying the item (or items) whose inventory represents the greatest cost to the company:

Total cost = (units on hand) × (average cost per unit)

Problem analysis

Let's begin with the following simple algorithm:

a. Prepare the inventory report.
b. Determine the item (or items) whose inventory represents the greatest cost.

Writing a program segment to produce a printed report such as the one required in step (a) is not new to us. After printing a report title and appropriate column headings for the values to be printed, we will process the data, item by item, to determine and print these values.

To carry out step (b), we must first find the greatest total cost of all items in stock and then compare the total cost for each item with this largest value. Thus step (b) can be broken down into the two simpler tasks (b1) and (b2) shown in the following refined algorithm:

a. Prepare the inventory report.
b1. Determine the greatest total cost of all items in stock.
b2. Print a report identifying each item whose inventory represents this greatest cost figure.

The task of finding the largest number in a set of numbers is likewise not new to us (see Example 6 of Section 9.1). We simply calculate the total cost of the items in stock, one at a time, always keeping track of the largest of the amounts encountered. To carry out step (b2), we must again calculate the total cost amounts, item by item, and then compare each with the largest amount found in step (b1).

Having identified what tasks must be performed, we must consider how to carry them out using the BASIC language. As described above, the given inventory data must be examined more than once. If we include these data in DATA lines, the RESTORE statement will allow us to examine the inventory data as often as needed. Let's agree to use one DATA line for the three values (item code, units on hand, and average cost per unit) associated with each stock item. A last DATA line containing the values XXXX, 0, 0 will be used to indicate the end of data.

```
500 DATA AA13, 844, 1.63
510 DATA MK21, 182, 5.93
         .
         .
         .
998 DATA XXXX,0,0
```

The next task is to choose variable names. To carry out step (a), we will need variables for the three values in a DATA line and a fourth to calculate the cost amounts required in the inventory report. In addition, we need a variable for the largest amount to be found in step (b1). These variable names are shown in lines 110 to 150 of the program.

The program

```
100 REM------INVENTORY PROGRAM------
110 REM    I$ = ITEM CODE
120 REM     Q = QUANTITY (IN UNITS) ON HAND
130 REM     C = AVERAGE COST PER UNIT
140 REM    T% = TOTAL COST (TO THE NEAREST DOLLAR)
145 REM              REPRESENTED BY ITEM I$
150 REM    L% = LARGEST OF ALL COST FIGURES
155 REM              (TO THE NEAREST DOLLAR)
160 REM ***** PREPARE AND PRINT INVENTORY REPORT *****
170 PRINT TAB(7); "WAREHOUSE INVENTORY REPORT"
180 PRINT
190 REM PRINT COLUMN HEADINGS.
200 PRINT "ITEM"; TAB(12);"UNITS";TAB(23);"AVERAGE";
205 PRINT TAB(35);"TOTAL"
210 PRINT "CODE";TAB(12);"ON HAND";TAB(23);"COST/UNIT";
215 PRINT TAB(35);"COST"
220 PRINT
230 REM PRINT TABLE VALUES.
240     READ I$,Q,C
250     IF I$="XXXX" THEN 290
260     LET T%=Q*C+0.5
270     PRINT I$;TAB(12);Q;TAB(23);C;TAB(35);T%
280 GOTO 240
290 PRINT
300 REM ***** DETERMINE THE LARGEST COST AMOUNT (L%) *****
310 LET L%=0
320 RESTORE
330     READ I$,Q,C
340     IF I$="XXXX" THEN 380
350     LET T%=Q*C+0.5
360     IF T%>L% THEN L%=T%
370 GOTO 330
380 REM PRINT REPORT OF ITEM OR ITEMS WHOSE
390 REM INVENTORY REPRESENTS THE GREATEST COST.
400 PRINT "MAXIMUM COST $";L%
```

```
41Ø RESTORE
42Ø    READ I$,Q,C
43Ø     IF I$="XXXX" THEN 999
44Ø     LET T%=Q*C+.5
45Ø IF T%=L% THEN PRINT "ITEM ";I$
46Ø GOTO 42Ø
998 DATA XXXX,Ø,Ø
999 END
```

If this program is run with the DATA lines

```
5ØØ DATA AA13,  844,  1.63
51Ø DATA MK21,  182,  5.93
52Ø DATA HJ43,  467,  4.37
53Ø DATA AC91,  764,  5.62
54Ø DATA YM15,  877,  4.73
55Ø DATA ST14,  636,  2.64
56Ø DATA LJ27,  292,  9.63
57Ø DATA LT51,1Ø67,  3.78
58Ø DATA WA19,  532,  7.41
59Ø DATA TK41,  1Ø3,11.53
```

it will produce the following report:

```
          WAREHOUSE INVENTORY REPORT

ITEM        UNITS       AVERAGE       TOTAL
CODE        ON HAND     COST/UNIT     COST

AA13        844         1.63          1376
MK21        182         5.93          1Ø79
HF43        467         4.37          2Ø41
AC91        764         5.62          4294
YM15        877         4.73          4148
ST14        636         2.64          1679
LJ27        292         9.63          2812
LT51        1Ø67        3.78          4Ø33
WA19        532         7.41          3942
TK41        1Ø3         11.53         1188

MAXIMUM COST $4294
ITEM AC91
```

Remark

The job of finding the greatest cost L% (lines 3ØØ to 37Ø) could have been accomplished by modifying the first program segment (lines 16Ø to 29Ø). The resulting program would have been slightly shorter, but not necessarily better. Indeed, combining tasks during the coding process can easily lead to serious programming errors. The problem analysis we carried out led us to consider three separate tasks. The program is segmented into three parts corresponding to these tasks. They are identified in the REM statements in lines 16Ø, 3ØØ, and 38Ø. As a result, the program is easy to read and understand, even though it may be longer than necessary. Moreover, because of the systematic way in which tasks were broken down into simpler tasks, we can be confident that the program is absolutely correct (barring syntax or typing errors).

The problem analysis carried out in the preceding example can be displayed in a diagram:

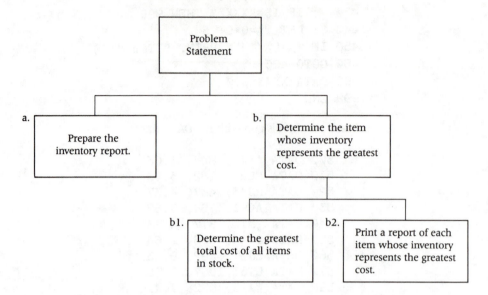

At the top is the problem statement—a complete description of what is to be done. The two tasks at the next lower level show how the problem was broken down into two slightly simpler tasks. The second of these, step (b), was broken down again, and it was then found that each of the terminal tasks, steps (a), (b1), and (b2), could easily be translated into a BASIC program. Hence no further subdivision was carried out.

The method of stepwise refinement is also called **top-down programming.** You start at the top (the problem statement), break this task down into simpler tasks, then break these tasks into even simpler ones, and continue this process, all the while knowing how the tasks at each level combine, until the tasks at the lowest level contain whatever detail is desired.

Let's summarize some of the main aspects of top-down programming:

1. Each algorithm is obtained from the preceding one by subdividing one or more of the individual tasks into simpler ones. At each step, or *level of refinement,* more details emerge to bring you closer to a solution—that is, closer to the desired program.
2. At the upper levels of refinement, dependence on the particular computer being used is avoided; the objective is to determine *what* tasks must be performed, not *how* to carry them out.
3. At the lower levels of refinement, it may be helpful to use terminology borrowed from the programming language being used. For instance, the algorithm shown on page 148 contains the step

   For MTH = 1 to 12 do the following:
      Read INC
      Add INC to SUM

   Writing the step this way is helpful since it suggests how to code it in BASIC.
4. At each level the algorithm must be debugged. If the algorithm at one level is correct, it should be a simple matter to debug the algorithm at the next lower level. You need only check to ensure that each task broken down into simpler tasks is broken down correctly. It is this aspect of the top-down approach that increases the likelihood that the final program will be correct.

We don't mean to imply that top-down programming will always lead directly to a "good" program. A level of refinement may be reached that, for some reason, is undesirable. When this happens, you may either start over at the top or go back one or more levels and continue from that point with a different refinement. Some problems may require you to back up in this manner several times before a satisfactory algorithm emerges.

The step-by-step process of segmenting complex tasks into simpler ones is not new; good programmers have always used such an approach. Giving a *name* to the process, however, has had two significant consequences. It has introduced the method of stepwise refinement to many people who previously programmed in a more or less haphazard fashion. As a result, better programs—that is, programs that are easy to read and likely to be correct—are being written. The second consequence is that the method of problem segmentation has been carefully studied and formulated into an orderly process, as illustrated in the worked-out examples. Since the way in which tasks are broken down into subtasks depends on who is carrying out this process, top-down programming is not an algorithm that will always lead to the same program. Rather, it is a *process* that brings order to an otherwise disorderly human activity— namely, programming. We might say that some structure has been introduced into the process of designing programs.

As noted, one of the benefits of using a top-down approach is that the resulting programs are more likely to be correct. But to know that a program is correct is another matter. Any serious consideration of this topic must necessarily concern the structure of the program itself, not just the structure of the process that leads to the program. It is in this context that the expression *structured programming* has emerged. Section 6.8 contains a brief discussion of structured programming and explains what constitutes a structured program. Although we suggested how a program's structure relates to the task of verifying its correctness, a complete discussion of this topic is beyond the scope of an introductory text such as this one. The principal concern of a beginning programmer is to write good programs. The following guidelines should help:

Guidelines for writing good (structured) programs

1. Use the method of top-down programming. If you follow the rules described in this chapter, you should obtain correct algorithms that are easily translated into correct and easy-to-read programs.
2. While constructing an algorithm, keep in mind the programming structures *sequence, selection,* and *repetition* described in Section 6.8. Each time you write a step that includes words such as *go to step (b)* or *repeat step (e),* ask yourself if this step is part of a selection or repetition structure. If it is not, try something else.
3. Code specific subtasks by using program segments with exactly one entry point and exactly one exit point. This means that a program segment should contain only one statement that initiates it and only one that gets you out. This is one of the basic rules of structured programming. Programs written in this way are said to be *block structured.*

We conclude this chapter by quoting Edsger W. Dijkstra, who gave structured programming its name* and who remains a central figure in the effort to discover the true nature of programs and the programming process.

Structured Programming, Software Engineering Techniques, by E. W. Dijkstra (Brussels: NATO Scientific Affairs Division, 1970), pp. 84–88.

We understand walls in terms of bricks, bricks in terms of crystals, crystals in terms of molecules, etc.

The only effective way to raise the confidence level of a program significantly is to give a convincing proof of its correctness. But one should not first make the program and then prove its correctness, because then the requirement of providing the proof would only increase the poor programmer's burden. On the contrary: the programmer should let the correctness proof and program grow hand in hand.[†]

10.1 Problems

It is intentional that no problems are included in this chapter. The method of top-down programming is not an isolated topic; it is an approach to problem solving that should be used in all programming tasks. The experience you gain in using the top-down approach with simple problems will prepare you for the more challenging problems ahead.

[†]"The Humble Programmer" (1972 ACM Turing Award Lecture), by E. W. Dijkstra, *Communications of the ACM*, vol. 15, no. 10, October 1972, pp. 859–866.

11

□ □ □ □ □ □ □ □ □ □ □ □ □ □ □

String and Numerical Functions

BASIC is designed to assist you in manipulating both numerical and string data. For this reason, the language includes several functions, called **built-in functions,** to carry out automatically certain common calculations with numbers and operations on strings. In addition, BASIC allows you to define your own *numerical* functions—functions that you may need but that are not part of the language. These are called **user-defined functions.** In this chapter we describe some of the more common string functions (Sections 11.1 and 11.2), the built-in numerical functions (Section 11.4), and the user-defined functions (Section 11.6).

11.1 String functions

Four of the most useful **string functions** included in Applesoft BASIC are described in this section. The first determines the length of a string, and the other three are used to examine individual characters or groups of characters in a string.

The string function LEN

If **s** denotes a string, then LEN(**s**), read length of **s**, is the number of characters contained in **s.** Thus LEN("JOHN AND MARY") has the value 13. And if Z$ = "JOHN AND MARY" then LEN(Z$) also has the value 13. As always, blanks are counted as characters. The **s** in LEN(**s**) is called the *argument* of the function and must be enclosed in parentheses as shown.

EXAMPLE 1. Here is a program to print only the strings that contain exactly three characters:

```
1Ø FOR I=1 TO 6
2Ø    READ X$
3Ø      IF LEN(X$)=3 THEN PRINT X$
4Ø NEXT I
5Ø DATA "THE","I DO","ONE","OLD ","THREE","127"
6Ø END
RUN

THE
ONE
127
```

Note that "I DO" has four characters—three letters and an embedded blank. Similarly, "OLD " has a trailing blank character.

EXAMPLE 2. Here is a program to print a column of words lined up on the right:

```
1ØØ  PRINT "123456789Ø123456789Ø"
11Ø REM READ WORDS AND PRINT RIGHT JUSTIFIED.
12Ø      READ A$
13Ø      IF A$="XXX" THEN 999
14Ø      PRINT TAB(15-LEN(A$));A$
15Ø GOTO 12Ø
16Ø DATA A,SHORT,LIST,OF,WORDS,XXX
999 END
RUN

123456789Ø123456789Ø
              A
          SHORT
           LIST
             OF
          WORDS
```

The TAB function tabs to position 15−1 to print A, to position 15−5 to print SHORT, and so on. This effectively prints the column of words with the last character of each word in column position 14.

The string function LEFT$

If **s** denotes a string and **n** a positive integer, then LEFT$(**s**,**n**) is the string consisting of the first **n** characters contained in **s**. Thus LEFT$("JOHN AND MARY",4) has the value JOHN.

EXAMPLE 3

```
1Ø LET Y$="SEVEN"
2Ø FOR N=1 TO LEN(Y$)
3Ø    PRINT LEFT$(Y$,N)
4Ø NEXT N
5Ø END
```

```
RUN

S
SE
SEV
SEVE
SEVEN
```

EXAMPLE 4. Here is a program to print only the words that begin with whatever prefix is input by the user:

```
11Ø INPUT "TYPE A PREFIX: ";P$
12Ø PRINT
13Ø FOR K=1 TO 1Ø
14Ø     READ A$
15Ø     IF LEFT$(A$,LEN(P$))=P$ THEN PRINT A$
16Ø NEXT K
17Ø DATA ENABLE,ENACT,ENGAGE,ENSURE,ENDORSE
18Ø DATA OBVERSE,OBDURATE,OBJECT,REACT,RECISION
19Ø END
RUN

TYPE A PREFIX: OB

OBVERSE
OBDURATE
OBJECT
```

The string function RIGHT$

If **s** denotes a string and **n** a positive integer, then RIGHT$(**s**,**n**) is the string consisting of the last **n** characters in **s**. Thus RIGHT$("JOHN AND MARY",4) has the value MARY.

EXAMPLE 5

```
1Ø LET Y$="SEVEN"
2Ø FOR N=1 TO LEN(Y$)
3Ø     PRINT RIGHT$(Y$,N)
4Ø NEXT N
5Ø END
RUN

N
EN
VEN
EVEN
SEVEN
```

The string function MID$

The MID$ function can be used in two forms. If **s** denotes a string and **m** and **n** denote positive integers, then:

1. MID$(**s,m,n**) is the string of **n** characters from **s** beginning with the **m**th character of **s**.
2. MID$(**s,n**) is the string consisting of all characters in **s** from the **n**th character on.

Thus MID$("JOHN AND MARY",6,3) has the value AND whereas MID$("JOHN AND MARY",10) has the value MARY.

EXAMPLE 6

```
1Ø LET Y$="ABCD"
2Ø FOR I=1 TO LEN(Y$)
3Ø    PRINT MID$(Y$,I,1),MID$(Y$,I)
4Ø NEXT I
5Ø END
RUN

A                ABCD
B                BCD
C                CD
D                D
```

EXAMPLE 7. Here is a program to count the number of A's in a string A$ of any length:

```
1ØØ LET C=Ø
11Ø INPUT A$
12Ø FOR I=1 TO LEN(A$)
13Ø    IF MID$(A$,I,1)="A" THEN C=C+1
14Ø NEXT I
15Ø PRINT "NUMBER OF A'S IS ";C
16Ø END
RUN

? ABRACADABRA
NUMBER OF A'S IS 5
```

11.2 Combining strings (concatenation)

The **concatenation operator +** allows you to combine two or more strings into a single string. Thus the statement

```
LET X$="PARA"+"MEDIC"
```

assigns the string "PARAMEDIC" to the variable X$. Similarly, if A$ = "PARA" and B$ = "MEDIC" the statement

```
LET X$=A$+B$
```

does exactly the same thing.

EXAMPLE 8. Here is a program to illustrate the concatenation operator:

```
1Ø LET X$="BIOLOGY"
2Ø LET Y$="ELECTRONICS"
3Ø LET Z$=LEFT$(X$,3)+RIGHT$(Y$,4)
4Ø PRINT Z$
5Ø END
RUN

BIONICS
```

Using only the functions LEFT$ and RIGHT$, we could have caused BIONICS to be printed, but we could not have assigned the string "BIONICS" to the variable Z$.

EXAMPLE 9. Here is a program to interchange the first and last names given in the string "EMILY DICKINSON":

```
1ØØ LET A$="EMILY DICKINSON"
11Ø PRINT A$
12Ø REM FIND THE POSITION I OF THE BLANK IN A$.
13Ø FOR I=1 TO LEN(A$)
14Ø    IF MID$(A$,I,1)=" " THEN 16Ø
15Ø NEXT I
16Ø REM STORE THE FIRST NAME IN F$ AND THE LAST NAME IN L$.
17Ø LET F$=LEFT$(A$,I-1)
18Ø LET L$=MID$(A$,I+1)
19Ø LET A$=L$+", "+F$
2ØØ PRINT A$
21Ø END
RUN

EMILY DICKINSON
DICKINSON, EMILY
```

Remark   The technique illustrated in this example has two immediate applications: it gives you additional control over the precise form of your output, and it allows you to alphabetize a list of names even if first names are given first. (Simply interchange first and last names and then use a standard sorting algorithm to alphabetize your list.) (See Section 13.3.)

EXAMPLE 10. Here is a program to assign the contents of A$ to B$, but in reverse order. For instance, if A$ = "AMNZ" then B$ will contain "ZNMA".

```
1ØØ LET A$="RORRIM"
11Ø LET B$="" : REM B$ IS THE EMPTY STRING.
12Ø REM USING THE CONCATENATION OPERATOR,
13Ø REM APPEND EACH OF THE CHARACTERS OF A$ TO B$.
14Ø FOR I=LEN(A$) TO 1 STEP -1
15Ø    LET B$=B$+MID$(A$,I,1)
16Ø NEXT I
17Ø PRINT A$;" IN REVERSE ORDER IS ";B$
18Ø END
RUN
```

```
RORRIM IN REVERSE ORDER IS MIRROR
```

Line 110 assigns a string containing no characters to B$. This step ensures that we will enter the FOR/NEXT loop that appends letters to B$ with nothing in B$.

Remark 1

The MID$ function allows you to print a string in reverse order. The concatenation operator is what allows you to assign the new string to B$.

Remark 2

As mentioned previously, when you type RUN the Apple sets all numerical variables to zero and all string variables to the empty string. We include line 110 for clarity just as we have consistently initialized numerical variables to zero when it is important that they have this initial value.

Remark 3

The program shown in this example illustrates the principal reason why programming languages such as BASIC allow the empty string. When you wish to determine a numerical sum by adding a list of numbers, you begin with a sum of zero; when you wish to build a new string by concatenating a list of characters or strings, you begin with the empty string.

11.3 Problems

1. Show the output of each program.
   a.
   ```
   1Ø LET A$="CYBERNETIC"
   2Ø PRINT LEFT$(A$,LEN(A$)/2)
   3Ø END
   ```

   b.
   ```
   1Ø LET B$="A TO Z"
   2Ø PRINT RIGHT$(B$,1);" TO ";LEFT$(B$,1)
   3Ø END
   ```

   c.
   ```
   1Ø LET A$="CONSTRUCTION"
   2Ø LET B$="SULTAN OF SWAT"
   3Ø LET C$=LEFT$(A$,3)+LEFT$(B$,5)+RIGHT$(A$,4)
   4Ø PRINT C$
   5Ø END
   ```

   d.
   ```
   1Ø LET A$="BIOLOGY"
   2Ø LET B$="PHYSICS"
   3Ø LET C$=LEFT$(A$,3)
   4Ø FOR I=1 TO LEN(B$)
   5Ø    LET C$=C$+MID$(B$,I,1)
   6Ø NEXT I
   7Ø PRINT C$
   8Ø END
   ```

2. Write a single program statement to perform each of the following tasks:
   a. Print the first character of A$.
   b. Print the second character of A$.
   c. Print the last character of A$.
   d. Print the first three characters of A$.
   e. Print the last three characters of A$.
   f. Print the first and last characters of A$.
   g. Transfer control to line 70 if A$ and B$ have the same number of characters.
   h. Transfer control to line 95 if the first character of A$ equals the last character of A$.
   i. Transfer control to line 160 if the first two characters of A$ are the same.
   j. Interchange the first two characters in S$ to obtain T$.
   k. Create a string F$ consisting of the first three characters of G$ and the last three characters of H$.
   l. Transfer control to line 150 if the first character of A$, the second character of B$, and the third character of C$ spell YES.

In Problems 3–13, write a program for each task specified.

3. Any five-character string typed at the keyboard is to be printed in reverse order. If the string does not contain exactly five characters, nothing is to be printed. The user should be allowed to try many strings, and the program should halt when the user types DONE.

4. Any string input at the keyboard is to be printed in reverse order. The program should halt only when the user types DONE.

5. All strings appearing in DATA lines are to be examined to determine and print those that begin with whatever letter is input at the keyboard. The user is to be allowed to try different letters during a single run and the program is to halt when ∗ is typed.

6. Two five-letter words are to be input at the keyboard. They are to be compared letter by letter. If two corresponding letters are different, a dollar sign should be printed. Otherwise the letter should be printed. If CANDY and CHIDE are input, for example, the output should be C$$D$.

7. Two words are to be input to obtain a listing of those letters in the second word that are also in the first. If STRING and HARNESS are typed, for example, the output should be RNSS, since these four letters in the second word HARNESS are also in the first.

8. A string containing two words separated by a comma is to be input. The two words are to be printed in reverse order without the comma. If "GARVEY, STEVE" is typed, for example, the output should be STEVE GARVEY. The program should halt only when the user types DONE.

9. Read a list of names from DATA lines. Each name is in the following form: last name, comma, first name, space, middle initial, period (BUNKER,ARCHIE Q.). The computer is to print the names with first name first (ARCHIE Q. BUNKER). Each full name is to be read into a single string variable. Use XXX as the EOD tag.

10. Input a string and change all occurrences of the letter Y to the letter M.

11. Read a list of words from DATA lines to determine the average number of letters per word.

12. Read a list of words from DATA lines, and print only the words with exactly N letters. N is to be input by the user, who should be allowed to try several different values for N during a single program run.

13. Read a list of strings appearing in DATA lines to determine how many times a particular letter or other character appears in this list. The letter or character is to be input by the user, who should be allowed to try several different characters during the same run. The program run should terminate whenever the user types END.

11.4 Built-in numerical functions

A list of the Applesoft BASIC numerical functions is provided in Table 11.1. These functions are an integral part of the BASIC language and can be used in any BASIC program. In this section we'll describe the ABS, INT, SQR, and SIN functions and show how they are used. The RND function (which is used somewhat differently from the other numerical functions) is considered in Chapter 16. The first sections of the RND chapter are written so that the material can be taken up at this time, should that be desired.

TABLE 11.1   Applesoft BASIC numerical functions

Function	Purpose
ABS(x)	Gives the absolute value of x.
INT(x)	Gives the greatest integer less than or equal to x.
SGN(x)	Returns the value 1 of x is positive, -1 if x is negative, and 0 if x is zero.
SQR(x)	Calculates the principal square root of x if $x \geq 0$; results in an error if x is negative.
RND(x)	Returns a pseudorandom number between 0 and 1 (see Chapter 16).
SIN(x)	Calculates the sine of x, where x is in radian measure.
COS(x)	Calculates the cosine of x, where x is in radian measure.
TAN(x)	Calculates the tangent of x, where x is in radian measure.
ATN(x)	Calculates the arctangent of x; $-\pi/2 \leq$ ATN $(x) < \pi/2$.
LOG(x)	Calculates the natural logarithm $\ln(x)$; x must be positive.
EXP(x)	Calculates the exponential e^x, where $e = 2.71828 \ldots$ is the base of the natural logarithms.

The numerical function ABS

ABS is the **absolute value function**: ABS(-3) = 3, ABS(7) = 7, and ABS($4-9$) = 5. In general, if **e** denotes a BASIC numerical expression, then ABS(**e**) is the absolute value of the value of the expression **e**. The next two examples illustrate the use of the ABS function.

EXAMPLE 11. Here is a program to print the absolute value of the sum of any two numbers:

```
10 PRINT "TYPE TWO NUMBERS PER LINE."
20 PRINT "TYPE 0,0 TO STOP."
30 INPUT X,Y
40    IF X=0 AND Y=0 THEN END
50    LET Z=ABS(X+Y)
60    PRINT "ABSOLUTE VALUE OF SUM: ";Z
70    INPUT "NEXT PAIR? ";X,Y
80 GOTO 40
RUN

TYPE TWO NUMBERS PER LINE.
TYPE 0,0 TO STOP.
? 7,3
ABSOLUTE VALUE OF SUM: 10
NEXT PAIR? 5,-9
ABSOLUTE VALUE OF SUM: 4
NEXT PAIR? 0,-92.7
ABSOLUTE VALUE OF SUM: 92.7
NEXT PAIR? 0,0
```

This program could have been written without using the ABS function. For example, if line 50 were replaced by the two lines

```
50 LET Z=X+Y
55 IF Z<0 THEN Z=-Z
```

the resulting program would work in the same way as the original. The first version is more desirable—its logic is transparent, whereas the logic of the second version is somewhat obscure. As a general rule you should use the built-in functions supplied with your system. Not only will your programs be easier to code but they will also be easier to understand and hence simpler to debug or modify, should that be required.

EXAMPLE 12. Let's write a program to count how many of 20 numbers in a data list are within 2.5 units of 7.

Problem analysis

We choose variable names as follows:

X = value being read
C = number of values read
N = number of values within 2.5 units of 7

It should not be hard to verify that the following algorithm describes what must be done.

Algorithm

a. Start with N = 0.
b. For C = 1 to 20, do the following:
   Read X.
   If X is within 2.5 units of 7, add 1 to N.
c. Print the count N and stop.

In this algorithm only the second step in (b) may be troublesome to code. To find how close a number X is to 7, we subtract X from 7 or 7 from X (depending on whether 7 is larger or smaller than X). Since we are interested only in how close X is to 7—not in which is larger—we simply examine the absolute value of X − 7. We find that X will be within 2.5 units of 7 if ABS(X − 7) is less than or equal to 2.5. Thus the last line of step (b) will be coded as

```
IF ABS(X-7)<=2.5 THEN N=N+1
```

The program

```
1Ø LET N=Ø
2Ø FOR C=1 TO 2Ø
3Ø    READ X
4Ø    IF ABS(X-7)<=2.5 THEN N=N+1
5Ø NEXT C
6Ø PRINT "OF THE 2Ø NUMBERS IN DATA LINES"
7Ø PRINT N;" ARE WITHIN 2.5 UNITS OF 7."
8Ø DATA 2.5, 3.9, 4.5, 5.7, 6, 7, 8, 9, 9.3, 1Ø
9Ø DATA 4, 4.4, 5, 5.9, 7.1, 8, 9.5, 9.8, 9, 9
99 END
RUN

OF THE 2Ø NUMBERS IN DATA LINES
12 ARE WITHIN 2.5 UNITS OF 7.
```

The numerical function INT

If INT(**e**) is used in a BASIC program, its value is the greatest integer less than or equal to the value of the expression **e.** For example, INT(2.6) = 2, INT(7) = 7, INT(7 − 3.2) = 3, and INT(− 4.35) = − 5. For this reason INT is called the **greatest-integer function.**

The INT function can be used to round off numbers. For example, suppose X satisfies the inequalities

$$36.5 \leq X < 37.5$$

Then X + 0.5 satisfies the inequalities

$$37 \leq X + 0.5 < 38$$

and we see that

```
INT(X+Ø.5)=37
```

That is, to round a number X to the nearest integer, use the BASIC expression

```
INT(X+Ø.5).
```

(You may recall that the command

```
LET N%=X+Ø.5
```

assigns the rounded value of X to N% if this rounded value is in the range − 32767 to 32767. By using

```
INT(X+Ø.5)
```

you are not restricted to numbers in this range.)

A slight modification of this method of rounding to the nearest integer can be used to round to any decimal position. We illustrate by rounding the number X = 67.382 to the nearest tenth to obtain 67.4:

X :	67.382	*(Number to be rounded.)*
1Ø*X :	673.82	*(Move decimal point to the right.)*
INT(1Ø*X+.5) :	674	*(Round to nearest integer.)*
INT(1Ø*X+.5)/1Ø :	67.4	*(Move decimal point back.)*

For more work with rounding numbers, see Problem 5 of Section 11.5.

EXAMPLE 13. Here is a program segment to tell whether or not an input value is an integer:

```
3ØØ INPUT A
31Ø IF A<>INT(A) THEN PRINT "NOT ";
32Ø PRINT "AN INTEGER"
```

The condition A<>INT(A) is true only when A is not an integer. Thus if A is an integer the command to print NOT in line 310 is skipped and the message AN INTEGER is printed.

EXAMPLE 14. This program segment tells whether a value is odd or even.

```
3ØØ INPUT N
31Ø IF N<>INT(N) THEN 3ØØ
32Ø PRINT "THE NUMBER IS ";
33Ø IF N/2=INT(N/2) THEN PRINT "EVEN."
34Ø IF N/2<>INT(N/2) THEN PRINT "ODD."
```

If the value typed is not an integer, line 310 transfers control back to the INPUT statement so that another value can be typed. If an integer is typed, control passes to line 320, which prints the partial output THE NUMBER IS. If N is even, N/2 is an integer and the condition in line 330 is true. If N is odd, N/2 is not an integer and the condition in line 340 is true. Thus the partial output is completed with the word EVEN if N is even or ODD if N is odd.

In the preceding example, an IF statement with the condition N/2 = INT(N/2) is used to tell whether an integer N is divisible by 2. To determine whether an integer N is divisible by an integer D that is not necessarily 2, the condition

N/D=INT(N/D)

may be used, since N/D is an integer only if N is exactly divisible by D.

Relational expression	*Truth value*
63/7 = INT(63/7)	true
6/4 = INT(6/4)	false
INT(1Ø5/15) = 1Ø5/15	true
INT(1ØØ/8) <> 1ØØ/8	true

Here we must add a word of caution. In BASIC the condition

```
N/D=INT(N/D)
```

is used to determine whether N/D is an integer only if both N and D are integers. If either is not an integer, you may get unexpected results. For instance, in Applesoft BASIC the condition

```
1/.1=INT(1/.1)
```

is false even though the fraction 1/.1 has the integer value 10. To see that this is so, type the immediate mode command

```
PRINT 1/.1, INT(1/.1)
```

The Apple will display 10 and 9. The reason for this discrepancy is that computers use an internal representation of numbers that does not allow all numbers to be stored exactly. (This should not be surprising; after all, the ordinary fraction 1/3 cannot be represented exactly as a finite decimal.) On most computers, including the Apple, .1 is one of these numbers. Thus calculations involving .1 may or may not be exact. The following short program with output produced by an Apple II computer illustrates this situation:

```
10 LET X=.1
20 LET X=X+.2
30 PRINT X/.1, INT(X/.1)
40 IF X<1 THEN 20
50 END
RUN

3          3
5          4
7          6
9          8
11         11
```

EXAMPLE 15. Here is a program to output a rectangular array of asterisks:

```
100 LET N=0
110    LET N=N+1
120    PRINT "*";
130    IF N/15=INT(N/15) THEN PRINT
140 IF N<45 THEN 110
150 END
RUN

**************
**************
**************
```

On each pass through the loop, line 110 adds 1 to N and line 120 displays an asterisk. The semicolon in line 120 suppresses the RETURN normally occurring after a PRINT command is executed. Then line 130 tests whether N is divisible by 15. If it is, the PRINT command causes a RETURN to be executed so that subsequent output will appear on the next line.

The INT function has many applications. We have shown that it can be used to round numbers (discussion preceding Example 13), to validate user input (Example 14), and to test for divisibility of one number by another (Example 15). As you work through the examples and problems in this and subsequent chapters you will find that the INT function is a valuable programming tool that can be used to simplify many programming tasks.

The numerical function SQR

SQR is called the **square root function.** Instead of writing N^0.5 to evaluate the square root of N you can write SQR(N). The principal advantage in doing this is that your programs will be easier to read—SQR(N) is *English-like* whereas N^0.5 is not. For instance, to evaluate the algebraic expression

$$\sqrt{b^2 - 4ac}$$

you can write

```
SQR(B^2-4*A*C)
```

instead of

```
(B^2-4*A*C)^0.5
```

(See Problem 24 in the next problem set for an application of the expression $\sqrt{b^2 - 4ac}$.) From left to right the first form reads "evaluate the square root of $B^2 - 4AC$" whereas the second reads "evalute $B^2 - 4AC$ to the one-half power." A second but minor advantage in using SQR is that the Apple executes SQR(N) more quickly than N^0.5.

In the next example we give a detailed analysis for a prime number program. The example illustrates the use of the SQR and INT functions and also discusses simple ways of speeding up program execution, should that be important.

EXAMPLE 16. Write a program to tell whether an integer typed at the keyboard is a prime number.

Problem analysis   Let N denote the number to be tested. A number N is prime if it is an integer greater than 1 whose only factors are 1 and N. To determine whether a number N is prime, you can divide it successively by 2, 3, . . . , N − 1. If N is divisible by none of these, then N is a prime. It is not necessary to check all the way to N − 1, however, but only to the square root of N. Can you see why? We will use this fact.

Let's construct a flowchart to describe this process in detail. Since all primes are at least as large as 2, we will reject any input value that is less than 2. Thus we can begin our flowchart as follows:

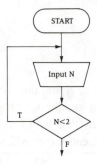

Next we must test all integers between 2 and $\sqrt{N}$, inclusive, as possible factors of N. If we test them in the order D = 2, 3, 4, and so on, we can stop testing when D > $\sqrt{N}$ or when D is a factor of N. Thus we can add the following segment to our partial flowchart:

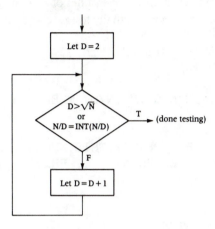

When we are done testing, we can be sure that N is prime if the last D value satisfies the condition D > $\sqrt{N}$, since this means that no factor less than or equal to $\sqrt{N}$ was found. On the other hand, if this last D value does not satisfy the condition D > $\sqrt{N}$, then it must satisfy the only other condition, N/D = INT(N/D), that can get us out of the loop. This means that D is a factor of N that lies between 2 and $\sqrt{N}$, inclusive; that is, N is not prime. We can now complete the flowchart as follows.

Prime number flowchart

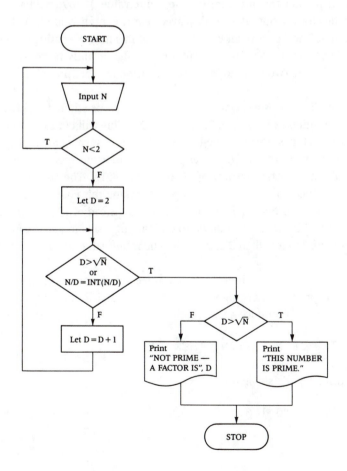

Remark   It is tempting to say that N is not a prime if the last value of D is a factor of N—that is, if N/D = INT(N/D) is true. If you use this condition (instead of the condition $D > \sqrt{N}$) to complete the flowchart, you will find that you have a bug. You should find it. (*Suggestion:* When debugging a program, test it for *extreme* values of any input variables. In this problem, the smallest value that the program will actually test is N = 2, so 2 is an extreme value here.)

The program

```
100 INPUT "TYPE AN INTEGER: ";N
110 IF N<2 THEN 100
120 LET D=2
130 IF D>SQR(N) OR N/D=INT(N/D) THEN 160
140    LET D=D+1
150 GOTO 130
160 IF D>SQR(N) THEN PRINT "THIS NUMBER IS PRIME."
170 IF D<=SQR(N) THEN PRINT "NOT PRIME - A FACTOR IS ";D
180 END
RUN

TYPE AN INTEGER: 37769
NOT PRIME - A FACTOR IS 179

RUN

TYPE AN INTEGER: 797513
THIS NUMBER IS PRIME.
```

Remark 1   When we ran this program for the input value 37769, we had to wait approximately 13 seconds for the output to be displayed. For the input value 797513 we had to wait about 45 seconds. The Apple spent essentially all of this time executing the loop in lines 130 to 150. It is often possible to reduce execution time significantly by making small changes in a loop.

Here are two ways to improve the prime number program:

1. Treat D = 2 as a special case before the loop is entered and use the loop to test only the odd numbers D = 3, 5, 7, . . . , SQR(N). This will cut execution time in half.
2. On each pass through the loop the Apple must calculate SQR(N) anew. This is very time consuming. To avoid these calculations include the line 115 ROOTN = SQR(N) and change all the other occurrences of SQR(N) to ROOTN. The change in line 130 is the important one since line 130 is in the loop. By making this change we obtained execution times of approximately 4 seconds and 12 seconds instead of 13 seconds and 45 seconds. When we made this change in addition to the one suggested in (1), the execution times were further reduced to less than 2 seconds for the input value 37769 and 8 seconds for 797513.

Remark 2   If this program is run, there is no guarantee that the user will type an integer. Line 110 ensures that the prime number algorithm will not be carried out for N < 2, but if 256.73 is input the algorithm will produce a silly result. To avoid this, you can insert the line

```
112 IF N<>INT(N) THEN 100
```

Remark 3   By inserting the single line

```
175 GOTO 100
```

many numbers can be tested without having to rerun the program each time. If you do this, however, you should tell a user how to stop the program. Remember, ctrl C is intended for use by programmers, not by users of programs.

The trigonometric functions

If **e** is a BASIC numerical expression, then SIN(**e**), COS(**e**), TAN(**e**), and ATN(**e**) evaluate the sine, cosine, tangent, and arctangent of the value of **e.** If the value of **e** denotes an angle, this value must be in radian measure.

EXAMPLE 17. Here is a program to determine SIN(D) for D = 0, 5, 10, . . . , 45°:

Since D denotes an angle in degrees, it must be changed to radian measure. Recalling the correspondence

1 degree = $\pi/180$ radians

we must multiply D by $\pi/180$ to convert to radian measure.

```
100 PRINT "DEGREES","SINE"
110 PRINT "--------","----"
120 FOR D=0 TO 45 STEP 5
130     LET Y=SIN(3.14159/180*D)
140     PRINT D,Y
150 NEXT D
160 END
RUN
```

DEGREES	SINE
0	0
5	.0871556693
10	.173648033
15	.258818832
20	.342019866
25	.422617928
30	.499999597
35	.573576014
40	.642787158
45	.707106312

EXAMPLE 18. Given side *a* and angles A and B in degrees, use the law of sines to determine side *b* of the following triangle:

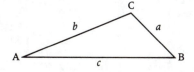

Problem analysis The law of sines states that

$$\frac{a}{\sin A} = \frac{b}{\sin B}$$

Solving for b, we obtain

$$b = \frac{a \sin B}{\sin A}$$

Since the angles A and B will be given in degrees, they must be changed to radian measure as required by the BASIC function SIN. In the following program, A1 and B1 denote the sides a and b, respectively.

The program

```
100 REM APPLICATION OF LAW OF SINES
110 INPUT "ENTER ANGLES A,B IN DEGREES ";A,B
120 INPUT "ENTER SIDE OPPOSITE ANGLE A ";A1
130 REM CONVERT TO RADIANS AND COMPUTE SIDE B1.
140 LET A=3.14159/180*A
150 LET B=3.14159/180*B
160 LET B1=A1*SIN(B)/SIN(A)
170 PRINT
180 PRINT "THE SIDE OPPOSITE ANGLE B"
190 PRINT "HAS LENGTH",B1
200 END
RUN

ENTER ANGLES A,B IN DEGREES 28,42
ENTER SIDE OPPOSITE ANGLE A 2

THE SIDE OPPOSITE ANGLE B
HAS LENGTH        2.85056953
```

11.5 Problems

1. Evaluate the following BASIC expressions.
a. ABS(3*(2-5))
b. ABS(-3*(-2))
c. ABS(2-30/3*2)
d. INT(26.1+0.5)
e. INT(-43.2+0.5)
f. INT(10*2.37+0.5)/10
g. 100*INT(1235.7/100+0.5)
h. ABS(INT(-3.2))
i. INT(ABS(-3.2))

2. Evaluate the following with A = −4.32, B = 5.93, and C = 2864.7144.
a. INT(ABS(A))
b. ABS(INT(A))
c. INT(B+0.5)
d. INT(A+0.5)
e. INT(C+0.5)
f. 10*INT(C/10+0.5)
g. 100*INT(C/100+0.5)
h. 1000*INT(C/1000+0.5)
i. INT(1000*C+0.5)/1000

3. Show the output for each program.
```
a. 100 FOR N=0 TO 4
   110     LET X=N*(N-1)
   120     LET Y=ABS(X-8)
   130     PRINT N,Y
   140 NEXT N
   150 END
```
```
b. 100 LET X=1.1
   110 LET Y=X
   120     LET Z=INT(Y)
   130     PRINT Y,Z
   140     LET Y=X*Y
   150 IF Y<=1.5 THEN 120
   160 END
```

```
c. 1Ø FOR X=3 TO 1Ø          d. 1ØØ LET N=63
   2Ø    PRINT "X";             11Ø LET D=1
   3Ø       IF X/4=INT(X/4) THEN PRINT   12Ø    LET D=D+1
   4Ø NEXT X                    13Ø    IF D>N/2 THEN 17Ø
   5Ø END                       14Ø    IF N/D<>INT(N/D) THEN 12Ø
                                15Ø    PRINT D
                                16Ø GOTO 12Ø
                                17Ø END

e. 1Ø LET M=24               f. 1ØØ LET S=13.99
   2Ø FOR D=2 TO 23 STEP 3      11Ø IF S>14 THEN 16Ø
   3Ø    PRINT "*";             12Ø    LET R=INT(1ØØ*S+Ø.5)/1ØØ
   4Ø       IF M/D=INT(M/D) THEN PRINT   13Ø    PRINT S,R
   5Ø NEXT D                    14Ø    LET S=S+Ø.ØØ3
   6Ø END                       15Ø GOTO 11Ø
                                16Ø END
```

4. Write a single BASIC statement for each task:
   a. For any two numbers A and B, print EQUAL if the absolute value of their sum is equal to the sum of their absolute values.
   b. For any two integers M and N, print DIVISIBLE if M is divisible by N.
   c. Transfer control to line 300 if X is a positive integer. (All you know about X is that it is a number.)
   d. Transfer control to line 400 if the integer K is divisible by either 7 or 11.
   e. Cause a RETURN to be executed if the integer L is even and also divisible by 25.
   f. For any integers A, B, and C, print OK if C is a factor of both A and B.

5. Using the INT function, write a single BASIC statement that will round off the value of X:
   a. to the nearest hundredth.
   b. to the nearest thousandth.
   c. to the nearest hundred.
   d. to the nearest thousand.

In Problems 6–14 write a program for each task specified. For tasks that require keyboard input, a user should be able to try different input values without having to rerun the program.

6. Find the sum and the sum of the absolute values of any input list. Print the number of values in the list as well as the two sums.

7. The deviation of a number N from a number M is defined to be ABS(M − N). Find the sum of the deviations of the numbers 2, 5, 3, 7, 12, −8, 43, −16 from M = 6. (All of these values are to be input during program execution.)

8. Find the sum of the deviations of numbers X from INT(X) where the Xs are input.

9. For any input list, sums S1 and S2 are to be found. S1 is the sum of the numbers, and S2 is the sum of the numbers each rounded to the nearest integer. Print both sums and also the number of values in the list.

10. Include the following information in DATA lines for a program to determine the batting average and slugging percentage for each player. In the table, 1B indicates a single, 2B a double, 3B a triple, HR a homerun, and AB the number of times a player has been at bat.

$$\text{batting average} = \frac{\text{number of hits}}{\text{AB}} \qquad \text{slugging percentage} = \frac{\text{total bases}}{\text{AB}}$$

Player	1B	2B	3B	HR	AB
Gomez	100	22	1	14	444
Boyd	68	20	0	3	301
Jackson	83	15	8	7	395
O'Neil	68	22	1	8	365
Struik	65	11	3	6	310
McDuffy	54	11	4	0	256
Vertullo	78	18	1	15	418
Ryan	25	1	1	0	104
Torgeson	49	15	0	11	301
Johnson	54	5	2	0	246

Your program is to print two tables: the first showing the players with their batting averages in adjacent columns, and the second showing the players with their slugging percentages. Each table is to have a title and each column a heading. The batting averages and slugging percentages are to be shown rounded to three decimal places.

11. Three positive integers are to be typed to determine whether the first is divisible only by the second, only by the third, by both the second and third, or by neither.

12. Determine and print all positive factors of a positive integer N input at the keyboard. (Include the factors 1 and N.)

13. A list of integers is to be input. Any integer less than 1 serves as the EOD-tag. Print the sum and a count of the even input values and also the sum and count of the odd ones.

14. Print the exact change received from a purchase of P dollars if an amount D is presented to the salesclerk. Assume that D is at most $100. The change should be given in the largest possible denominations of bills and coins, but $50 and $2 bills are not to be used. If P = 26.68 and D = 100, for example, the change D − P = 73.32 would be:

> 3 $20 bills
> 1 $10 bill
> 3 $1 bills
> 1 quarter
> 1 nickel
> 2 pennies

(*Suggestion:* Let C denote the change in pennies. Then N = INT(C/2000) gives the number of $20 bills. You would then subtract 2000 * N from C and proceed to the next lower denomination.)

In Problems 15–27 write a program for each task specified. (These are for the mathematically inclined reader.)

15. Determine and print all prime numbers that do not exceed N. N is to be input.

16. Determine and print all prime numbers between A and B. A and B are to be input and are to be rejected if either is not a positive integer.

17. Recall from arithmetic that, when you divide a positive integer A by a positive integer B, you get a quotient Q and a remainder R ($0 \le R < B$) according to the equation

$$A/B = Q + R/B \quad \text{(or, equivalently, } A = BQ + R).$$

For example, if A = 11 and B = 4, then Q = 2 and R = 3, since 11/4 = 2 + 3/4. Determine Q and R for any positive integers A and B. (Use the INT function.)

18. Add the digits in any three-digit positive integer. For example, if 378 is input, then 18 (3 + 7 + 8) should be printed. The program should reject typed-in values that are not integers greater than 99 and less than 1000. (*Hint:* 8 = 378 − 10*INT(378/10).)

19. Add the digits in any positive integer. (See Problem 18.)

20. Print the prime factorization of any positive integer greater than 1 typed at the keyboard. For example, if 35 is input, the output should be 35 = 5*7; if 41 is input, the output should be 41 IS PRIME; if 90 is input, the output should be 90 = 2*3*3*5.

21. Write a program to input a decimal constant containing fewer than five fractional digits, and print it as a quotient of two integers. For example, if 23.79 is input, the output should be 2379/100. (Remember, the computer may store only a close approximation of the input value; see the discussion following Example 14 in Section 11.4. Be sure that your program works in all cases.)

22. Write a program to input a decimal constant as in Problem 21, and print it as a quotient of two integers that have no common factors. For example, if 4.40 is input, the output should be 22/5.

23. The distance d of a point (x, y) in the plane from the line $ax + by + c = 0$ is given by

$$d = \frac{|ax + by + c|}{\sqrt{a^2 + b^2}}$$

Write a program to input the coefficients a, b, and c, and compute the distance d for any number of points (x, y) typed at the keyboard. Be sure that all input requests and all output values are labeled.

24. If a, b, and c are any three numbers with $a \neq 0$, the quadratic equation

$$ax^2 + bx + c = 0$$

can be solved for x by using the formula

$$x = \frac{-b \pm \sqrt{b^2 - 4ac}}{2a}$$

If $b^2 - 4ac > 0$, the formula gives two solutions; if $b^2 - 4ac = 0$, it gives one solution. If $b^2 - 4ac < 0$, however, there are no real solutions. Your program is to solve the quadratic equation for any input values a, b, and c, with $a \neq 0$.

25. Produce a two-column table showing the value of X and the cotangent of X for all values of X from zero to $\pi/2$ in increments of 0.05. (The case X = 0 must get special treatment.)

26. Referring to the diagram in Example 18, write a program to determine side c if sides a and b and angle C are given. (Use the law of cosines: $c^2 = a^2 + b^2 - 2ab \cos(C)$.)

27. An object moves so that its distance d from a fixed point P at time t is

$$d = \frac{1}{1 - 0.999 \cos t}$$

Produce a table (with column headings) of the d values for t between zero and 2π in increments of 0.1.

11.6 User-defined functions: The DEF statement

In addition to providing the built-in functions, BASIC allows you to define and name your own numerical functions. These functions, called **user-defined functions,** can be referenced in any part of your program much as the built-in functions are referenced. We'll illustrate with a simple example. The statement

```
1ØØ DEF FN G(X)=1+X^2
```

defines a function whose name is G and whose value for any number X is $1 + X^2$. The keyword DEF is an abbreviation for *define* and FN stands for *function*. To reference this function, you must use the form

FN G(**argument**)

where **argument** denotes any numerical expression whose value is to be substituted for X in the function definition. Thus if the expression FN G(3) is used in the program, its value will be $1 + 3^2 = 10$. Similarly, if the variable Y has been assigned the value 3, then FN G(Y) will again have the value 10. The following short program employs this user-defined function to produce a table of values for the expression $1 + X^2$:

```
1ØØ DEF FN G(X)=1+X^2
11Ø PRINT " X ","1+X^2"
12Ø PRINT "---","-----"
13Ø FOR Z=Ø TO 2 STEP Ø.5
14Ø    LET Y=FN G(Z)
15Ø      PRINT Z,Y
16Ø NEXT Z
17Ø END
RUN
```

X	1+X^2
Ø	1
.5	1.25
1	2
1.5	3.25
2	5

While typing this program you don't have to include a space after FN. In listings, however, the Apple always separates FN from the function name.

There are several advantages in defining your own functions:

1. A program containing a user-defined function is easily modified to treat different functions. For instance, if you change line 100 in the preceding program to

   ```
   1ØØ DEF FN G(X)=5+7*X^3
   ```

   the program will produce a table of values for the expression $5 + 7X^3$.
2. The numerical expression defining a function is written only once even though it is used several times in a program (see the next example).
3. By assigning a name to a numerical expression, programs can often be written so that they are easier to read and their logic is simpler to follow.

EXAMPLE 19. Here is a program to convert centimeters to inches and then to feet. The function R rounds values to two decimal places.

```
1ØØ DEF FN R(X)=INT(1ØØ*X+.5)/1ØØ
11Ø PRINT "CENTIMETERS","INCHES","FEET"
12Ø PRINT
13Ø REM MAKE THE CONVERSIONS:
14Ø REM CENTIMETERS (C) TO INCHES (I)
15Ø REM AND INCHES (I) TO FEET (F).
16Ø FOR C=1Ø TO 1ØØ STEP 1Ø
17Ø     LET I=C/2.54
18Ø     LET F=I/12
19Ø     LET I=FN R(I)
2ØØ     LET F=FN R(F)
21Ø     PRINT C,I,F
22Ø NEXT C
23Ø END
RUN
```

CENTIMETERS	INCHES	FEET
1Ø	3.94	.33
2Ø	7.87	.66
3Ø	11.81	.98
4Ø	15.75	1.31
5Ø	19.69	1.64
6Ø	23.62	1.97
7Ø	27.56	2.3

```
8Ø              31.5            2.62
9Ø              35.43           2.95
1ØØ             39.37           3.28
```

The function named R rounds values to two decimal places. Since this must be done for both inches and feet, it makes sense to employ a user-defined function.

Remark

The variable name X used in the definition in line 1ØØ could have been any simple numerical variable name. It is called a **dummy variable** or **dummy argument** because it serves only to define the function; if used later in the program, it is treated the same as any other variable. For example, if the DEF statement in this program were changed to

```
1ØØ DEF FN R(I)=INT(1ØØ*I+.5)/1ØØ
```

the program would behave just as before. No conflict would arise because of the appearance of the variable I elsewhere in the program. In contrast, the variables I and F in the function references FN R(I) and FN R(F) in lines 19Ø and 2ØØ do supply values to the function. For this reason they are called **actual arguments.**

The general form of the DEF statement is

ln DEF FN **name(v) = e**

where **name** denotes any string allowed as a real numerical variable name, **v** denotes a simple numerical variable, and **e** denotes a BASIC numerical expression defining a function of the variable **v.** The function is referenced by using the form

FN **name**(*argument*)

where *argument* denotes any numerical expression.

The following rules govern the use of the DEF statement and user-defined functions:

1. A function definition must be given in a line numbered lower than any program statement that references the function.
2. A user-defined function may be referenced as an operand in any numerical expression.
3. Applesoft distinguishes between function names, as between variable names, by using only their first two characters. As always, reserved words must be avoided when you are selecting function names.
4. The numerical expression **e** used in a DEF statement may contain variables other than the dummy variable. When such a function is referenced, the current values of these variables are used in the evaluation. Thus if the function EVAL is defined by

   ```
   1ØØ DEF FN EVAL(S)=5*S+T
   ```

   the programming line

   ```
   2ØØ LET T=1ØØØ : PRINT FN EVAL(7)
   ```

   will output the value 1Ø35 (EVAL(7) = 5 * 7 + 1ØØØ = 1Ø35).
5. The numerical expression **e** used in a DEF statement may involve built-in functions and user-defined functions. A function may not be defined in terms of itself, however.

Thus the two lines

```
1ØØ DEF FN Y(X)=X+3
11Ø DEF FN Z(S)=S*FN Y(S)
```

are admissible. The reference FN Z(4) will have the value 28
(Z(4)=4*FN Y(4)=4*(4+3)=28). The line

```
1ØØ DEF FN Y(N)=N+FN Y(N-1)
```

is not allowed since the expression to the right of the equals sign involves the function Y that is being defined.

6. The DEF statement can be used only in deferred execution mode.

EXAMPLE 20. Salaried employees are to receive an end-of-year bonus of $100 plus 1% of their annual salaries. The following program calculates the bonus amounts for any salary figures entered at the keyboard:

```
1ØØ DEF FN B(S)=1ØØ+.Ø1*S : REM CALCULATES BONUS
11Ø DEF FN R(X)=INT(X+.5) : REM ROUNDING FUNCTION
12Ø PRINT "TYPE Ø TO STOP."
13Ø REM ***DETERMINE BONUS B FOR ANY SALARY S***
14Ø    PRINT
15Ø    INPUT "SALARY? ";S
16Ø    IF S=Ø THEN 999
17Ø    LET B=FN B(S)
18Ø    LET B=FN R(B)
19Ø    PRINT "YEAR-END BONUS",B
2ØØ GOTO 14Ø
999 END
RUN

TYPE Ø TO STOP.

SALARY? 13Ø28
YEAR-END BONUS   23Ø

SALARY? 1256Ø
YEAR-END BONUS   226

SALARY? Ø
```

This program shows that more than one user-defined function can be included in a single program. Here the function B calculates the bonus amount and the function R is used to round this figure to the nearest whole-dollar amount.

Lines 170 and 180 can be replaced by the single line

```
17Ø LET B=FN R(FN B(S))
```

The program will behave exactly as before.

11.7 Problems

1. Each of these short programs contains an error—either a syntax error that will cause an error message to be printed or a programming error that the computer will not recognize but that will cause incorrect results. In each case, find the error and tell which of the two types it is.

   a.
   ```
   1Ø REM PRINT 6 PERCENT
   2Ø REM OF ANY NUMBER
   3Ø DEF FN Z(U)=.Ø6*U
   4Ø INPUT X
   5Ø LET V=FN Z(U)
   6Ø PRINT V
   7Ø END
   ```

   b.
   ```
   1Ø REM A TABLE OF SQUARES
   2Ø DEF FN S(I)=X^2
   3Ø FOR I=1 TO 9
   4Ø    LET S=FN S(I)
   5Ø     PRINT I,S
   6Ø NEXT I
   7Ø END
   ```

   c.
   ```
   1Ø REM BONUS CALCULATION
   2Ø DEF BONUS(S)=2ØØ+Ø.Ø2*S
   3Ø INPUT "SALARY? ";S
   4Ø LET B=BONUS(S)
   5Ø PRINT "BONUS IS ";B
   6Ø END
   ```

   d.
   ```
   1Ø DEF FN ADD2(X)=X+2
   2Ø DEF FN ADD5(X)=X+5
   3Ø LET I=3
   4Ø PRINT FNADD2(I),FNADD5(I)
   5Ø END
   ```

2. What will be printed when each program is run?

   a.
   ```
   1Ø DEF FN Q(A)=A+1
   2Ø DEF FN R(A)=A+2
   3Ø FOR X=Ø TO 3
   4Ø     LET A=FN R(FN Q(X))
   5Ø      PRINT X,A
   6Ø NEXT X
   7Ø END
   ```

   b.
   ```
   11Ø DEF FN I(R)=P*R/1ØØ*T
   12Ø LET T=1/2
   13Ø LET P=1ØØØ
   14Ø FOR R=1Ø TO 16 STEP 2
   15Ø     LET I=FN I(R)
   16Ø      PRINT I
   17Ø NEXT R
   18Ø END
   ```

3. Write a user-defined function that:
   a. converts degrees Celsius to degrees Fahrenheit (F = (9/5)C + 32).
   b. converts degrees Fahrenheit to degrees Celsius.
   c. converts feet to miles.
   d. converts kilometers to miles (1 mi = 1609.3 m).
   e. converts miles to kilometers
   f. gives the average speed in miles per hour for a trip of D miles that takes T hours. Use D as the dummy variable.
   g. gives the selling price if an article whose list price is X dollars is selling at a discount of Y%. Use X as the dummy variable.
   h. gives the cost in dollars of a trip of X miles in a car that averages 15 mph if gasoline costs Y cents per gallon. Use X as the dummy variable.
   i. rounds N to the third decimal place.
   j. gives the area of a circle of radius R.
   k. gives the volume of a sphere of radius R.
   l. gives the sine of an angle of A degrees.

In Problems 4–10, write a program to perform each task specified.

4. Produce a three-column table showing the conversions from feet F to miles and then to kilometers for the values F = 1000, 2000, 3000, . . . , 20,000. All output values are to be rounded to three decimal places. Write user-defined functions to perform the two conversions required and to do the rounding.

5. Produce a three-column table as follows. The first column is to contain the mileage figures 10, 20, . . . , 200 mi. The second and third columns are to give the time in minutes required to travel these distances at the respective speeds of 40 mph and 55 mph. All output values are to be rounded to the nearest minute. Write user-defined functions to calculate the times and to do the rounding.

6. Produce a three-column table showing the conversions from grams G to ounces and then to pounds (1 oz = 28.3495 g) for G = 20, 40, 60, . . . , 400. All output values are to be rounded to three decimal places. Employ a user-defined function to do the rounding.

7. Produce a three-column table showing the values of t, x, and y for $t = 0, 1, 2, . . . , 10$, where $x = 5/(1 + t)$ and $y = \sqrt{x^2 + 1}$. Determine x and y with user-defined functions.

8. Determine the area in square centimeters of any rectangle whose length and width in inches are typed by the user. Use a function to convert inches to centimeters.

9. Write a user-defined function AC to determine the area of a circle with circumference L. Also write a function AS to determine the area of a square with perimeter L. Use these two functions in a program to produce a three-column table showing L and the values of AC and AS for L = 1, 2, 3, . . . , 10. The values of AC and AS are to be rounded to three decimal places.
10. A thin wire of length L is cut into two pieces of lengths L1 and L2. One piece is bent into the shape of a circle and the other into a square. Decide how the wire should be cut if the sum of the two enclosed areas is to be as small as possible. (Use the functions AC and AS described in Problem 9.) How should the wire be cut if the sum of the areas is to be as large as possible?

11.8 Review true-or-false quiz

1. If A is any number, LEN(A) gives the number of digits in A.   T   F
2. If LEN(X$) = LEN(Y$), then X$ = Y$.   T   F
3. LEN(X$ + Y$) = LEN(X$) + LEN(Y$).   T   F
4. If X$ has the value MADAM, then MID$(X$,3,3) has the value D.   T   F
5. B$ = LEFT$(B$,LEN(B$)).   T   F
6. Although it may be convenient to use the functions LEFT$ and RIGHT$, they are not needed. The function MID$ can always be used in their place.   T   F
7. If there is a built-in function that performs a needed task, you should use it even if it is a simple matter to write your own programming lines to perform this task.   T   F
8. If N and D are positive numbers, but not necessarily integers, BASIC allows you to use the logical expression INT(N/D) = N/D to determine whether dividing N by D gives an integer.   T   F
9. ABS(INT(−2.3)) = INT(ABS(−2.3)).   T   F
10. The relational expression INT(N) = N is true if N is either zero or a positive integer and is false in all other cases.   T   F
11. If the variable Y is used as the dummy variable in a DEF statement, then Y may be used for some other purpose in the program.   T   F
12. There is nothing wrong with the statement

    ```
    100 DEF FN REC(Y)=Y+FN REC(Y-1)
    ```
                                                                                    T   F

13. The expression SIN(37 * 3.14159/180) may be used to find the sine of 37 degrees.   T   F

12

□ □ □ □ □ □ □ □ □ □ □ □

Arrays

Suppose we wish to examine all the numbers in a data list to determine counts of those less than 50 and those greater than 50 and then perform some calculation on these counts. To do so two variable names must be used to store the two counts. If more than two counts are involved, more than two variables must be used. This situation poses a real problem when only the simple BASIC variables considered to this point are available. Imagine the complexity of a program using as many as 100 different simple variables. To be useful, a programming language must provide the means for handling such problems efficiently. BASIC meets this requirement with the inclusion of **subscripted variables.** These variables may be referenced simply by specifying their numerical subscripts. They not only resolve the difficulty cited but also greatly simplify numerous programming tasks involving large quantities of data. In this chapter we consider the application of subscripted variables to programming tasks involving the processing of numbers. The use of subscripted *string* variables is described in Chapter 13.

12.1 One-dimensional arrays

A **one-dimensional array,** or **list,** is an ordered collection of items in the sense that there is a first item, a second item, and so on. If you have taken five quizzes during a semester and received grades of 71, 83, 96, 77, and 92, for example, you have a list in which the first grade is 71, the second grade is 83, and so forth. In mathematics we might use the following subscripted notation:

$$g_1 = 71$$
$$g_2 = 83$$
$$g_3 = 96$$
$$g_4 = 77$$
$$g_5 = 92$$

However, since the BASIC character set does not include subscripts, the notation is changed:

$$G(1) = 71$$
$$G(2) = 83$$
$$G(3) = 96$$
$$G(4) = 77$$
$$G(5) = 92$$

We say that the *name* of the array is G, that G(1), G(2), G(3), G(4), and G(5) are *subscripted variables*, and that 1, 2, 3, 4, and 5 are the *subscripts* of G. We read G(1) as **G sub 1,** and in general G(I) is read **G sub I.** G(1), G1, and G are all different variables and can be used in the same program; the computer has no problem distinguishing among them, even though people often do.

The array G can be visualized as follows:

	1	2	3	4	5
G	71	83	96	77	92

The name of the array appears to the left, the subscripts are above each entry, and the entries are inside, just below their subscripts. Names that are acceptable for simple variables are also admissible array names.

The value of a subscripted variable—that is, an entry in an array—is referenced in a program just as the values of simple variables are referenced. For example, the two statements

```
LET G(1)=71
LET G(6)=G(1)+12
```

assign 71 to the subscripted variable G(1) and 83 to G(6).

Arrays provide one significant advantage over simple variables—namely, the subscripts may be variables or other numerical expressions rather than just integer constants. We illustrate by example.

EXAMPLE 1. Here is a program segment to assign values to G(1), G(2), G(3), G(4), and G(5):

```
100 FOR I=1 TO 5
110    READ G(I)
120 NEXT I
130 DATA 71,83,96,77,92
```

On each pass through the loop, the index I of the loop serves as the subscript. The first time through the loop, I has the value 1; hence the statement in line 110 assigns the value 71 to G(1). Similarly, G(2) through G(5) are assigned their respective values during the remaining four passes through the loop.

EXAMPLE 2. Here is a program segment to calculate the sum S of the odd-numbered entries in array G. The sum is stored in G(0).

```
140 LET S=0
150 FOR K=1 TO 3
160    LET S=S+G(2*K-1)
170 NEXT K
180 LET G(0)=S
```

On the first pass through the loop the control variable K is 1, so the subscript $2*K - 1$ has the value $2*(1) - 1 = 1$. Thus $G(2*K - 1)$ refers to $G(1)$, and this value is added to S. On the second pass, $2*K - 1$ has the value $2*(2) - 1 = 3$, so $G(3)$ is added to S. Similarly, $G(5)$ is added to S on the third pass. After the loop has been satisfied, the value of S is assigned to $G(0)$. At this point both S and $G(0)$ have the same value.

The subscript that appears within the parentheses to indicate the position in an array (I in Example 1 and $2*K - 1$ in Example 2) may be any BASIC numerical expression. Thus the following are all admissible:

```
A(7)        X(I+1)
B(7+3/2)    Z(100-N)
```

When the computer encounters a subscript, the subscript is evaluated; if it is not an integer, its decimal part is ignored and this resulting integer is used. The smallest subscript allowed in Applesoft BASIC is zero. If the Apple encounters a negative subscript, a fatal error condition that causes the diagnostic

```
?ILLEGAL QUANTITY ERROR IN ____
```

is created. In the next section we discuss the largest subscript allowed. For now we'll assume the top limit to be 10.

When storing a list of numbers in array A, it is common practice to store them beginning in $A(1)$ and not $A(0)$. Programs are more easily understood if the first entry in a list is stored in $A(1)$, the second in $A(2)$, and the Nth in $A(N)$. Moreover, if you do this then $A(0)$ can be used for some other purpose—for instance, in Example 2 we used $G(0)$ to store the sum of the odd-numbered entries in array G.

Subscripted variables, as we have seen, may be assigned values by READ statements (line 110 in Example 1) and LET statements (line 180 in Example 2). They may also be assigned values by INPUT statements. For example, the loop

```
FOR I=1 TO 5
    INPUT G(I)
NEXT I
```

can be used to input values for $G(1)$ through $G(5)$ during program execution.

Values assigned to subscripted variables are retained until changed in another program statement, just as is the case with simple variables.

EXAMPLE 3

```
100 FOR I=1 TO 5
110     READ G(I)
120 NEXT I
130 PRINT G(1),G(3)
140 LET G(3)=G(1)
150 PRINT G(1),G(3)
160 DATA 71,83,96,77,92
170 END
RUN
```

```
71                    96
71                    71
```

When line 140 is executed, the value 71 of G(1) is assigned to G(3), but G(1) is not changed. After execution of this line, G(1) and G(3) have the same value 71 as shown in the output. Note that the previous value 96 of G(3) is lost.

The appearance of the same array name (G in the following example) in two FOR/NEXT loops, each using a different control variable (I and J in the example), often causes difficulty for the beginning programmer.

EXAMPLE 4. Here is a program segment that increases each entry of the array G by 2 and stores the resulting values in a second array M, but in the reverse order:

```
200 FOR I=1 TO 5
210    LET G(I)=G(I)+2
220 NEXT I
230 FOR J=1 TO 5
240    LET M(J)=G(6-J)
250 NEXT J
```

Let's assume that prior to execution of this program segment, the array G is read as in Example 1. Pictorially we have

	1	2	3	4	5
G	71	83	96	77	92

The first loop (the I loop) adds 2 to each entry in G:

	1	2	3	4	5
G	73	85	98	79	94

The second loop (the J loop) creates a new array M. For $J = 1$, the assignment statement is LET M(1) = G(5); for $J = 2$, LET M(2) = G(4); and so on. After execution of this second loop, M is as follows:

	1	2	3	4	5
M	94	79	98	85	73

Remark 1

Creating new arrays that are modifications of existing arrays is a common programming task. In this example, the entries in array M are a rearrangement of the entries in array G. Note that the creation of array M by the J loop in no way modifies the existing array G.

Remark 2   Although it is common practice to refer to the symbols G(I) and M(J) as variables, remember that the actual variable names are G(1), G(2), G(3), and so on. Each time the LET statements are executed, I and J have specific values indicating which of these variables is being referenced.

12.2 The DIM statement

Whenever a subscripted variable—say Z(1)—appears in a program, memory space is automatically reserved for the 11 variables Z(0), Z(1), Z(2), ..., Z(10). If subscripts larger than 10 are needed, you must ensure that more space is reserved in memory. This you can do with the DIM statement.

EXAMPLE 5. Here is a program segment to read values for the N variables B(1), B(2), ..., B(N):

```
100 DIM B(35)
110 INPUT N
120 FOR I=1 TO N
130    READ B(I)
140 NEXT I
```

Line 100 reserves memory space for the 36 variables B(0) to B(35). If 35 is input for N at line 110, the FOR/NEXT loop will read values from DATA lines for B(1), B(2), ..., B(35). If 20 is input for N, the FOR/NEXT loop will assign values only to the variables B(1), B(2), ..., B(20); the remaining variables, B(0), B(21), ..., B(35), although available, are simply not used. If a number 36 or larger is input for N, however, the attempt to read a value for B(36) will cause the fatal error condition that displays the message

```
?BAD SUBSCRIPT ERROR IN 130
```

This message tells you that a subscript in line 130 is out of range.

As illustrated in the preceding example, the DIM statement specifies the dimensions (sizes) of arrays. For this reason, it is called the **dimension statement.** When only one subscript is included (two or more subscripts are considered in Section 12.6), we say that the array is **one-dimensional** and the DIM statement serves only to specify an upper limit for the subscript. Thus DIM B(35) specifies a one-dimensional array B that can store 36 numbers (subscripts 0 to 35). When the Apple executes this DIM statement, we say that the array B has been **dimensioned.**

Although BASIC requires that you dimension only those arrays whose subscripts exceed 10, it is an excellent programming practice to dimension *every* array in your programs. Doing so facilitates the debugging process since a DIM statement explicitly establishes which variables are arrays and indicates their dimensions.

When coding a program that will read input data into an array, you must ensure that the DIM statement specifies an array large enough to accommodate all the input values. If you know in advance that your program will never be required to read more than 1000 numbers into an array A, the statement

```
DIM A(1000)
```

will suffice. However, this statement actually reserves memory space for the 1001 variables A(0) to A(1000); that is, your program will tie up this memory space whether or not a particular run of the program uses it. This means that you must not only ensure that your array is large enough, but you should keep it as small as possible. For this purpose, Applesoft allows you to use numerical expressions other than constants to specify dimensions for arrays. For example, you can write

```
200 INPUT N
210 DIM A(N)
```

and then specify the dimension of array A during program execution. This capability, called **dynamic storage allocation,** can be useful if the available memory space on your Apple system is severely limited. (By issuing DIM commands in immediate mode you can get a rough estimate of how many variables you can have in a program. For instance, if DIM A(5000) gives you no error message, your Apple has memory space for 5001 real variables. If your program is not too long, most of this space is available for variables. If you type DIM A(20000) you will most likely get the message ?OUT OF MEMORY. This is self-explanatory. Specifying a dimension greater than 32767 will give you the message ?ILLEGAL QUANTITY ERROR.)

The program segment in Example 5 shows how data can be read into an array when the number of values to be read is known in advance; in the example, this number is the first input value. Many programming applications require that data terminated with an EOD tag be read into an array. The following example shows one way to do this.

EXAMPLE 6. Here is a program segment to read a list of numbers into an array K:

```
100 DIM K(100)
110 LET I=0
120 REM READ NEXT VALUE INTO ARRAY K.
130    LET I=I+1
140    READ K(I)
150 IF K(I)<>9999 THEN 130
160 REM N DENOTES ACTUAL LENGTH OF LIST.
170 LET N=I-1
```

The variable I is used to keep track of the subscript. Each time a value is read for K(I) it is compared with the EOD tag 9999. If K(I) does not equal 9999, the subscript I is increased by 1 and another value is read. When the EOD tag is read, we have K(I) = 9999; that is, the EOD tag is in the Ith position of the array. Control then passes to the statement LET $N = I - 1$ so that N specifies the number of values, exclusive of the EOD tag, read into the array. In any further processing of this array we would use N to specify its length.

Remark

Note that this program segment will cause program execution to terminate if the EOD tag 9999 is not one of the first 100 numbers read. Should this happen, a user will be confronted with the message

```
?ILLEGAL QUANTITY ERROR IN 140
```

Such messages are intended for you the programmer, not for users of your programs; hence, they should be avoided if possible. In this example, replacing line 150 by the three lines

```
150 IF K(I)<>9999 AND I<100 THEN 130
152 IF K(I)=9999 THEN 160
154 PRINT "I CAN HANDLE ONLY 99 NUMBERS,": END
```

accomplishes this. Now control will pass to line 152 if K(I) = 9999 or if I = 100. If K(I), the last value read, is 9999, control passes to line 160 as before. If K(I) is not 9999, I must be 100; that is, 100 numbers were read without encountering the EOD tag 9999. Control then passes to line 154, which displays the more informative message

```
I CAN HANDLE ONLY 99 NUMBERS
```

before the program stops.

More than one DIM statement may appear in a program, and each DIM statement may be used to dimension more than one array. The programming line

```
1ØØ DIM A(1ØØ),X(5Ø),Z(5)
```

is admissible and will reserve memory space for the arrays A, X, and Z.

The general form of the DIM statement as it applies to one-dimensional arrays (lists) is

ln DIM **a**(**e**), **b**(**f**), . . . , **c**(**g**)

where **a, b, c** denote array names and **e, f, g** denote BASIC numerical expressions.

Here are some key points concerning the use of DIM statements:

1. A DIM statement must appear before any reference is made to the array (or arrays) being dimensioned. The customary practice is to place DIM statements near the beginning of a program unless they are used for dynamic storage allocation.

2. If an array has been dimensioned, either explicitly with a DIM statement or implicitly by usage, it cannot be dimensioned again. Any attempt to do so will produce the diagnostic ?REDIM'D ARRAY ERROR and program execution will terminate.

3. The numerical expressions **e, f,** and **g** shown in the general form are usually positive-integer constants or simple variables whose values are positive integers. If a noninteger value is specified, it will be truncated to obtain an integer dimension.

At the outset of this chapter we mentioned that subscripted variables are useful in programming tasks that require us to determine many counts. The following example illustrates this use of subscripted variables.

EXAMPLE 7. A list of integers, all between 1 and 100, is contained in DATA lines. Let's write a program to determine how many of each integer are included. We'll assume that 9999 terminates the list.

Problem analysis We must determine 100 counts: the number of 1s, the number of 2s, and so on. Let's use C(1), C(2), . . . , C(1ØØ) to store these counts. Now, each value appearing in the DATA lines must be read to determine which of the 100 integers it is. If it is 87, then C(87) must be increased by 1; if it is 24, then C(24) must be increased by 1. Using X to denote the value being read, we may write the following algorithm:

a. Initialize: C(I) = 0 for I = 1 to 100.
b. Read a value for X.
c. If X = 9999, print the results and stop.
d. Add 1 to C(X) and go to step (b).

Let's print two columns containing I and C(I) but suppress the output whenever C(I) = 0 (that is, if I is not in the given list). The following flowchart segment shows how to create this output:

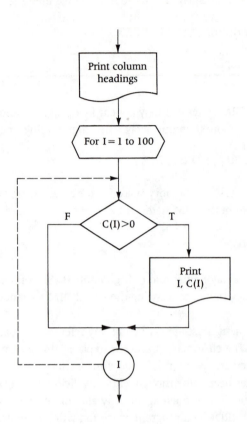

The program

```
100 REM INITIALIZE COUNTERS.
110 DIM C(100)
120 FOR I=1 TO 100
130     LET C(I)=0
140 NEXT I
150 REM READ X AND ADD 1 TO C(X) UNTIL
160 REM THE EOD TAG 9999 IS ENCOUNTERED.
170     READ X
180     IF X=9999 THEN 210
190     LET C(X)=C(X)+1
200 GOTO 170
210 REM PRINT THE FREQUENCY TABLE.
220 PRINT "DATUM","FREQUENCY"
230 PRINT "-----","---------"
240 FOR I=1 TO 100
250     IF C(I)>0 THEN PRINT I,C(I)
260 NEXT I
500 DATA 80,80,80,80,80,60,60,50
510 DATA 50,50,45,45,50,50,50,32
998 DATA 9999
999 END
RUN
```

DATUM	FREQUENCY
32	1
45	2
5Ø	6
6Ø	2
8Ø	5

12.3 Problems

1. Show the output of each program.

a.
```
1Ø LET I=2
2Ø READ X(I),X(1)
3Ø FOR I=1 TO 2
4Ø    PRINT X(I)
5Ø NEXT I
6Ø DATA 4,5,7,3
7Ø END
```

b.
```
1Ø LET J=1
2Ø READ X(J)
3Ø FOR I=1 TO 3
4Ø    READ X(I+1)
5Ø    PRINT X(I);" ";
6Ø NEXT I
7Ø DATA 3,1,5,6,8
8Ø END
```

c.
```
11Ø READ J
12Ø FOR J=5 TO 7
13Ø    READ M(J)
14Ø NEXT J
15Ø READ B,C
16Ø FOR K=B TO C
17Ø    PRINT M(K);" ";
18Ø NEXT K
19Ø DATA 2,9,8,4,6,6,3
2ØØ END
```

d.
```
1Ø FOR I=1 TO 3
2Ø    READ A(I)
3Ø NEXT I
4Ø FOR I=1 TO 2
5Ø   LET A(I)=A(I+1)
6Ø   LET A(I+1)=A(I)
7Ø   PRINT A(I),A(I+1)
8Ø NEXT I
9Ø DATA 7,8,3
99 END
```

2. Explain what is wrong with each of the following.

a.
```
1Ø FOR A=9 TO 12
2Ø    READ M(A)
3Ø    PRINT M(A);" ";
4Ø NEXT A
5Ø DATA 7,3,5,2,9,1,-3,-2
6Ø END
```

b.
```
1Ø READ A(1),A(2),A(3)
2Ø PRINT A(3),A(2),A(1)
3Ø DIM A(2)
4Ø READ A(1),A(2)
5Ø PRINT A(2),A(1)
6Ø DATA 1,2,3,4,5
7Ø END
```

c.
```
3ØØ REM PROGRAM SEGMENT TO REVERSE THE
31Ø REM ORDER IN AN ARRAY L OF LENGTH 1Ø
32Ø FOR K=1 TO 1Ø
33Ø    LET L(11-K)=L(K)
34Ø NEXT K
```

d.
```
4ØØ REM PROGRAM SEGMENT TO FIND THE
41Ø REM LARGEST NUMBER L IN AN ARRAY A
42Ø REM OF LENGTH N
43Ø FOR J=1 TO N
44Ø    IF L<A(J) THEN LET A(J)=L
45Ø NEXT J
```

In Problems 3–14, write a program to perform each task specified. Don't use the RESTORE statement in any of these problems.

3. Input an array A of undetermined length and print the values in reverse order. Use an EOD tag to terminate the input list. (You may assume that the input list will contain fewer than 50 numbers.)

4. Five numbers are to be input into an array B as follows. The first value is to be assigned to B(1) and B(1Ø), the second to B(2) and B(9), and so on. The array B is then to be printed, and five more values are to be input in the same manner. This process is to continue until the user types Ø. When this happens, program execution is to terminate with no further output.

5. Ten values are to be read into an array Y. Then a new array X containing 20 values is to be created so that the odd-numbered entries in X contain 1s and the even-numbered entries are the entries of Y in the same order. Print both arrays.

6. Read 20 values into an array A and print three columns as follows. Column 1 contains the 20 values in the original order; column 2 contains the 20 values in reverse order; column 3 contains the average of the corresponding elements in columns 1 and 2.

7. The following DATA lines show the annual salaries of all the employees in Division 72 of the Manley Corporation. The last value (72) is an EOD tag.

```
5ØØ DATA 14ØØØ, 162ØØ, 1Ø195, 18432, 1336Ø
51Ø DATA 193ØØ, 1645Ø, 1218Ø, 2564Ø,  842Ø
52Ø DATA 89ØØ,  927Ø,  962Ø,  994Ø, 112ØØ
53Ø DATA 72
```

Calculate and print the average salary of all employees in Division 72, and then print a list of the salaries exceeding this average.

8. Read the salary data shown in Problem 7 into array S. Then create a new array T as follows. T(I) is to be obtained by subtracting S(I) from the average of all the salaries. Arrays S and T are then to be printed as a two-column table with appropriate headings.

9. Use the salary data shown in Problem 7 to create two arrays as follows. Array A is to contain all salaries less than $14,000, and B is to contain the rest. Arrays A and B are then to be printed as columns with appropriate headings. (The columns need not be adjacent.)

10. An undetermined number of values is to be input into arrays P and N so that array P contains those that are positive and N contains those that are negative. Zeros are to be ignored and 999 is to serve as the EOD tag. When the EOD tag is encountered, the two lists are to be printed in adjacent columns with the headings POSITIVES and NEGATIVES.

11. A number of scores, each lying in the range from 0 to 100, are given in a collection of DATA lines. These scores are to be used to create an array C as follows:

C(1) = a count of scores S satisfying $S \leq 20$
C(2) = a count of scores S satisfying $20 < S \leq 40$
C(3) = a count of scores S satisfying $40 < S \leq 60$
C(4) = a count of scores S satisfying $60 < S \leq 80$
C(5) = a count of scores S satisfying $80 < S \leq 100$

The results should be printed in tabular form as follows:

Interval	Frequency	
0–20	C(1)	(actually the value of C(1))
20–40	C(2)	
40–60	C(3)	
60–80	C(4)	
80–100	C(5)	

12. Problem 11 asked for a count of the number of scores in each of five equal-length intervals. Instead of using five intervals, allow a user to type a positive integer N to produce a similar frequency table using N equal-length intervals.

13. Calculate and print the mean M and standard deviation D of a set of numbers contained in data lines. Use the following method to compute D. If the numbers are $x_1, x_2, x_3, \ldots, x_n$, then $D = \sqrt{S1/(n-1)}$, where

$$S1 = (x_1 - M)^2 + (x_2 - M)^2 + \cdots + (x_n - M)^2$$

14. A correspondence between x and y is given by the following table. (Each y entry corresponds to the x entry just above it.)

x	0	2	4	6	8	10	12	14	16	18	20
y	−5	3	27	67	123	195	283	387	507	643	795

Your program is to allow a user to type two numbers—a 0, 1, or 2 and a value for x in the range 0 to 20. (Any other input values should be rejected and two new values requested.) The computer is to respond as follows:

0: If the first number typed is zero, the y value corresponding to x is to be printed. If the x value is not in the table, the message NOT FOUND should be printed. The user should then be allowed to type in two more numbers.

1: If the first number typed is 1, the y value corresponding to x should be printed. However, if x is not in the table, a linear interpolation should be performed to determine y. If x_1 and x_2 are successive values in the list with x lying between them, and if y_1 and y_2 are the corresponding y values, the value y to be printed is given by

$$y = y_1 + \frac{x - x_1}{x_2 - x_1}(y_2 - y_1)$$

The user should again be allowed to type two more numbers.

2: If the first number typed is 2, the program should terminate. If the first number typed is not 0, 1, or 2, or if the second number is not between 0 and 20, the two values just typed should be rejected and new values requested.

12.4 Sorting

Many programming tasks require sorting (arranging) arrays according to some specified order. When lists of numbers are involved, this usually means arranging them according to size—from smallest to largest or from largest to smallest. For example, you may be required to produce a salary schedule in which salaries are printed from largest to smallest. When lists of names are involved, you may wish to arrange them in alphabetical order. In this section we show how arrays of numbers can be arranged in ascending or descending order. In Chapter 13 we'll show how algorithms for sorting arrays of numbers are easily modified to sort arrays containing strings (for instance, names).

The first sorting algorithm we will describe, called the **bubble sort,** takes any list A(1), A(2), . . . , A(N) of numbers and rearranges them in ascending order—that is, arranges them so that

$$A(1) \leq A(2) \leq \cdots \leq A(N)$$

We'll demonstrate the steps with a short array A containing only four values:

    4   3   5   1

First we compare the values in positions 1 and 2. If they are in the proper order (the first is less than or equal to the second), we leave them alone. If not, we interchange them:

    4   3   5   1   becomes   **3   4**   5   1

Next we compare the values in positions 2 and 3 in the same manner:

    3   **4   5**   1   remains   3   **4   5**   1

Then we compare the values in positions 3 and 4:

    3   4   **5   1**   becomes   3   4   **1   5**

The effect of these three comparisons is to move the largest value to the last position. This process is now repeated—except that this time the final comparison is omitted because the largest value is already in the last position:

    3   4   1   5   remains   **3   4**   1   5
    3   **4   1**   5   becomes   3   **1   4**   5

We repeat the process once more, this time noting that the final two comparisons are unnecessary because the correct numbers are already in the last two positions:

3 1 4 5   becomes   1 **3** 4 5

The array is now in the proper order.

To summarize, array A contains four values and we make three passes through the array:

On pass 1, we compare A(I) with A(I + 1) for I = 1, 2, 3.
On pass 2, we compare A(I) with A(I + 1) for I = 1, 2.
On pass 3, we compare A(I) with A(I + 1) for I = 1.

If an array contains N values instead of 4, we make N − 1 passes through the array. In this case the following comparisons are made:

On pass 1, compare A(I) with A(I + 1) for I = 1, 2, . . . , N − 1.
On pass 2, compare A(I) with A(I + 1) for I = 1, 2, . . . , N − 2.
On pass 3, compare A(I) with A(I + 1) for I = 1, 2, . . . , N − 3.

$$\cdot$$
$$\cdot$$
$$\cdot$$

On pass N − 2, compare A(I) with A(I + 1) for I = 1, 2.
On pass N − 1, compare A(I) with A(I + 1) for I = 1.

Note that on each pass through the array, one fewer comparison is made. We make N − 1 comparisons the first time (I = 1, 2, . . . , N − 1), N − 2 the second (I = 1, 2, . . . , N − 2), N − 3 the third, and so on.

In general, on the Jth pass through the array, N − J comparisons are made—one for each I = 1, 2, 3, . . . , N − J. Since J, the pass number, takes on the successive values 1 through N − 1, all necessary comparisons can be accomplished with the nested FOR/NEXT loops:

```
FOR J=1 TO N-1
  FOR I=1 TO N-J
    .
    .
    .
  NEXT I
NEXT J
```

The actual method of comparison is as follows: if A(I) is greater than A(I + 1), we must interchange them. The three statements

```
LET T=A(I)
LET A(I)=A(I+1)
LET A(I+1)=T
```

accomplish this. If A(I) is not greater than A(I + 1), these three lines must be skipped. The flowchart in Figure 12.1 displays the process just described. The corresponding program segment, shown in Figure 12.2, can be used to sort, in ascending order, any one-dimensional array A of N numbers.

Figure 12.1
Flowchart to perform a
bubble sort.

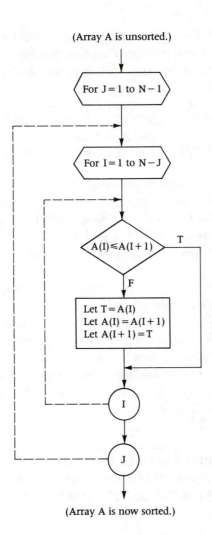

(Array A is unsorted.)

For J = 1 to N − 1

For I = 1 to N − J

A(I) ≤ A(I + 1)   T

F

Let T = A(I)
Let A(I) = A(I + 1)
Let A(I + 1) = T

I

J

(Array A is now sorted.)

Figure 12.2
Program segment to
perform a bubble sort.

```
500 REM BUBBLE SORT TO ARRANGE THE N
510 REM TERMS OF ARRAY A IN ASCENDING ORDER
520 FOR J=1 TO N-1
530    FOR I=1 TO N-J
540       IF A(I)<=A(I+1) THEN 580
550          LET T=A(I)
560          LET A(I)=A(I+1)
570          LET A(I+1)=T
580       NEXT I
590 NEXT J
600 REM ARRAY A IS SORTED.
```

If the comparisons are reversed, with line 540 being changed to

```
540 IF A(I)>=A(I+1) THEN 580
```

The program segment in Figure 12.2 will sort the array in descending rather than ascending order. This accounts for the name bubble sort—the smaller or lighter values are "bubbled" to the top.

Remark

You may have noticed that if no swaps (lines 550 to 570) are made on a pass through the array (the I loop), the array must have been in order. This fact is easily incorporated into the bubble sort by using a counter C to keep track of the number of swaps made on each pass. Simply add the following lines:

```
525 LET C=Ø : REM A NEW PASS IS TO BE MADE.
575 LET C=C+1 : REM A SWAP WAS MADE.
585 IF C=Ø THEN 6ØØ : REM NO SWAPS WERE MADE.
```

Although many programmers use this "improved" bubble sort, we do not recommend it on the Apple. Most often there will be no improvement whatever. Indeed, the likelihood of making a complete pass (the I loop) with no swaps early in the algorithm (the early passes use most of the time) is very slim unless the array is "almost" in order. Moreover, inserting three extra statements that must be repeated many times can slow execution of an Applesoft program considerably.

Many applications requiring arrays to be sorted involve more than one array. Suppose, for example, that C and P denote one-dimensional arrays with each pair C(I), P(I) giving an item code number and the price of the item. If the contents of these two arrays must be printed in a two-column report of item codes and prices, with the item codes appearing from smallest to largest, the list of pairs C(I), P(I) must be sorted so that the entries in C are in increasing order. This can be accomplished by modifying a bubble sort that sorts array C. Simply insert lines that interchange P(I) and P(I + 1) whenever C(I) and C(I + 1) are interchanged. The next example demonstrates the procedure.

EXAMPLE 8. Several pairs of numbers are included in DATA lines. The first of each pair is a quality point average (QPA); the second gives the number of students with this QPA. Write a program to produce a table with the column headings QPA and FREQUENCY. The frequency counts in the second column are to appear in descending order.

Problem analysis

Two lists are given in the DATA lines. Let's use Q to denote the QPAs and F to denote the frequency counts. The following algorithm shows the three subtasks that must be performed:

    a. Read arrays Q and F.
    b. Sort the two arrays so that the frequencies appear in descending order.
    c. Print the two arrays as a two-column table.

To code step (a), we must remember that the lists are presented in DATA lines as pairs of numbers. Thus we will read values for Q(I) and F(I) for I = 1, 2, and so on, until all pairs have been read. We'll use an F value of 0 as an EOD tag.

To code step (b), we will use a bubble sort to arrange array F in descending order. Since a pair Q(I), F(I) must not be separated, however, we will interchange Q values whenever the corresponding F values are interchanged.

The program

```
1ØØ REM READ ARRAYS Q AND F.
11Ø DIM Q(5Ø),F(5Ø)
12Ø LET I=Ø
13Ø     LET I=I+1
14Ø     READ Q(I),F(I)
15Ø IF F(I)<>Ø AND I<5Ø THEN 13Ø
16Ø IF F(I)=Ø THEN 18Ø
17Ø PRINT "I CAN HANDLE ONLY 49 PAIRS.": END
18Ø LET N=I-1
```

```
19Ø REM SORT ARRAYS Q AND F ACCORDING
2ØØ REM TO DECREASING F VALUES.
21Ø FOR J=1 TO N-1
22Ø     FOR I=1 TO N-J
23Ø         IF F(I)>=F(I+1) THEN 3ØØ
24Ø         LET T=F(I)
25Ø         LET F(I)=F(I+1)
26Ø         LET F(I+1)=T
27Ø         LET T=Q(I)
28Ø         LET Q(I)=Q(I+1)
29Ø         LET Q(I+1)=T
3ØØ     NEXT I
31Ø NEXT J
32Ø REM PRINT COLUMN HEADINGS AND TABLE VALUES.
33Ø PRINT "QPA","FREQUENCY"
34Ø PRINT
35Ø FOR I=1 TO N
36Ø     PRINT Q(I),F(I)
37Ø NEXT I
5ØØ DATA 4.ØØ,2,3.75,16,3.4Ø,41,3.2Ø,38,3.ØØ,92
51Ø DATA 2.75,162,2.3Ø,352,2.ØØ,28Ø,1.7Ø,81,1.5Ø,27
998 DATA Ø,Ø
999 END
RUN
```

QPA	FREQUENCY
2.3	352
2	28Ø
2.75	162
3	92
1.7	81
3.4	41
3.2	38
1.5	27
3.75	16
4	2

Lines 27Ø to 29Ø were inserted in the bubble sort to interchange Q values whenever the corresponding F values were interchanged.

The bubble sort is one of the easiest sorting algorithms to understand, to remember, and to code. For this reason many beginners tend to use it exclusively. This is fine if the lists to be sorted are short and the program will see only limited use, but the bubble sort is very inefficient for long lists. The Apple, using the bubble sort shown in Figure 12.2, takes less than 4 seconds to sort a list of 20 numbers—but it takes about 5.5 minutes for a list of 200 numbers and nearly 2 hours for a list of 800 numbers. These sorting times are unacceptably slow and clearly show the need for faster sorting algorithms.

Much attention has been given to the problem of sorting, and many fast sorting algorithms have been developed. The reasons for this activity go deeper than the need to produce well-formatted output documents with values printed in a certain order. A common task is that of searching an array A(1), A(2), . . . , A(N) for some specified value V. If the array is not arranged in a known order, the best we can do is to compare V with A(1), then with A(2), and so on, until V is found or the entire list has been examined. This is called a **sequential search** and is easily coded:

```
500 FOR I=1 TO N
510    IF V=A(I) THEN 550
520 NEXT I
530 PRINT V;" NOT FOUND."
540 END
550 PRINT V;" HAS THE INDEX ";I
```

If a long array A is to be searched for many different values V (the usual situation), and if you use a sequential search, you and others waiting to use the Apple may have a long wait. However, if the array A is sorted (say, in ascending order), a much more efficient search can be made for V. (To turn to page 216 of this book, for instance, you would not start from page 1 and turn pages until you found page 216; you would use a more efficient method.) Principally, it is this need for a fast searching algorithm that prompted all the attention given to sorting algorithms.

Although a detailed discussion of fast sorting and searching algorithms is beyond the scope of an introductory text such as this, we do include two efficient algorithms you may wish to use. The first (Figure 12.3) is a fast sorting algorithm known as **Shellsort,**[*] and the second (Figure 12.4) is an efficient search algorithm called the **binary search.** They are presented here as alternatives to the bubble sort and the sequential search, should you have a need for them.[†] The following table shows comparative sorting times on an Apple for the bubble sort and the Shellsort:

Length of list	Bubble sort	Shellsort
20	4 seconds	3 seconds
40	13 seconds	5 seconds
100	1.3 minutes	17 seconds
200	5.5 minutes	40 seconds
300	13 minutes	1 minute
400	22 minutes	1.5 minutes
800	1.8 hours	3.6 minutes
1600	7.2 hours	8.3 minutes

[*]"A High-Speed Sorting Procedure," by Donald L. Shell, *Communications of the ACM*, vol. 2, July 1959, pp. 30–32.

[†]A detailed explanation of how and why the two algorithms work may be found in our text *BASIC: An Introduction to Computer Programming*, 2nd ed. (Monterey, Calif.: Brooks/Cole, 1982).

Figure 12.3
Program segment to
perform a Shellsort.

```
500 REM SHELLSORT TO SORT ARRAY A WITH
510 REM N TERMS INTO ASCENDING ORDER
520 LET S=N
530     LET S=INT(S/2)
540     IF S<1 THEN 670
550     FOR K=1 TO S
560         FOR I=K TO N-S STEP S
570             LET J=I
580             LET T=A(I+S)
590             IF T>=A(J) THEN 630
600             LET A(J+S)=A(J)
610             LET J=J-S
620             IF J>=1 THEN 590
630             LET A(J+S)=T
640         NEXT I
650     NEXT K
660 GOTO 530
670 REM LIST A IS NOW SORTED.
```

Figure 12.4
Program segment to
perform a binary search.

```
700 REM BINARY SEARCH TO SEARCH LIST A
710 REM OF LENGTH N FOR V.  M IS SET EQUAL
720 REM TO THE INDEX I FOR WHICH A(I)=V.
730 REM M=0 MEANS V WAS NOT FOUND.
740 LET L=1 : R=N
750     LET M=INT((L+R)/2)
760     IF V=A(M) THEN 810
770     IF V<A(M) THEN R=M-1
780     IF V>A(M) THEN L=M+1
790 IF L<=R THEN 750
800 LET M=0
810 REM SEARCH IS COMPLETE.
```

The Shellsort algorithm is easily modified to sort two arrays A and B so that the pairs A(I), B(I) are not separated (see Example 8). Simply add the following three lines:

```
585 LET T1=B(I+S)
605 LET B(J+S)=B(J)
635 LET B(J+S)=T1
```

12.5 Problems

In Problems 1–12, write a program to perform each task specified.

1. Print, in ascending order, any five input values L(1), L(2), L(3), L(4), and L(5). Your program should process many such sets of five integers during a single run. Test your program with the following input data:

5	4	3	2	1
5	1	2	3	4
−1	−2	−3	−4	−5
2	1	4	3	5
15	19	14	18	10
1	2	3	4	5

2. Modify your program for Problem 1 so that each group of five integers is printed in descending order. (Only one line needs to be changed.)

3. Any list of numbers typed at the keyboard is to be printed in ascending order. The value 9999, when typed, is to indicate that the entire list has been entered.

4. A list of numbers is to be read to obtain a two-column printout with the column headings ORIGINAL LIST and SORTED LIST. The first column is to contain the list values in the order in which they are read; the second column is to contain the same values printed from largest to smallest. Use the following algorithm:
   a. Input the list values into identical arrays A and B.
   b. Sort array A into descending order.
   c. Print the table as described.
   Try your program using the following DATA lines:

```
5ØØ DATA 8Ø, 7Ø, 4Ø, 9Ø, 95, 38, 85, 42, 6Ø, 7Ø
51Ø DATA 4Ø, 6Ø, 7Ø, 2Ø, 18, 87, 23, 78, 85, 23
998 DATA 9999
```

5. Several numbers, ranging from 0 to 100, are to be read and stored in two arrays A and B. Array A is to contain the numbers less than 50; the others are to be stored in array B. Arrays A and B are then to be sorted in descending order and printed side by side with the column headings LESS THAN 50 and 50 OR MORE. Test your program by using the input data shown in Problem 4.

6. Read an array L and sort it in ascending order. Then create a new array M containing the same values as L but with no repetitions. If $L(1) = 7$, $L(2) = L(3) = 8$, and $L(4) = L(5) = L(6) = 9$, for example, the array M is to have $M(1) = 7$, $M(2) = 8$, and $M(3) = 9$. Print both arrays. Run your program using the DATA lines shown in Problem 4.

7. Read an array L and sort it in ascending order. Then modify L by deleting all values appearing more than once. If $L(1) = 7$, $L(2) = L(3) = 8$, and $L(4) = L(5) = L(6) = 9$, for example, the new array is to have $L(1) = 7$, $L(2) = 8$, and $L(3) = 9$. Run your program using the DATA lines shown in Problem 4.

8. A study of the Tidy Corporation's annual reports for the years 1972–1980 yielded the following statistics:

Year	Gross sales (in thousands)	Earnings per share
1972	$19,500	$0.27
1973	18,350	−0.40
1974	18,400	−0.12
1975	18,000	−0.84
1976	18,900	0.65
1977	20,350	0.78
1978	24,850	1.05
1979	24,300	0.68
1980	27,250	0.88

Include the second and third columns of this table in DATA lines for a program to print two columns with the same headings as those shown. However, the earnings-per-share figures are to appear in ascending order. (Use the method described in Example 8.)

9. Include all three columns given for the Tidy Corporation (Problem 8) in DATA lines for a program to produce a three-column table with the same headings. However, the gross sales figures are to appear in descending order.

10. Following is the weekly inventory report of a sewing supply wholesaler:

Item	Batches on hand Monday	Batches sold during week	Cost per batch	Sales price per batch
Bobbins	220	105	$8.20	$10.98
Buttons	550	320	5.50	6.95
Needles—1	450	295	2.74	3.55
Needles—2	200	102	7.25	9.49
Pins	720	375	4.29	5.89
Thimbles	178	82	6.22	7.59
Thread—A	980	525	4.71	5.99
Thread—B	1424	718	7.42	9.89

Include the five columns of this report in DATA lines by using one DATA statement for each item. Use the line numbers 800, 810, 820, . . . , 870. Your program is to produce a three-column report showing, for each item, the number of batches on hand at the end of the week and the income generated by that item. However, the income column is to appear in descending order.

11. Using the inventory report shown in Problem 10, produce a five-column report showing the item names, the cost per batch, the sales price per batch, the dollar markup per batch, and the percent markup per batch. The figures in the last column should appear in descending order. (The percentages in the fifth column are given by (M/C)*100, where M denotes the markup and C denotes the cost.)

12. N pairs of numbers are to be read so that the first of each pair is in array A and the second is in array B. Sort the pairs A(I), B(I) so that $A(1) \le A(2) \le \cdots \le A(N)$ and so that $B(I) \le B(I + 1)$ whenever $A(I) = A(I + 1)$. Print the modified arrays in two adjacent columns with the headings LIST A and LIST B. *Hint:* If $A(I) > A(I + 1)$, a swap is necessary; if $A(I) < A(I + 1)$, no swap is necessary; otherwise—that is, if $A(I) = A(I + 1)$—swap only if $B(I) > B(I + 1)$.

12.6 Higher-dimensional arrays

Data to be processed by the computer are often presented in tabular form. Suppose you wish to write a program to analyze the following data, which summarize the responses of college students to a hypothetical opinion poll concerning the abolition of grades.

Class	In favor of abolishing grades	Not in favor of abolishing grades	No opinion
Freshmen	207	93	41
Sophomores	165	110	33
Juniors	93	87	15
Seniors	51	65	8

If you wanted to determine the number of sophomores who were polled, you would add the three entries in the second row; to determine the percentage of sophomores polled who are not in favor of abolishing grades, you would divide the entry 110 by this sum. Many calculations of this sort may be desired, and the computer is ideally suited for such tasks. What you need is a convenient way to present these data to the computer. First we will introduce some terminology to make it easier to refer to such tables of values.

A **two-dimensional array** is a collection of items arranged in a rectangular fashion. That is, there is a first (horizontal) row, a second row, and so on, and a first (vertical) column, a second column, and so on. An array with *m* rows and *n* columns is called an *m-by-n array* (also written *m × n array*). Thus the opinion poll data are presented as a 4 × 3 array.

An item in an array is specified simply by giving its row number and column number. For example, the item in the third row and second column of the opinion poll table is 87. By convention, when specifying an item in an array we give the row number first. In the opinion poll table, 33 is in the 2,3 position and 51 is in the 4,1 position. In mathematical notation we could write

$$P_{1,1} = 207 \qquad P_{1,2} = 93 \qquad P_{1,3} = 41$$

to indicate the values in the first row of our table. Since the BASIC character set does not include subscripts, this notation is changed as it was for one-dimensional arrays. Thus the values in the opinion poll table would be written as follows:

$$
\begin{array}{lll}
P(1,1) = 207 & P(1,2) = 93 & P(1,3) = 41 \\
P(2,1) = 165 & P(2,2) = 110 & P(2,3) = 33 \\
P(3,1) = 93 & P(3,2) = 87 & P(3,3) = 15 \\
P(4,1) = 51 & P(4,2) = 65 & P(4,3) = 8
\end{array}
$$

We say that P is the *name* of the array, that P(1,1), P(1,2), . . . are *doubly subscripted* variables, and that the numbers enclosed in parentheses are the *subscripts* of P. The symbol P(I,J) is read "P sub I comma J" or simply "P sub IJ."

The 4 × 3 array P can be visualized as follows:

		(Column)	
P	1	2	3
1	207	93	41
2	165	110	33
3	93	87	15
4	51	65	8

(Row) labels rows 1, 2, 3, 4.

This schematic displays the array name P, the row number for each item, and the column numbers.

The value of a doubly subscripted variable—that is, an array entry—is referenced in a program just as values of singly subscripted variables are referenced. The subscripts can be integer constants, variables, or expressions. For example, the FOR/NEXT loop

```
FOR J=1 TO 3
    LET P(1,J)=5*J
NEXT J
```

assigns the values 5, 10, and 15 to the first row P(1,1), P(1,2), P(1,3) of P. Similarly,

```
LET K=1
FOR I=1 TO 4
    LET P(I,K)=P(I,K)+6
NEXT I
```

adds 6 to each entry in the first column P(1,1), P(2,1), P(3,1), P(4,1) of P.

EXAMPLE 9. Here is a program segment to read the opinion poll data into an array P:

```
100 REM READ VALUES FOR THE 4-BY-3 ARRAY P.
110 FOR I=1 TO 4
120    REM READ VALUES FOR THE ITH ROW OF P.
130    FOR J=1 TO 3
140        READ P(I,J)
150    NEXT J
160 NEXT I
500 DATA 207,93,41
510 DATA 165,110,33
520 DATA 93,87,15
530 DATA 51,65,8
```

When the first FOR statement (line 110) is executed, I is assigned the initial value 1. The J loop then reads the first three data values 207, 93, and 41 for the variables P(1,1), P(1,2), and P(1,3), respectively. That is, when I = 1, values are read into the first row of P. Similarly, when I = 2, values are read into the second row, P(2,1), P(2,2), P(2,3), of P and so on until all 12 values have been assigned to P.

Remark

The data do not have to be given in four lines as shown here. The single line

```
500 DATA 207, 93, 41, 165, 110, 33, 93, 87, 15, 51, 65, 8
```

could replace lines 500 through 530. It is only the order in which they appear that matters.

EXAMPLE 10. Let's use the program segment of Example 9 in a program to count the number of students in each class who participated in the opinion poll survey.

Problem analysis

The following algorithm describes one way to carry out the specified task:

a. Read the opinion poll data into array P (done in Example 9).
b. Determine and print how many students in each class participated in the survey.

Since all three entries in any row of P correspond to students in one of the four classes, the task in step (b) is to add the three entries in each row of P and print these four sums. Let's use S(1) to denote the sum of the entries in the first row and S(2), S(3), and S(4) for the other three row sums. These sums can be determined as follows:

```
LET S(1)=P(1,1)+P(1,2)+P(1,3)
LET S(2)=P(2,1)+P(2,2)+P(2,3)
LET S(3)=P(3,1)+P(3,2)+P(3,3)
LET S(4)=P(4,1)+P(4,2)+P(4,3)
```

However, note that S(I), for I = 1, 2, 3, and 4, is obtained by summing P(I,J) for J = 1, 2, and 3. This is exactly the order of subscripts determined by the nested FOR/NEXT loops:

```
FOR I=1 TO 4
   FOR J=1 TO 3
      •
      •
      •
   NEXT J
NEXT I
```

The following program can now be written. Lines 100 to 160, which carry out step (a) of the algorithm, are simply the program segment shown in Example 9. To this we add lines 170 to 320, which represent one way to carry out step (b) of the algorithm.

The program

```
100 REM READ VALUES FOR THE 4-BY-3 ARRAY P.
110 FOR I=1 TO 4
120    REM READ VALUES FOR THE ITH ROW OF P.
130    FOR J=1 TO 3
140       READ P(I,J)
150    NEXT J
160 NEXT I
170 REM DETERMINE AND PRINT THE ROW SUMS OF P.
180 PRINT "PARTICIPATION IN SURVEY BY CLASS"
190 PRINT "----------------------------------"
200 FOR I=1 TO 4
210    LET S(I)=0
220 NEXT I
```

```
23Ø FOR I=1 TO 4
24Ø    FOR J=1 TO 3
25Ø       LET S(I)=S(I)+P(I,J)
26Ø    NEXT J
27Ø    IF (I=1) THEN PRINT "FRESHMEN",
28Ø    IF (I=2) THEN PRINT "SOPHOMORES",
29Ø    IF (I=3) THEN PRINT "JUNIORS",
3ØØ    IF (I=4) THEN PRINT "SENIORS",
31Ø    PRINT S(I)
32Ø NEXT I
5ØØ DATA 2Ø7,93,41
51Ø DATA 165,11Ø,33
52Ø DATA 93,87,15
53Ø DATA 51,65,8
999 END
RUN
```

```
PARTICIPATION IN SURVEY BY CLASS
---------------------------------
FRESHMEN        341
SOPHOMORES      3Ø8
JUNIORS         195
SENIORS         124
```

Remark   This program could have been written with only one pair of nested FOR/NEXT loops by inserting appropriate lines in the program segment

```
1ØØ REM READ VALUES FOR THE 4-BY-3 ARRAY P.
11Ø FOR I=1 TO 4
12Ø    REM READ VALUES FOR THE ITH ROW OF P.
13Ø    FOR J=1 TO 3
14Ø       READ P(I,J)
15Ø    NEXT J
16Ø NEXT I
```

that was used to carry out step (a) of the algorithm. Specifically, inserting the line

```
115 LET S(I)=Ø
```

serves to initialize the counters S(1), S(2), S(3), and S(4); if the line

```
145 LET S(I)=S(I)+P(I,J)
```

is included, the required row sums S(1), S(2), S(3), and S(4) will be calculated. The lines that print the caption

```
PARTICIPATION IN SURVEY BY CLASS
---------------------------------
```

can be placed anywhere before line 11Ø and, finally, the lines that print the counts S(I) with the identifying labels can be placed just after S(I) is determined—that is, between lines 15Ø and 16Ø.

Although these changes result in a shorter program, it is not necessarily better. In the program as given, each of the two subtasks (steps (a) and (b)) in the algorithm occupies its own part of the program. (The REM statements in lines 100 and 170 identify these program segments.) That the resulting program may not be the shortest possible is of little consequence. The longer program obtained by segmenting is easier to read and certainly easier to modify, should that be required. The axiom "the shorter the better" is not always valid in programming.

When a subscripted variable such as B(1,1) is used in a program, the smallest subscript allowed is 0 and the largest is 10. However, just as for singly subscripted variables, the DIM statement may be used to specify larger subscripts. If A is to be an array with as many as 50 rows and 20 columns, for example, the statement

```
DIM A(50,20)
```

would be used. Both one-dimensional and two-dimensional arrays may be dimensioned with the same DIM statement.

```
10 DIM Z(15),M(15,10)
```

is a proper DIM statement. It reserves memory space for the one-dimensional array Z of 16 real numbers and for the two-dimensional array M of 176 (16 × 11) real numbers.

Many programming applications involve rearranging the entries in arrays. We saw one such situation in Section 12.4 where the entries in a one-dimensional array were rearranged to yield an array whose entries were in increasing or decreasing order. The next two examples illustrate the rearrangement of entries in two-dimensional arrays.

EXAMPLE 11. Here is a program segment to interchange rows K and L of an N × N array A:

```
200 FOR J=1 TO N
210    LET T=A(K,J)
220    LET A(K,J)=A(L,J)
230    LET A(L,J)=T
240 NEXT J
```

When $J = 1$, the three statements in the range of the loop cause A(K,1) and A(L,1), the first entries in the Kth and Lth rows of A, to be interchanged. When $J = 2$, the second entries A(K,2) and A(L,2) are interchanged. Similar statements apply for $J = 3, 4, \ldots, N$.

EXAMPLE 12. Here is a self-explanatory program:

```
100 DIM A(4,4)
110 REM READ VALUES FOR ARRAY A, ROW BY ROW.
120 FOR I=1 TO 4
130    FOR J=1 TO 4
140       READ A(I,J)
150    NEXT J
160 NEXT I
170 REM FIND THE ROW NUMBER K OF THE ROW OF A
180 REM WITH THE LARGEST FIRST VALUE A(K,1).
190 LET K=1
200 FOR I=2 TO 4
210    IF A(I,1)>A(K,1) THEN LET K=I
220 NEXT I
230 REM INTERCHANGE ROW K AND ROW 1.
240 FOR J=1 TO 4
250    LET T=A(K,J)
260    LET A(K,J)=A(1,J)
270    LET A(1,J)=T
280 NEXT J
290 REM PRINT THE MODIFIED ARRAY A, ROW BY ROW.
300 FOR I=1 TO 4
310    FOR J=1 TO 4
320       PRINT A(I,J);"  ";
330    NEXT J
340    PRINT
350 NEXT I
500 DATA 22.25,21.75,28.63,29.84
510 DATA 61.23,55.47,59.55,62.33
520 DATA 33.35,42.78,39.25,48.62
530 DATA 44.45,43.25,27.62,39.04
999 END
RUN

61.23   55.47   59.55   62.33
22.25   21.75   28.63   29.84
33.35   42.78   39.25   48.62
44.45   43.25   27.62   39.04
```

Applesoft BASIC does not restrict you to one or two subscripts. For example, the statement

```
DIM A(2,2,2)
```

specifies a three-dimensional array whose entries can be referenced by using A(I,J,K), where the subscripts I, J, and K can be any of the integers 0, 1, or 2. Similarly,

```
DIM B(3,3,3,3,3)
```

specifies a five-dimensional array whose entries can be referenced by B(I,J,K,L,M), where the five subscripts can be any of the values 0, 1, 2, or 3.

Arrays with more than two dimensions are sometimes used in technical engineering and mathematical applications, but they are rarely used in nontechnical programming tasks. For this reason, they are not illustrated here.

12.7 Problems

1. What will be printed when each program is run?

a.
```
100 FOR I=1 TO 4
110     FOR J=1 TO 4
120         LET M(I,J)=I*J
130     NEXT J
140 NEXT I
150 FOR K=1 TO 4
160     PRINT M(K,K);" ";
170 NEXT K
180 END
```

b.
```
100 FOR I=1 TO 3
110     FOR J=1 TO 2
120         READ A(I,J)
130         LET B(J,I)=A(I,J)
140     NEXT J
150 NEXT I
160 PRINT B(2,1);B(2,2);B(2,3)
170 DATA 1,2,3,4,5,6,7,8,9
180 END
```

c.
```
100 FOR K=1 TO 3
110     FOR L=1 TO K
120         READ S(K,L)
130         LET S(L,K)=S(K,L)
140     NEXT L
150 NEXT K
160 FOR N=1 TO 3
170     PRINT S(N,2);" ";
180 NEXT N
190 DATA 1,1,1,2,2,2,3,3,3
200 END
```

d.
```
110 READ X,Y
120 FOR J=1 TO X
130     FOR K=1 TO Y-J
140         READ M(J,K)
150         PRINT M(J,K)-K;" ";
160     NEXT K
170     PRINT
180 NEXT J
190 DATA 2,3,9,3,6,8,2,4,3,1
200 END
```

2. Find and correct the errors in the following program segments. Assume that values have already been assigned to the 5 × 5 array A.

a.
```
200 REM PRINT THE SUM S
210 REM OF EACH ROW OF A.
220 LET S=0
230 FOR I=1 TO 5
240     FOR J=1 TO 5
250         LET S=S+A(I,J)
260     NEXT J
270     PRINT S
280 NEXT I
```

b.
```
200 REM INTERCHANGE THE ROWS
210 REM AND COLUMNS OF A.
220 FOR I=1 TO 5
230     FOR J=1 TO 5
240         LET T=A(I,J)
250         LET A(I,J)=A(J,I)
260         LET A(J,I)=T
270     NEXT J
280 NEXT I
```

In Problems 3–19, write a program to perform each task specified.

3. Read 16 values into the 4 × 4 array M. The array M is then to be printed. Further, the four column sums are to be printed below their respective columns.

4. Repeat Problem 3 for an N × N array M in which N can be any integer up to 6.

5. Read 16 values into the 4 × 4 array M. Then print the array. Row sums are to be printed to the right of their respective rows and column sums below their respective columns.

6. Repeat Problem 5 for an N × N array M in which N can be any number up to 6.

7. Values are to be read into an N × N array A. Then the sum of the entries in the upper-left to lower-right diagonal of A is to be printed. This sum is called the *trace* of array A. (N is to be input before the array values are read. Assume that N will never exceed 6.)

8. Values are to be read into an N × N array A. The product of the entries in the upper-left to lower-right diagonal of A is to be printed. (Assume N ≤ 6.)

9. The *transpose* B of an N × N array A is the N × N array whose rows are the columns of A in the same order. Read the entries of A from DATA lines, and print the transpose B. (Assume that N will be less than 6.)

10. The *sum* S of two N × N arrays A and B is the N × N array whose entries are the sums of the corresponding entries of A and B. Read A and B from DATA lines, and print arrays A, B, and S. (Assume that N will be less than 6.)

11. Create the following 5 × 5 array N:

$$
\begin{array}{ccccc}
0 & 1 & 1 & 1 & 1 \\
-1 & 0 & 1 & 1 & 1 \\
-1 & -1 & 0 & 1 & 1 \\
-1 & -1 & -1 & 0 & 1 \\
-1 & -1 & -1 & -1 & 0
\end{array}
$$

The values N(I,J) are to be determined during program execution without using READ or INPUT statements. Array N should be printed. (*Hint:* The value to be assigned to N(I,J) can be determined by comparing I with J.)

12. Read values into a 5 × 3 array N. Then print the subscripts corresponding to the largest entry in N. If this largest value appears in N more than once, more than one pair of subscripts must be printed. Use the following algorithm:

  a. Read values for array N.
  b. Determine M, the largest number in array N.
  c. Print the subscripts I, J for which $N(I,J) = M$.

13. Read values into a 5 × 3 array N. Print the row of N with the smallest first entry. If this smallest value is the first entry in more than one row, print only the first of these rows. Then interchange this row with the first row and print the modified array N. Use the following algorithm:

  a. Read values for array N.
  b. Find the first K such that row K has the smallest first entry.
  c. Print row K.
  d. Interchange rows 1 and K.
  e. Print the modified array N.

14. Read values into a 5 × 3 array A. Rearrange the rows of A so that their first entries are in ascending order. Print the modified array row by row. (Use a bubble sort to place the first-column entries A(1,1), A(2,1), A(3,1), A(4,1), A(5,1) in ascending order. Instead of swapping only A(I,1) and A(I + 1,1) whenever they are out of order, you must interchange all of row I with row I + 1.)

15. Modify your program for Problem 14 to handle M × N arrays rather than just 5 × 3 arrays.

16. Read N pairs of numbers into an N × 2 array A. Sort these pairs (that is, the rows of A) so that the first-column entries are in ascending order and so that $A(I,2) \leqslant A(I + 1,2)$ whenever $A(I,1) = A(I + 1,1)$. Use a bubble sort that will place the first-column entries A(1,1), A(2,1), . . . , A(N,1) in ascending order with the following modification. If $A(I,1) > A(I + 1,1)$, swap rows I and I + 1; if $A(I,1) < A(I + 1,1)$, no swap is necessary; otherwise—that is, if $A(I,1) = A(I + 1,1)$—swap only if $A(I,2) > A(I + 1,2)$.

17. An N × N array of numbers is called a *magic square* if the sums of each row, each column, and each diagonal are all equal. Test any N × N array in which N will never exceed 10. Values for N and array values should be input. Be sure to print out and identify all row, column, and diagonal sums, the array itself, and a message indicating whether or not the array is a magic square. Try your program on the following arrays:

a.
11	10	4	23	17
18	12	6	5	24
25	19	13	7	1
2	21	20	14	8
9	3	22	16	15

b.
4	139	161	26	174	147
85	166	107	188	93	12
98	152	138	3	103	157
179	17	84	165	184	22
183	21	13	175	89	170
102	156	148	94	8	143

18. Five numbers are to be input to produce a five-column table as follows. The first column is to contain the five numbers in the order they are input. The second column is to contain the four differences of successive values in the first column. If the first column contains 2 4 8 9 3, for example, the second column will contain 2 4 1 −6. In the same way, each of columns 3 through 5 is to contain the differences of successive values in the column before it. If the values 1, 5, 9, 6, 12 are input, the output should be

1	4	0	−7	−23
5	4	−7	16	
9	−3	9		
6	6			
12				

In the following suggested algorithm, K denotes a 5 × 5 array:

  a. Input the first column of K.
  b. Generate the remaining four columns of K as specified in the problem statement.
  c. Print the table as specified.

19. N numbers are to be input to produce a table of differences as described in Problem 18. Assume that N is an integer from 2 to 10.

12.8 Review true-or-false quiz

1. Dimension statements may appear anywhere in a program as long as they appear before the arrays being dimensioned are used.   T   F
2. The two programming lines

```
100 DIM A(25)
110 LET A=0
```

will assign the value 0 to all 25 positions in the array A.   T   F

3. Once array L is assigned values in a program, the statement PRINT L is sufficient to cause the entire array to be displayed.   T   F
4. The programming line 50 LET A(I) = 7 could never cause an error message to be displayed.   T   F
5. The statement LET A(7) = 25 can never cause an error message to be displayed.   T   F
6. If a noninteger subscript is encountered during program execution, an error message will be displayed and the program run will terminate.   T   F
7. Array values may be assigned by READ, INPUT, or LET statements.   T   F
8. Since two-dimensional arrays make use of two subscripts, they must be used in nested loops.   T   F
9. If both one-dimensional and two-dimensional arrays are to be used in a program, two DIM statements must be used.   T   F
10. The bubble sort is used only to arrange the terms of a list in ascending order. T   F

12.8 Review true-or-false quiz

13
□ □ □ □ □ □ □ □ □ □ □ □ □
More on Processing String Data

In the foregoing chapters we've shown how string values can be assigned to string variables, how these values can be printed, how strings can be compared by using the operators = and < >, how the functions LEN, LEFT$, RIGHT$, and MID$ can be used to examine the individual characters in strings, and how the concatenation operator (+) can be used to build new strings from old ones.

In this chapter the topic of string variables is expanded. You will see how strings can be compared by using any of the relational operators =, <>, <, <=, >, and >= (Section 13.1), and how lists of strings can be processed by using subscripted string variables (Section 13.3). Other built-in functions used to process string data are described in Section 13.5.

13.1 Strings in relational expressions

You will recall that strings can be compared for equality in IF statements. The following program reviews how BASIC tests for equality:

```
1Ø PRINT "TYPE FINI TO END THIS PROGRAM."
2Ø     INPUT A$
3Ø     IF A$="FINI" THEN 6Ø
4Ø     PRINT A$
5Ø GOTO 2Ø
6Ø PRINT "ADIOS"
7Ø END
RUN
```

```
TYPE FINI TO END THIS PROGRAM
? HELLO
HELLO
? GOODBYE
GOODBYE
? "    FINI"
    FINI
? FINI
ADIOS
```

Recall that for two strings to be equal, they must be identical. Thus "   FINI" is not equal to "FINI" since the first begins with blanks and the second does not. Remember that when strings appear in relational expressions ("FINI" in line 30), quotation marks must be used.

BASIC allows strings to be compared by using any of the relational operators $=$, $<>$, $<$, $<=$, $>$, and $>=$. Thus M\$ $<$ A\$ is an admissible relational expression. But to understand when one string is less than another string, you should have some knowledge of the method used to store a string in memory. Whenever a program requires the use of a string, each character of the string is assigned a numerical value called its **numeric code.** It is these numerical values that are compared. As one would expect, the numeric code for the letter A is smaller than that for B, the numeric code for B is smaller than that for C, and so on. But it is not only letters that can be compared; each BASIC character has its own unique numeric code so that any two characters may be compared. One BASIC character is less than a second character if the numeric code of the first is less than the numeric code of the second.

The numeric codes used in Applesoft BASIC are those of the American Standard Code of Information Interchange (ASCII). This *ordering* or *collating* sequence is presented in Tables 13.1 and 13.2. The first table gives the numeric codes for all the display characters—that is, for letters, digits, the space bar, and other symbols that can be displayed on the screen. The numeric codes shown in Table 13.2 do not correspond to display characters; they are used for other purposes—for instance, you already know the meaning of RETURN, ←, →, and ctrl C.

TABLE 13.1 ASCII numeric codes 32–94 (display characters)

Numeric code	Character	Numeric code	Character	Numeric code	Character
32	(blank)	53	5	74	J
33	!	54	6	75	K
34	"	55	7	76	L
35	#	56	8	77	M
36	$	57	9	78	N
37	%	58	:	79	O
38	&	59	;	80	P
39	'	60	<	81	Q
40	(	61	=	82	R
41	)	62	>	83	S
42	*	63	?	84	T
43	+	64	@	85	U
44	,	65	A	86	V
45	−	66	B	87	W
46	.	67	C	88	X
47	/	68	D	89	Y
48	0	69	E	90	Z
49	1	70	F	91	[
50	2	71	G	92	\
51	3	72	H	93	]
52	4	73	I	94	∧

TABLE 13.2 ASCII numeric codes 0–31 (control characters and special keys)

Numeric code	Keyboard entry	Numeric code	Keyboard entry	Numeric code	Keyboard entry
0	ctrl @	11	ctrl K *monitor cmd*	22	ctrl V
1	ctrl A	12	ctrl L	23	ctrl W
2	ctrl B	13	ctrl M(RETURN)	24	ctrl X
3	ctrl C *-break*	14	ctrl N	25	ctrl Y
4	ctrl D *- Dos command*	15	ctrl O	26	ctrl Z
5	ctrl E	16	ctrl P *- monitor cmd.*	27	ESC
6	ctrl F	17	ctrl Q	28	n/a
7	ctrl G *- BELL*	18	ctrl R	29	ctrl shift-M
8	ctrl H(←)	19	ctrl S *- stop scroll*	30	ctrl ∧
9	ctrl I	20	ctrl T	31	n/a
10	ctrl J	21	ctrl U(→)	95	n/a

Using this ASCII ordering sequence, we have:

"G" < "P" since 71 < 80
"4" < "Y" since 52 < 89
"$" < "∧" since 36 < 94
"8" < "?" since 56 < 63

If strings containing more than one character are to be compared, they are compared character by character beginning at the left. Strings consisting only of letters of the alphabet are ordered just as they would appear in a dictionary. Here are some relational expressions and their truth values:

Relational expression	Truth value
"AMA" > "AM"	true
"XYZW" > "XYZZE"	false
"1234" <= "1234"	true
"13N" > "14A"	false
"M24" <= "M31"	true
"P1" < "M394"	false
"BEAL TOM" < "BEALS TOM"	true

In the last expression, the fifth character in "BEAL TOM" is the blank character (ASCII code 32), whereas the fifth character in "BEALS TOM" is S (ASCII code 83). Since 32 < 83, the relational expression is true.

EXAMPLE 1. Here is a program to print the words appearing in a data list that begin with a letter from D to M:

```
100 READ W$
110    IF W$="END OF LIST" THEN 999
120    IF (W$>="D") AND (W$<"N") THEN PRINT W$
130 GOTO 100
500 DATA WHITE,BLACK,YELLOW,RED,BLUE,ORANGE,GREEN
510 DATA PINK,GRAY,MAGENTA,BEIGE,BROWN,VIOLET,LIME
998 DATA  END OF LIST
999 END
RUN
```

```
GREEN
GRAY
MAGENTA
LIME
```

A word from the data list is read into W$ and is compared with the EOD tag END OF LIST. (This EOD tag is not a member of the list being searched.) If W$<"D" it is not printed since its first letter must be an A, B, or C. Similarly, if W$> = "N" it is rejected because its first letter must be N, O, P, . . . , or Z.

EXAMPLE 2. Here is a program segment to print the value of W$ if it contains only letters of the alphabet:

```
3ØØ LET N=Ø : REM N COUNTS NUMBER OF LETTERS IN W$.
31Ø FOR I=1 TO LEN(W$)
32Ø    LET L$=MID$(W$,I,1)
33Ø      IF L$>="A" AND L$<="Z" THEN N=N+1
34Ø NEXT I
35Ø IF N=LEN(W$) THEN PRINT W$
```

Line 320 assigns the Ith character of W$ to L$ and line 330 increases N by 1 if this character is a letter. Thus lines 300 to 340 determine the number N of letters in W$. Line 350 prints W$ only if N = LEN(W$); that is, only if each character in W$ is a letter.

13.2 Problems

1. Show the output of each program.

a.
```
1Ø FOR I=1 TO 3
2Ø    READ A$,B$
3Ø      IF A$<=B$ THEN PRINT A$
4Ø NEXT I
5Ø DATA A,AA,M,MO,M,KANT
6Ø END
```

b.
```
1Ø FOR J=1 TO 3
2Ø    READ C$,D$
3Ø      IF C$>D$ THEN C$=D$
4Ø    PRINT C$,D$
5Ø NEXT J
6Ø DATA CAT,DOG,7,9,MAN,BEAST
7Ø END
```

c.
```
1Ø LET M$="MIDDLE"
2Ø    READ A$
3Ø      IF A$="*" THEN END
4Ø      IF (A$>M$) AND (A$<"ZZZ") THEN A$="LAST"
5Ø PRINT A$
6Ø GOTO 2Ø
7Ø DATA HARRY,ALICE,PAUL,ROSE,*
8Ø END
```

In Problems 2–7, write a program for each task specified.

2. A list of English words is presented in DATA lines. First print those words beginning with a letter from A to M, then print the rest. (Use a RESTORE statement.)

3. A program is to contain the following DATA lines.

```
8ØØ DATA 9
81Ø DATA MARIAN EVANS,JAMES PAYN,JOSEPH CONRAD
82Ø DATA EMILY DICKINSON,HENRY THOREAU,JOHN PAYNE
83Ø DATA JOHN FOX,MARY FREEMAN,GEORGE ELIOT
```

The names are to be read twice. On the first pass, only those names with a last name beginning with a letter from A to M are to be printed. The remaining names are to be printed in the second pass.

4. For any string typed at the keyboard, the computer is to print THE FIRST CHARACTER IS A LETTER or THE FIRST CHARACTER IS NOT A LETTER, whichever message is correct. A user should be allowed to type many strings during a single program run, and the program should halt when DONE is typed.

5. A list of English words is presented in DATA lines. A user should be allowed to type any two words to obtain a listing of all words alphabetically between them. The program should halt when both input words are the same.

6. Repeat Problem 5 but this time assume that the words are in alphabetical order and make use of this fact.

7. A list of strings is presented in DATA lines. Each string consists of display characters as shown in Table 13.1 and possibly control characters as shown in Table 13.2. Produce a three-column table showing the strings, the number of display characters in each string, and the number of control characters in each string. The columns are to have appropriate headings.

13.3 Subscripted string variables

BASIC allows you to use arrays to process lists of strings, such as names, rather than just lists of numbers. Any admissible string variable name can be used as the name of an array whose entries are strings.

The entries in string arrays are referenced just as entries in numerical arrays are referenced. Thus, if A$ denotes a one-dimensional array, the subscripted variable A$(7) denotes the seventh entry in A$, counting from A$(1). If J = 7, then A$(J) denotes the same entry. As with numerical arrays, using a subscript larger than 10 requires that the array be dimensioned.

EXAMPLE 3. Here is a program to read ten names into an array A$ and then search this array for any names typed at the keyboard. The program will terminate when the word DONE is typed.

```
100 REM READ NAMES INTO THE ARRAY A$.
110 FOR I=1 TO 10
120    READ A$(I)
130 NEXT I
140 REM SEARCH A$ FOR ANY NAME TYPED AT THE KEYBOARD.
150 PRINT "TYPE NAMES EXACTLY AS FOLLOWS:"
160 PRINT "FIRST NAME (SINGLE SPACE) LAST NAME"
170 PRINT "TYPE 'DONE' WHEN FINISHED."
180    PRINT
190    INPUT N$
200    IF N$="DONE" THEN 999
210    LET FOUND$="FALSE"
220    FOR I=1 TO 10
230       IF N$=A$(I) THEN FOUND$="TRUE": GOTO 250
240    NEXT I
250    PRINT N$;" IS ";
260    IF FOUND$="FALSE" THEN PRINT "NOT ";
270    PRINT "IN THE LIST."
280 GOTO 180
500 DATA ABRAHAM LINCOLN, ANDREW JOHNSON
510 DATA ULYSSES GRANT, RUTHERFORD HAYES
520 DATA JAMES GARFIELD, CHESTER ARTHUR
530 DATA GROVER CLEVELAND, BENJAMIN HARRISON
540 DATA WILLIAM MCKINLEY, THEODORE ROOSEVELT
999 END
RUN
```

```
TYPE NAMES EXACTLY AS FOLLOWS:
FIRST NAME (SINGLE SPACE) LAST NAME
TYPE 'DONE' WHEN FINISHED.

? LINCOLN
LINCOLN IS NOT IN THE LIST.

? ABRAHAM LINCOLN
ABRAHAM LINCOLN IS IN THE LIST.

? DONE
```

EXAMPLE 4

Let's write a program to help a chemistry student learn the abbreviations for 12 of the basic elements in the periodic table. The computer is to display the element name, and the student is to respond with the correct abbreviation. If the abbreviation is wrong, the message INCORRECT should be printed with the correct abbreviation before the student goes on to the next element.

Problem analysis

Let's use the following variable names:

E$(I) = Ith basic element in the periodic table
A$(I) = abbreviation of the Ith element
  B$ = abbreviation the student will type

The arrays E$ and A$ will be read from DATA lines that contain the elements and their standard abbreviations. Then the element names will be printed one at a time by a FOR/NEXT loop. After each E$(I)—that is, each element—is printed, the student will type an abbreviation for the element, which will be assigned to B$. B$ will then be compared with A$(I). If they are equal, the next E$(I) will appear. If not, the message will be printed according to the problem description. The following algorithm also determines a count of the number of correct answers.

Algorithm

a. Print a message to the user describing what the program does.
b. Initialize T = 0 (counts number of wrong answers).
c. Read the elements and abbreviations into arrays E$ and A$, respectively.
d. Print the element names one by one, asking for the appropriate abbreviation. If the answer is incorrect, add 1 to T and print the correct abbreviation before going on to the next element.
e. Print the student's score (12 − T) and stop.

The program

```
100 PRINT "THIS PROGRAM WILL PRINT THE NAMES OF 12"
110 PRINT "ELEMENTS FROM THE PERIODIC TABLE. YOU ARE"
120 PRINT "TO RESPOND WITH THE CORRECT ABBREVIATIONS."
130 PRINT
140 REM T COUNTS THE NUMBER OF WRONG ANSWERS.
150 LET T=0
```

```
16Ø REM READ ELEMENTS/ABBREVIATIONS INTO ARRAYS E$ AND A$.
17Ø DIM E$(12),A$(12)
18Ø FOR I=1 TO 12
19Ø    READ E$(I),A$(I)
2ØØ NEXT I
21Ø REM PRINT THE ELEMENTS ONE BY ONE AND WAIT
22Ø REM FOR AN ABBREVIATION TO BE INPUT.
23Ø FOR I=1 TO 12
24Ø    PRINT E$(I);
25Ø    INPUT B$
26Ø    IF B$=A$(I) THEN 29Ø
27Ø    PRINT "INCORRECT",A$(I)
28Ø    LET T=T+1
29Ø NEXT I
3ØØ PRINT
31Ø PRINT "YOUR SCORE IS ";12-T;" CORRECT OUT OF 12."
5ØØ DATA ALUMINUM,AL,GOLD,AU,SILVER,AG
51Ø DATA BORON,B,BROMINE,BR,CARBON,C
52Ø DATA COPPER,CU,CALCIUM,CA,COBALT,CO
53Ø DATA CHROMIUM,CR,CHLORINE,CL,HYDROGEN,H
999 END
RUN

THIS PROGRAM WILL PRINT THE NAMES OF 12
ELEMENTS FROM THE PERIODIC TABLE. YOU ARE
TO RESPOND WITH THE CORRECT ABBREVIATIONS.

ALUMINUM? AL
GOLD? GO
INCORRECT          AU
SILVER? AG
BORON? B
BROMINE? BR
CARBON? C
COPPER? CU
CALCIUM? CAL
INCORRECT          CA
COBALT? CO
CHROMIUM? CR
CHLORINE? CHL
INCORRECT          CL
HYDROGEN? H

YOUR SCORE IS 9 CORRECT OUT OF 12.
```

The string functions LEN, LEFT\$, RIGHT\$, and MID\$ presented in Chapter 11 can also be used with arrays whose entries are strings. For example, if L\$ has been dimensioned as a string array, then:

LEN(L\$(I))   gives the number of characters in the string L\$(I).

LEFT\$(L\$(I),3)   gives the three-character string consisting of the first three characters in L\$(I).

RIGHT$(L$(I),5)   gives the string consisting of the last five characters in L$(I).

MID$(L$(I),M,N)   gives the string of N characters in L$(I) beginning with the Mth character.

MID$(L$(I),N)   gives the string of all characters in L$(I) from the Nth character on.

The next example illustrates the use of string functions with arrays.

EXAMPLE 5. A list of ten words appears in DATA lines. Print the words containing the four-letter sequence TION followed by those containing the two-letter sequence IS.

Problem analysis

Let's begin with the following simple algorithm:

a. Read the ten words into an array L$.
b. For I = 1 to 10, print L$(I) if L$(I) contains TION.
c. For I = 1 to 10, print L$(I) if L$(I) contains IS.
d. Stop.

Step (a) is easily coded:

```
1ØØ REM READ 1Ø WORDS INTO ARRAY L$.
11Ø DIM L$(1Ø)
12Ø FOR I=1 TO 1Ø
13Ø    READ L$(I)
14Ø NEXT I
```

Writing a program segment to carry out step (b) requires that we compare the successive four-character sequences in L$(I) with the string TION. If L$(I) = "EXHIBITIONIST", for example, we can compare the string TION with EXHI, XHIB, HIBI, and so on. The first of these four-character sequences is given by MID$(L$(I),1,4), the second by MID$(L$(I),2,4), the third by MID$(L$(I),3,4), and so on. Since LEN(L$(I)) denotes the number of characters in L$(I), the last four-character sequence in L$(I) is given by MID$(L$(I),LEN(L$(I))−3,4). Thus to determine whether LS(I) contains TION, we can compare TION with MID$(L$(I),J,4) for J = 1,2, . . . , LEN(L$(I))−3. If a match is found, L$(I) should be printed and no further comparisons made. Lines 150 to 220 of the following program use this method to carry out step (b) of the algorithm. A similar analysis applies to step (c), whose code is shown in lines 230 to 310 of the program.

The program

```
1ØØ REM ***** READ 1Ø WORDS INTO ARRAY L$ *****
11Ø DIM L$(1Ø)
12Ø FOR I=1 TO 1Ø
13Ø    READ L$(I)
14Ø NEXT I
15Ø REM ***** PRINT WORDS IN L$ THAT CONTAIN "TION"
16Ø PRINT "WORDS CONTAINING TION"
17Ø PRINT
18Ø FOR I=1 TO 1Ø
19Ø    FOR J=1 TO LEN(L$(I))-3
2ØØ       IF MID$(L$(I),J,4)="TION" THEN PRINT L$(I): GOTO 22Ø
21Ø    NEXT J
22Ø NEXT I
```

```
230 REM ***** PRINT WORDS IN L$ THAT CONTAIN "IS"
240 PRINT
250 PRINT "WORDS CONTAINING IS"
260 PRINT
270 FOR I=1 TO 10
280    FOR J=1 TO LEN(L$(I))-1
290       IF MID$(L$(I),J,2)="IS" THEN PRINT L$(I): GOTO 310
300    NEXT J
310 NEXT I
500 DATA EXHIBITIONIST,DUPLICATION,DISARM,HATEFUL,LISTEN
510 DATA MULTIPLICATION,PARIS,PREDICTION,ISOLATION,MISER
999 END
RUN

WORDS CONTAINING TION

EXHIBITIONIST
DUPLICATION
MULTIPLICATION
PREDICTION
ISOLATION

WORDS CONTAINING IS

EXHIBITIONIST
DISARM
LISTEN
PARIS
ISOLATION
MISER
```

Remark   Since TION most often occurs at the end of a word, the program could be made slightly more efficient by examining the four-character sequences in L$(I) from last to first. The single change

```
190 FOR J=LEN(L$(I))-3 TO 1 STEP -1
```

accomplishes this.

In Examples 3, 4, and 5 we used string arrays to store the data contained in DATA lines. We did this to illustrate string arrays, not because it was essential to use them. (In the next problem set you are asked to rewrite these three programs without using arrays.) There are times, however, when string arrays are required. The most common situation involves sorting lists of strings in some specified order (for example, lists of names in alphabetical order). We conclude this section by showing how a simple modification of the sorting algorithms shown in Section 12.4 can be used with lists of strings.*

---

*It is with some hesitation that we say a particular method (in this case, using arrays) *must* be used in a programming task. Indeed, if data are stored on external storage devices (the subject of the next chapter), it is possible to sort these data without using arrays. The technique required to do so is an advanced programming technique, however, and is not described in this book.

EXAMPLE 6. Here is a program to alphabetize any list of words typed at the keyboard. The list is to be terminated by typing FINI.

```
100 REM BUBBLE SORT AS APPLIED TO STRINGS
110 DIM A$(50)
120 PRINT "ENTER YOUR LIST. TYPE FINI TO END."
130 LET I=0 : REM NUMBER OF INPUT VALUES
140     LET I=I+1
150     INPUT A$(I)
160 IF A$(I)<>"FINI" AND I<50 THEN 140
170 IF A$(I)="FINI" THEN 190
180 PRINT "I CAN HANDLE ONLY 49 WORDS." : END
190 LET N=I-1 : REM LENGTH OF LIST
200 REM ALPHABETIZE THE N WORD ARRAY A$.
210 FOR J=1 TO N-1
220     FOR I=1 TO N-J
230         IF A$(I)<=A$(I+1) THEN 270
240         LET T$=A$(I)
250         LET A$(I)=A$(I+1)
260         LET A$(I+1)=T$
270     NEXT I
280 NEXT J
290 REM PRINT THE ALPHABETIZED LIST.
300 PRINT
310 PRINT "THE ALPHABETIZED LIST:"
320 FOR I=1 TO N
330     PRINT A$(I)
340 NEXT I
999 END
RUN

ENTER YOUR LIST. TYPE FINI TO END.
? LINCOLN
? JOHNSON
? GRANT
? HAYES
? GARFIELD
? FINI

THE ALPHABETIZED LIST:
GARFIELD
GRANT
HAYES
JOHNSON
LINCOLN
```

The algorithm in lines 200 to 280 is the bubble sort algorithm described in Section 12.4 with the array name A changed to A$. Note also that the variable T in lines 240 and 260 is changed to T$. Strings must be assigned to string variables and numbers to numerical variables.

Everything we said in Section 12.4 about the slow execution of loops that process numbers applies also to string processing. In the preceding example, the bubble sort was adequate because the program was written to handle lists of at most 49 words. If you should need a faster algorithm to sort lists of strings, the Shellsort (Figure 12.3) can be used. Simply change the numerical variables A and T to A$ and T$ as we did for the bubble sort.

13.4 Problems

1. Show the output of each program.

   a.
   ```
   1Ø FOR I=1 TO 3
   2Ø    READ M$(I)
   3Ø NEXT I
   4Ø FOR J=3 TO 1 STEP -1
   5Ø    IF M$(J)<="ROBERTS" THEN PRINT M$(J)
   6Ø NEXT J
   7Ø DATA ALBERT,ZIP,ROBERT
   8Ø END
   ```

   b.
   ```
   1Ø FOR J=1 TO 4
   2Ø    READ X$
   3Ø    IF X$="HAT" THEN RESTORE : GOTO 4Ø
   35    LET A$(J)=X$
   4Ø NEXT J
   5Ø FOR J=1 TO 4 STEP 2
   6Ø    PRINT A$(J);
   7Ø NEXT J
   8Ø DATA AB,MAN,SCAM,HAT
   9Ø END
   ```

   c.
   ```
   1Ø FOR J=1 TO 4
   2Ø    READ F$(J),L$(J)
   3Ø NEXT J
   4Ø FOR I=4 TO 1 STEP -1
   5Ø    PRINT L$(I);",";F$(I)
   6Ø NEXT I
   7Ø DATA JOHN,CASH,ELTON,JOHN
   8Ø DATA JOHN,DENVER,JOHN,PAYCHECK
   9Ø END
   ```

   d.
   ```
   1ØØ FOR I=1 TO 5
   11Ø    READ A$(I)
   12Ø NEXT I
   13Ø FOR I=1 TO 5
   14Ø    FOR J=1 TO LEN(A$(I))
   15Ø       IF MID$(A$(I),J,1)="S" THEN PRINT A$(I): GOTO 17Ø
   16Ø    NEXT J
   17Ø NEXT I
   18Ø DATA SAM,HARRY,JESS,SANDI,OLIVER
   19Ø END
   ```

In Problems 2–8, write a program to perform each task specified. No sorting is required for these problems.

2. Rewrite the program in Example 3 without using arrays.
3. Rewrite the program in Example 4 without using arrays.
4. Rewrite the program in Example 5 without using arrays.
5. Allow a user to create an array L$ of words as follows. The computer is to request (INPUT statement) that a word be typed. If the word has not already been typed, it should be added to the array; if it has, it should be ignored. In either case the user should then be allowed to enter another word. If the user types the word LIST, however, the array L$ created to that point should be printed and another request made. If the user types END, the program run should terminate.
6. A list of N names appears in DATA lines ("Last,First"). The last datum is the EOD tag XXXX. Separate the names into three arrays. The first array is to contain all names A through K, the second all names L through Q, and the third all names R through Z. The three arrays are to be printed one under the other with the three headings A–K, L–Q, and R–Z.

7. Allow the user to input the names of the residents of the town of Plymouth who attended the June Town Meeting. The names are to be entered in the order in which the people arrived at the meeting. After each name the voting precinct of that resident is to be typed. (There are four precincts in Plymouth.) A typical entry would therefore be ALDEN PRISCILLA, 3. When the user types DONE,Ø the program should print four lists according to precinct.

8. Write a program to produce each of the following designs. When needed, the strings A, B, C, . . . , G are to be read from DATA lines.

a. A
   BB
   CCC
   DDDD
   EEEEE
   FFFFFF

b. ABCDEFG
   BCDEFG
   CDEFG
   DEFG
   EFG
   FG
   G

c. A A A A
    B B B
    C C C C
     D D D
    E E E E

d.   A
     BBB
    CCCCC
   DDDDDDD
   EEEEEEEEE

In Problems 9–16, write a program for each task specified. Sorting is required for these problems.

9. A list of English words is presented in DATA lines. The last datum is the EOD tag XXXX. The user should be allowed to issue any of the following commands: LIST, to print the list in the order given in the DATA lines; SORTLIST, to print the list in alphabetical order; and DONE, to terminate the run. After any command other than DONE, the user should be allowed to issue another command.

10. A list of words as described in Problem 9 is to be printed in two adjacent columns with the column headings A–M and N–Z. The words in each column are to appear in alphabetical order.

11. Last year's sales report of the J. T. Pencil Company reads as follows:

January	$32,350	July	$22,000
February	$16,440	August	$43,500
March	$18,624	September	$51,400
April	$26,100	October	$29,000
May	$30,500	November	$20,100
June	$28,600	December	$27,500

Produce a two-column report with the headings MONTH and SALES. Sales figures are to appear in descending order. Include the given data in DATA lines with the months JANUARY through DECEMBER appearing first and the 12 sales figures following.

12. Compute the semester averages for all students in a psychology class. A separate DATA line should be used for each student and should contain the student's name and five grades. A typical DATA line might read

    7ØØ DATA LINCOLN JOHN,72,79,88,97,9Ø

The output should be in tabular form with the column headings STUDENT and SEMESTER AVERAGE. Semester averages are to appear in descending order.

13. Modify Problem 12 so that the table is printed with the students' names in alphabetical order.

14. Modify Problem 12 as follows. After averages are rounded to the nearest integer, letter grades should be given according to this table:

Average	*Grade*
90–100	A
80–89	B
70–79	C
60–69	D
Below 60	E

The five strings A, B, C, D, and E should be read into an array N$. The output should be in tabular form with the column headings STUDENT and LETTER GRADE.

15. A program is to contain the following DATA lines.

```
800 DATA 9
810 DATA MARIAN EVANS,JAMES PAYN,JOSEPH CONRAD
820 DATA EMILY DICKINSON,HENRY THOREAU,JOHN PAYNE
830 DATA JOHN FOX,MARY FREEMAN,GEORGE ELIOT
```

Use the following algorithm to alphabetize this list of names.

a. Read the names into an array A$.
b. Create a new array B$ containing the names in A$ but with last names first. (See Example 9 of Section 11.2.)
c. Sort B$ into alphabetical order. When a swap is made in B$, make the corresponding swap in A$.
d. Print array A$.

16. English prose can be written in DATA lines by representing each line of text as a string occupying a single DATA line. When this is done, the last DATA line should contain a dummy value such as "END OF TEXT" as an EOD tag.

```
500 DATA "WHEN IN THE COURSE OF HUMAN EVENTS, IT BECOMES"
501 DATA "NECESSARY FOR ONE PEOPLE TO DISSOLVE THE POLITICAL"
            •
            •
            •
998 DATA "END OF TEXT"
```

Write a program to determine some or all of the following statistics.

a. A count of the number of words of text.
b. A count of the number of N-letter words for N = 1,2,3, ...
c. A two-column table giving each word used and its frequency. The column of words should be in alphabetical order.
d. A total count of the number of articles and conjunctions used. For this you should create a list of articles and conjunctions and determine how many of the words are in this list. (Be sure you include *a, an, the, and, but, however, or, nor.*)

13.5 The Applesoft conversion functions

In this section we describe four additional built-in functions: the CHR$ and ASC functions which are used to convert between numerical codes and characters, and the STR$ and VAL functions which are used to convert between numbers and strings whose contents denote numbers.

The CHARACTER function CHR$

This function converts numeric codes to their corresponding characters. Thus, in light of Table 13.1, CHR$(65) = "A" and CHR$(43) = " + ".

EXAMPLE 7. This example illustrates the CHR$ function.

```
10 PRINT "THE SEQUENCE OF CHARACTERS CORRESPONDING TO THE"
20 PRINT "NUMERIC CODES CONTAINED IN THE DATA LINES IS:"
30 PRINT
40    READ N
50    IF N=0 THEN 99
60    PRINT CHR$(N);
70 GOTO 40
80 DATA 42,42,42,72,79,87,68,89,42,42,42
90 DATA 0
99 END
RUN

THE SEQUENCE OF CHARACTERS CORRESPONDING TO THE
NUMERIC CODES CONTAINED IN THE DATA LINES IS:

***HOWDY***
```

EXAMPLE 8. Here is a program to print the English alphabet:

```
10 FOR K=65 TO 90
20    PRINT CHR$(K);
30 NEXT K
40 FOR L=1 TO 5
50    PRINT CHR$(7);
60 NEXT L
70 END
RUN

ABCDEFGHIJKLMNOPQRSTUVWXYZ
```

Lines 40 to 60 output the Apple's bell character (ctrl G) five times. If the output is directed to the video screen, a bell will ring (actually, the Apple's speaker will beep) five times. If the output is directed to a printer, a bell will ring only if the printer has one.

Remark

It is sometimes helpful to include the statement PRINT CHR$(7); in a program so that the bell will alert you when a certain point has been reached during program execution. To estimate the execution time of a loop, for instance, simply place this statement just before and just after the loop. Doing so will have no effect on the displayed output. Control characters, such as ctrl G, are not only nonprinting but they cause no space to appear on a screen or printer. Of course, the semicolon is necessary to suppress the RETURN.

The ASCII function ASC

The ASC function converts the first character in a string to its numeric code. For example, ASC("MARY") = 77, the numeric code for M. When used with a one-character string, ASC converts the character to its numeric code. Thus ASC("A") = 65 and ASC("+") = 43.

EXAMPLE 9. This program illustrates the ASC function:

```
100 INPUT "TYPE A LETTER: ";L$
110 IF L$<"A" OR L$>"Z" THEN 160
120 LET N=ASC(L$)-ASC("A")+1
130 PRINT "ITS POSITION IN ALPHABET IS ";N
140 PRINT
150 GOTO 100
160 PRINT "NOT A LETTER"
170 END
RUN

TYPE A LETTER: C
ITS POSITION IN ALPHABET IS 3

TYPE A LETTER: Z
ITS POSITION IN ALPHABET IS 26

TYPE A LETTER: +
NOT A LETTER
```

The numeric codes for the letters A, B, C, . . . , Z are 65, 66, 67, . . . , 90, respectively. Thus if L$ = "C" then ASC(L$) = 67, so that line 120 gives N = 67 − 65 + 1 = 3.

Remark

To guard against the user's typing more than one character, you can insert the line

```
115 IF LEN(L$)<>1 THEN 160
```

In addition to the numeric codes 0–95 shown in Tables 13.1 and 13.2, Applesoft BASIC allows the codes 96–255. Some of these (97–122) are used by the Apple to transmit lowercase letters to output devices capable of printing or displaying them. To print a lowercase letter, simply add 32 to the numeric code of the corresponding uppercase letter. Thus if L$ = "A" the statement

```
PRINT CHR$(ASC(L$)+32)
```

will produce the lowercase letter *a*. If the output of a program that prints lowercase letters is directed to your video screen, it will be unreadable—the PRINT statement shown will display ! and not *a* or A.

Other than the exception described in the preceding paragraph, you should avoid using numeric codes greater than 95—they can lead to unexpected results. Both of the statements PRINT CHR$(65) and PRINT CHR$(193) will output the letter A, for example, but the logical expression CHR$(65) = "A" will be true whereas the logical expression CHR$(193) = "A" will be false.

The STRING function STR$

The STR$ function converts a numerical value to a string. For example, the programming line

```
25 LET A$=STR$(234.6)
```

assigns the string "234.6" to A$. The STR$ function is especially useful when columns of numbers must line up according to the decimal point. The following example shows one way to do this.

EXAMPLE 10. Here is a program to print the costs of 1, 2, . . . , 15 items selling seven for $5.00:

```
100 PRINT "NUMBER","COST"
110 PRINT
120 LET UNIT=5.00/7
130 FOR N=1 TO 15
140     LET C=N*UNIT : REM COST OF N ITEMS AS A DECIMAL
150     LET C=INT(100*C+0.5) : REM COST IN CENTS
160     REM INSERT DECIMAL POINT.
170     LET C$=STR$(C)
180     IF LEN(C$)=1 THEN C$="0.0"+C$ : GOTO 220
190     IF LEN(C$)=2 THEN C$="0."+C$ : GOTO 220
200     IF LEN(C$)>2 THEN C$=LEFT$(C$,LEN(C$)-2)+"."+RIGHT$(C$,2)
210     REM PRINT NTH ROW OF TABLE.
220     HTAB 5-LEN(STR$(N)) : PRINT N;
230     HTAB 21-LEN(C$) : PRINT C$
240 NEXT N
999 END
RUN
```

NUMBER	COST
1	0.71
2	1.43
3	2.14
4	2.86
5	3.57
6	4.29
7	5.00
8	5.71
9	6.43
10	7.14
11	7.86
12	8.57
13	9.29
14	10.00
15	10.71

For each value of N, line 140 determines the cost C of N items and line 150 converts C to an integer giving the equivalent cost in cents. Line 170 changes this integer to a string and lines 180 to 200 insert a decimal point in the proper position of the string: line 180 inserts 0.0 before single-digit numbers (5 would become 0.05); line 190 inserts 0. before two-digit numbers (71 becomes 0.71); and line 200 correctly places the decimal point in numbers with three or more digits (143 becomes 1.43 and 1000 becomes 10.00). Finally, lines 220 and 230 print the two columns lined up on the right in column positions 4 and 20.

The VALUE function VAL

The VAL function reverses the process just described for STR$. It converts a string up to its first nonnumerical character into its numerical value. For example:

BASIC statement	Value assigned to A
LET A=VAL("29.Ø4")	29.Ø4
LET A=VAL("537.2 FEET")	537.2
LET A=VAL("1.234E2XYZ")	1.234E2 or 123.4
LET A=VAL("THREE")	Ø

If no number occurs before the first nonnumerical character, VAL gives the value Ø. Thus VAL("THREE") = Ø as shown.

Programs should be designed to prevent incorrect input data from influencing the results. If a user enters 6 for an interest rate when the correct entry should be 0.06, for example, any calculation using this rate will be in error. The next example illustrates how the VAL function, together with other string functions, can be used to detect just such erroneous input.

EXAMPLE 11. Here is a program segment to input prices for N items ITEM$(1), ITEM$(2), . . . , ITEM$(N). The prices are stored in PRICE(1), PRICE(2), . . . , PRICE(N).

```
5ØØ PRINT "FOR EACH ITEM, ENTER ITS PRICE"
51Ø PRINT "IN THE FORM XXXX.XX"
52Ø PRINT
53Ø FOR K=1 TO N
54Ø    PRINT ITEM$(K)
55Ø    INPUT "PRICE $";P$ : REM STORE PRICE AS STRING.
56Ø    IF LEN(P$)<3 THEN PRINT "INCORRECT FORM" : GOTO 54Ø
57Ø    LET D$=MID$(P$,LEN(P$)-2,1)
58Ø    IF D$<>"." THEN PRINT "INCORRECT FORM" : GOTO 54Ø
59Ø    PRICE(K)=VAL(P$)
6ØØ NEXT K
```

Line 540 prints the item names stored in the array ITEM$. For each item the selling price is entered in the string variable P$. Line 560 rejects any entry of less than three characters. Line 570 assigns the third from last character of P$ to D$. If this character is not the decimal point, line 580 rejects the input value P$. Any string in the specified form is changed to its numerical value by the VAL function in line 590 and stored in the numerical array PRICE.

13.6 Problems

1. Show the output of each program.

a.
```
1Ø LET A$="31"
2Ø LET B$="31"
3Ø PRINT A$;"+";B$;"=";
4Ø PRINT VAL(A$)+VAL(B$)
5Ø END
```

b.
```
1Ø LET L$="E"
2Ø LET N=ASC(L$)-ASC("A")+1
3Ø PRINT L$, N
4Ø END
```

c.
```
1Ø LET D$="7"
2Ø LET N=ASC(D$)-ASC("Ø")
3Ø PRINT D$,N
4Ø END
```

d.
```
1Ø FOR K=48 TO 58
2Ø    PRINT CHR$(K):
3Ø NEXT K
4Ø END
```

```
e. 1Ø REM W=NUMBER OF WINS
   2Ø REM G=NUMBER OF GAMES PLAYED
   3Ø LET W=42
   4Ø LET G=63
   5Ø LET B$=STR$(W)+" WINS"
   6Ø LET C$=" AND "+STR$(G-W)+" LOSSES"
   7Ø LET D$=" GIVES A PERCENTAGE OF "+STR$(INT(1ØØØ*W/G+Ø.5)/1ØØØ)
   8Ø PRINT B$;C$;D$
   9Ø END
```

In Problems 2–7, write a program for each task specified.

2. For any input string, two columns are to be output. The first column is to contain the characters in the string and the second their numeric codes. The user should be allowed to try many strings during a single program run.

3. Produce a table displaying the 63 numeric codes 32–94 with their corresponding characters (as shown in Table 13.1). The table should have an appropriate title and column headings.

4. For any input string, two columns are to be output. The first is to show the letters appearing in the string; the second is to show how many times these letters occur in the string. For example, if the string "BOB, ROB, OR BO" is typed, the output should be

```
B  4
O  4
R  2
```

Use an array DIM F(26) to store the required counts. Example 9 illustrates the technique that allows you to do this.

5. Each of many DATA lines contains a single string (it may be long). The last string is the EOD tag END-OF-DATA. Produce a two-column table as described in Problem 4 for all letters appearing in all DATA lines but the last. The columns are to be labeled LETTER and FREQUENCY.

6. Input any decimal, and print the sequence of digits without the decimal point. For example, if 764.38 is input, 76438 should be output.

7. Input two positive integers A and B for which A<B. The program should print the decimal expansion of A/B to N places where the positive integer N is also input during execution.

13.7 Review true-or-false quiz

1. It now makes sense to use the condition A<"B" in an IF statement.   T   F
2. The BASIC statement

   ```
   IF A$>="A" AND A$<="Z" THEN PRINT "OK"
   ```

   will print OK whenever the first character in A$ is a letter of the alphabet.   T   F
3. The BASIC statement PRINT CHR$(1) will print the letter A.   T   F
4. ASC("Z") − ASC("A") = 26.   T   F
5. ASC("3") = ASC("2") + 1.   T   F
6. ASC(CHR$(32)) = 32.   T   F
7. VAL(STR$(55.23)) = 55.23.   T   F
8. The BASIC statement

   ```
   IF STR$(VAL(A$))=A$ THEN PRINT "OK"
   ```

   will print OK whatever the value of A$.   T   F

14

□ □ □ □ □ □ □ □ □ □ □ □ □ □

Data Files

Although DATA statements provide the means for presenting large quantities of data to the computer, situations do arise in which they prove inadequate. Sometimes, for example, the output values of one program are required as the input values of another program or perhaps several other programs. For this reason BASIC allows input data to come from sources external to the program (other than the keyboard) and permits the output to be stored on secondary storage devices for later use. This storage is accomplished by the use of data files.

A **data file** is a named collection of related data that can be referenced by a program.

On Apple computer systems, data files are called **text files**—this use of the word *text* is explained in Section 14.1. They are stored on diskettes and later retrieved as input files by including special DOS commands in your programs. In this chapter we assume that your system contains at least one disk unit and that DOS is operational as described in Appendix B.

The disk operating system allows you to use two types of text files: **sequential-access files** (or simply *sequential files*) and **random-access files.** The contents of both types of files are ordered in sequence—there is a first entry, a second entry, a third, and so on. There are two main differences in the uses of sequential and random-access files:

1. Data in a sequential file are accessed in order, beginning with the first datum, whereas data in a random-access file are accessed directly.
2. Data are added only at the end of a sequential file. This means that to change an entry

in an existing file you would create a completely new file that contains this change.*
With random-access files, individual entries can be changed and there is no need to
create a completely new file each time a file must be changed.

In this chapter we show how to create both sequential and random-access files and explain
how they are used in several programming applications. Sequential files are described first
(Sections 14.1 and 14.3) because they are somewhat easier to use and are adequate for most
applications encountered by beginning programmers. Random-access files are considered in
Section 14.5.

14.1 Sequential-access files

Brief descriptions of the DOS commands most often used in programs to process sequential
files are as follows.

OPEN **fn**   establishes a communication link between a program and a text file named
fn. We say that **fn** has been *opened*.

WRITE **fn**   specifies that subsequent PRINT statements will transmit output to the file
fn rather than to the screen or printer. We say that **fn** is a WRITE file.

READ **fn**   specifies that subsequent INPUT statements will obtain values from the file
fn and not from the Apple's keyboard. We say that **fn** is a READ file.

CLOSE **fn**   terminates the communication link established by the OPEN statement. We
say that **fn** has been *closed*. Every file that has been opened with an OPEN
command must be closed before program execution terminates. Failure to
do so may result in a loss of data.

To include any of these commands in a BASIC program, you must use a PRINT statement
to output the special DOS character ctrl D (CHR$(4)) followed by the command itself. The
program statements

```
100 PRINT CHR$(4);"OPEN FILE1"
110 PRINT CHR$(4);"WRITE FILE1"
```

will open a file named FILE1 (line 100) and specify that subsequent output is to be directed
to this file (line 110).

The Apple interprets the nonprinting character ctrl D as a DOS command only if ctrl D
is the first character output to a line. For example, the statements

```
100 PRINT "HELLO"
110 PRINT CHR$(4);"OPEN FILE1"
```

will display the string HELLO and then open FILE1, whereas the statements

```
100 PRINT "HELLO";
110 PRINT CHR$(4);"OPEN FILE1"
```

will not open FILE1 since ctrl D is the sixth and not the first character output to a line. In this
case, the two statements will simply produce the output

```
HELLOOPEN FILE1
```

---

*Applesoft BASIC provides the means for changing data in a sequential file. This practice, however, represents
an advanced programming technique and is not described in this book.

EXAMPLE 1. Here is a program to create a file named DATA1:

```
100 LET D$=CHR$(4): REM CTRL D
110 PRINT D$;"OPEN DATA1"
120 PRINT D$;"WRITE DATA1"
130 PRINT "SOME NUMBERS"
140 FOR N=1 TO 10 STEP 3
150     PRINT N
160 NEXT N
170 PRINT D$;"CLOSE DATA1"
180 END
```

Before running this program, place a diskette that is not write-protected (see Section B.4) in your disk unit. Then type

```
DELETE DATA1
```

to ensure that the diskette does not contain a file named DATA1. Once you have done this, the action of the program will be as follows.

First, lines 110 and 120 open a WRITE file named DATA1. Since the name DATA1 is not already in the diskette catalog (we deleted it), it is automatically placed there.

Then lines 130 to 160 output the following five lines to the file DATA1. (The use of the term *lines* as it applies to files will be explained shortly.)

```
SOME NUMBERS
1
4
7
10
```

Then line 170 properly closes the file DATA1.

Remark 1

When this program is run, the output is directed only to the disk unit and not to the screen or printer. The disk operating system allows you to see what values are being output to disk by using the disk monitor command MON O. (The O is for output.) Let's do this.

```
]MON O
]RUN
SOME NUMBERS
1
4
7
10
```

To cancel the effect of the MON O command, type

```
NOMON O
```

The MON and NOMON commands are used principally as debugging aids. Indeed, if a program error occurs while a file is open as a WRITE file, you will see the error message only if MON O is in effect. The error message will be output to the file and not to the screen or printer. Thus if you are having trouble with a program that uses files, one of the first things you should do is run the program with MON O in effect. Other uses of the monitor commands are described after Example 2.

Remark 2   If you issue the CATALOG command, you will see that DATA1 is now included with its name preceded by the letter T. This indicates that it is a text file created by an OPEN command. The Applesoft commands LOAD and RUN cannot be used with text files. This means that you cannot LIST a text file since to LIST a file it must first be loaded. To "see" what is on a text file (other than creating it with MON O in effect) you can write a program to retrieve and display its contents.

EXAMPLE 2. Here is a program to display the contents of the text file DATA1 created by the program in Example 1:

```
100 LET D$=CHR$(4): REM CTRL D
110 PRINT D$;"OPEN DATA1"
120 PRINT D$;"READ DATA1"
130 INPUT A$
140 PRINT A$
150 FOR I=1 TO 4
160    INPUT NUM
170    PRINT NUM
180 NEXT I
190 PRINT D$;"CLOSE DATA1"
RUN

SOME NUMBERS
1
4
7
10
```

Lines 110 and 120 open DATA1 as a READ file. Since DATA1 already exists on disk, the OPEN statement positions this file at its beginning.

Line 130 assigns the first value (the string SOME NUMBERS) from file DATA1 to A$ and line 140 displays this value. Each time the INPUT statement at line 160 is executed, the next value from the file is assigned to NUM. Line 170 displays these values as shown in the output.

Line 190 properly closes the file DATA1.

As shown by the program run in Example 2, values being input from disk (lines 130 and 160) are not displayed. If you wish to see this disk input, issue the disk monitor command MON I. (The I is for input.) Let's do this for the program in Example 2.

```
]MON I
]RUN
?SOME NUMBERS
SOME NUMBERS
?1
1
?4
4
?7
7
?10
10
```

Note that the question mark associated with INPUT statements is displayed when you monitor disk input. To cancel the effect of MON I, simply type NOMON I.

When you are debugging programs that use disk files, it sometimes helps to know what DOS commands are being carried out at the time. The monitor command MON C (C is for command) is used for this purpose. In the following run of the program of Example 2, we assume that MON I is not in effect:

```
]MON C
]RUN
OPEN DATA1
READ DATA1
SOME NUMBERS
1
4
7
1Ø
CLOSE DATA1
```

The MON and NOMON commands can be used with any one of the specifiers O, I, and C or any combination of them. Thus to monitor both disk input and DOS commands you can use

```
MON I
MON C
```

or the equivalent single command

```
MON I,C
```

To cancel the effect of this command, type

```
NOMON I,C
```

At the outset of this chapter we mentioned that data files used with Apple computer systems are called text files. The term *text* indicates that data are stored as sequences of individual characters—more precisely, as numerical codes associated with individual characters. On the Apple, these numerical codes are the ASCII codes given in Tables 13.1 and 13.2 of Section 13.1. If a file is currently open as a WRITE file, for example, the statement

```
2ØØ PRINT "SAM"
```

will transmit the characters S, A, and M (ASCII codes 83, 65, and 77) to the output file. The statement

```
2Ø1 PRINT 31.5
```

will transmit the *characters* 3, 1, period, and 5 (ASCII codes 51, 49, 46, and 53). Moreover, since these two PRINT statements do not have a final semicolon or comma, each also transmits the RETURN character (ASCII code 13) to the output file. Here is a schematic representation of the part of the output file generated by these two PRINT statements ($\circlearrowleft$ denotes the RETURN character):

| • | • | • | S | A | M | $\circlearrowleft$ | 3 | 1 | . | 5 | $\circlearrowleft$ | • | • | • |

Because of the RETURN characters, it is customary to view this portion of the file as containing the distinct lines

```
SAM
31.5
```

Each of these "lines" of the file, together with its RETURN character, is called a **field.** On Apple computer systems, sequential files consist of fields terminated with a RETURN character.

EXAMPLE 3. Here is a program to create a text file and then display its contents:

```
100 LET D$=CHR$(4): REM CTRL D
110 PRINT D$;"OPEN SCORES"
120 PRINT D$;"WRITE SCORES"
130 FOR N=1 TO 3
140     READ A$,S
150     PRINT A$
160     PRINT S
170 NEXT N
180 PRINT D$;"OPEN SCORES"
190 PRINT D$;"READ SCORES"
200 FOR N=1 TO 3
210     INPUT A$
220     INPUT S
230     PRINT A$,S
240 NEXT N
250 PRINT D$;"CLOSE SCORES"
260 DATA NICKLAUS,206
270 DATA MILLER,208
280 DATA WATSON,205
290 END
RUN

NICKLAUS        206
MILLER          208
WATSON          205
```

Here is a schematic representation of the file SCORES after execution of lines 100 to 170:

Again, because of the RETURN characters, we would visualize this file as containing six distinct lines:

```
NICKLAUS
2Ø6
MILLER
2Ø8
WATSON
2Ø5
```

Remark 1   We did not include line 18Ø simply to open the file SCORES; line 11Ø does this. Rather, its purpose is to position the file at its beginning. Without line 18Ø, the READ command in line 19Ø will specify SCORES as the READ file, but the current file position will not be changed. Consequently, the next INPUT statement (line 21Ø) will attempt to obtain input data with the file positioned at its end. This attempt will result in an END OF DATA error and program execution will halt.

Remark 2   This program illustrates that it is not necessary to use the CLOSE command to close a file before it is opened a second time. When line 18Ø is encountered, the Apple will automatically close the WRITE file SCORES before carrying out the OPEN command.

File INPUT statements obtain values from the fields of a file in exactly the same way that ordinary INPUT statements obtain values from lines typed at the Apple's keyboard. Thus in the program in Example 3 we could have used the single statement

```
21Ø INPUT A$,S
```

in place of the two statements

```
21Ø INPUT A$
22Ø INPUT S
```

A single field of a text file can contain more than one value. However, if these values are to be assigned to distinct variables, they must be separated by commas, just as you use commas to separate input values typed at the keyboard. Thus to print the values of A$ and S in one field of a file you would use

```
PRINT A$;",";S
```

and not

```
PRINT A$;S     or     PRINT A$,S
```

That is, the comma must actually be printed on the file. When the file is used later as an input file, the Apple recognizes the comma as separating two distinct input values.

If you modify the program shown in Example 3 by replacing the statements

```
15Ø PRINT A$
16Ø PRINT S
```

by the single statement

```
15Ø PRINT A$;",";S
```

the output file SCORES will consist of three distinct fields:

```
NICKLAUS,2Ø6
MILLER,2Ø8
WATSON,2Ø5
```

Any program that uses this file as an input file should use INPUT statements that are consistent with this data structure. The statement INPUT A$,S would be appropriate.

Since every comma appearing in a file is interpreted by the Apple as separating distinct input values, only commas *intended* for this purpose should be output to a file. Thus if X$ = "DOE,JANE" the statement PRINT X$ will produce the field

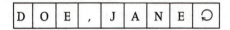

But if you later use INPUT X$ to input a value from this field, DOE will be assigned to X$ and JANE will be ignored (causing the diagnostic message EXTRA IGNORED).

Note the use of semicolons in the statement

```
PRINT A$;",";S
```

When output is being directed to a disk file, you can use commas instead of semicolons with no change whatever in the action of a program. The Apple will treat the commas as if they were semicolons. Although there is no change in the action of the program, there is a difference in what is displayed when MON O is in effect. If commas are used, the monitored output will be displayed in the format specified by the commas. For this reason, most programmers consistently use semicolons so that the monitored output will give an accurate picture of what is actually being output to disk.

It is often convenient to use keyboard INPUT statements to enter values to be stored in a file, rather than including these values in DATA lines as in Example 3. When using this method of data entry you must observe the following rule:

NEVER ALLOW A WRITE COMMAND TO BE IN EFFECT WHILE DATA ARE BEING INPUT AT THE KEYBOARD.*

There are two clear and compelling reasons why this rule must be strictly observed:

1. When a WRITE command is in effect, all output generated by the Apple is sent to the active WRITE file. But all keyboard input is accompanied by output—users must receive a prompt of some kind, usually a printed message but sometimes a simple question mark. This output is sent to the active file, leaving its contents useless.
2. An INPUT statement cancels a WRITE command, but only after sending the input prompt to the output file—again rendering the output file useless.

---

*Most difficulties (and frustrations) encountered by beginners writing programs to process DOS files can be traced to violations of this single rule.

With Apple computer systems, the usual way to create files from values typed at the keyboard involves two steps:

1. Input and store all data in one or more arrays.
2. Output the array values to a file.

The file that will store these data can be opened during step 1, but not as a WRITE file. The first action required by step 2 is to open a WRITE file or, if it is already open, to declare it as the output file in a WRITE command.

EXAMPLE 4. Here is a program to create a file INVTRY at the keyboard:

```
100 LET D$=CHR$(4): REM CTRL D
110 DIM ITEM$(50),QTY(50),PRICE(50)
120 PRINT "TO STOP, TYPE XXX FOR ITEM NAME."
125 PRINT "ENTER NO MORE THAN 49 ITEMS."
130 PRINT "TO IGNORE AN ENTRY, TYPE 0 FOR PRICE."
140 FOR N=1 TO 50
150    PRINT
160    INPUT "ITEM NAME: ";ITEM$(N)
170    IF ITEM$(N)="XXX" THEN 220
180    INPUT "UNITS ON HAND: ";QTY(N)
190    INPUT "PRICE PER UNIT: ";PRICE(N)
200    IF PRICE(N)=0 THEN 150
210 NEXT N
215 PRINT "ONLY 49 ITEMS ALLOWED": END
220 LET N=N-1: REM NUMBER OF ITEMS
230 REM ***CREATE FILE INVTRY***
240 PRINT D$;"OPEN INVTRY"
250 PRINT D$;"WRITE INVTRY"
260 PRINT N
270 FOR K=1 TO N
280    PRINT ITEM$(K);",";QTY(K);",";PRICE(K)
290 NEXT K
300 PRINT D$;"CLOSE INVTRY"
310 END
```

Let's run this program with MON O in effect:

```
]MON O
]RUN
TO STOP, TYPE XXX FOR ITEM NAME.
ENTER NO MORE THAN 49 ITEMS.
TO IGNORE AN ENTRY, TYPE Ø FOR PRICE.

ITEM NAME: HAMMER
UNITS ON HAND: 45Ø
PRICE PER UNIT: 8.99

ITEM NAME: PLIERS
UNITS ON HAND: 845
PRICE PER UNIT: 3.59

ITEM NAME: SAW
UNITS ON HAND: 15Ø
PRICE PER UNIT: Ø

ITEM NAME: SAW
UNITS ON HAND: 25Ø
PRICE PER UNIT: 11.88

ITEM NAME: XXX
3
HAMMER,45Ø,8.99
PLIERS,845,3.59
SAW,25Ø,11.88
```

Lines 110 to 210 assign input values to the three arrays ITEM$, QTY, and PRICE. Note the special use of Ø described in line 130. It allows you to retype the three values associated with an item if a transcription error is noticed before all three values have been entered. In the run given here, we did this for the item SAW.

Line 220 assigns to N the number of different items to be output to the file INVTRY.

Lines 240 to 300 create the file INVTRY. Since MON O was in effect for the run, the four fields output to the file are displayed (the last four lines).

Remark

To use INVTRY as an input file for another program, you would open INVTRY as a READ file, use a statement such as INPUT N to input the count, and then use a loop to retrieve and process the inventory data contained in the next N fields of the file. The INPUT statement that retrieves these data must be consistent with the data structure of the file. The statement INPUT I$,Q,C would be appropriate.

Each text file contains a special **end-of-file mark** following its last field. This end-of-file mark serves two purposes:

1. While reading data from a file, the computer will detect the end-of-file mark. Any attempt to read information beyond this end-of-file mark will result in an END OF DATA error and program execution will terminate.
2. Applesoft BASIC contains the special error-detecting command

```
ONERR GOTO ln
```

Once this command is executed, any *fatal error*—that is, any error that would otherwise cause an error message and halt program execution—will cause an immediate transfer of control to the specified line number **ln.** Of particular interest here is its use in detecting any attempt to read beyond an end-of-file mark.

In the following example, we illustrate how the ONERR GOTO command can help us count how many fields are in a file that includes neither a count as its first entry (as in Example 4) nor an EOD tag as its last entry.

EXAMPLE 5. This example illustrates the ONERR GOTO command. A file DATA5 contains many fields, each including first a string value and then two numerical values. This program determines the number COUNT of fields in the file:

```
100 LET D$=CHR$(4): REM CTRL D
110 PRINT D$;"OPEN DATA5"
120 PRINT D$;"READ DATA5"
130 REM ***COUNT THE NUMBER OF FIELDS IN DATA5***
140 LET COUNT=0
150 ONERR GOTO 190
160     INPUT A$,X,Y
170     LET COUNT=COUNT+1
180 GOTO 160
190 PRINT "DATA5 CONTAINS ";COUNT;" FIELDS."
200 PRINT D$;"CLOSE DATA5"
210 END
```

Line 150 instructs the Apple to transfer control to line 190 if an error should occur. In this program, only one error will occur—namely, the attempt by line 160 to obtain input data from the file DATA5 after the end-of-file mark has been sensed.

Remark 1   Programs that use the ONERR GOTO command to detect an END OF DATA error must otherwise be free of bugs. If the command ONERR GOTO **ln** is in effect, *any* fatal error (not just END OF DATA errors) will transfer control to the same line number **ln.**

Remark 2   Programs using ONERR GOTO **ln** must be written so that **ln** specifies a programming line outside of any FOR/NEXT loop or subroutine that may be active when an error occurs. (Subroutines are described in Chapter 15.) The reason for this rule is that all active FOR/NEXT loops and subroutines are disturbed when the Apple detects a fatal error. (If a program handles an error and then encounters a NEXT statement before the corresponding FOR statement, a NEXT WITHOUT FOR error will occur.)

Here are some further points concerning the use of DOS commands:

1. File names can be specified by using string variables. For example, if F$ has the string value DATA the statement

```
PRINT CHR$(4);"OPEN ";F$
```

will output the DOS character ctrl D followed by the sequence of characters OPEN DATA. But this is exactly what the statement

```
PRINT CHR$(4);"OPEN DATA"
```

does, so the two statements are equivalent.

The following programming lines allow you to enter the name of an output file during program execution:

```
100 LET D$=CHR$(4): REM CTRL D
110 INPUT NAME$
120 PRINT D$;"OPEN ";NAME$
130 PRINT D$;"WRITE ";NAME$
```

To declare NAME$ as an input file you would write

```
130 PRINT D$;"READ ";NAME$
```

2. When you are creating a new file, be sure that you start with an empty file. If you don't, any information output to the file is written over the information already there and you may end up with a file containing the new data followed by some of the old. The easiest way to ensure that you begin with an empty file is to issue the CATALOG command and if the name you plan to use is there, delete it from the diskette or choose another name. This method cannot always be used, however. You may have to use a file as an input file, make changes in the input values, and then create a file with the same name but containing the modified data. (Modifying existing files is the subject of Section 14.3.) The following program segment ensures that the FILE1 is an empty WRITE file:

```
300 LET D$=CHR$(4): REM CTRL D
310 PRINT D$;"OPEN FILE1"
320 PRINT D$;"DELETE FILE1"
330 PRINT D$;"OPEN FILE1"
340 PRINT D$;"WRITE FILE1"
```

Line 320 deletes FILE1 from the diskette catalog so that line 330 opens an empty file. Line 310 is included to ensure that there will be a file FILE1 for line 320 to delete. An attempt to delete a nonexistent file will result in a FILE NOT FOUND error that terminates program execution.

3. More than one file can be open at the same time. For instance, the program segment

```
100 LET D$=CHR$(4): REM CTRL D
110 PRINT D$;"OPEN F1"
120 PRINT D$;"OPEN F2"
130 PRINT D$;"READ F1"
```

opens files F1 and F2 and specifies F1 as the READ file. If the Apple later encounters the statement

```
300 PRINT D$;"WRITE F2"
```

file F2 becomes the WRITE file, but only after the effect of the READ command in line 13Ø is canceled. (Any DOS cmmand cancels the effect of READ and WRITE commands. Because of this, at any instance during program execution at most one file will be active as a READ or WRITE file.) At this point, both F1 and F2 are open. Before the program ends, both should be closed.

4. Only advanced programming applications require that two files be open simultaneously. The usual practice is to open a file, use it, and then close it before opening another. If you adopt this practice, your programs will be easier to read and their action easier to follow.

5. If a file is currently open as a READ file, the question mark associated with certain INPUT statements is displayed if the screen cursor (or printer mechanism) is not positioned at the left margin of a display line. For instance, if a file containing the three lines

```
    45
    57
    34
```

is open as a READ file, the program segment

```
3Ø PRINT "SOME NUMBERS: ";
4Ø FOR N=1 TO 3
5Ø    INPUT N
6Ø    PRINT N;" ";
7Ø NEXT N
```

will produce the output

```
SOME NUMBERS: ?45 ?57 ?34
```

To avoid this cluttered output you can use the statement INPUT " ";N since no question mark is associated with INPUT statements containing string constants. If you do so you will get

```
SOME NUMBERS: 45 57 34
```

6. As indicated in note 5, INPUT statements containing string constants can be used for file input. For example, if a file containing the two fields

```
SAM SAWYER
75,8Ø
```

is open as a READ file, the program segment

```
4Ø INPUT "NAME: ";N$
5Ø PRINT N$
6Ø INPUT "SCORES: ";A,B
7Ø PRINT A;" ";B
```

will produce the output

```
NAME: SAM SAWYER
SCORES: 75 8Ø
```

14.2 Problems

1. Here is a program to create a sequential file:

```
100 LET D$=CHR$(4)
110 PRINT D$;"OPEN GRADES"
120 PRINT D$;"WRITE GRADES"
130     READ A$,N1,N2
140     PRINT A$;",";N1;",";N2
150     IF A$="X" THEN 170
160 GOTO 130
170 PRINT D$;"CLOSE GRADES"
180 DATA JOAN,80,90
190 DATA SAM,100,80
200 DATA GREG,80,40
210 DATA MARY,70,30
220 DATA MARK,50,90
230 DATA X,0,0
240 END
```

What output is produced by each program in parts (a) to (c)?

a.
```
10 LET D$=CHR$(4)
20 PRINT D$;"OPEN GRADES"
30 PRINT D$;"READ GRADES"
40     INPUT B$,A,B
50     IF A=0 THEN 80
60     IF A>B THEN PRINT B$
70 GOTO 40
80 PRINT D$;"CLOSE GRADES"
90 END
```

b.
```
10 LET D$=CHR$(4)
20 PRINT D$;"OPEN GRADES"
30 PRINT D$;"READ GRADES"
40     INPUT N$,X,Y
50     IF N$="X" THEN 95
60     LET A=(X+2*Y)/3
70     IF A>65 THEN 90
80 PRINT N$,"FAIL": GOTO 40
90 PRINT N$,"PASS": GOTO 40
95 PRINT D$;"CLOSE GRADES"
99 END
```

c.
```
10 LET D$=CHR$(4)
20 PRINT D$;"OPEN GRADES"
30 PRINT D$;"READ GRADES"
40 ONERR GOTO 80
50     INPUT P$
60     PRINT P$
70 GOTO 50
80 PRINT D$;"CLOSE GRADES"
90 END
```

In Problems 2–17, write a program to carry out each task specified.

2. A sequential file WORDS contains many fields, each containing a single English word. The last entry is the EOD tag XXX. Print all words beginning with a letter A through M and follow this list by two counts—a count of how many words are in the file and a count of how many words were printed.

3. Given a file WORDS as described in Problem 2, create two files—one containing all words beginning with a letter A through M and the other containing the remaining words. Use the names A–M and N–Z for the two files.

4. Create a file NAMES containing up to 50 names typed at the keyboard. If a name is typed a second time, an appropriate message should be printed and the name should not be stored a second time. If at any time LIST is typed, all names entered to that point are to be printed. If END is typed, program execution is to halt. (*Suggestions:* Input names into an array and create the file NAMES only after the user types END. Include a count of how many names are stored as the first entry of NAMES.)

5. Create a file of names exactly as described in Problem 4. This time, however, the user should be required to input a name for the file. (*Hint:* Refer to notes 1 and 2 at the end of Section 14.1.)

6. Create two files named ALPHA and BETA. ALPHA is to contain all numbers from 1 to 200 that are multiples of either 2, 3, 5, or 7. The rest of the numbers from 1 to 200 go in file BETA. Include a first entry in each file telling how many numbers it contains.

7. Each field but the last in file STAT contains a string followed by either one, two, or three

numbers. The last field contains the EOD tag ENDSTAT. Determine how many fields are contained in the file. Do not use the ONERR GOTO command. (*Hint:* It is not necessary to read all of the data.)

8. You are given a file STAT as described in Problem 7. You are also told that the string in each field containing numbers ends with a digit 1, 2, or 3 indicating how many numbers are in the field. You are to display the contents of STAT. Do not use the ONERR GOTO command.

9. The following table describes an investor's stock portfolio:

Name of stock	Number of shares	Last week's closing price	Current week's closing price
STERLING DRUG	800	$16.50	$16.125
DATA GENERAL	500	56.25	57.50
OWEN ILLINOIS	1200	22.50	21.50
MATTEL INC	1000	10.75	11.125
ABBOTT LAB	2000	33.75	34.75
FED NATL MTG	2500	17.75	17.25
IC GEN	250	43.125	43.625
ALO SYSTEMS	550	18.50	18.25

Write a program to create a file named STOCKS that contains precisely the given information.

10. Using the file STOCKS created in Problem 9, produce a two-column report showing each stock name and the equity based on the current week's closing price.
(Equity = number of shares × price.)

11. Using the file STOCKS created in Problem 9, prepare a four-column report showing the stock name, the equity at the close of business last week, the equity this week, and the dollar change in equity. Conclude the report with a message showing the total net gain or loss for the week.

12. Create a file named LIBEL containing the following information about employees of the Libel Insurance Company:

ID	Sex	Age	Years of service	Annual salary
2735	1	47	13	$20,200
2980	2	33	6	14,300
3865	2	41	15	23,900
4222	1	22	2	11,400
4740	1	59	7	19,200
5200	2	25	3	13,000
5803	1	33	13	21,500
7242	2	28	4	13,400
7341	1	68	30	25,500
8004	1	35	6	14,300
9327	2	21	3	9,200

Problems 13–17 refer to the file LIBEL created in Problem 12.

13. Print a five-column report with a title and appropriate column headings displaying the employee information contained in the file LIBEL. (The sex column is to contain MALE or FEMALE, not 1 or 2.)

14. Print two reports showing the employee information contained in LIBEL by sex. Each report is to be titled and is to have four appropriately labeled columns.

15. Print a two-column report showing ID numbers and annual salaries of all employees whose annual salary exceeds $15,000. In addition to printing column headings, be sure the report has an appropriate title.

16. Print a two-column report as described in Problem 15 for all employees whose annual salaries exceed the average annual salary of all Libel employees. Following the report, display the total annual salary earned by these employees. The title of the report should include the average salary of all Libel employees.

17. Print a report showing the ID numbers, years of service, and salaries of all employees who have been with the firm for more than 5 years.

14.3 Maintaining sequential files

Updating existing data files is a common programming application. In this section we give two examples illustrating this practice. The first involves making changes in a short simplified inventory file; the second involves creating and updating research files. In practice, however, data files are usually long and require complex programs to maintain them. Our objective here is simply to show that file maintenance is possible. A complete discussion of the many techniques used in file-maintenance programs is beyond the scope of an introductory text such as this one.

EXAMPLE 6. A sequential file named INVTRY contains the following data:

```
8
A10010,2000
A10011,4450
C22960,1060
D40240,2300
X99220,500
X99221,650
Y88000,1050
Y88001,400
```

The first line contains a count of how many items are included in the file. The first entry in each line other than the first denotes an item code, and the second entry gives the quantity on hand. Our task is to write a program that allows the user to update INVTRY to reflect all transactions since the last update.

Problem analysis

Let's assume that the user must specify, for each item to be changed, the item code, the number of units shipped since the last update, and the number of units received since the last update. Thus the user might come to the computer armed with a list like this:

Item code	Shipped	Received
A10010	1200	1000
A10011	1000	550
D40240	1800	2000
Y88000	300	0

A person carrying out this task by hand might proceed as follows:

a. Read an item code.
b. Search the file INVTRY for this code, and change the units-on-hand figure as required.
c. If more changes are to be made, go to step (a).
d. Have the updated copy of INVTRY typed.

This algorithm is not suitable for the task at hand, however. INVTRY is a sequential file and individual entries in a sequential file are not changed as stated in step (b). First we will input the data from INVTRY into arrays and then make the necessary changes in these arrays. After we've done this for each item requiring a change, we will make a completely new copy of the file INVTRY. Before writing an algorithm suitable for processing sequential files, let's choose variable names:

C\$ = array of item codes from INVTRY
Q = corresponding array of quantities from INVTRY
N = number of items in INVTRY
X\$ = item code to be typed
S = quantity shipped
R = quantity received

In the following algorithm we require the user to type END after all changes have been made.

Algorithm

a. Input arrays C\$ and Q from the file INVTRY.
b. Enter an item code X\$.
c. If X\$ = END, make a new copy of INVTRY and stop.
d. Find I such that C\$(I) = X\$. If X\$ is not in the list, print an appropriate message and then repeat step (b).
e. Enter the quantities S and R corresponding to item X\$.
f. Let Q(I) = Q(I) + R − S, and go to step (b).

This algorithm contains sufficient detail to be coded directly to a BASIC program.

The program

```
100 REM INVENTORY UPDATE PROGRAM
110 REM     C$ = ARRAY OF ITEM CODES FROM FILE INVTRY
120 REM     Q  = ARRAY OF QUANTITIES FROM FILE INVTRY
130 REM     N  = NUMBER OF ITEMS IN FILE INVTRY
140 REM     X$ = ITEM CODE TO BE INPUT
150 REM     S  = QUANTITY SHIPPED (OF ITEM X$)
160 REM     R  = QUANTITY RECEIVED (OF ITEM X$)
170 LET D$=CHR$(4): REM CTRL D
180 REM ***INPUT ARRAYS C$ AND Q FROM INVTRY***
190 PRINT D$;"OPEN INVTRY"
200 PRINT D$;"READ INVTRY"
210 INPUT N
220 DIM C$(N),Q(N)
230 FOR K=1 TO N
240    INPUT C$(K),Q(K)
250 NEXT K
260 PRINT D$;"CLOSE INVTRY"
270 REM ***UPDATE ARRAYS C$ AND Q***
280    PRINT
290    INPUT "ITEM CODE? ";X$
300    IF X$="END" THEN 420
310    REM ***SEARCH ARRAY C$ FOR X$***
320    FOR K=1 TO N
330       IF C$(K)=X$ THEN 370
340    NEXT K
350    PRINT X$;" IS NOT A CORRECT ITEM CODE."
360 GOTO 280
370    REM ***ENTER S AND R TO UPDATE Q(K)***
380    INPUT "UNITS SHIPPED? ";S
390    INPUT "UNITS RECEIVED? ";R
400    LET Q(K)=Q(K)+R-S
410 GOTO 280
420 REM ***MAKE A NEW COPY OF INVTRY***
430 PRINT D$;"DELETE INVTRY"
```

```
44Ø PRINT D$;"OPEN INVTRY"
45Ø PRINT D$;"WRITE INVTRY"
46Ø PRINT N
47Ø FOR K=1 TO N
48Ø     PRINT C$(K);",";Q(K)
49Ø NEXT K
5ØØ PRINT D$;"CLOSE INVTRY"
51Ø PRINT "INVTRY IS UPDATED."
52Ø END
RUN

ITEM CODE? A1ØØ1Ø
UNITS SHIPPED? 12ØØ
UNITS RECEIVED? 1ØØØ

ITEM CODE? A1ØØ11
UNITS SHIPPED? 1ØØØ
UNITS RECEIVED? 55Ø

ITEM CODE? D4Ø42Ø
D4Ø42Ø IS NOT A CORRECT ITEM CODE.

ITEM CODE? D4Ø24Ø
UNITS SHIPPED? 18ØØ
UNITS RECEIVED? 2ØØØ

ITEM CODE? Y88ØØØ
UNITS SHIPPED? 3ØØ
UNITS RECEIVED? Ø

ITEM CODE? END
INVTRY IS UPDATED.
```

Remark 1

The purpose of the CLOSE command in line 26Ø is to cancel the effect of the READ command (line 2ØØ) so that the next INPUT statement (line 29Ø) will obtain a value from the keyboard and not the file.

Remark 2

The last output line INVTRY IS UPDATED is intended to reassure us that the file has been correctly updated. To see that this is so, we could have run the program with MON O in effect or we could use a short program like this one:

```
1ØØ REM ***DISPLAY CONTENTS OF INVTRY***
11Ø LET D$=CHR$(4): REM CTRL D
12Ø PRINT D$;"OPEN INVTRY"
13Ø PRINT D$;"READ INVTRY"
14Ø PRINT "ITEM CODE","UNITS ON HAND"
15Ø INPUT N
16Ø FOR K=1 TO N
17Ø     INPUT X$,Q
18Ø     PRINT X$,Q
19Ø NEXT K
2ØØ PRINT D$;"CLOSE INVTRY"
21Ø END
RUN
```

ITEM CODE	UNITS ON HAND
A1ØØ1Ø	18ØØ
A1ØØ11	4ØØØ
C2296Ø	1Ø6Ø
D4Ø24Ø	25ØØ
X9922Ø	5ØØ
X99221	65Ø
Y88ØØØ	75Ø
Y88ØØ1	4ØØ

In the next example we modify an existing sequential file by adding data to the end of it. Changing a sequential file in this way does not require making a completely new copy of the file—if you open a file as a READ file, read all its data so that the file is positioned at its end, and then declare the file as a WRITE file, subsequent output will be stored at the end of the file. You don't have to go to all this trouble, however. The DOS command APPEND opens an existing sequential file, but positions it at the end. Thus, to add data at the end of file F1, you can use the two statements

```
1ØØ PRINT CHR$(4);"APPEND F1"
11Ø PRINT CHR$(4);"WRITE F1"
```

Subsequent output will be written at the end of the file. F1 *must* be an existing file. Any attempt to open a new file with APPEND will result in a fatal FILE NOT FOUND error.

EXAMPLE 7. A researcher has compiled a large collection of measurements and wishes to store this information in such a way that it can be processed by many different computer programs. We are told that the data are organized in groups; each group consists of a string identifying the group and then a list of measurements. The length of the list depends on the group, but we are told that no list will contain more than 100 measurements. Let's write a program to assist the researcher in this task.

Problem analysis

Since the data are to be processed by more than one program, we should use files rather than DATA statements. Since we are told that the entire collection of measurements is very large, we cannot expect all data to be typed during a single session at the keyboard. Each group contains no more than 100 measurements, however, so we can require that only complete groups be entered at any input session. Here is one way to input and store on file the data for any group of measurements:

1. Input the group name.
2. Input all measurements for the current group terminating the list with the end-of-group indicator 9999. Store all input values, including 9999, in an array.
3. Write the group name and the array of numbers on the output file.

Since the data collection is very large, more than one file may be needed. To allow for this we will use the variable F$ to denote the file name, and each time the program is run the user will type the name of the file to be used. This feature should please the researcher since it will allow further organization of the compiled data—for instance, related groups can be stored in the same file. Adding this feature poses a slight problem. If F$ is an existing file in which additional data are to be stored, it should be opened with the APPEND command.

However, if F$ denotes a new file to be created, it must be opened with the OPEN command—remember, APPEND can be used only to open files that alredy exist on a diskette.

To resolve this difficulty, we'll use an OPEN command to open file F$ whether it is a new file name or an existing one. Then when we are ready to transmit data to F$ (step 3) we'll use an APPEND command to open it again so that the data will be written at the end of the file. This is appropriate whether the file is a new one or an old one.

With this detail out of the way, and in light of the three-step process described for handling the input data for a group, writing an algorithm for the task at hand is not difficult. To ensure a concise algorithm that is easily coded to a BASIC program, let's choose variable names as follows:

F$ = name of output file
GP$ = name of current group
MEAS = array containing measurements for group GP$ (its last value will be 9999)

Algorithm

a. Input F$ and open a file with the name F$.
b. Input GP$.
c. Stop if GP$ = "END".
d. Input MEAS(N) for N = 1, 2, . . . , until 9999 is input.
e. Open F$ as a WRITE file (use APPEND and WRITE commands).
f. Output GP$ and the array MEAS (including 9999) to the file F$.
g. Go to step (b).

Note that step (c) allows the person doing the typing to end an input session by typing END, but only when the computer is ready to accept data for a new group. *Remember:* It was agreed that only complete groups were to be entered at an input session.

There is one more detail to take care of. Note that steps (b) and (d) require keyboard input. Because of this, the WRITE command must be canceled before control passes back to step (b)—remember the rule stated in Section 14.1: *Never allow a* WRITE *command to be in effect while data are being input at the keyboard.* The following modification of step (g) shows one way to cancel the WRITE command.

g. Close F$ and go to step (b).

The program

```
100 LET D$=CHR$(4): REM CTRL D
110 INPUT "ENTER FILE NAME: ";F$
120 PRINT D$;"OPEN ";F$
130 DIM MEAS(101)
140 REM *****DATA ENTRY*****
150     PRINT
160     INPUT "GROUP NAME? TYPE END WHEN DONE: ";GP$
170     IF GP$="END" THEN END
180     PRINT "ENTER MEASUREMENTS, ONE PER LINE."
190     PRINT "TYPE 9999 WHEN DONE."
200     LET N=0: REM COUNT OF NUMBERS IN LIST
210         LET N=N+1
220         INPUT MEAS(N)
230     IF MEAS(N)<>9999 AND N<=100 THEN 210
240     IF MEAS(N)=9999 THEN 270
250     PRINT "TOO MANY MEASUREMENTS--SEE PROGRAMMER."
260     END
270     REM ****APPEND DATA TO FILE****
280     PRINT D$;"APPEND ";F$
290     PRINT D$;"WRITE ";F$
300     PRINT GP$
310     FOR K=1 TO N
320         PRINT MEAS(K)
330     NEXT K
340     PRINT D$;"CLOSE ";F$
350 GOTO 150
RUN

ENTER FILE NAME: NORTHEAST

GROUP NAME? TYPE END WHEN DONE: BERKSHIRES
ENTER MEASUREMENTS, ONE PER LINE.
TYPE 9999 WHEN DONE.
?12.43
?19.65
?9999

GROUP NAME? TYPE END WHEN DONE: CAPE COD
ENTER MEASUREMENTS, ONE PER LINE.
TYPE 9999 WHEN DONE.
?31.5
?30.82
?28.06
?9999

GROUP NAME? TYPE END WHEN DONE: END
```

Remark 1

Files created by using this program will not contain a count of how many groups are included nor will they contain an EOD tag at the end of the file. To determine what groups are included and how many there are, you can use the ONERR GOTO command described in Section 14.1 or you can write a short program to display and count the group names as they are encountered and simply accept the END OF DATA error. Because of the end-of-group indicator's 9999 output to the file, you will know when the next field contains a group name instead of a number.

Remark 2 After all data compiled by the researcher have been stored, a new copy of each file should be made—one that contains a count of how many groups are included.

14.4 Problems

Problems 1–4 refer to the file EMPLOY maintained by the Hollis Investment Corporation. The contents of EMPLOY are as follows:

Name	*Age*	*Years of service*	*Monthly salary*
Murray George	53	21	$2100
Ritchie Albert	41	13	1850
Galvin Fred	62	35	2475
Cummings Barbara	37	16	1675
Gieseler Norma	41	20	2200
Hughes Bette	52	18	2050
Meland Ralph	29	5	1550
Tibeau Frances	30	7	1340

1. Include these data in DATA lines for a program to create the file EMPLOY. Conclude your program with a segment that displays the contents of the file.
2. Using the file EMPLOY as an input file, create a file EMPLOY2 that contains precisely the information in EMPLOY but with the names in alphabetical order. After EMPLOY2 has been created, its contents should be displayed.
3. A 5% across-the-board salary increase has been negotiated for all Hollis employees. Update the file EMPLOY to reflect this increase.
4. Delete Fred Galvin from the file EMPLOY and add the following:

```
BING MELINDA  23  Ø  12ØØ
DEREK SUSAN   24  Ø  18ØØ
```

Problems 5–7 refer to a product survey. A manufacturing company sends a package consisting of eight new products to ten families and asks them to rate each product on the following scale:

0 = poor   1 = fair   2 = good   3 = very good   4 = excellent

Here are the results in tabular form:

		Family number									
		1	2	3	4	5	6	7	8	9	10
	1	0	1	1	2	1	2	2	1	0	1
	2	2	3	3	0	3	2	2	3	4	1
	3	1	3	4	4	4	1	4	2	3	2
	4	3	4	2	4	3	1	3	4	2	4
Product number	5	0	1	3	2	2	2	1	3	0	1
	6	4	4	4	3	2	1	4	4	1	1
	7	1	3	1	3	2	4	1	4	3	4
	8	2	2	3	4	2	2	3	4	2	3

5. Create a file RATE containing the information in this table. Then use the file to print a two-column report showing the product numbers and the average rating for each product.
6. Use the file RATE to print a two-column report. The first column is to give the product numbers receiving at least six ratings of 3 or better. The second column is to give the number of these ratings obtained.
7. An error in the transcription of the numbers in the survey is discovered. The correct results for families 1 and 7 are as follows:

Family 1	3	2	4	2	2	4	1	3
Family 7	2	3	4	4	2	4	3	2

Update the file RATE to include these corrected values.

Problems 8–11 refer to the following files maintained by the Sevard Company:

	File SST				File WEEKLY	
Employee ID	Year-to-date income	Hourly rate			Employee ID	This week's hours
24168	$12,442.40	$ 7.35			24168	40
13725	17,250.13	11.41			13725	36
34104	10,425.00	6.50			34104	32
28636	11,474.25	6.75			28636	40
35777	15,450.35	10.45			35777	40
15742	14,452.00	10.05			15742	30

8. Write a program to create files SST and WEEKLY.

9. A Social Security tax deduction of 6.7% is taken on the first $35,700 earned by an employee. Once this amount is reached, no further deduction is made. Using the files SST and WEEKLY, produce a report giving the ID number, the current week's gross pay, and this week's Social Security deduction for each employee.

10. Modify the program written for Problem 9 to update the year-to-date income in the file SST.

11. Using the files SST and WEEKLY, print a list of the ID numbers of all employees who have satisfied the Social Security tax requirement for the current year. With each ID number printed, give the year-to-date income figure.

In Problems 12–15, write programs as specified.

12. Write a program to allow a user to create a file containing whatever words are typed at the keyboard or to add new words to an existing file. Each file created or modified by your program must contain as its first entry a count of how many words are included. Use the following algorithm:
   a. Input a file name and specify whether it is an old file or a new one.
   b. If an old file is specified, store its contents in an array A$. (Arrange things so that no file will contain more than 200 words.)
   c. At this point the user is allowed to issue any of the following commands:

   ADD—to add one or more words. If a word is already in array A$, it should be ignored.
   LIST—to obtain a listing of all words in array A$.
   DELETE—to delete one or more words.
   END—to update the file named in step (a) and halt.

   After each command other than END, step (c) is repeated.

13. Write a program as described in Problem 12 with the following changes:
   i. Instead of storing words, any *strings* are to be stored. (Avoid commas in strings.)
   ii. Change the commands in step (c) of the algorithm to the following:

   ADD—to add one or more strings. (You need not check to see if a string was previously entered.)
   LIST— to obtain a listing of all strings contained in A$. In this listing, each string is to be preceded by the subscript indicating its position in the array.
   CHANGE—to change a string by first typing the number of the string (as given by the LIST command). If the empty string is specified (a simple RETURN will do this), the array entry should be deleted by moving all subsequent strings up one position in the array.
   END—to update the file named in step (a) of the algorithm and halt.

14. Modify the program of Problem 13 by allowing the user to specify the following additional command in step (c) of the algorithm:

   COPY—to obtain a listing of all strings from string number M to string number N. String numbers are not to be printed as with the LIST command. (After the user types COPY, the computer should request values for M and N.)

15. A file GRADE contains the following information:

2		
Edwards	75	93
Lebak	91	65
Myers	41	83
Nolan	89	51
Post	78	63
Sovenson	56	87
Block	82	82

The two numbers following each name represent grades, and the first value—the number 2—tells how many grades have been recorded on the file for each student. Write a program to allow the user to enter any of the following commands:

LIST— to obtain a printout of the current contents of the file GRADE.
AVERAGE—to obtain a listing of student names and averages.
ADD—to add an additional grade for each student. (Each student's name should be printed to allow the user to enter the next grade.)
DONE—to terminate the run. When this command is issued, an updated file GRADE should be created.

14.5 Random-access files

Random-access and sequential-access files are alike in many ways:

1. Both are text files—that is, data are stored as sequences of individual characters.
2. The DOS commands OPEN, READ, WRITE, and CLOSE are used with both types of files, but in slightly different forms.
3. INPUT and PRINT statements are used for I/O operations with both types of files, and in much the same way.

There are differences between them, however:

1. Sequential files consist entirely of *fields* terminated by a RETURN character, whereas random-access files consist of equal-length subdivisions called **records.** These records are numbered in sequence starting from zero—that is, there is a record 0, a record 1, a record 2, and so on.
2. The fields in a sequential file are accessed in order, beginning with the first, whereas records are accessed directly by specifying the record number (much as array entries are accessed by specifying subscripts).
3. In a sequential file, data are added only at the end. In a random-access file, data can be stored in any record and later changed without affecting the rest of the file.
4. APPEND is used only with sequential files.

We'll begin our discussion of random-access files with a description of the DOS commands used with them. First, the OPEN command must specify the length of each record in the file. The statement

```
1ØØ PRINT CHR$(4);"OPEN F1, L15Ø"
```

specifies that file F1 is to consist of equal-length records of length 150. This means that each record can store up to 150 characters. If you change L150 to L50, each record can store up to 50 characters.

When used with random-access files, the WRITE command must specify the name of the output file and the number of the output record. The specifier R5 in the statement

```
11Ø PRINT CHR$(4);"WRITE F1, R5"
```

specifies record 5 as the output record. That is, subsequent PRINT statements will transmit the output to record 5 of file F1.

EXAMPLE 8. Here is a program to store data in records 1 and 5 of file RF:

```
100 LET D$=CHR$(4): REM CTRL D
110 PRINT D$;"OPEN RF,L50"
120 PRINT D$;"WRITE RF,R1"
130 PRINT "NICKLAUS"
140 PRINT 206
150 PRINT D$;"WRITE RF,R5"
160 PRINT "MILLER"
170 PRINT 208
180 PRINT D$;"CLOSE RF"
190 END
```

Assuming that a file named RF is not in the diskette catalog, the action of this program is as follows.

Line 110 opens a random-access file RF with records of length 50. Since RF is not in the disk catalog, it is automatically placed there.

Line 120 declares RF as the WRITE file and specifies record 1 as the output record.

Lines 130 and 140 output the values NICKLAUS and 206 to record 1. Since these two PRINT statements have no terminating comma or semicolon, RETURN characters are also output to record 1. At this point, record 1 can be visualized as follows (remember that random-access files are *text* files):

(*record 1*)
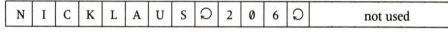

| ← positions 14–50 → |

Similarly, line 150 specifies record 5 as the output record and lines 160 and 170 give

(*record 5*)
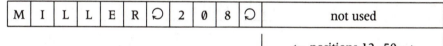

| ← positions 12–50 → |

Line 180 properly closes file RF. The form of the CLOSE command is exactly the same for both random-access files and sequential files.

Remark   We transmitted data to records 1 and 5, skipping records 2, 3, and 4, only to show that any record can be specified as the output record. Most often data are transmitted to successive records of a file.

To retrieve information from a random-access file, the record from which input data are to be obtained must be specified in a READ command. The statement

```
PRINT CHR$(4);"READ RF, R5"
```

specifies that subsequent INPUT statements are to obtain values from record 5 of file RF.

EXAMPLE 9. Here is a program to display the information previously stored in records 1 and 5 of file RF:

```
100 LET D$=CHR$(4): REM CTRL D
110 PRINT D$;"OPEN RF,L50"
120 PRINT D$;"READ RF,R5"
130 INPUT A$
140 INPUT S
150 PRINT A$,S
160 PRINT D$;"READ RF,R1"
170 INPUT A$
180 INPUT S
190 PRINT A$,S
200 PRINT D$;"CLOSE RF"
210 END
RUN

MILLER          208
NICKLAUS        206
```

Remark 1

This program illustrates that records can be accessed in any order. The program inputs values from record 5 first and then from record 1.

Remark 2

Since the program of Example 8 that created file RF stored data only in records 1 and 5, this program reads data only from those records. Any attempt to obtain data from an empty record, like any attempt to obtain data from an empty sequential file, will result in an END OF DATA error.

Remark 3

In Example 8 we used the graphic representation

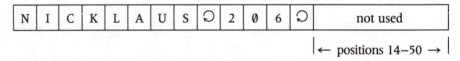

|←— positions 14–50 —→|

to display the contents of record 1. As with sequential files, we say that this record contains two distinct *lines* (or *fields*):

```
NICKLAUS
206
```

Also, as with sequential files, INPUT statements obtain values from the fields of a record in exactly the same way that ordinary INPUT statements obtain values from lines typed at the keyboard. Thus lines 130 and 140 of the program can be replaced by 130 INPUT A$,S. A similar statement applies to lines 170 and 180.

In the preceding examples we used R1 and R5 in READ and WRITE commands to specify that records 1 and 5 were to be used. DOS allows you to specify record numbers by using variables or other numerical expressions, rather than just constants. If N = 17, for example, the statement

```
PRINT CHR$(4);"WRITE FILE1, R";N
```

will output the ctrl D character followed by the characters WRITE FILE1, R17. But this is exactly what the statement

```
PRINT CHR$(4);"WRITE FILE1, R17"
```

does, so the two statements are equivalent.

EXAMPLE 10. Here is a program to write the information contained in DATA lines on a random-access file:

```
100 LET D$=CHR$(4): REM CTRL D
110 PRINT D$;"OPEN STAT-60,L60"
120 LET N=0
130    READ A$,X,Y
140    IF A$="XXX" THEN 190
150    LET N=N+1
160    PRINT D$;"WRITE STAT-60,R";N
170    PRINT A$;",";X;",";Y
180 GOTO 130
190 PRINT D$;"WRITE STAT-60,R0"
200 PRINT N
210 PRINT D$;"CLOSE STAT-60"
500 DATA PINS,1200,1.49
510 DATA NEEDLES,530,2.35
520 DATA BOBBINS,255,2.73
530 DATA THREAD,1550,.84
540 DATA XXX,0,0
999 END
```

Here is a run of this program with MON O,C in effect:

```
]MON O,C
]RUN
OPEN STAT-60,L60
WRITE STAT-60,R1
PINS,1200,1.49
WRITE STAT-60,R2
NEEDLES,530,2.35
WRITE STAT-60,R3
BOBBINS,255,2.73
WRITE STAT-60,R4
THREAD,1550,.84
WRITE STAT-60,R0
4
CLOSE STAT-60
```

All displayed values are monitored information. Without MON O,C in effect, nothing will be displayed.

Lines 160 and 170 are executed four times with the successive N values 1, 2, 3, and 4. On each of these four passes, line 160 specifies record N as the output record and line 170 outputs three values read from DATA lines to this record. As shown in the monitored output, these values are output as one field containing the three values separated by commas.

When the EOD tag XXX is encountered, control passes to line 190 and the count N of how many records were used is output to record 0. Using record 0 of a random-access file to store information about the file is a common programming practice.

Remark

As noted, a single field containing three values is output to records 1 through 4. To use this file as an input file, you must use INPUT statements consistent with this data structure. The statement INPUT ITEM$,QTY,PRICE would be correct.

EXAMPLE 11. Here is a program to add new data typed at the keyboard to the file STAT-60. In this program we use the usual method of handling input data that are to be output to a file. Specifically the input data are stored in arrays and not output to disk until all keyboard entries have been made.

```
100 LET D$=CHR$(4): REM CTRL D
110 DIM A$(30),X(30),Y(30)
120 PRINT "TYPE XXX FOR ITEM NAME WHEN DONE."
125 PRINT "MAKE AT MOST 29 ENTRIES."
130 FOR N=1 TO 30
140     PRINT
150     INPUT "ITEM NAME: ";A$(N)
160     IF A$(N)="XXX" THEN 200
170     INPUT "QUANTITY: ";X(N)
180     INPUT "COST PER UNIT: ";Y(N)
190 NEXT N
195 PRINT "ONLY 29 ENTRIES ALLOWED.":END
200 LET N=N-1: REM NUMBER OF NEW ENTRIES
210 PRINT D$;"OPEN STAT-60,L60"
220 PRINT D$;"READ STAT-60,R0"
230 INPUT COUNT: REM LARGEST RECORD NUMBER USED
240 PRINT
250 FOR K=1 TO N
260     PRINT D$;"WRITE STAT-60,R";COUNT+K
270     PRINT A$(K);",";X(K);",";Y(K)
280 NEXT K
290 PRINT D$;"WRITE STAT-60,R0"
300 PRINT COUNT+N
310 PRINT D$;"CLOSE STAT-60"
320 END
RUN

TYPE XXX FOR ITEM NAME WHEN DONE.
MAKE AT MOST 29 ENTRIES.

ITEM NAME: SPINDLES
QUANTITY: 2200
COST PER UNIT: 2.23

ITEM NAME: SCISSORS
QUANTITY: 1600
COST PER UNIT: 3.89

ITEM NAME: XXX
```

Remark 1

Besides adding new data to the file STAT-60, this program changes the value previously stored in record 0. (Line 300 does this.) As mentioned at the outset of this section, any record in a random-access file can be changed—but you must not cause more data to be output to a record than allowed by the record length for the file.

Remark 2

The record length specified for a file in an OPEN statement must be the same each time the file is used. Otherwise you may introduce errors that will halt program execution; in any case you will obtain incorrect results. Including the record length of a random-access file as part of its name (as in STAT-60) is a good way to document this information.

Random-access files are preferred to sequential-access files for many programming applications. Following are two file characteristics that suggest the use of random-access files. You will note that these characteristics concern how a file is to be used rather than how the data are organized.

1. Frequent changes must be made to selected data stored on the file. (This may involve periodic updating of selected items.)
2. Speedy access to selected data is required.

The following example illustrates a typical application of random-access files. The programming exercises in the next problem set indicate other situations for which random-access files can be used to advantage.

EXAMPLE 12. Let's write a program to allow a user to create and modify a mailing list file.

Problem analysis

To process a mailing list effectively a program must be able to carry out three essential steps: add new entries to the list, delete entries from the list, and produce a copy of all entries in the list. To allow a user to specify these three steps or to stop the processing, we'll write our program so the following commands can be entered.

ADD	to add new names to the list.
DEL	to delete a list entry.
LIST	to obtain a listing of all entries.
END	to stop the program.

It is not difficult to write an algorithm for this task if we omit details. The following algorithm makes use of a file named MAIL.

Algorithm

a. Initialize necessary variables. (Although we have yet to consider variables, it is a safe assumption that this step will be needed. If it is not, no harm is done.)
b. Enter one of the commands ADD, DEL, LIST, or END.
c. Carry out the command entered in step (b). After ADD, LIST, or DEL is carried out, go to step (b). (Any changes to the mailing list are to be made directly on the file MAIL.)

The specification in step (c) that changes are to be made directly on the file MAIL requires us to open MAIL as a random-access file. Thus we must specify the record length. If we agree to store the following five fields in each record, a record length of 100 should suffice.

Field 1   *name*
Field 2   *street address*
Field 3   *city or town*
Field 4   *state*
Field 5   *zip code*

By using separate fields for *city or town* and *state* we avoid the comma that occurs between the city or town and the state in an address. (Remember, a comma appearing on a file serves only to separate values.) Let's consider step (c) in greater detail. We must show how the computer is to respond to each of the commands ADD, DEL, LIST, and END. To do this, we should be more specific about how information will be stored on the file. We have already agreed that a single record will be used for each mailing list entry. We'll use records 1, 2, 3, and so on for these entries. In record 0 we'll keep two numbers, a count of how many addresses are in the list and the highest record number in use. As explained below, these two numbers will not always be the same.

With these file details out of the way, we can now describe how the commands ADD, DEL, LIST, and END can be carried out.

ADD   After typing ADD, the user will type five strings: *name, street address, city or town, state,* and *zip code.* This information will be written on a new record and the two numbers showing the number of list entries and the highest record number in use will be increased by 1. The user will then make another entry. This process of data entry will be repeated until the user types DONE.

Let's agree to use the following variables for this step.

A\$(1), A\$(2), . . . , A\$(5) = five entries for an address
NL = number of entries in mailing list
NR = highest record number in use

In addition to these variables, let's use an array to store five input prompts for the five values A\$(1), A\$(2), . . . , A\$(5).

P\$(1) = "NAME? "
P\$(2) = "STREET ADDRESS? "
P\$(3) = "CITY OR TOWN? "
P\$(4) = "STATE? "
P\$(5) = "ZIP CODE? "

Note that the variables NL and NR and the array P\$ must be assigned initial values. The values for P\$ are as shown. The initial values for NL and NR will be zero if the file MAIL is being created, but they must be read from record 0 if MAIL is an existing file to be modified.

DEL   After typing DEL, the user will type the record number of the mailing list entry to be deleted. (Record numbers will be displayed when the user enters the LIST command.) The computer will "delete" this record by storing the word DELETED as its first entry and by subtracting 1 from NL. The user will then enter another record number. This process of record deletion will continue until the user types Ø.

LIST   After the user types LIST, the computer will print the entire mailing list with each entry preceded by its record number. The contents of records containing the word DELETED will not be printed.

END   When this command is typed, we must close file MAIL and stop the program. Before doing this, however, we will write the values of NL and NR in record Ø. Doing this means that record Ø does not have to be changed each time a new name is added or an old name is deleted.

Now that we know how each step in the algorithm can be carried out, writing a BASIC program is not difficult. A careful review of this problem analysis shows that two additional variables are needed: one to store commands typed by the user (we'll use C$) and one to store the number of a record to be deleted (we'll use D). Variable names are summarized in lines 120 to 170 of the program.

The program

```
100 REM ***** MAILING LIST PROGRAM *****
110 REM
120 REM   A$ = ARRAY TO STORE AN ADDRESS
130 REM   P$ = ARRAY OF PROMPTS FOR ENTRIES OF A$
140 REM   C$ = A COMMAND TYPED BY THE USER
150 REM   NL = NUMBER OF NAMES IN MAILING LIST
160 REM   NR = HIGHEST RECORD NUMBER IN USE
170 REM    D = NUMBER OF A RECORD TO BE DELETED
180 REM
190 REM ***** INITIALIZE NL, NR, AND P$ *****
200 LET D$ = CHR$(4) : REM CTRL D
210 INPUT "IS THIS A NEW FILE (YES OR NO)? "; C$
220 IF C$ = "YES" THEN NL = Ø : NR = Ø : GOTO 270
230 PRINT D$;"OPEN MAIL, L100"
240 PRINT D$;"READ MAIL, RØ"
250 INPUT NL, NR
260 PRINT D$;"CLOSE MAIL"
270 LET P$(1) = "NAME? "
280 LET P$(2) = "STREET ADDRESS? "
290 LET P$(3) = "CITY OR TOWN? "
300 LET P$(4) = "STATE? "
310 LET P$(5) = "ZIP CODE? "
320 REM
330 REM ***** USER COMMAND SECTION *****
340 PRINT : INPUT "COMMAND? "; C$
350 IF C$ = "ADD" THEN 430
360 IF C$ = "DEL" THEN 600
370 IF C$ = "LIST" THEN 750
380 IF C$ = "END" THEN 930
390 PRINT "COMMANDS ALLOWED ARE:"
400 PRINT "ADD  DEL  LIST  END"
410 GOTO 340
420 REM
430 REM ***** DATA ENTRY SECTION *****
440 PRINT "TYPE DONE WHEN ALL ENTRIES HAVE"
450 PRINT "BEEN MADE. USE NO COMMAS."
460 PRINT
```

```
47Ø FOR I=1 TO 5
48Ø    INPUT P$(I); A$(I)
49Ø    IF A$(I) = "DONE" THEN 34Ø
5ØØ NEXT I
51Ø LET NL = NL+1 : NR = NR+1
52Ø PRINT D$;"OPEN MAIL, L1ØØ"
53Ø PRINT D$;"WRITE MAIL, R"; NR
54Ø FOR I=1 TO 5
55Ø    PRINT A$(I)
56Ø NEXT I
57Ø PRINT D$;"CLOSE MAIL"
58Ø GOTO 46Ø
59Ø REM
6ØØ REM ***** DELETE SECTION *****
61Ø PRINT "TYPE NUMBER OF ENTRY TO BE DELETED."
62Ø INPUT "TYPE Ø WHEN DONE: "; D
63Ø IF D<Ø OR D>NR THEN 61Ø
64Ø IF D=Ø THEN 34Ø
65Ø PRINT D$;"OPEN MAIL, L1ØØ"
66Ø PRINT D$;"READ MAIL, R";D
67Ø INPUT A$(1)
68Ø IF A$(1) = "DELETED" THEN 72Ø
69Ø PRINT D$;"WRITE MAIL, R";D
7ØØ PRINT "DELETED"
71Ø LET NL = NL - 1
72Ø PRINT D$;"CLOSE MAIL"
73Ø PRINT : GOTO 61Ø
74Ø REM
75Ø REM ***** LIST SECTION *****
76Ø PRINT D$;"OPEN MAIL, L1ØØ"
77Ø PRINT
78Ø FOR I = 1 TO NR
79Ø    PRINT D$;"READ MAIL, R"; I
8ØØ    INPUT A$(1)
81Ø    IF A$(1) = "DELETED" THEN 89Ø
82Ø    FOR J = 2 TO 5
83Ø       INPUT A$(J)
84Ø    NEXT J
85Ø    PRINT : PRINT I
86Ø    PRINT A$(1)
87Ø    PRINT A$(2)
88Ø    PRINT A$(3);",";A$(4);",";A$(5)
89Ø NEXT I
9ØØ PRINT D$;"CLOSE MAIL"
91Ø GOTO 34Ø
92Ø REM
93Ø REM ***** END SECTION *****
94Ø PRINT D$;"OPEN MAIL, L1ØØ"
95Ø PRINT D$;"WRITE MAIL, RØ"
96Ø PRINT NL : PRINT NR
97Ø PRINT D$;"CLOSE MAIL"
98Ø END
```

Although this program is longer than the programs considered to this point, its action is not hard to follow. The REM statements in lines 190 and 330 correspond to steps (a) and (b) of the algorithm developed in the problem analysis, and the individual tasks needed to carry out step (c) are identified by the REM statements in lines 430, 600, 750, and 930.

A careful reading of this program will show that certain statements are included that are not specified in the algorithm. In each case, however, the added statements serve only to validate data being processed. Specifically:

1. Lines 390 to 410 ensure that the user types only admissible commands.
2. Line 630 ensures that the user does not type an inadmissible record number.
3. Lines 660 to 680 ensure that the number NL of entries will not be decreased by 1 if the user inadvertently tries to delete an entry more than once.

14.6 Problems

1. Write a program to create a random-access file INVTRY containing the following information.

Item code	Units on hand	Warehouse number
A2000	7	39
A3500	25	39
C2255	0	39
D4296	100	46
E7250	19	46
P2243	5	39

The information in this table is to be stored in records 1 through 6 and record 0 is to contain 6, the highest record number in use.

2. Write a program to allow a user to modify the file INVTRY created in Problem 1. The user should be able to issue the following commands:

ADD—to add new items to the file.

SORT—to make a new copy of file INVTRY with the item codes ordered according to the Apple's ordering of strings. (To do this, read all data into arrays, sort the arrays, and then copy this information back onto the file.)

END—to stop the program.

3. Write a program to allow a person to use the file INVTRY in the following ways.

   a. If the user types S (for search) the computer is to request a single item code. The user would then type an item code to obtain the units on hand amount and the warehouse number for that item.

   b. If the user types C (for change) the computer should request an item code and a number. The units on hand figure for the specified item is to be decreased by this number.

   c. If the user types E (for end) the program is to stop.

   Be sure to guard against erroneous values typed by the user. (*Suggestion:* Use a binary search to find the record containing the specified item. This is why the item codes shown in Problem 1 are ordered, and why the SORT command is included in Problem 2.)

4. Modify the mailing list program shown in Example 12 to allow a user to specify the file name.

Problems 5 and 6 refer to file MAIL created by the program in Example 12. You will recall that record 0 contains two numbers: the number of addresses stored in the file and the highest record number in use. Each of the other records contains five values as follows:

   Field 1   name
   Field 2   street address
   Field 3   city or town
   Field 4   state
   Field 5   zip code

or else the single value DELETED.

5. Write a program to get rid of all records containing DELETED.
6. Write a program to produce a listing of the entire mailing list with zip codes appearing in ascending order.

14.7 Review true-or-false quiz

1. The only way to delete file F from a diskette is to type the immediate mode command DELETE F.   T   F
2. If a program uses a file as an input file, then the program cannot also use this file as an output file.   T   F
3. Input data for a program cannot be read from a file and also from DATA lines. These two methods of supplying input data are incompatible.   T   F
4. A number stored on a sequential access file is stored as a sequence of codes, with each code representing a single character.   T   F
5. Sequential files and random-access files are called text files.   T   F
6. Certain files are called random-access files because information stored on the files is accessed by randomly searching parts of the file until the desired data are found.   T   F
7. The DOS commands OPEN, READ, WRITE, CLOSE, and APPEND are used with both sequential and random-access files.   T   F
8. The ONERR GOTO command obviates the need to use an EOD tag as the last entry or a count as the first entry in a data file.   T   F

15

□ □ □ □ □ □ □ □ □ □ □ □ □ □

Subroutines

In Chapter 11 you saw that when a function is needed in a program, it is sufficient to define the function once in a DEF statement. The function may then be referenced as many times as necessary. Often you'll find that you need the same *sequence* of statements in several places in a program. With BASIC you can include this sequence of statements just once in a program, even though it is to be used in several different places. Such a sequence of statements is called a **subroutine.** This chapter describes the GOSUB and RETURN statements, which allow you to write and use BASIC subroutines.

15.1 The GOSUB and RETURN statements

The GOSUB statement is used to transfer control to a subroutine, and the RETURN statement is used to transfer control back from the subroutine. A BASIC subroutine is any sequence of BASIC programming lines to carry out a specific task. It *must* contain at least one RETURN statement. Here is a subroutine to print a row of dashes.

```
5ØØ REM ***SUBROUTINE TO PRINT 3Ø DASHES***
51Ø FOR I=1 TO 3Ø
52Ø    PRINT "-";
53Ø NEXT I
54Ø PRINT
55Ø RETURN
```

Program control is transferred to this subroutine each time the statement GOSUB 5ØØ is encountered during program execution. For example, in a program containing this subroutine, the three lines

```
200 GOSUB 500
210 PRINT "TODAY'S STARTING LINEUP"
220 GOSUB 500
```

will cause the output

```
-----------------------------------
TODAY'S STARTING LINEUP
-----------------------------------
```

Line 200 transfers control to line 500 (the subroutine) and a row of dashes is output. The RETURN statement in line 550 then transfers control back to line 210, the first line following the GOSUB statement just used. When line 220 is encountered, control again passes to the subroutine and another row of dashes is output. This time the RETURN statement transfers control back to the programming line following 220.

EXAMPLE 1. Here is a program to print the average of any two input values and also the average of their squares:

```
100 INPUT "TYPE TWO NUMBERS: ";A,B
110 GOSUB 300
120 LET A=A*A
130 LET B=B*B
140 PRINT "SQUARES ARE: ";A;"   ";B
150 GOSUB 300
160 END
300 REM ***SUBROUTINE TO PRINT THE AVERAGE OF A AND B***
310 LET M=(A+B)/2
320 PRINT "THEIR AVERAGE IS ";M
330 RETURN
RUN

ENTER TWO NUMBERS: 3,4
THEIR AVERAGE IS 3.5
SQUARES ARE: 9   16
THEIR AVERAGE IS 12.5
```

The subroutine consists of lines 300 to 330. Line 110 transfers control to line 300, and 3.5, the average of 3 and 4, is printed. The RETURN statement then transfers control back to line 120, the line following the GOSUB statement just used. Lines 120 and 130 assign the squares (9 and 16) to A and B, and line 140 prints these squares. When line 150 is encountered, a second transfer is made to the subroutine and 12.5, the average of 9 and 16, is printed. This time the RETURN statement transfers control back to line 160, which in this program terminates execution.

Remark 1   The END statement (line 160) ensures that the subroutine is entered only under the control of a GOSUB statement.

Remark 2   When the GOSUB statement in line 110 or line 150 is executed, we say that the subroutine has been *called*.

Remark 3   The GOSUB statement differs from the GOTO statement in that it causes the computer to "remember" which statement to execute next when it encounters a RETURN statement. This is the statement immediately following the GOSUB statement used to call the subroutine.

Remark 4   Note that we used M (for mean) and not A (for average) in the subroutine. If line 310 is changed to

```
310 LET A=(A+B)/2
```

the original value of A will be destroyed during the first subroutine call and incorrect results will be printed. When writing subroutines you must make sure that the variable names you use do not conflict with variable names used in other parts of the program for different purposes.

The GOSUB statement is always used in the form

```
GOSUB ln
```

where **ln** denotes the first line of the subroutine. The RETURN statement is always used in a subroutine to transfer control back to the line following the most recently executed GOSUB statement.

A subroutine may be called from within another subroutine. Following is a schematic representation of a program that does this. The action of the program is indicated by the arrows labeled **a, b, c,** and **d.**

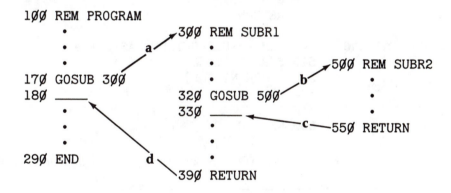

EXAMPLE 2. Here is a program to print a short report for each employee whose name and annual salary are included in DATA lines. Two subroutines are used. The first prints the report for one employee. The second simply prints a row of dashes and is called by the first subroutine.

```
100 REM SALARY PROGRAM
110 REM N$=EMPLOYEE'S NAME
120 REM  A=ANNUAL SALARY OF N$
130    READ N$,A
140    IF N$="END-OF-DATA" THEN 290
150    REM PRINT ANNUAL AND WEEKLY SALARIES.
160    PRINT
170    GOSUB 300
180 GOTO 130
200 DATA "S.J.BRYANT",18500
210 DATA "T.S.ENDICOTT",25700
220 DATA "END-OF-DATA",0
290 END
```

The first subroutine
```
300 REM ***PRINT SHORT SALARY REPORT***
310 REM    W=WEEKLY SALARY
320 GOSUB 500
330 LET W=A/52
340 LET W=INT(W*100+0.5)/100
350 PRINT "EMPLOYEE NAME: ";N$
360 PRINT "ANNUAL SALARY: ";A
370 PRINT "WEEKLY SALARY: ";W
380 GOSUB 500
390 RETURN
```

The second subroutine
```
500 REM ***SUBROUTINE DASHES***
510 FOR I=1 TO 30
520    PRINT "-";
530 NEXT I
540 PRINT
550 RETURN
```

For the given DATA lines (200 to 220), this program produces the following printout:

```
------------------------------
EMPLOYEE NAME: S.J.BRYANT
ANNUAL SALARY: 18500
WEEKLY SALARY: 355.77
------------------------------


------------------------------
EMPLOYEE NAME: T.S.ENDICOTT
ANNUAL SALARY: 25700
WEEKLY SALARY: 494.23
------------------------------
```

Remark

Many programming applications call for long printed reports. If confronted with such a programming task you will do well to examine the requirements carefully to see if the long report in fact consists of several short reports that are to be repeated several times. Such short reports are often ideal candidates for subroutines.

In the preceding chapters we have stressed the importance of segmenting programming tasks into smaller, more manageable subtasks. A program can often be made more readable if subtasks are performed by subroutines, even though they may be referenced in only one programming line. An instance of this practice is the subroutine used in the preceding example to print a salary report for one employee. Note that it is referenced only in line 170 of the program.

The following comments apply to the use of subroutines:

1. The first lines of a subroutine should describe the task being performed.
2. A subroutine must contain one or more RETURN statements.
3. A subroutine must be entered only by using a GOSUB statement. This may require using an END statement to avoid entering a subroutine inadvertently.
4. A subroutine should be used if it will make your program easier to read and understand.
5. A subroutine can contain a GOSUB statement transferring control to another subroutine. A subroutine should not call itself, however.

The following two examples further illustrate the use of subroutines. The first is an application to economics; the second concerns a game played by two users.

EXAMPLE 3. An airline charter service estimates that it will need ticket sales of $1000 to break even on a certain excursion. It thus makes the following offer to an interested organization. If ten people sign up, the cost will be $100 per person. For each additional person, the cost per person will be reduced by $3. Produce a table showing the cost per customer and the profit to the airline for N = 10, 11, 12, . . . , 30 customers. Further, a message is to be printed giving the number of customers that will maximize the profit for the airline. Column headings, underlined by a row of dashes, are to be used, and a row of dashes must precede and follow the final message.

Problem analysis   The output values specified in this problem statement are as follows:

N = number of people who sign up for excursion (N will range from 10 to 30)
C = cost per person (if N people sign up, $C = 130 - 3 \times N$)
P = profit to airline (if N people sign up, $P = N \times C - 1000$)
$N1$ = number of people yielding maximum profit to airline
$P1$ = maximum profit to airline (initially, $P1 = 0$)

According to the problem statement, three rows of dashes are to be printed. Rather than writing a loop that does this three times, we will use a subroutine (lines 500–550 of the program).

Producing a table of values with column headings is not new to us. After printing the column headings (line 130), we can use a FOR/NEXT loop initiated with FOR N = 10 TO 30 to produce the table values (lines 160–230 of the program).

Finally, the program must determine the number $N1$ of customers that yields a maximum profit $P1$ to the airline. Each time a new profit P is computed, it will be compared with $P1$, the largest profit obtained to that point. If P is larger, we will let $P1 = P$ and $N1 = N$; if not, $N1$ and $P1$ will not be changed. To keep our main program as uncluttered as possible, we'll also do this in a subroutine (lines 600–630).

The program

```
100 REM PROGRAM TO PRINT A TABLE OF AIRLINE EXCURSION RATES
110 REM AND DETERMINE THE MAXIMUM PROFIT TO THE AIRLINE
120 LET P1=0
130 PRINT "PASSENGERS  COST/PERSON   PROFIT"
140 GOSUB 500
150 REM COMPUTE AND PRINT THE TABLE VALUES.
160 FOR N=10 TO 30
170     LET C=130-3*N
180     LET P=N*C-1000
190     HTAB  5 : PRINT N;
200     HTAB 17 : PRINT C;
210     HTAB 29 : PRINT P
220     GOSUB 600
230 NEXT N
240 GOSUB 500
250 PRINT N;" PASSENGERS YIELD A"
260 PRINT "MAXIMUM PROFIT OF $";P1
270 GOSUB 500
280 END
500 REM ***SUBR TO PRINT A ROW OF DASHES***
510 FOR I=1 TO 32
520     PRINT "-";
530 NEXT I
540 PRINT
550 RETURN
600 REM ***SUBR TO RECORD THE NUMBER N1 OF CUSTOMERS
610 REM YIELDING THE MAXIMUM PROFIT P1***
620 IF P>P1 THEN P1=P : N1=N
630 RETURN
RUN
```

```
PASSENGERS   COST/PERSON    PROFIT
----------------------------------
    10          100          0
    11           97          67
    12           94          128
    13           91          183
    14           88          232
    15           85          275
    16           82          312
    17           79          343
    18           76          368
    19           73          387
    20           70          400
    21           67          407
    22           64          408
    23           61          403
    24           58          392
    25           55          375
    26           52          352
    27           49          323
    28           46          288
    29           43          247
    30           40          200

----------------------------------
22 PASSENGERS YIELD A
MAXIMUM PROFIT OF $408
----------------------------------
```

EXAMPLE 4. A program is desired for the following game. Two players alternate in typing a whole number from 1 to 5. The computer assigns a point value (unknown to the players) for each number typed according to the table given. The first player to accumulate a total of 15 points or more wins.

Number chosen	Point value
1	3
2	2
3	2
4	1
5	2
Any other	0

Problem analysis

The input and output values for this program are as follows.

Input: A sequence of numbers alternately typed by the two players

Output: The scores of the two players when one of them has a score of 15 or more

It is not hard to devise an algorithm for this task if we leave out the details. In the algorithm we'll use the following variable names:

FIRST = accumulated score of first player
SECND = accumulated score of second player
   X = most recent input value
  PT = point value of X

Algorithm

a. Initialize FIRST and SECND to 0.
b. Input the first player's selection X.
c. Add the point value of X to FIRST.
d. If FIRST >= 15, go to step (i)—the game is over.
e. Input the second player's selection X.
f. Add the point value of X to SECND.
g. If SECND >= 15, go to step (i)—the game is over.
h. Go to step (b).
i. Print the results and stop.

In coding this algorithm, only steps (c) and (f) may be troublesome. Since the point value of X is the same whether X is typed by the first player (step b) or the second (step e), we can use the following subroutine to obtain the point value PT of X:

```
REM SUBR TO DETERMINE POINT VALUE OF X
LET PT=∅
IF X=1 THEN PT=3
IF X=2 OR X=3 OR X=5 THEN PT=2
IF X=4 THEN PT=1
RETURN
```

With this subroutine the required program is easily coded directly from the algorithm. This task is left as an exercise (see Problem 15).

15.2 Problems

1. Show the output of each program.

a.
```
10 READ X,Y
20 IF X=0 THEN 70
30 GOSUB 80
40 PRINT X,Y,Z
50 GOTO 10
60 DATA 4,2,3,-7,0,8
70 END
80 LET Z=3*X+2*Y
90 RETURN
```

b.
```
110 READ A,B
120 IF A=B THEN 190
130 IF A<B THEN 150
140 GOSUB 200
150 GOSUB 210
160 GOTO 110
170 DATA 2,4,8,6,5,5
190 END
200 PRINT A-B
210 PRINT B-A
220 RETURN
```

c.
```
100 FOR I=1 TO 4
110     GOSUB 200
120     PRINT S
130 NEXT I
140 END
200 LET S=0
210 FOR J=1 TO I
220     LET S=S+J
230 NEXT J
240 RETURN
```

d.
```
110 LET M=5
120 GOSUB 300
130 PRINT M
140 END
300 LET M=M+1
310 GOSUB 400
320 RETURN
400 LET M=(M+1)*(M+1)^2
410 RETURN
```

In Problems 2–10, write a subroutine to carry out each task given. In each case, test your subroutine by writing a short program that uses it.

2. For any number N, assign OK to C$ if N is an integer in the range 0 to 100 and assign BAD DATA to C$ in every other case. (Be sure that the subroutine works for the cases $N = -1$, $N = 101$, and $N = 43.74$.)

3. Determine the sum S of the next N values appearing in DATA lines. (You may assume that only numbers appear in DATA lines.)

4. For any numbers A, B, and C, determine and print the largest of the three values $(A+B+C)/3$, $(A+B+2*C)/4$, and $(B+C)/2$.

5. For any number X, assign a value to V as follows:

X	V
1, 3, 5, 7, 9	1
2, 4, 6, 8	2
Negative	−1
Anything else	0

6. For any string A$, assign to C$ the value LETTERS if A$ consists entirely of letters. If A$ contains characters other than letters, assign BAD DATA to C$.

7. For any string X$, determine the count C of how many alphanumeric characters (letters A–Z and digits 0–9) are contained in X$.

8. N! (read "N factorial") is defined as the product

$$N! = 1 \times 2 \times 3 \times \cdots \times N$$

if N is a positive integer and it is defined as 1 if $N = 0$. For any integer $N \geq 0$, assign the value N! to the variable FACT.

9. Determine the greatest common divisor (GCD) of the two positive integers A and B. Use the following algorithm (and convince yourself that it works):
   a. Start with GCD = smaller of A and B.
   b. If GCD is a factor of both A and B, RETURN.
   c. Subtract 1 from GCD and repeat step (b).

10. Use the following algorithm to find the GCD of two positive integers A and B:
    a. Let R = integer remainder when A is divided by B. (R is given by A − INT(A/B)∗B.)
    b. If R = 0, let GCD = B and RETURN.
    c. Assign B to A and R to B.
    d. Repeat step (a).
    The algorithm in Problem 9 can be slow for large numbers; this algorithm, the so-called Euclidean algorithm, is very fast.

In Problems 11–20, write a program for each task specified.

11. A data list contains many sets of scores S1, S2, and S3. The three values 0, 0, 0 are used to terminate the data list. Produce a four-column report: the three scores are to appear in the first three columns; the fourth is to contain the larger of the two values (S1 + S2 + S3)/3 and (S1 + S2 + 2∗S3)/4. Use a subroutine to find the two "averages" and determine which is larger. The subroutine is to contain no print statements.

12. For any list of numbers typed at the keyboard, print two adjacent columns. The first is to contain the numbers in the order in which they are typed. Each entry in the second column is to show how many numbers in the entire list are less than the corresponding number in the first column. Use the following algorithm:
    a. Input the array A.
    b. For each number A(I) in the list, determine the count C(I) of how many numbers are less than A(I).
    c. Print the arrays A and C side by side.
    Use a subroutine to carry out step (b). (Don't assume that the numbers will be typed in increasing order.)

13. Write a program to print all numbers in a data list and then print them again, this time in ascending order. Assume that the first datum is a count of how many numbers are included. Use the following algorithm:
    a. Read the count N and the array A.
    b. Print A.
    c. Sort A into ascending order.
    d. Print the sorted array A.
    e. Stop.
    Use a subroutine to carry out steps (b) and (d).

14. Write a program to allow the user to create an array L as follows. The user is allowed to input as many numbers X as desired. When a value for X is entered, the following is to happen:
    a. If X = 0, the entire array created to that point is to be printed and the program is to halt.
    b. If X is negative, the array to that point is to be printed and the user is to be allowed to enter another number.
    c. If X is positive and not already in the array, it should be added to L and the user is to be allowed to enter another number. (Note that the very first positive value typed will be placed in L(1).)
    d. If X is already in array L, the index I for which L(I) = X is to be printed and the user is to enter another number.
    Use a subroutine to search array L for the value X. The subroutine is not to print anything and is not to be used to add X to the array.

15. Code the algorithm shown in Example 4. Be sure to begin your program with PRINT statements that describe the game to be played.

16. An apple orchard occupying 1 acre of land now contains 25 apple trees, and each tree yields 450 apples per season. For each new tree planted, the yield per tree will be reduced by 10 apples per season. How many additional trees should be planted so that the total yield is as large as possible? Produce a table showing the yield per tree and the total yield if N = 1, 2, 3, . . . , 25 additional trees are planted. Use column headings underlined by a row of dashes. Separate the message (telling how many additional trees to plant) from the table by a row of dashes.

17. An organization can charter a ship for a harbor cruise for $9.75 a ticket provided that at least 200 people agree to go. However, the ship's owner agrees to reduce the cost per ticket by 25¢ for each additional ten people signing up. Thus if 220 people sign up, the cost per person will be $9.25. Write a program to determine the maximum revenue the ship's owner can receive if the ship's capacity is 400 people. Moreover, prepare a table showing the cost per person and the total amount paid for N = 200, 210, 220, . . . , 400 people. Use column headings under-lined by a row of dashes. The maximum revenue the ship's owner can receive should be printed following the table and separated from it by a row of dashes.

18. A merchant must pay the fixed price of $1 a yard for a certain fabric. From experience it is known that 1000 yd will be sold each month if the material is sold at cost and also that each 10¢ increase in price means that 50 fewer yards will be sold each month. Write a program to produce a table showing the merchant's profit for each selling price from $1 to $3 in increments of 10¢. Moreover, a message giving the selling price that will maximize the profit is to be printed. Use column headings underlined with a row of dashes, and separate the table from the final message with a row of dashes.

19. The binomial coefficients

$$\binom{n}{r} = \frac{n!}{(n-r)!r!}$$

occur in many different contexts. Here it is assumed that n and r are integers such that $0 \le r \le n$.

a. Write a subroutine to evaluate $\binom{n}{r}$. Test your subroutine to be sure it works correctly for

n as large as 20. (You must not use the factorial subroutine of Problem 8. On the Apple it will correctly evaluate $n!$ only for $n \le 12$—try it and see.)

b. For any input integer N from 0 to 20, print the N + 1 values

$$\binom{N}{0}, \binom{N}{1}, \binom{N}{2}, \ldots, \binom{N}{N}$$

c. Produce a two-column table as follows. The first column is to show the sum

$$S = \binom{N}{0} + \binom{N}{1} + \binom{N}{2} + \ldots + \binom{N}{N}$$

for each integer N from 0 to 20. The second column is to show the value of $2 \wedge N$ for these same integers N.

d. For each N from 0 to 10, print the N + 1 values

$$\binom{N}{0}, \binom{N}{1}, \binom{N}{2}, \ldots, \binom{N}{N}$$

on a single line. Make sure the output appears as follows:

```
1
1   1
1   2   1
1   3   3   1
```

and so on. (This triangular array of numbers is called Pascal's triangle.)

20. For any four positive integers typed at the keyboard, your program is to determine two integers X and Y for which

A/B + C/D = X/Y

and X/Y is reduced to lowest terms. For example, if 3, 4, 5, and 6 are input, the output should be

3/4 + 5/6 = 19/12

Here is one way to do this:

a. Find the least common multiple (LCM) of B and D. (For this you can use the GCD subroutine of Problem 9 or 10. If GCD is the greatest common divisor of B and D, then LCM = B × D/GCD.)

b. Determine P and Q such that A/B = P/LCM and C/D = Q/LCM. This will give A/B + C/D = (P + Q)/LCM.

c. Reduce (P + Q)/LCM to lowest terms. (Simply divide the numerator and denominator by their GCD.)

15.3 Review true-or-false quiz

1. A program need not contain the same number of GOSUB statements as RETURN statements.   T   F

2. The GOSUB statement is really unnecessary, since the GOTO statement will accomplish the same thing.   T   F

3. An END statement must appear on the line that immediately precedes the first line of each subroutine.   T   F

4. If one subroutine calls a second subroutine, the first must appear in the program before the second.   T   F

5. Subroutines should be used only when a group of statements is to be performed more than once.   T   F

6. Subroutines that perform no numerical calculations are of little use in programming.   T   F

7. Subroutines can be useful even if their only purpose is to improve a program's readability.   T   F

16

□ □ □ □ □ □ □ □ □ □ □ □

Random Numbers and Their Application

If you toss a coin several times, you'll obtain a sequence such as HTTHTHHHTTH, where H denotes a head and T a tail. We call this a **randomly generated sequence** because each letter is the result of an experiment (tossing a coin) and could not have been determined without actually performing the experiment. Similarly, if you roll a die (a cube with faces numbered 1 through 6) several times, you'll obtain a randomly generated sequence such as 5315264342. The numbers in such a sequence are called **random numbers.**

BASIC contains a built-in function called RND used to generate sequences of numbers that have the appearance of being randomly generated. Although these numbers are called random numbers, they are more accurately referred to as **pseudo-random numbers** because the RND function does not perform an experiment such as tossing a coin to produce a number; rather, it uses an algorithm carefully designed to generate sequences of numbers that emulate random sequences. This ability to generate such sequences makes it possible for us to use the computer in many new and interesting ways. Using "random-number generators," people have written computer programs to simulate the growth of a forest, to determine the best location for elevators in a proposed skyscraper, to assist social scientists in their statistical studies, to simulate game playing, and to perform many other tasks.

16.1 The RND function

The RND function is used somewhat differently than the other BASIC functions. For any number X, RND(X) has a value from zero up to, but not including, 1:

$$0 \leq RND(X) < 1$$

If $X > 0$, the value assumed by RND(X) is unpredictable—it will appear to have been selected randomly from the numbers between 0 and 1. In this section we illustrate the use of RND(X) for the case $X > 0$. The use of RND(X) with $X \leq 0$ is considered in Section 16.2.

EXAMPLE 1. Here is a program to generate and print eight random numbers lying between 0 and 1:

```
11Ø FOR I=1 TO 8
12Ø    PRINT RND(1)
13Ø NEXT I
14Ø END
RUN

.2Ø48Ø4811
5.85Ø88613E-Ø3
.784193965
.594331536
.13Ø72565Ø7
.834264561
.567285335
.92Ø549918
```

Observe that each time line 120 is executed a different number is output, even though the same expression RND(1) is used. If you run this program a second time, a different list of eight numbers will be output. This happens whenever you use only RND(X) with X > 0 to generate random numbers.

EXAMPLE 2. Here is a program to generate 1000 random numbers between 0 and 1 and determine how many are in the interval from 0.3 to 0.4:

```
1Ø LET C=Ø : REM C DOES THE COUNTING.
2Ø FOR I=1 TO 1ØØØ
3Ø    LET R=RND(2)
4Ø     IF (R>.3) AND (R<.4) THEN C=C+1
5Ø NEXT I
6Ø PRINT "OF 1ØØØ NUMBERS GENERATED,"
7Ø PRINT C;" WERE BETWEEN .3 AND .4."
8Ø END
RUN

OF 1ØØØ NUMBERS GENERATED,
1Ø4 WERE BETWEEN .3 AND .4.
```

Each time line 30 is executed, RND(2) takes on a different value, which is then assigned to R. The IF statement at line 40 determines whether R lies in the specified interval. In this example it was necessary to assign the value of RND(2) to a variable R so that the comparisons could be made. If we had written

```
4Ø IF (RND(2)>.3) AND (RND(2)<.4) THEN C=C+1
```

the two occurrences of RND(2) would have different values—which is not what we wanted in this situation.

Remark

In Example 1 we used RND(1) to generate random numbers between 0 and 1, and in this example we used RND(2). The effect is the same; the only requirement is that the argument of RND be positive. In subsequent examples we will use the form RND(1) whenever a positive argument for RND is needed.

The numbers generated by the RND function are nearly uniformly distributed between 0 and 1. If many numbers are generated, approximately as many will be less than 0.5 as are greater than 0.5, approximately twice as many will be between 0 and 2/3 as are between 2/3 and 1, approximately one-hundredth of the numbers will be between 0.37 and 0.38, and so on. The examples throughout the rest of this chapter illustrate how this property of random-number sequences can be put to use by a programmer.

EXAMPLE 3. Let's write a program to simulate tossing a coin 20 times. An H is to be printed each time a head occurs and a T each time a tail occurs.

Problem analysis

Since RND(1) will be less than 0.5 approximately half the time, let's say that a head is tossed whenever RND(1) is less than 0.5. The following program is then immediate:

```
1Ø FOR I=1 TO 2Ø
2Ø    IF RND(1)<.5 THEN PRINT "H"; : GOTO 4Ø
3Ø    PRINT "T";
4Ø NEXT I
5Ø END
RUN

HHTHTTTHTTHTHTHHHTTH
```

Remark

If you wish to simulate tossing a bent coin that produces a head twice as often as a tail, you could say that a head is the result whenever RND(1) < .66667. Thus one change in line 2Ø allows the same program to work in this case.

The next example shows how the RND function can be used to simulate a real-life situation.

EXAMPLE 4. A professional softball player has a lifetime batting average of .365. Assuming she will come to bat four times in each of her next 100 games, estimate in how many games she will go hitless, have one hit, have two hits, have three hits, and have four hits.

Problem analysis

To simulate one time at bat, we will generate a number RND(1) and concede a hit if RND(1) < .365. For any one game we will compare four such numbers with .365. If in a particular game H hits are made ($0 \le H \le 4$), we will record this by adding 1 to the counter C(H). Thus, C(0) counts the number of hitless games, C(1) the games in which one hit is made, and so on. This problem analysis suggests how to code step (b) of the following algorithm. Steps (a) and (c) are routine.

Algorithm

a. Set counters C(0), C(1), . . . , C(4) to zero.
b. Repeat the following 100 times:
     Simulate one game to obtain the number H of hits.
     Add 1 to C(H).
c. Print the results C(0), C(1), . . . , C(4) and stop.

The program

```
100 REM INITIALIZE COUNTERS TO ZERO.
110 FOR K=0 TO 4
120    LET C(K)=0
130 NEXT K
140 REM SIMULATE 100 GAMES.
150 FOR GAME=1 TO 100
160    REM H COUNTS HITS IN ONE GAME.
170    LET H=0
180    FOR I=1 TO 4
190       IF RND(1)<.365 THEN H=H+1
200    NEXT I
210    LET C(H)=C(H)+1
220 NEXT GAME
230 REM PRINT THE RESULTS.
240 PRINT "HITS PER GAME","FREQUENCY"
250 PRINT
260 FOR H=0 TO 4
270    PRINT TAB(7);H;SPC(12);C(H)
280 NEXT H
999 END
RUN
```

```
HITS PER GAME    FREQUENCY

     0              16
     1              39
     2              35
     3               9
     4               1
```

Remark 1

This program is easily modified to handle different batting averages. Simply make these two changes:

```
105 INPUT "BATTING AVERAGE? ";BAV
190 IF RND(1)<BAV THEN H=H+1
```

If you also add the line

```
290 PRINT : GOTO 105
```

the performance of many players can be simulated during a single program run. Although lines 110 to 130 were not actually needed in the original program, they are needed if this change is made.

Remark 2

In this example we concede a hit if the condition RND(1) < .365 in line 190 is true. If we change this condition to RND(1) <= .365, essentially the same results will occur; it is extremely unlikely that RND(1) will ever take on the exact value .365. In fact, if BAV denotes any number it is extremely unlikely that RND(1) will take on the exact value BAV. But even if it does, it will happen so rarely that there will be no significant change in the simulation being carried out.

16.2 Repeating a random process

In this section we show how zero and negative arguments for RND can be used to repeat previously generated random numbers.

A zero argument always produces the last random number generated by your Apple. If you type

```
PRINT RND(1) : LET B=RND(Ø)
```

the value generated for RND(1) will be printed and then assigned to B. Similarly, the following line will print a single random number three times:

```
PRINT RND(1);" ";RND(Ø);" ";RND(Ø)
```

Since you can always use a variable to "remember" the most recent random number—instead of using RND(1) in an expression, assign RND(1) to R and then use R in the expression— you will have little need to use RND(Ø). As we now show, *negative* arguments for RND can be useful.

Each negative argument of RND has associated with it a fixed number between 0 and 1. If you type

```
PRINT RND(-1),RND(-4)
```

you will always obtain the same (predictable) numbers. We did this and got the numbers

```
2.99196472E-Ø8    2.99214662E-Ø8
```

These particular values are of no significance, however. What is important is that using RND with a negative argument will cause subsequent random numbers generated with positive arguments to follow a specific sequence associated with this negative argument. Thus the program

```
1ØØ PRINT RND(-1)
11Ø FOR I=1 TO 5ØØ
12Ø    PRINT RND(1)
13Ø NEXT I
14Ø END
```

will produce exactly the same output each time it is run. It is not necessary that RND(-1) be output; it simply must be used. Thus if line 1ØØ is changed to

```
1ØØ LET Q=RND(-1)
```

the loop will produce exactly the same 500 random numbers as before.

EXAMPLE 5. This program illustrates RND with a negative argument.

```
100 LET Q=RND(-1)
110 PRINT "THREE NUMBERS:"
120 FOR K=1 TO 3
130    PRINT RND(1)
140 NEXT K
150 PRINT
160 LET Q=RND(-1)
170 PRINT "THE SAME THREE:"
180 FOR L=1 TO 3
190    PRINT RND(1)
200 NEXT L
210 END
RUN

THREE NUMBERS:
.738207502
.272707136
.299733446

THE SAME THREE:
.738207502
.272707136
.299733446
```

Each time this program is run, it will produce exactly the same output. Moreover, because lines 100 and 160 use RND with the same negative argument, the three numbers output by the L loop repeat those output by the K loop.

Remark

It isn't necessary to use the same positive argument in line 190 that we used in line 130. Replacing RND(1) in line 190 by RND(2) will not change the output. Indeed, since L takes on only positive values in the loop, you can use RND(L) in line 190 without changing the output.

The principal use of RND with negative arguments is to assist at the debugging stage. First write your program using RND with positive arguments—for instance, RND(1)—and run it. If you are not convinced that the program is correct, include a statement such as PRINT RND(−1) as the first line. The program will now produce the same sequence of random numbers each time it is run and this may help you find errors. When you are convinced that the program is correct, delete this PRINT statement. To reflect what happens in real-life situations, your programs—no matter how often they are run—should generate different random sequences.

16.3 Problems

1. Approximately how many asterisks are output by each program segment?

   a. ```
      1Ø FOR I=1 TO 1ØØ
      2Ø   IF RND(1)<.8 THEN 4Ø
      3Ø   PRINT"*";
      4Ø NEXT I
      ```

   b. ```
      1Ø FOR J=1 TO 1Ø
      2Ø     IF RND(1)=RND(1) THEN 4Ø
      3Ø     PRINT "*";
      4Ø NEXT J
      ```

   c. ```
      1Ø FOR K=1 TO 1ØØ
      2Ø   IF RND(1)<.4 THEN 5Ø
      3Ø   IF RND(Ø)>.7 THEN 5Ø
      4Ø PRINT "*";
      5Ø NEXT K
      ```

   d. ```
      1Ø LET X=RND(-4)
      2Ø FOR L=1 TO 1Ø
      3Ø     LET A(L)=RND(1)
      4Ø NEXT L
      5Ø LET Y=RND(-4)
      6Ø FOR N=1 TO 1Ø
      7Ø     IF RND(2)<>A(N) THEN 9Ø
      8Ø     PRINT "*";
      9Ø NEXT N
      ```

2. Which of these logical expressions are always true? Which are always false? Which may be true or false?

   a. `RND(1)>=Ø`

   b. `4*RND(1)<4`

   c. `RND(1)<RND(2)`

   d. `RND(1)+RND(1)=2*RND(1)`

   e. `RND(1)+1>RND(1)`

   f. `INT(RND(1))=Ø`

In Problems 3–12, write a program to perform each task specified.

3. Print approximately one-fourth of all values appearing in DATA lines. A decision to print or not to print should be made as the number is read.

4. Print approximately 1% of all integers from 1000 to 9999, inclusive. They are to be selected randomly.

5. Simulate tossing two coins 100 times. The output should be a count of the number of times each of the possible outcomes HH, HT, TH, and TT occurs.

6. Simulate tossing three coins ten times. The output should be a list of ten terms such as HHH, HTH, HHT, and so on.

7. Simulate tossing K coins N times. The output should be a list of N terms in which each term is a sequence of K H's and T's. N and K are to be input.

8. A game between players A and B is played as follows. A coin is tossed three times or until a head comes up, whichever occurs first. As soon as a head comes up, player A collects $1 from player B. If no head comes up on any of the three tosses, player B collects $6 from player A. In either case, the game is over. Your program is to simulate this game 1000 times to help decide whether A or B has the advantage (or if it is a fair game).

9. Generate an array L of 1000 random numbers between 0 and 1. Using L, determine an array C as follows. C(1) is a count of how many entries of L are between 0 and 0.1, C(2) a count of those between 0.1 and 0.2, and so on. Array C should then be printed.

10. The first three hitters in the Bears' batting order have lifetime batting averages of .257, .289, and .324, respectively. Simulate their first trip to the plate for the next 100 games, and tabulate the number of games in which they produce zero, one, two, and three hits.

11. Jones and Kelley are to have a duel at 20 paces. At this distance Jones will hit the target on the average of two shots in every five and Kelley will hit one in every three. Kelley shoots first. Who has the best chance of surviving? Use a FOR/NEXT loop to run the program 20 times and print the results.

12. (Drunkard's Walk) A poor soul, considerably intoxicated, stands in the middle of a 10-ft-long bridge that spans a river. The inebriate staggers along, either toward the left bank or toward the right, but fortunately cannot fall off the bridge. Assuming that each step taken is exactly

1 ft long, how many steps will the drunkard take before a bank is reached? Assume that it is just as likely that a step will be toward the left bank as toward the right.

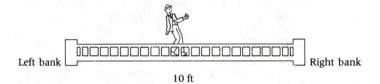

Left bank   Right bank

10 ft

You must do three things:

a. Find how many steps are taken in getting off the bridge.
b. Tell which bank is reached.
c. Let the drunkard go out for several nights and arrive at the same point (the center) on the bridge. Find, on the average, how many steps it takes to get off the bridge.

16.4 Random integers

Many computer applications require generating random *integers* rather than just random numbers between 0 and 1. Suppose a manufacturer estimates that a proposed new product will sell at the rate of 10 to 20 units each week and wants a program to simulate sales figures over an extended period of time. To write such a program, you must be able to generate random integers from 10 to 20 to represent the estimated weekly sales. To do this you can multiply RND(1), which is between 0 and 1, by 11 (the number of integers from 10 to 20) to obtain

$$0 \leqslant 11*RND(1) < 11$$

If many numbers are obtained by using 11*RND(1), they will be nearly uniformly distributed between 0 and 11. This means that the value of INT(11 * RND(1)) will be one of the integers 0, 1, 2, . . . , 10. If you then add 10 to this expression, you will get an integer from 10 to 20:

$$10 \leqslant INT(11*RND(1)) + 10 \leqslant 20$$

The important thing here is that integers generated in this manner will appear to have been chosen randomly from the set of integers {10, 11, 12, . . . , 20}.

In general, if A and B are integers with A < B, then

$$INT((B - A + 1)*RND(1))$$

will generate an integer from zero to B − A. (Note that B − A + 1 gives the number of integers between A and B, inclusive.) Adding A to this expression, we obtain

$$INT((B - A + 1)*RND(1)) + A$$

whose value is an integer chosen randomly from the set {A, A + 1, A + 2, . . . , B}. The following table illustrates how to obtain a random integer within specified bounds.

Expression	Value of the expression
`INT(1Ø*RND(1))`	A random integer from 0 to 9
`INT(N*RND(1))`	A random integer from 0 to N − 1
`INT(N*RND(1))+1`	A random integer from 1 to N
`INT(51*RND(1))+1ØØ`	A random integer from 100 to 150
`INT(11*RND(1))-5`	A random integer from −5 to 5

EXAMPLE 6. Here is a program to generate 15 numbers randomly selected from the set {1, 2, 3, 4, 5}:

```
1Ø FOR I=1 TO 15
2Ø    PRINT INT(5*RND(1))+1;" ";
3Ø NEXT I
4Ø END
RUN

1 2 5 1 5 5 4 3 5 3 3 4 2 4 2
```

EXAMPLE 7. If a pair of dice is rolled, the sum of the top faces is an integer from 2 to 12. Let's write a program to simulate rolling a pair of dice 1000 times and determine a count of how many times each of the possible sums occurs.

Problem analysis

It is not enough simply to generate numbers from 2 to 12 by using the expression $INT(11*RND(1)) + 2$. If we did this, each of the 11 numbers would have approximately an equal chance of occurring—but anyone who has rolled dice knows that this is not what actually happens. To obtain realistic results, we should try to simulate what really takes place.

When a single die is rolled, a random number from 1 to 6 is obtained. We can simulate this rolling of a single die by using the expression $INT(6*RND(1)) + 1$. For the task at hand, two such numbers should be generated and added to obtain a number from 2 to 12. The following flowchart describes an algorithm for rolling a pair of dice 1000 times. In the flowchart, S denotes the sum obtained from one roll of the two dice, and C(S), for S = 2 to 12, is a count of how many times a sum of S occurred. The program was coded directly from this flowchart.

The program

```
100 REM SIMULATE ROLLING DICE.
110 DIM C(12)
120 FOR S=2 TO 12
130    LET C(S)=0
140 NEXT S
150 REM ROLL DICE 1000 TIMES.
160 FOR I=1 TO 1000
170    LET R1=INT(6*RND(1))+1
180    LET R2=INT(6*RND(1))+1
190    LET S=R1+R2
200    LET C(S)=C(S)+1
210 NEXT I
220 REM PRINT FREQUENCY TABLE.
230 PRINT "SUM","FREQUENCY"
240 PRINT
250 FOR S=2 TO 12
260    PRINT S,C(S)
270 NEXT S
280 END
RUN
```

SUM	FREQUENCY
2	26
3	49
4	81
5	111
6	122
7	161
8	166
9	114
10	92
11	60
12	18

The flowchart

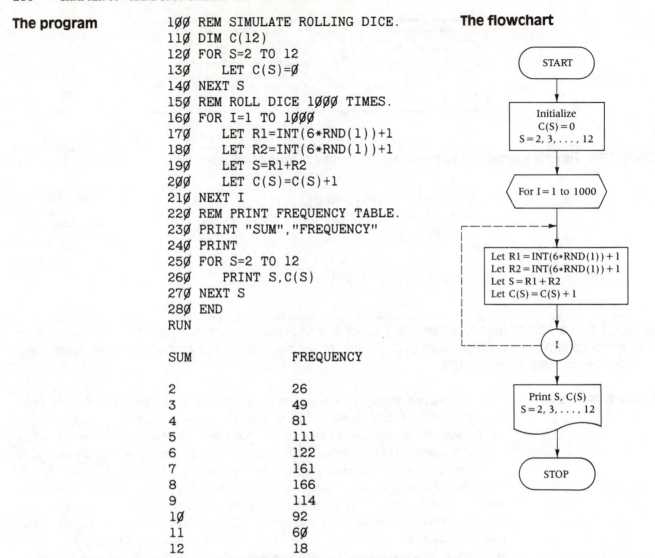

16.5 Simulation

Example 4 of Section 16.1 shows how the RND function can be used to simulate a ballplayer's future performance based on past performance. The example illustrates a major category of simulation problems encountered in computer programming—namely, the simulation of future events based on data obtained by observing the results of similar or related previous events. In this section we show how such a simulation can be used to advantage in a business setting.

EXAMPLE 8. A retail store will soon handle a new product. A preliminary market survey indicates that between 500 and 1000 units will be sold each month. (The survey is no more specific than this.) Write a program to simulate sales for the first 6 months. The retail store management is to be allowed to experiment by specifying two values: the number of units to be purchased initially and the number to be purchased on the first of each subsequent month.

Problem analysis

The input values are:

$$IPUR = \text{initial inventory purchase}$$
$$PUR = \text{inventory purchase for subsequent months}$$

The problem statement does not specify the nature of the output. Let's agree to print a four-column report showing the following items:

$$MNTH = \text{month } (1, 2, \ldots, 6)$$
$$SALES = \text{estimated sales } (500-1000) \text{ for 1 month}$$
$$FIRST = \text{quantity on hand at beginning of month (initially, IPUR)}$$
$$LAST = \text{quantity on hand at end of month (initially 0)}$$

After the initial and periodic purchase quantities (IPUR and PUR) are input, we will print column headings and then assign the input value IPUR to FIRST so that the simulation can begin. The actual simulation of sales for each of the 6 months (MNTH = 1 TO 6) can be carried out as follows:

1. Estimate sales for 1 month (SALES = INT (501*RND(1)) + 500).
2. Determine the quantity on hand at the end of the month (LAST = FIRST − SALES).
3. Print MNTH, SALES, FIRST, LAST.
4. Determine the quantity on hand at the start of the next month
   (FIRST = LAST + PUR).

The program

```
100 INPUT "INITIAL INVENTORY PURCHASE? ";IPUR
110 INPUT "SUBSEQUENT MONTHLY PURCHASE? ";PUR
120 PRINT
130 PRINT "                    INVENTORY"
140 PRINT "                 ------------------"
150 PRINT "MONTH     ESTIMATED   START OF    END OF"
160 PRINT "NUMBER     SALES      MONTH       MONTH"
170 PRINT
180 LET FIRST=IPUR: REM START OF MONTH
190 FOR MNTH = 1 TO 6
200    LET SALES=INT(501*RND(1))+500: REM SALES FOR MONTH
210    LET LAST=FIRST-SALES: REM INVENTORY AT END-OF-MONTH
220    HTAB 3: PRINT MNTH;
230    HTAB 12: PRINT SALES;
240    HTAB 22: PRINT FIRST;
250    HTAB 33: PRINT LAST
260    LET FIRST=LAST+PUR: REM START OF NEXT MONTH
270 NEXT MNTH
280 END
RUN
```

```
INITIAL INVENTORY PURCHASE? 1ØØØ
SUBSEQUENT MONTHLY PURCHASE? 85Ø
```

		INVENTORY	
MONTH	ESTIMATED	START OF	END OF
NUMBER	SALES	MONTH	MONTH
1	717	1ØØØ	283
2	584	1133	549
3	564	1399	835
4	518	1685	1167
5	798	2Ø17	1219
6	877	2Ø69	1192

Remark

A user would run this program many times and use the results as a guide to determining a reasonable purchasing strategy. The increasingly larger values in the last column of the output suggest only that a monthly purchase of 850 units is excessive.

We wrote the new-product simulation program so that sales of 500 to 1000 units would be selected with equal likelihood. We did this not because it is realistic, but because the preliminary market analysis gave no further information. A more careful market analysis would probably show that the number of units would range from 500 to 1000—with sales near 750 more likely than sales near the extremes 500 and 1000. We'll now show how random numbers that cluster about a specific number can be generated.

The subroutine

```
5ØØ LET R=Ø
51Ø FOR K=1 TO 5
52Ø    LET R=R+RND(1)
53Ø NEXT K
54Ø LET R=R/5
55Ø RETURN
```

generates a random number R from 0 to 1 by averaging five random numbers RND(1). If many numbers R are generated by this subroutine, they will tend to cluster about the midpoint 0.5 of the interval from 0 to 1 with fewer occurring toward the endpoints 0 and 1. (The distribution of random numbers generated by this method of averaging is called a **binomial distribution.** If a number larger than 5 is used in the subroutine, the numbers generated will cluster more closely around the midpoint 0.5.)

With R obtained from this subroutine, the statement

```
LET DEV=INT(5Ø1*R)-25Ø
```

assigns to DEV (for deviation) a random integer from -250 to 250 that is more likely to be near the midpoint (0) than the extremes -250 and 250. Adding 750 to DEV

```
LET SALES=DEV+75Ø
```

we obtain a number from 500 to 1000 that is more likely to be near the midpoint (750) than the extremes 500 and 1000. The program shown in Example 8 is easily modified to generate SALES by this method. Simply add the given subroutine and change line 2ØØ to

```
2ØØ GOSUB 5ØØ
2Ø2 LET DEV=INT(5Ø1*R)-25Ø
2Ø4 LET SALES=DEV+75Ø
```

or to the equivalent single line

```
2ØØ GOSUB 5ØØ : SALES=INT(5Ø1*R)+5ØØ
```

Here is a run of the program after these changes were made:

```
RUN

INITIAL INVENTORY PURCHASE? 8ØØ
SUBSEQUENT MONTHLY PURCHASE? 75Ø


                        INVENTORY
               ---------------------
MONTH    ESTIMATED  START OF   END OF
NUMBER     SALES     MONTH     MONTH

  1        711        8ØØ        89
  2        776        839        63
  3        8Ø1        813        12
  4        613        762       149
  5        828        899        71
  6        713        821       1Ø8
```

16.6 Problems

1. Write BASIC statements to print the following:
   a. A nonnegative random number (not necessarily an integer) less than 4
   b. A random number less than 11 but not less than 5
   c. A random number less than 3 but not less than -5
   d. A random integer between 6 and 12, inclusive
   e. A random number from the set $\{0, 2, 4, 6, 8\}$
   f. A random number from the set $\{1, 3, 5, 7, 9\}$
2. What values can be assumed by each of the following expressions? For each expression, tell whether the possible values are all equally likely to occur.

   a. `INT(2*RND(1)+1)`
   b. `3*INT(RND(1))`
   c. `INT(5*RND(1))-2`
   d. `INT(2*RND(1)+1)+INT(2*RND(1)+1)`
   e. `INT(6*RND(1)+1)+INT(6*RND(1)+1)`
   f. `INT(3*RND(1)+1)*(INT(3*RND(1))+1)`

In Problems 3–16, write a program to perform each task specified.

3. Print a sequence of 20 letters that are selected randomly from the word RANDOM.
4. Randomly select and print an integer from 1 to 100 and then another from the remaining 99.
5. Create an array B of exactly 20 different integers from 1 to 100. The integers are to be chosen randomly. The array should be printed, but only after it is completely determined.
6. Read 20 different English words into an array A$. Then create another array B$ containing exactly 10 different words randomly selected from those in array A$.
7. Starting with $D(1) = 1, D(2) = 2, D(3) = 3, \ldots, D(52) = 52$, rearrange the entries of D as follows: select an integer K from 1 to 52 and swap $D(K)$ with $D(52)$, select K from 1 to 51 and swap $D(K)$ with $D(51)$, select K from 1 to 50 and swap $D(K)$ with $D(50)$, and so on. The last step in this process is to select K from 1 to 2 and swap $D(K)$ with $D(2)$. Then print the entries of D in four columns, each containing 13 numbers. Explain in what sense your program shuffles a standard bridge deck and deals one hand in bridge.
8. Print 20 sets of three integers D, L, and F with $0 \leq D < 360$, $5 \leq L \leq 15$, and $1 \leq F \leq 4$. (*Note:* If we interpret D as a direction and L as a length, we can create a design using these numbers. Starting at a point on our paper, we draw a line of length L in the direction given by D. At the end of this line segment we draw one of four figures as specified by F—for example,

different colored circles the sizes of a dime, nickel, quarter, and half dollar. Using the end of this first line segment as our starting point, we repeat the process by using the second of our 20 triples D, L, F. This process illustrates, in a very elementary way, what some people refer to as random art.)

9. A retail store will soon carry a new product. A preliminary market analysis indicates that between 300 and 500 units will be sold each week. (The survey is no more specific than this.) Assuming that each unit costs the store $1.89, write a program to simulate sales for the next 16 weeks. The store management is to be allowed to specify the selling price to obtain a printout showing the week, the estimated sales in number of units, the total revenue, the income (revenue − cost), and the cumulative income. The user should be allowed to try many different selling prices during a single program run.

10. Carry out the task specified in Problem 9, but this time assume that the market analysis says the number of units sold per week (300–500) will follow a binomial distribution as described in Section 16.5.

11. Write a subroutine to generate random numbers between 0 and 1 by averaging N random numbers rather than 5 as in Section 16.5. Include this subroutine in a program that allows the user to specify a positive integer N to obtain a frequency table showing counts of how many of 500 random numbers generated by the subroutine are in each of the ten intervals 0–0.1, 0.1–0.2, . . . , 0.9–1. The user should be allowed to obtain tables for many positive integers N during a single program run. The program should halt when the user types zero. (Be sure to try the cases N = 1, 10, and 20.)

12. The IDA Production Company will employ 185 people to work on the production of a new product. It is estimated that each person can complete between 85 and 95 units each working day. Experience shows that the absentee rate is between 0 and 15% on Mondays and Fridays and between 0 and 7% on the other days. Simulate the production for 1 week. The results of this simulation are to be printed in four columns showing the day of the week, the number of workers present, the number of units produced, and the average number produced per worker.

13. Two knights begin at diagonally opposite corners of a chessboard and travel randomly about the board but always making legitimate knight moves. (The knight moves either one step forward or backward and then two steps to the right or left or else two steps forward or backward and one step to the right or left.) Calculate the number of moves before one knight captures the other. However you number the squares, each knight's move should be printed as it is taken.

14. A single trip for a knight is defined as follows. The knight starts in one corner of the chessboard and randomly makes N knight moves to arrive at one of the 64 squares of the chessboard. (See Problem 13 for a description of an admissible knight move.) Write a program to simulate 1000 such trips for a knight to determine how many times each square was reached at the end of a trip. These counts should be presented as an 8 × 8 table displaying the counts for the 64 squares. A value for N is to be supplied by the user, who is allowed to obtain a frequency table for many values of N during a single program run.

15. SIM is a game in which two players take turns drawing lines between any two of the six dots numbered 1 through 6 in the following diagram:

```
        1        2
        •        •
   6 •              • 3
        •        •
        5        4
```

Lines drawn by the first player are colored red; the second player's are colored blue. The loser is the first player to complete a triangle with three of these six dots as vertices. For example, if the second player draws a line (blue) between dots 2 and 4, 6 and 4, and 2 and 6, this player has completed a blue triangle and hence loses. Write a program in which the computer is the second player. The computer is to record all moves and announce the end of each game with a message stating who won. (Hint: Use a 6 × 6 array H(I,J) to record the moves. If the first player types 3, 5 to indicate that a red line is drawn between these two dots, set H(3,5) and H(5,3) to 1. If the computer picks 2,6 (to be done randomly), then set H(2,6) and H(6,2) to 2. Note that a triangle of one color has been completed when there are three different numbers I, J, K for which H(I,J), H(J,K), and H(K,I) are equal.)

16. Write a program for the game of SIM described in Problem 15, but this time the second player is a person, not the computer.

16.7 A statistical application

Programmers are often confronted with tasks that simply cannot be programmed to run within a specified time limit. When this happens, it is not always necessary to abandon the task. Sometimes satisfactory results can be obtained by doing only part of the job. The following example, which illustrates one such situation, makes use of the statistical fact that the average of a large collection of numbers can be estimated by taking the average of only a fraction of the numbers, provided that the numbers are chosen randomly.

EXAMPLE 9. A researcher has compiled three lists A, B, and C of 500 measurements each and wishes to determine the average of all possible sums obtained by adding three measurements, one from each of the three lists. We are to write a program to assist the researcher in this task.

Problem analysis

On the surface this appears to be a simple programming task. For each set A(I), B(J), C(K) of measurements, we can add A(I) + B(J) + C(K) to a summation accumulator S and then divide S by the number of sets A(I), B(J), C(K) used. The following program segment will do this:

```
300 LET S=0
310 FOR I=1 TO 500
320    FOR J=1 TO 500
330       FOR K=1 TO 500
340          LET S=S+A(I)+B(J)+C(K)
350       NEXT K
360    NEXT J
370 NEXT I
380 LET AV=S/500^3
```

If you use this program segment to find the required average AV, however, you'll have a long wait. To see that this is so, precede the program segment with the line

```
290 DIM A(500),B(500),C(500)
```

and type RUN. (The Apple takes just as long to add zeros—which is what will happen here—as other numbers.) We did this and after one minute used ctrl C to stop program execution. The immediate mode command

```
PRINT I,J,K
```

gave the values I = 1, J = 10, and K = 407. This means that J × 500 + K = 5407 passes through the triply nested loops were made in one minute. Since 500^3 = 125,000,000 passes must be made in all, the estimated execution time is 125,000,000 ÷ 5407 = 23,118.18 minutes—which is approximately 385 hours, or sixteen 24-hour days.

About the only way out of this dilemma is to treat only a fraction of the 125 million sets A(I), B(J), C(K) and use the average of *their* sums as an estimate of the average desired. Using 1 in 10,000 of these sets will take approximately 2.3 minutes (23,118.18 ÷ 10,000). To ensure that the average obtained will be a reliable estimate of the average desired, the sets A(I), B(J), C(K) must be chosen randomly. In the following program segment we use the expression INT(500 * RND(1)) + 1 to select subscripts from 1 to 500 randomly. The statement FOR N = 1 TO 12500 is appropriate since using 1 in 10,000 of the sets A(I), B(J), C(K) means that a total of 125,000,000 ÷ 10,000 = 12,500 sets will be used.

```
3ØØ LET S=Ø
31Ø FOR N=1 TO 125ØØ
32Ø    LET I=INT(5ØØ*RND(1))+1
33Ø    LET J=INT(5ØØ*RND(1))+1
34Ø    LET K=INT(5ØØ*RND(1))+1
35Ø    LET S=S+A(I)+B(J)+C(K)
36Ø NEXT N
37Ø LET AV=S/125ØØ
```

When this program segment is executed, the same subscripts I, J, K may be selected more than once. Since each set A(I), B(J), C(K) has an equal chance of being selected, however, the effect on the final average will be statistically insignificant.

16.8 Monte Carlo

The speed of modern computing machines, together with their ability to generate good random sequences, allows us to approach many problems in ways not previously possible. The following example illustrates one such method, called the **Monte Carlo method.** When you complete the example, you should have little difficulty explaining why this name is applied to the technique involved.

EXAMPLE 10

Consider the following figure of a circle inscribed in a square:

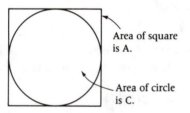

Area of square is A.

Area of circle is C.

If darts are randomly tossed at this figure and tosses landing outside the square are ignored, we can expect the number of darts falling within the circle to be related to the number falling on the entire square as the area C of the circle is related to the area A of the square. We will use this observation to approximate the area C of a unit circle (circle of radius 1).

Problem analysis

Let's suppose that N darts have landed on the square and that M of these are in the circle. Then, as noted in the problem statement, we will have the approximation

$$M/N \doteq C/A$$

or, solving for C,

$$C \doteq M \times A/N$$

The more darts thrown (randomly), the better we can expect this approximation to be. The problem, then, is to simulate this activity and keep an accurate count of M and N. To simplify this task, let's place our figure on a coordinate system with its origin at the center of the circle:

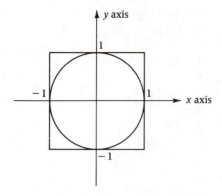

A point (x,y) will lie in the square if both x and y lie between -1 and $+1$. Such a point will lie within the circle if

$$x^2 + y^2 < 1$$

To simulate tossing a single dart, we randomly generate two numbers x and y between -1 and $+1$. The following algorithm describes this process for N = 1000 tosses. The approximate area of the circle M × A/N is output for the vaues N = 100, 200, 300, . . . , 1000.

   a. Let M = 0. (M counts the darts falling within the circle.)
   b. For N = 1 to 1000, do the following:
       Generate x and y between -1 and 1.
       If $x^2 + y^2 < 1$, add 1 to M.
       If N is a multiple of 100, print N and M × A/N.
   c. Stop.

Since 2*RND(1) $-$ 1 gives a random number between -1 and $+1$, and since the area A of the square is 4, the above algorithm translates rather easily into the following program:

The program

```
1ØØ REM A MONTE CARLO SIMULATION
11Ø PRINT "NUMBER OF        ESTIMATED AREA"
12Ø PRINT "DARTS THROWN     OF UNIT CIRCLE"
13Ø PRINT "-------------    ---------------"
14Ø LET M=Ø : A=4
15Ø FOR N=1 TO 1ØØØ
16Ø     LET X=2*RND(1)-1
17Ø     LET Y=2*RND(1)-1
18Ø     IF X^2+Y^2<1 THEN M=M+1
19Ø     IF N=1ØØ*INT(N/1ØØ) THEN PRINT N,M*A/N
2ØØ NEXT N
21Ø END
RUN
```

```
NUMBER OF              ESTIMATED AREA
DARTS THROWN           OF UNIT CIRCLE
------------           --------------
100                    3.48
200                    3.2
300                    3.29333334
400                    3.19
500                    3.208
600                    3.22666667
700                    3.2
800                    3.17
900                    3.12888889
1000                   3.112
```

Remark

The accuracy obtainable from using the RND function in Monte Carlo simulations is limited because of the way in which the RND function generates numbers. For example, the final result (3.112) obtained in this problem is accurate to one decimal place. The area of a circle of radius 1 is π (approximately 3.1416). Using RND, this is about the best you can do.

16.9 Problems

In Problems 1–3, write a program for each task specified.

1. A principle of statistics tells us that the mean (average) of a large collection of numbers can be approximated by taking the mean of only some of the numbers, provided that the numbers are chosen randomly. Generate a one-dimensional array L containing 500 numbers (any numbers will do), and print the mean M of these 500 numbers. To test the stated principle of statistics, randomly select approximately 30 numbers from L and print their mean. Use a loop to repeat this process 20 times. The 20 means obtained should cluster about M.

2. Let L be an array of N numbers between 0 and 1. Using array L, determine an array C as follows: C(1) is a count of how many entries of L are between 0 and 0.1, C(2) a count of those between 0.1 and 0.2, and so on. If L emulates a random sequence, we can expect each C(J) to be approximately E = N/10. In statistics, the value

$$X = \frac{(C(1) - E)^2}{E} + \frac{(C(2) - E)^2}{E} + \cdots + \frac{(C(10) - E)^2}{E}$$

is called the *chi-square statistic* for C. If it is small, it means that the C(J) do not differ drastically from the expected value E. For the present situation, statistics tells us that if $X \geq 16.92$, we can be 95% confident that L does not emulate a random sequence. Thus, unless $X < 16.92$, we should reject L as a potential random sequence.

   a. Assuming that N and the list C are known, write a subroutine to compute and print the chi-square statistic X.

   b. Use the subroutine of part (a) in a program to test RND as a random-number generator. For any positive integer $N \geq 200$, the program is to determine the counts C(1), C(2), . . . , C(10) for N numbers generated by RND(1) and then determine and print the chi-square statistic. The program should halt if a value of N less than 200 is typed.

   (*Note:* If C gives a count of numbers in intervals other than (0, 0.1), (0.1, 0.2), and so on, a critical value other than 16.92 must be used. The test described here is called a *chi-square goodness-of-fit test* and is described in most introductory statistics books.)

3. Let a function $y = f(x)$ have positive values for all x between A and B as in the following diagram:

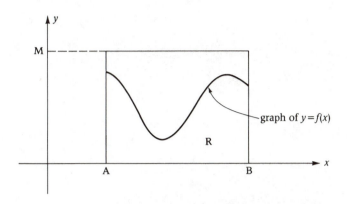

A point (x,y) with $A < x < B$ will lie in the region R if $0 < y < f(x)$. If M is a number such that $f(x) \leq M$ for all such x, the area of the rectangle of height M shown in the diagram is $M*(B - A)$. Use the Monte Carlo method to approximate the area R. Try your program for the following cases:
a. $y = 1 - x^3$, A = 0, B = 1
b. $y = \sin(x)$, A = 0, B = $\pi/2$
c. $y = \sin(x)/x$, A = 0, B = 1

16.10 Review true-or-false quiz

1. The RND function generates sequences of numbers by using a well-defined algorithm.   T   F
2. If 100 numbers are generated by the statement LET R = RND(1), then approximately half these numbers will be less than 50.   T   F
3. With equal likelihood, the expression INT(2*RND(1)) will have the value 0 or 1.   T   F
4. With equal likelihood, the expression

```
INT(3*RND(1))+INT(2*RND(1))
```

will have one of the values 1, 2, 3, 4, or 5.   T   F
5. Let L$ be an array of 100 different names. If we wish to select exactly 20 of these names randomly, we can generate 100 random numbers between 0 and 1 and select the Ith name in array L$ if the Ith number generated is less than 0.2.   T   F
6. A certain experiment has two possible outcomes: Outcome 1 and Outcome 2. To simulate this experiment on the computer, we can generate a number R = RND(1) and specify that Outcome 1 occurs if R is less than 0.5 and Outcome 2 occurs otherwise.   T   F
7. RND(1)/RND(1) = 1.   T   F
8. Although the RND function can be used to generate negative numbers, this is never done.   T   F
9. The value of the expression INT(17*RND(1)) + 1 is an integer from 1 to 17.   T   F
10. The value of the expression INT(5*RND(1)) + 5 is an integer from 5 to 10.   T   F

17

□ □ □ □ □ □ □ □ □ □ □ □ □ □

Graphics

Screen output thus far has comprised letters, numbers, and certain other special characters from the BASIC character set. The Apple also allows you to display graphic images by illuminating in color individual blocks (low-resolution) or points (high-resolution) on the screen. This chapter illustrates both the Apple's low-resolution graphics (Sections 17.1, 17.2, and 17.3) and high-resolution graphics (Section 17.5).

17.1 Low-resolution graphics

To this point, the Apple's video screen has been used to display 24 horizontal lines of 40 characters each (Figure 17.1a). This is referred to as operating in **text mode.** The term **text window** is used to describe the portion of the screen used to display text—thus up to now, the text window has been the full screen. In Apple's low-resolution **mixed-screen graphics mode** (Figure 17.1b), the screen is divided into two parts. The **graphics area** comprises the part of the screen normally used to display text lines 1 through 20 and the text window is reduced to the last four lines on the screen. (In Section 17.2 we'll show you how you can use the full screen for graphics.)

The graphics area is divided into a 40-column by 40-row grid of blocks sometimes called **picture elements** (or **pixels**). Two pixels, one on top of the other, take up the equivalent screen space of one text character. The columns in the grid are numbered 0 to 39 from left to right; the rows are numbered 0 to 39 from top to bottom (Figure 17.2).

An individual pixel is specified by giving its column number followed by its row number. As shown in Figure 17.2, (0,0) identifies the block in the upper-left corner, the block (0,20) is located 20 positions below this corner block, (32,35) is the block in column 32 and row 35 (since positions are numbered from zero, this is the thirty-third column and thirty-sixth row), (20,20) is located at about the center of the graphics area, and (39,6) is in the far right column.

Figure 17.1
Display modes for the
Apple's video screen.

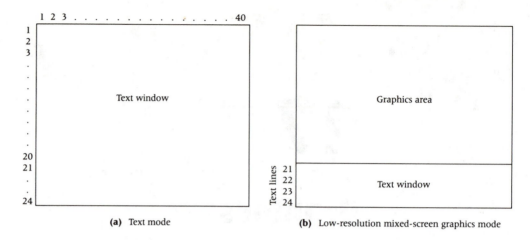

(a) Text mode   (b) Low-resolution mixed-screen graphics mode

The two numbers used to specify a block in the grid are called its *coordinates*. The first is the *x* or *horizontal* coordinate; the second is the *y* or *vertical* coordinate. This terminology is borrowed from mathematics. We can also refer to the top row as the *x* axis (labeled 0 to 39 from left to right), the left-hand column as the *y* axis (labeled 0 to 39 from top to bottom), and the block (0,0) in the upper-left corner as the origin.

To enter the Apple's low-resolution graphics mode of operation, use the command GR; to return to text mode, use TEXT. (All graphics commands can be issued in either immediate mode or deferred mode.)

Figure 17.2
Low-resolution graphics area

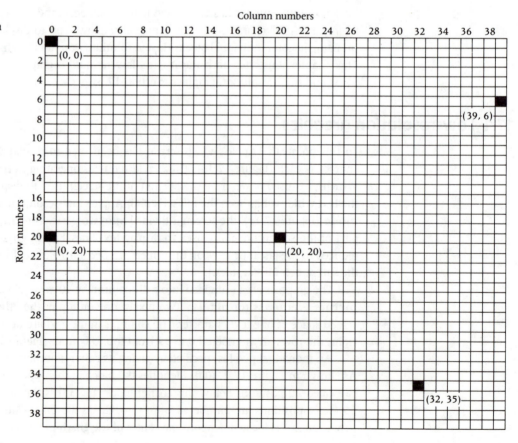

GR   Clears the 40-column by 40-row graphics area (color it black) and positions the cursor in the text window near the bottom of the screen. This command also selects the color black for subsequent graphics output.

After typing the immediate mode command GR, type a few lines—even illegal commands will do—and note their rapid disappearance as they are scrolled through the four-line text window at the bottom of the screen.

TEXT   Sets the screen to the normal full-screen text mode and displays the Applesoft prompt] on the last line (line 24) of the screen.

Issuing the TEXT command while in low-resolution graphics mode will leave you with a cluttered screen; the graphics area will be filled with seemingly meaningless text characters. But these are of no concern and will scroll from the screen as new lines are typed. If you wish to return to text mode with a clear screen, use the Applesoft command HOME, which clears the current text window and positions the cursor at the beginning of this text window. Thus to return to text mode with a clear screen use

TEXT:HOME

To enter graphics mode with a clear four-line text window, use

GR:HOME

Once in graphics mode, you can create displays by using the following low-resolution graphics commands:

COLOR =   to specify a color
PLOT   to color (or illuminate) a single block
HLIN   to color a horizontal row of blocks
VLIN   to color a vertical column of blocks

Illuminating a specific block is called **plotting the point** (another term borrowed from mathematics). To plot a point, first choose one of the 16 colors permitted in low-resolution graphics (Table 17.1).

TABLE 17.1   Low-resolution colors

Number	Color	Number	Color
0	black	8	brown
1	magenta	9	orange
2	dark blue	10	gray
3	purple	11	pink
4	dark green	12	green
5	gray	13	yellow
6	medium blue	14	aqua
7	light blue	15	white

The command

```
COLOR=3
```

selects the color purple and

```
PLOT 1Ø,1Ø
```

plots the point with coordinates (10,10). Thus the program segment

```
1ØØ GR
11Ø COLOR=3
12Ø PLOT 1Ø,1Ø
```

will clear the graphics area and then illuminate the block at (10,10) in purple. (If we had not specified a color, the point (10,10) would be colored black, the background color, and hence would not be visible.) Similarly, typing the immediate mode commands

```
GR
COLOR=7
PLOT Ø,Ø
PLOT 39,Ø
PLOT Ø,39
PLOT 39,39
COLOR=2:PLOT 2Ø,2Ø
```

in the given order will color the four corner blocks of the graphics area in light blue and the block (20,20) in dark blue. (If your screen is designed to display only black and white, the different colors will show varying amounts of brightness. If your screen does display colors but they are not precisely as stated, try adjusting the color controls for your screen.)

EXAMPLE 1. Here is a program to allow you to experiment with the GR, COLOR = , and PLOT commands:

```
1ØØ GR:REM ENTER THE GRAPHICS MODE.
11Ø HOME:REM CLEAR THE 4-LINE TEXT WINDOW.
12Ø    INPUT "SPECIFY A COLOR: ";C
13Ø    COLOR=C
14Ø    INPUT "SELECT A POINT: ";X,Y
15Ø    PLOT X,Y
16Ø PRINT:GOTO 12Ø
```

When this program is run, all input prompts, input values, and error messages will be displayed in the four-line text window.

In response to line 120 you would type an integer from 0 to 15 for the variable C. Line 130 selects whatever color you specified. (You cannot use the statement INPUT COLOR to specify a color. COLOR is not a variable; rather COLOR= is a command that must be used in the form COLOR = *numerical expression*.) In response to line 140 you would type the coordinates of the point to be plotted. These coordinates should be in the range 0 to 39. After line 150 plots the specified point in the color C, line 160 sets up a loop so that other points and colors can be tried.

At this point you should type and run the program. In addition to selecting colors and points as described (integers 0 to 15 for C and coordinates 0 to 39 for X and Y), try other values to see what happens. Try, for example, the following:

Point (1.2,1.9)	PLOT X,Y truncates to obtain integer coordinates. Thus (1,1) is plotted.
Point (40,0)	Causes an ILLEGAL QUANTITY error. X must be in the range 0 to 39.99999. After the error message, use RUN 120 or GOTO 120 to restart the program without clearing the graphics area.
Point (20,45)	When the full screen is used for graphics (Section 17.2), the Y coordinate can be in the range 0 to 47. Since you are using mixed-screen graphics, (20,45) specifies a block in the text window. PLOT 20,45 will cause an unwanted character to be displayed in this block and program execution will continue.
Color 18	This is out of the range 0 to 15, but the color dark blue (2) is selected. This is obtained by subtracting 16 from 18 to obtain a color code in the range 0 to 15. If an integer from 0 to 255 is typed for C, the Apple interprets it modulo 16 by using the color code C − 16*INT(C/16). This is the same as repeatedly subtracting 16 from C until an integer in the range 0 to 15 is obtained. If an integer not in the range 0 to 255 is used to specify a color, an ILLEGAL QUANTITY error will occur.
Color 2.9	The color dark blue (2) is selected. The command COLOR = C truncates C to obtain an integer color code.

The general forms of the COLOR = and PLOT commands are as follows:

COLOR = **n**	**n** denotes a numerical expression whose value is truncated (if necessary) to an integer. If this integer is in the range 0 to 255, it is reduced modulo 16 (as described in Example 1) to obtain a color code from 0 to 15. If the integer is not in the range 0 to 255, an ILLEGAL QUANTITY error occurs.
PLOT **m,n**	**m** and **n** denote numerical expressions whose values are truncated (if necessary) to integers. Let M and N denote these two integers. If both are in the range 0 to 39, the point (M,N) is plotted. If M is from 0 to 39 and N is from 40 to 47, an unwanted character is displayed in the text window unless full-screen graphics are being used (see Section 17.2). In any other case, an ILLEGAL QUANTITY error occurs.

The low-resolution graphics commands HLIN and VLIN are used to plot horizontal and vertical lines, respectively. The command

```
HLIN 7,21 AT 30
```

will plot a horizontal line at Y = 30 from X = 7 to X = 21:

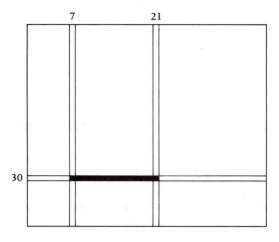

The command

```
VLIN 12,25 AT 4
```

will produce a vertical line at X = 4 from Y = 12 to Y = 25:

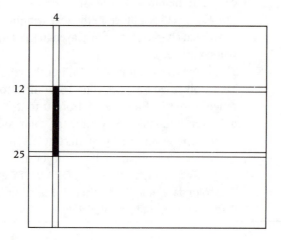

EXAMPLE 2. Here is a program to outline the graphics area of the screen:

```
1Ø  GR:HOME
2Ø  COLOR=7
3Ø  HLIN Ø,39 AT Ø
4Ø  VLIN Ø,39 AT 39
5Ø  HLIN 39,Ø AT 39
6Ø  VLIN 39,Ø AT Ø
7Ø  END
```

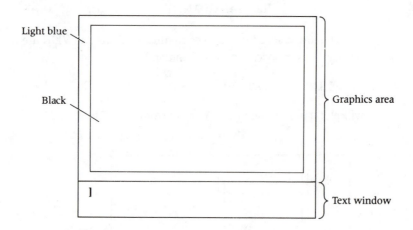

Remark 1

Line 5Ø draws the horizontal line across the bottom of the graphics area from right to left. If this line were changed to

```
5Ø  HLIN Ø,39 AT 39
```

the finished display would be the same but the bottom line would be drawn from left to right.

Remark 2   The vertical lines in this display will be thicker than the horizontal lines because blocks are wider than they are tall.

The general forms of the HLIN and VLIN commands are as follows:

```
HLIN a,b AT c
VLIN a,b AT c
```

Here **a, b,** and **c** denote numerical expressions whose values are truncated (if necessary) to integers. Let A, B, and C denote these integers. The HLIN command plots a horizontal row of blocks from (A,C) to (B,C) and the VLIN command plots a vertical column of blocks from (C,A) to (C,B). Since the integers A, B, and C are used to specify coordinates of points, they must satisfy the conditions for coordinates as described for the PLOT command.

EXAMPLE 3. Here is a program to display a square centered in the graphics area. Colors for the square and the background are specified by the user. The action of this program is described by the REM statements in lines 100, 130, 190, and 240.

```
100 REM ***INPUT COLORS FOR THE DESIGN***
110 INPUT "BACKGROUND COLOR? ";B
120 INPUT "COLOR OF THE SQUARE? ";SQ
130 REM ***COLOR THE BACKGROUND***
140 GR:HOME
150 COLOR=B
160 FOR Y=0 TO 39
170    HLIN 0,39 AT Y
180 NEXT Y
190 REM  ***COLOR THE CENTER SQUARE***
200 COLOR=SQ
210 FOR Y=11 TO 30
220    HLIN 11,30 AT Y
230 NEXT Y
240 REM ***SELECT AND DISPLAY A TITLE***
250 FOR C=0 TO B
260    READ B$
270 NEXT C
280 RESTORE
290 FOR C=0 TO SQ
300    READ SQ$
310 NEXT C
320 PRINT "TITLE: ";SQ$;" ON ";B$
330 DATA BLACK,RED,BLUE,PURPLE,GREEN,GRAY
340 DATA BLUE,BLUE,BROWN,ORANGE,GRAY
350 DATA PINK,GREEN,YELLOW,AQUA,WHITE
360 END
RUN
```

BACKGROUND COLOR? 13
COLOR OF THE SQUARE? 12

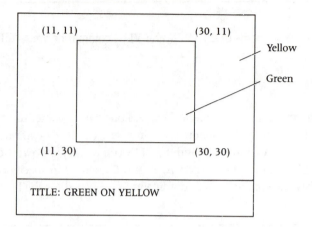

TITLE: GREEN ON YELLOW

The HLIN and VLIN commands are used only to display horizontal and vertical lines. To draw other lines, you must cause each individual point on the line to be plotted by using the PLOT command.

EXAMPLE 4. Here is a program to draw intersecting diagonal lines:

```
10  GR:HOME
20  COLOR=7
30  FOR X=0 TO 38
40      PLOT X,X
50      PLOT X,38-X
60  NEXT X
70  END
RUN
```

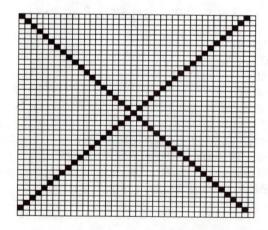

As X goes from 0 to 38, line 40 plots the points whose X and Y coordinates are equal. These are precisely the points on the upper-left to lower-right diagonal. Line 50 plots the points whose coordinates add up to 38: (0,38), (1,37), . . . , (38,0). These are the points on the lower-left to upper-right diagonal.

Remark   If actual lines are needed rather than lines of blocks, you must use the Apple's high-resolution graphics (Section 17.5).

17.2 Full-screen graphics

To extend the graphics area to the full screen, follow the GR command with the command

```
POKE -16302,0
```

This command stores (pokes) the number 0 in a memory location of the Apple's main memory (RAM) that is related to the number −16302. Doing so instructs the Apple to use the full screen for a 40-column by 48-row grid of blocks. The rows are numbered 0 to 47 and the columns are again numbered 0 to 39. The companion command

```
POKE -16301,0
```

returns you from full-screen to mixed-screen graphics.

EXAMPLE 5. Here is a program to color the full screen white:

```
10 REM ***SELECT FULL-SCREEN GRAPHICS***
20 GR:POKE -16302,0
30 REM ***COLOR THE SCREEN WHITE***
40 COLOR=15
50 FOR Y=0 TO 47
60    HLIN 0,39 AT Y
70 NEXT Y
80 END
```

17.3 Low-resolution graphics applications

In this section we give three examples further illustrating the use of the Apple's low-resolution graphics. The first concerns plotting a bar chart showing grade distributions of students, the second uses the RND function to generate changing kaleidoscopic designs, and the third illustrates a technique used in some video games. In each case we use the Apple's mixed-screen graphics mode so that descriptive text can be included with the graphic displays.

EXAMPLE 6. The number of students receiving the grades of A, B, C, D, and E at Easy University are given below. Write a program to display a bar chart showing the relative size of the five groups.

Number of students	Grade
432	A
567	B
673	C
123	D
53	E

Problem analysis

To keep things as simple as possible, we'll include the five input values (432, 567, 673, 123, and 53) in a DATA statement. Since no specific details of the output are given in the problem statement, let's agree to produce a chart like the one shown here. (The column numbers 11, 15, 19, 23, and 27 are for reference only.)

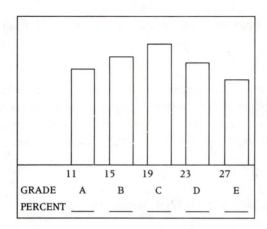

A simple two-step algorithm to produce this output is as follows.

    a. Display the vertical bars in the graphics area.
    b. Print the two lines of text in the text window and stop.

To display the bars we need to know the height of each rectangle. The height should represent the fraction F of students receiving a particular grade. If we use 40 × F vertical blocks, we can be sure that each rectangle will fit in the graphics area. (F is between 0 and 1 so 40 × F is between 0 and 40.)

Step (b) of the two-step algorithm is not difficult. It requires only that data be output in specified columns. We will use HOME to clear the text window and then the TAB function in PRINT statements to display the two lines.

Step (a) requires more detail. To this end let's choose variable names:

    NUM = number of students receiving a certain grade
      TTL = total number of grades given
        F = fraction of TTL for a certain grade (F = NUM/TTL)
    COL = column position in the 40 × 40 grid
    HGT = height of rectangle to be constructed

If we use HGT = 40*F to specify the number of blocks in a rectangle (vertical bar), the Apple will first truncate HGT. The bar chart will more accurately represent the given data if we round 40*F. Thus we will use

    HGT=INT(4Ø*F+Ø.5)

Algorithm (refined)

    a1. Sum the five counts NUM to obtain TTL.
    a2. For each of the five counts NUM:
            Calculate F = NUM/TTL.
            Calculate HGT = INT(40*F + Ø.5).
            Display a vertical bar HGT blocks high.
    b.   Print the two lines of text in the text window and stop.

From the diagram we see that the bars begin at column position COL = 11, 15, 19, 23, and 27. To display them three columns wide, we'll use the VLIN command three times—once each at COL, COL + 1, and COL + 2.

The program

```
100 REM ***GRADE REPORT BAR CHART***
110 REM
120 REM DETERMINE TOTAL NUMBER TTL OF GRADES.
130 LET TTL=0
140 FOR K=1 TO 5
150     READ NUM:TTL=TTL+NUM
160 NEXT K
170 REM DISPLAY A BAR FOR EACH GRADE.
180 RESTORE
190 GR:COLOR=7
200 LET COL=11:REM POSITION FOR A BAR
210 FOR K=1 TO 5
220     READ NUM
230     LET F=NUM/TTL
240     LET HGT=INT(40*F+0.5)
250     VLIN 39,39-HGT AT COL
260     VLIN 39,39-HGT AT COL+1
270     VLIN 39,39-HGT AT COL+2
280     COL=COL+4
290 NEXT K
300 REM DISPLAY IDENTIFYING TEXT FOR BAR CHART.
310 HOME
320 PRINT "GRADE";TAB(12);"A";TAB(16);"B";
330 PRINT TAB(20);"C";TAB(24);"D";TAB(28);"E"
340 RESTORE
350 PRINT "PERCENT";
360 LET COL=12
370 FOR K=1 TO 5
380     READ NUM
390     PRINT TAB(COL);INT(100*NUM/TTL+.5);
400     LET COL=COL+4
410 NEXT K
420 DATA 432,567,673,123,53
430 END
RUN
```

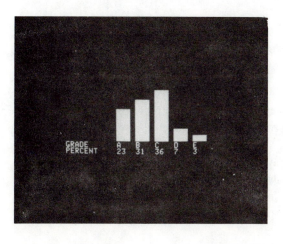

EXAMPLE 7. Kaleidoscope designs.

Kaleidoscopic designs make use of reflections to produce symmetrical sets of images. In this example we obtain the required symmetry as follows. First we divide the graphics area into four quadrants by means of imaginary horizontal and vertical lines that meet in the center:

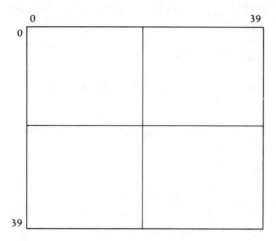

Next we select a point (X,Y) in the upper-left quadrant and plot the following four symmetrical points:

$$(X, Y) = \text{point selected}$$
$$(39 - X, Y) = \text{reflection of } (X, Y) \text{ in the vertical line}$$
$$(X, 39 - Y) = \text{reflection of } (X, Y) \text{ in the horizontal line}$$
$$(39 - X, 39 - Y) = \text{reflection of } (39 - X, Y) \text{ in the horizontal line}$$

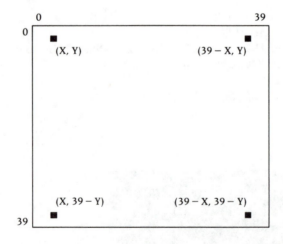

The following steps show one way to produce changing kaleidoscopic designs with the symmetries just described:

a. Randomly select a point (X,Y) in the upper-left quadrant.
b. Randomly select a color (0–15).
c. Plot the four symmetrical points associated with (X,Y).
d. Go to step (a).

The program

```
100 GR:HOME
110 PRINT "KALEIDOSCOPE---TYPE CTRL C TO STOP."
120     REM SELECT A POINT IN FIRST QUADRANT.
130     LET X=INT(20*RND(1))
140     LET Y=INT(20*RND(1))
150     REM SELECT A COLOR.
160     COLOR=INT(16*RND(1))
170     REM PLOT 4 SYMMETRICAL POINTS.
180     PLOT X,Y:PLOT 39-X,Y
190     PLOT X,39-Y:PLOT 39-X,39-Y
200 GOTO 120
RUN
```

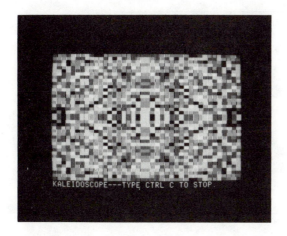

Remark

On black and white screens, pleasing designs are obtained by selecting one color (say, black) more often than the others. To select black 50% of the time, include the line

```
165 IF RND(1)<.5 THEN COLOR=0
```

Many video games involve a moving ball capable of rebounding off a wall. The moving ball can be simulated by plotting a point, causing a short delay, erasing the point (plot it in the color of the background), and moving on to the next point. The program segment

```
300 GR
310 LET X=0:Y=5:REM STARTING POINT
320     COLOR=7:PLOT X,Y:REM PLOT THE POINT.
330     FOR DLAY=1 TO 5:NEXT DLAY
340     COLOR=0:PLOT X,Y:REM ERASE THE POINT.
350     LET X=X+1
360 IF X<=39 THEN 320
```

simulates a ball moving from left to right along the horizontal line Y = 5. If you keep X fixed and vary Y, the ball will move along a vertical line. The delay (line 330) is necessary for two reasons: it extends the length of time the ball is visible so that it can easily be seen, and it controls the speed of the ball.

By changing both X and Y, the ball can be made to move in directions other than the horizontal and vertical. For example, the program segment

```
3ØØ GR
31Ø LET X=Ø:Y=39
32Ø    COLOR=7:PLOT X,Y
33Ø    FOR DLAY=1 TO 5:NEXT DLAY
34Ø    COLOR=Ø:PLOT X,Y
35Ø    LET X=X+2:Y=Y-1
36Ø IF X<=39 AND Y>=Ø THEN 32Ø
```

simulates a ball moving from the lower-left corner of the graphics area along the line containing the successive points (0,39), (2,38), (4,37), (6,36), and so on.

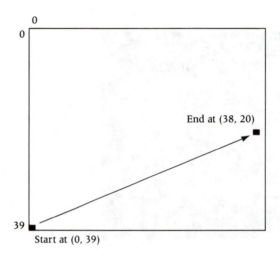

Assume now that a wall one block thick is constructed at each of the four boundaries of the graphics area—X = 0, X = 39, Y = 0, and Y = 39—and that a ball approaches one of these walls. To simulate a rebounding ball, two things must be done: we must detect when a wall has been encountered, and then we must start the ball off in a new direction just as if it were a real ball meeting a barrier.

Determining when a wall is encountered is easy. Since the walls were placed at X = 0, X = 39, Y = 0, and Y = 39, a wall is encountered when the next position (X,Y) of the moving ball satisfies one of the following conditions:

$X \geq 39$ right wall is encountered
$X \leq 0$ left wall is encountered
$Y \geq 39$ bottom wall is encountered
$Y \leq 0$ top wall is encountered

To describe a method for selecting a new direction for a rebounding ball, let's assume that the ball moves by changing its coordinates X and Y by the respective amounts XCHANGE and YCHANGE. Having just plotted the ball in position (X,Y), we give the next position by the two commands

```
LET X=X+XCHANGE
LET Y=Y+YCHANGE
```

Let's assume that $X \geq 39$—that is, the ball has reached the right vertical wall. To start it in the opposite direction, we'll let X = 38 and continue it in the new direction by letting

XCHANGE = −XCHANGE. Similar remarks apply as the ball approaches the other three boundaries. The following program segment ensures that a moving ball will rebound when it reaches any of the four boundaries:

```
500 REM REBOUND
510    IF X>=39 THEN X=38:XCHANGE=-XCHANGE
520    IF X<=0 THEN X=1:XCHANGE=-XCHANGE
530    IF Y>=39 THEN Y=38:YCHANGE=-YCHANGE
540    IF Y<=0 THEN Y=1:YCHANGE=-YCHANGE
550    COLOR=7:PLOT X,Y
560    FOR DLAY=1 TO 5:NEXT DLAY
570    COLOR=0:PLOT X,Y
580    LET X=X+XCHANGE:Y=Y+YCHANGE
590 GOTO 510
```

For a number of reasons, including the large size of the blocks in the 40 × 40 grid, it is impossible to write a program that simulates the motion of a bouncing ball exactly. The method presented here gives an approximation of this motion that is adequate for beginning programming tasks. To improve significantly on this method would require a detailed mathematical analysis that is beyond the scope of this book.

EXAMPLE 8. A simple video game.

The program in this example makes use of the rebounding ball simulation and introduces one other element. There is a vertical column of bricks at position $X = 32$. The ball is given an initial position and direction and then allowed to rebound off the four walls and also the brick wall. If the ball hits a brick, however, it knocks the brick out of the column (to the tune of a beep) as it rebounds. Should the ball arrive at a position in the column from which it has previously knocked out the brick, it is allowed to pass through the column to the other side. The program also keeps score of how many bricks were knocked out.

To determine whether a brick remains or has been removed from the original column of bricks, we will need the Applesoft built-in function

SCRN(X,Y)

which returns the color code of the point (X,Y). Initially we will color the bricks purple (color code 3) and recolor them black (the background color) as they are hit. This strategy will allow us to use the condition SCRN(X,Y) = 3 to tell whether a brick remains at position (X,Y).

Lines 100 to 320 of the program describe the game and tell the user how it is played. The GET command that immediately follows these PRINT statements (line 330) is widely used in graphics and game programs to allow the user time to read instructions appearing on the screen. Any character typed at the keyboard in response to GET A$, although not displayed, will be assigned to A$ and allow execution to continue. The user can take as long as necessary to read the instructions since the program will not continue until a key is pressed. (Note: Although pressing any key allows program execution to resume, no carriage return is generated. To avoid certain difficulties with DOS commands, GET commands should be followed by PRINT commands as shown in line 330.) In this program, note that as soon as a key is pressed, the very next line (line 340) causes the instructions to disappear. The action of the rest of the program is described by the REM statements in lines 350, 410, 430, and 520 and also by the INPUT prompts.

The program

```
100  PRINT "IN THIS GAME A BALL BOUNCES OFF THE"
110  PRINT "BOUNDARIES OF AN ENCLOSED AREA AND"
120  PRINT "ALSO OFF A BRICK WALL IN THIS AREA."
130  PRINT "EACH TIME A BRICK IS HIT, IT IS"
140  PRINT "REMOVED LEAVING A HOLE THROUGH WHICH"
150  PRINT "THE BALL CAN PASS ANOTHER TIME."
160  PRINT
170  PRINT "THE OBJECT OF THE GAME IS TO SELECT"
180  PRINT "A STARTING POSITION AND DIRECTION"
190  PRINT "FOR THE BALL SO THAT THE"
200  PRINT "GREATEST NUMBER OF BRICKS WILL BE"
210  PRINT "REMOVED IN A FIXED TIME LIMIT."
220  PRINT
230  PRINT "YOU WILL SELECT A STARTING POSITION"
240  PRINT "ALONG THE LEFT WALL BY TYPING A"
250  PRINT "NUMBER FROM 1 TO 38.(1 FOR THE TOP.)"
270  PRINT
280  PRINT "YOU WILL SELECT A STARTING DIRECTION"
290  PRINT "BY TYPING A NUMBER FROM 0 TO 4. (4"
300  PRINT "GIVES THE GREATEST DECLINATION.)"
310  PRINT
320  PRINT "PRESS ANY KEY TO CONTINUE:";
330  GET A$ : PRINT
340  GR : HOME
350  REM ***DRAW THE BOUNDARY WALLS***
360  COLOR=7
370  HLIN 0,39 AT 0
380  HLIN 0,39 AT 39
390  VLIN 0,39 AT 0
400  VLIN 0,39 AT 39
410  REM ***BUILD THE BRICK WALL***
420  COLOR=3: VLIN 1,38 AT 32
430  REM ***SET STARTING VALUES***
440  LET X=1: REM START AT LEFT WALL.
450  INPUT "SELECT STARTING POSITION (1-38): ";Y
460  IF Y<1 OR Y>38 THEN 450
470  COLOR=7: PLOT X,Y
480  LET XCHANGE=1
490  INPUT "SELECT STARTING DIRECTION (0-4): ";YCHANGE
500  COUNT=0: REM COUNTS NUMBER OF BRICKS REMOVED.
510  VTAB 23: PRINT TAB(28);"SCORE  ";COUNT
520  REM ***MOVE THE BALL 1000 TIMES***
530  COLOR=0: PLOT X,Y : REM ERASE STARTING POINT.
540  FOR N=1 TO 1000
550      LET X=X+XCHANGE:Y=Y+YCHANGE
560      IF X>=39 THEN X=38:XCHANGE=-XCHANGE
570      IF X<=0 THEN X=1:XCHANGE=-XCHANGE
580      IF Y>=39 THEN Y=38:YCHANGE=-YCHANGE
590      IF INT (Y)<=0 THEN Y=1:YCHANGE=-YCHANGE
600      IF SCRN(X,Y)<>3 THEN 660
610      REM ***A BRICK IS HIT***
620      LET COUNT=COUNT+1
630      VTAB 23: PRINT TAB(28);"SCORE  ";COUNT
640      LET XCHANGE=-XCHANGE
```

```
650    PRINT CHR$(7);:REM RING THE BELL.
660    COLOR=7: PLOT X,Y
670    FOR DLAY=1 TO 7: NEXT DLAY
680    COLOR=0: PLOT X,Y : REM ERASE PREVIOUS POINT.
690 NEXT N
700 INPUT "DO YOU WISH TO PLAY AGAIN? ";C$
710 IF C$="YES" THEN TEXT : HOME : GOTO 340
720 TEXT : HOME : END
RUN
```

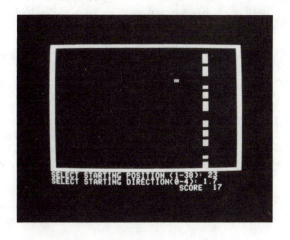

Remark

This program executes the line

```
650 PRINT CHR$(7);: REM RING THE BELL.
```

each time a brick is hit. Some find this sound annoying, but Applesoft BASIC provides the means for producing softer and different sounds. To do so, you must use the expression

```
PEEK(-16336)
```

Normally the PEEK function is used to examine the contents of individual memory locations in the Apple's main memory just as POKE (see Section 17.2) is used to place information in individual memory locations. The location associated with the number -16336 is special, however. It is connected to the Apple's speaker in such a way that the speaker will click each time PEEK(-16336) is encountered in a program. To see that this is so, type the immediate mode command

```
A=PEEK(-16336)
```

and listen carefully. To produce a more audible sound, you can cause a rapid sequence of clicks. The single line

```
100 FOR I=1 TO 20 : A=PEEK(-16336) : NEXT I
```

will produce clicks in rapid succession that you may find a welcome substitute for the bell. The line

```
200 FOR I=1 TO 10 : A=PEEK(-16336)+PEEK(-16336) : NEXT I
```

will also produce rapid clicks but with a different timbre. By experimenting you should be able to cause different sounds for different events—for instance, one sound for bouncing off a boundary wall and another for hitting a brick.

17.4 Problems

1. What graphics display results from each program?

a.
```
1Ø GR
2Ø COLOR=7
3Ø FOR Y=Ø TO 1Ø
4Ø     HLIN Ø,Y AT Y
5Ø NEXT Y
6Ø END
```

b.
```
1Ø GR
2Ø COLOR=7
3Ø FOR Y=Ø TO 1Ø
4Ø     HLIN 1Ø-Y,1Ø AT Y
5Ø NEXT Y
6Ø END
```

c.
```
1Ø GR : HOME
2Ø COLOR=7
3Ø FOR X=1 TO 9 STEP 4
4Ø     VLIN 1Ø,3Ø AT X
5Ø NEXT X
6Ø HLIN 1,5 AT 2Ø
7Ø HLIN 8,1Ø AT 1Ø
8Ø HLIN 8,1Ø AT 3Ø
9Ø END
```

d.
```
1ØØ GR : COLOR=7
11Ø LET X=7 : Y=7 : GOSUB 2ØØ
12Ø LET X=X+2Ø : GOSUB 2ØØ
13Ø LET Y=Y+2Ø : GOSUB 2ØØ
14Ø LET X=X-2Ø : GOSUB 2ØØ
15Ø END
2ØØ VLIN Y,Y+3 AT X
21Ø HLIN X,X+4 AT Y+3
22Ø VLIN Y,Y+5 AT X+3
23Ø RETURN
```

In Problems 2–11, write a program to produce each display described. (A color screen is not required. Black and white displays will show the different colors in distinguishable shadings.)

2. Color the left half of the graphics area dark blue and the right half orange.
3. Divide the graphics area into four quadrants. Color the upper-left quadrant yellow, the upper-right green, the lower-left dark green, and the lower-right red (magenta).
4. Color all blocks on or below the upper-left to lower-right diagonal in dark blue. Color all other blocks in light blue.
5. Divide the graphics area into ten equal rows each four blocks thick. Color every other row purple, beginning with the first. Color the remaining rows yellow.
6. Divide the graphics area into ten equal columns each four blocks wide. Color every other column purple, beginning with the first. Color the remaining columns white.
7. Construct a low-resolution color chart by using columns 1 through 32 of the graphics area. Beginning at the left, color every successive pair of columns a different color according to the color codes 0 to 15. Label these 16 columns in the text window.
8. Display the message HALT! in large block letters centered in the graphics area.
9. Fill the graphics area with an 8 × 8 checkerboard pattern. The two colors should be specified by the user during program execution.
10. Use the full screen to display a 6 × 5 checkerboard pattern of 8-block by 8-block squares. The two colors should be specified by the user during program execution.
11. Produce a display as in Problem 10 except that the border squares should all be of one color. Thus the user must specify three colors—two for the inner squares and one for the border.

In Problems 12–15, write a program for each task specified.

12. Produce a bar chart to display the following sales figures graphically. The years and the sales amounts should be displayed in the text window. (Assume that a bar 40 blocks high represents the sales amount $1500 million.)

Year	Sales in millions
1978	$1235
1979	$1421
1980	$1251
1981	$1025
1982	$843

13. Produce changing kaleidoscopic designs by modifying the program of Example 7 in one or more of the following ways:

a. If a randomly selected point (X,Y) satisfies the condition X + Y < 19, reject it and select another. (The designs will no longer occupy the full graphics area.)

b. If a randomly selected point (X,Y) satisfies the condition

$$(X - 19)^2 + (Y - 19)^2 > 15^2$$

reject it and select another. (The designs will appear in a circle centered on the screen. If you change > to <, the designs will appear outside this circle.)

c. For each point (X,Y) randomly selected from the first quadrant, plot (X,Y) and (Y,X)—its reflection in the upper-left to lower-right diagonal. Then plot the symmetrical points obtained by reflecting these two points as described in Example 7. Thus for each point (X,Y) you will plot the following eight points:

(X,Y)	(Y,X)
(39 − X,Y)	(39 − Y,X)
(X, 39 − Y)	(Y, 39 − X)
(39 − X, 39 − Y)	(39 − Y, 39 − X)

14. Simulate the motion of two rebounding balls. The user should specify starting positions and directions for the two balls during program execution. One ball is to start along the left wall and the other along the right. If the balls meet, program execution should halt.

15. Simulate the following video game. The graphics area is bordered by a wall and also contains columns of bricks in columns 15, 18, 21, and 24 that divide the graphics area into separate compartments. Two players are to specify starting positions and directions for two balls: one along the left wall of the leftmost compartment and the other along the right wall of the rightmost compartment. As soon as this is done, the two balls are to be set in motion as described in Example 8. Each time a brick in one of the center columns is hit, the ball is to rebound after knocking out the brick. The first player to get through to the other player's compartment wins. (Do not allow either player to specify the horizontal direction.)

17.5 High-resolution graphics

In this section we'll assume that you are familiar with the Apple's low-resolution graphics as described in Section 17.1—and, of course, that your Apple computer system allows high-resolution graphics (most do). The main differences between low-resolution and high-resolution graphics, as well as certain similarities, are summarized in Tables 17.2 and 17.3.

TABLE 17.2 Comparison of low-resolution and high-resolution graphics

Feature	Low-resolution graphics	High-resolution graphics
Picture element	Block	Point (size of period)
Graphics area (mixed screen)	40 columns by 40 rows of blocks	280 columns by 160 rows of points
Graphics area (full screen)	40 columns by 48 rows of blocks	280 columns by 192 rows of points
To initiate graphics mode	GR	HGR (mixed screen) HGR2 (full screen)
To select a color	COLOR = (16 colors: Table 17.1)	HCOLOR = (8 colors: Table 17.3)
To plot a point	PLOT X,Y	HPLOT X,Y
To plot a line	HLIN (horizontal) VLIN (vertical)	HPLOT X1,Y1 TO X2,Y2 (to plot any line, not just horizontal and vertical)

TABLE 17.3 High-resolution colors

Number	Color	Number	Color
0	black1	4	black2
1	green (depends on video screen)	5	(depends on video screen)
2	blue (depends on video screen)	6	(depends on video screen)
3	white1	7	white2

Note: White1 and white2 do not always produce white. On black and white screens, 0 and 3 are good choices.

In high-resolution mixed-screen graphics, the 280 columns are numbered from 0 to 279 from left to right and the 160 rows are numbered from 0 to 159 from top to bottom (see Figure 17.3). As in low-resolution graphics a point is specified by giving its column number followed by its row number. Several labeled points are shown in Figure 17.3. Note that (140,80) is approximately at the center of the graphics area.

Because of the similarities between low-resolution and high-resolution graphics indicated in Table 17.2, it should be evident that the commands

```
HGR
HCOLOR=3
HPLOT 0,80
HPLOT 140,80
```

will illuminate the points (0,80) and (140,80) shown in Figure 17.3. Thus using HPLOT to illuminate single points in the graphics area presents no difficulty.

When you type HGR, the graphics area will be cleared but the cursor may not be visible in the four-line text window as it is when GR is typed. If you don't see the cursor, simply press the RETURN key until it appears. (This slight difference between low-resolution and high-resolution graphics is discussed in Remark 2 of Example 10.)

As shown in Table 17.2 Applesoft BASIC contains two commands to initiate high-resolution graphics mode: HGR and HGR2. When HGR is used, display information is stored in a part of the Apple's random-access memory referred to as *high-resolution graphics Page 1.* When HGR2 is used, this information is stored in a different part of RAM referred to as *Page 2.* Your Apple system may require you to use HGR2 because Page 1 is used for another purpose. If you must use HGR2, the full screen is used for a 280-column by 192-row graphics area with no text window. This means that all graphics commands should be issued in deferred

Figure 17.3
High-resolution graphics area.

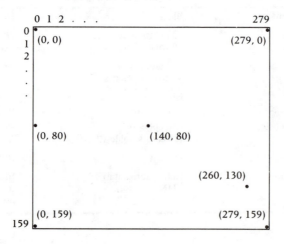

mode—that is, from within programs that are typed while in text mode. (If you do issue the immediate mode command HGR2, any subsequent commands that you type will be carried out but the commands themselves will not be displayed.)

Here is a program segment to illuminate the four corner points of the graphics area:

```
10 HGR : REM OR HGR2
20 HCOLOR=3
30 HPLOT 0,0
40 HPLOT 279,0
50 HPLOT 279,159
60 HPLOT 0,159
```

The four points are plotted clockwise, starting from the upper-left corner point. As with low-resolution graphics, coordinates are truncated to integers to obtain screen coordinates. Thus

```
HPLOT 15,40
```

and

```
HPLOT 15.2,40.999
```

both plot the point (15,40).

You may have noticed that in each illustration we use the color code 3 (white1). When you are using a black and white screen, colors other than black (0 or 4) and white (3 or 7) may result in unexpected displays. To see that this is so, select any other color—say green (color code 1)—and try plotting a few points. You will undoubtedly find that some of the points are not displayed. On our own black and white screen, we've found that the most reliable results are obtained by using color code 3 for white rather than 7.

In high-resolution graphics, HPLOT is the only plotting command. It is used to plot not only individual points but entire line segments. The command

```
HPLOT 143,50 TO 84,148
```

plots the line segment from the point (143,50) to the point (85,148). The command

```
HPLOT 84,148 TO 143,50
```

plots the same line segment but in the opposite direction. The line produced by this command can also be drawn by using the form HPLOT X,Y to plot each of its points. This requires that you tell the Apple a method for determining what points must be plotted—not an easy task for those unfamiliar with the mathematical equations of lines. Using

```
HPLOT 143,50 TO 84,148
```

alleviates this difficulty. (If you plot the line from (143,50) to (84,148) by either method, the line will not be a solid straight line but somewhat jagged. The reason for this discrepancy is discussed in Remark 3 of Example 10.)

EXAMPLE 9. Here is a program to draw several squares with a common center:

```
100 HGR : REM OR HGR2
110 HCOLOR=3
120 LET L=120 : REM SIDE LENGTH
130 LET Y=20 : REM TOP EDGE
140 FOR X=80 TO 140 STEP 10
150     REM PLOT SQUARE STARTING
160     REM AT CORNER (X,Y).
170     HPLOT X,Y TO X+L,Y
180     HPLOT X+L,Y TO X+L,Y+L
190     HPLOT X+L,Y+L TO X,Y+L
200     HPLOT X,Y+L TO X,Y
210     LET L=L-20 : REM NEW LENGTH
220     LET Y=Y+10 : REM NEW TOP EDGE
230 NEXT X
240 END
RUN
```

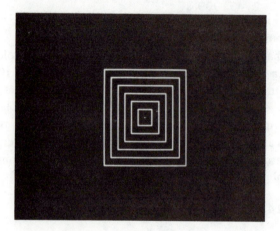

Remark   The last time through the loop, (X,Y) = (140,80) and L = 0. This means that the last square plotted by lines 170 to 200 has (140,80) for each vertex. Thus it is plotted as a point as shown in the display.

Previously we used the command

```
HPLOT 143,50 TO 84,148
```

to plot a line from (143,50) to (84,148). Applesoft allows you to plot this line by using

```
HPLOT 143,50
HPLOT TO 84,148
```

The second of these commands plots a line from the last point plotted—in this case, (143,50)—to the point (84,148) in whatever color was used to plot the first point. With this new form of the HPLOT command, lines 170 to 200 of the preceding program (which plot a square) can be replaced by

```
170 HPLOT X,Y
180 HPLOT TO X+L,Y
190 HPLOT TO X+L,Y+L
200 HPLOT TO X,Y+L
205 HPLOT TO X,Y
```

thus simplifying somewhat the job of typing the program.

The form

```
HPLOT A,B TO C,D
```

is most often used when isolated line segments are to be plotted. The form

```
HPLOT TO X,Y
```

is intended for applications requiring a sequence of connecting line segments for which the coordinates of the endpoints must be determined during program execution. The method just described for drawing squares is an illustration. (Another is shown in Example 10.) The most common application of this method involves plotting a single point and then many connecting line segments (perhaps hundreds) starting from the first point. To do this you would plot the starting point, say (X,Y), using

```
HPLOT X,Y
```

Then, for each new (X,Y) determined during program execution, you would use

```
HPLOT TO X,Y
```

to plot the next segment. The first point *must* be plotted. Unless you first plot some point, the statement HPLOT TO X,Y will display nothing. When this method is used to plot connecting line segments, they will all be plotted in whatever color was used for the very first point— even if a different HCOLOR= command is executed while plotting the line segments.

EXAMPLE 10. Here is a program to join a sequence of points (X,Y) with connecting line segments:

The sequence of points (X,Y) to be connected is described in lines 110 to 130 of the program. You may check that these points are (0,80), (40,92), (80,56), (120,116), (160,32), (200,130), and (240,8)—all of which lie in the graphics area.

```
100 REM JOIN THE POINTS X,Y GIVEN BY
110 REM      X=40C
120 REM      X=80+12C (FOR C=1,3,5)
130 REM      Y=80-12C (FOR C=0,2,4,6)
140 REM
150 REM *****BEGIN THE DISPLAY*****
160 HGR : HCOLOR=3
170 REM ***PLOT THE FIRST POINT***
180 LET X=0 : Y=80 : REM CASE C=0
190 HPLOT X,Y
200 REM ***PLOT CONNECTING LINE SEGMENTS***
210 LET SIGN=1 : REM WILL ALTERNATE BETWEEN +1 AND -1
```

```
22Ø FOR C=1 TO 6
23Ø    LET X=4Ø*C : Y=8Ø+SIGN*12*C
24Ø    HPLOT TO X,Y
25Ø    LET SIGN=-SIGN
26Ø NEXT C
27Ø REM ***DISPLAY A TITLE***
28Ø HOME
29Ø VTAB 22 : PRINT "A LINE DRAWING"
3ØØ END
RUN
```

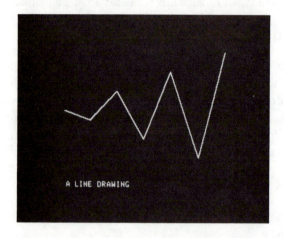

Remark 1

If your Apple system requires that you use HGR2 rather than HGR, you would not include lines 27Ø to 29Ø, which display a title in the text window. *Remember:* With HGR2 there is no text window.

Remark 2

When you are using mixed-screen high-resolution graphics, use the VTAB command to specify a screen line for any output to be displayed in the text window. In this program the VTAB command in line 29Ø is absolutely essential. The HOME command in line 28Ø clears the text window but does not position the cursor in this window as it does in low-resolution graphics mode. Rather, the cursor is positioned as if it were at the top of the screen behind the graphics area. Since PRINT statements cause screen output to begin at the current cursor position, failure to use VTAB 22 (or 21, 23, or 24) means that the output string A LINE DRAWING would not be displayed. To help understand this point, we recommend that you experiment by typing the following sequence of immediate mode commands:

```
HGR           (Select high-resolution graphics.)
HOME          (Everything will disappear.)
PRINT "HELLO" (Type carefully. Nothing will be displayed—not even HELLO.)
REM ANYTHING
TEXT          (When you press the RETURN key, everything you typed after HOME
               will be visible as well as the output string HELLO.)
```

Remark 3

Notice that the six line segments shown in the display are not solid lines. Rather, each segment has missing points and a somewhat jagged appearance. Although the Apple's use of color can in fact cause missing points, the principal reason for this discrepancy is that the number of different points that can be plotted on the Apple's video screen is inadequate for displaying most segments. Consider, for example, the two commands

```
HCOLOR=3
HPLOT Ø,Ø TO 1,5Ø
```

As the Apple plots the segment from (0,0) to (1,50), the only X coordinates available are 0 and 1. Since these two X coordinates designate adjacent vertical lines on the screen, each point displayed will lie on one of these lines. Recalling that the Apple truncates reals to obtain integer screen coordinates, we see that a vertical line is plotted from (0,0) to (0,49) and then the point (1,50) is plotted. Moreover, the vertical line will appear as a sequence of distinguishable dots and not as a solid line. With the Apple, only horizontal lines appear as solid lines. If any other line must be made to appear solid, you will have to plot it with one or more lines adjacent to it.

On some, but not all, Apple systems, you can use a single HPLOT command to plot two or more connecting line segments. The command

```
HPLOT A,B TO C,D TO E,F
```

will plot a line from (A,B) to (C,D) and then another from (C,D) to (E,F). Thus the command is equivalent to the two commands

```
HPLOT A,B TO C,D
HPLOT C,D TO E,F
```

or to

```
HPLOT A,B
HPLOT TO C,D
HPLOT TO E,F
```

If your system allows this extended form of the HPLOT command, you may find it useful in producing simple figures consisting of only a few connected line segments. For example,

```
HPLOT A,B TO C,D TO E,F TO A,B
```

will draw a triangle with the three included points as vertices. Similarly,

```
HPLOT X,Y TO X+24,Y+72 TO X-38,Y+28 TO
X+38,Y+28 TO X-24,Y+72 TO X,Y
```

will plot a five-point star:

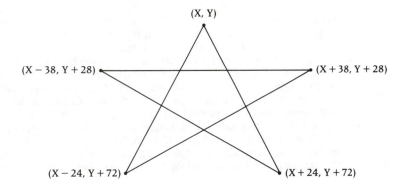

The general forms of the HPLOT command are as follows:

```
HPLOT a,b
HPLOT a,b TO c,d {TO e,f}
HPLOT TO a,b
```

The numerical expressions **a, b, c, d, e,** and **f** are truncated (if necessary) to obtain integer screen coordinates. Only certain Apple systems (those that use firmware Applesoft) allow you to include three or more points in the second of the three forms.

Here are some further points concerning high-resolution graphics:

1. Although the two coordinates (X,Y) of a point are normally from 0 to 279 and 0 to 159, respectively, the Y coordinate can be any integer from 0 to 191 without causing an error diagnostic. If mixed-screen graphics mode (HGR) is used, points with Y coordinates from 160 to 191 simply will not be displayed. If you use HGR2, the full screen is used for graphics so that these points are displayed.

2. In Section 17.2 we used the command POKE −16302,0 to convert the screen from mixed-screen mode (graphics plus text) to full-screen graphics. This can also be done with high-resolution graphics. Simply issue the HGR command and then the POKE command.

3. Some printers are capable of producing good printed copy of what appears on the high-resolution graphics screen. It's worth finding out if your printer can do this. (The Apple company's Silentype printer can produce such copy. Simply type PR#1—assuming the printer is plugged into slot 1—and then type ctrl Q. To obtain the best copy possible, you would naturally consult the Silentype manual.)

17.6 Problems

Write a program to perform each task.

1. Draw a boundary, four points wide, around the graphics area.
2. Color the region of the graphics area below the upper-left to lower-right diagonal.
3. Color the upper-left and lower-right quadrants of the graphics area by drawing only lines that pass through the point (140,80).
4. Color the triangular region bounded by the three line segments connecting (140,0), (0,159), and (279,159). (Draw only lines that emanate from the point (140,0).)
5. Divide the graphics area into eight triangular regions by drawing four lines through (140,80). Two of these should be screen diagonals; the others should be horizontal and vertical. Then draw a borderline along the entire screen boundary.
6. Color the eight triangular regions described in Problem 5 in alternating colors.
7. Divide the graphics area into five regions by drawing four squares of side lengths 40, 80,120, and 160. Each square is to have the point (0,0) as one of its corner points.
8. Assuming the graphics area to be divided into five regions as in Problem 7, use two colors to color these regions. Adjacent regions are to be colored differently. If you use black and white, color the smallest region white.
9. Assuming the graphics area to be divided into seven regions as shown in Example 9, use two colors to color these regions. Adjacent regions are to be colored differently. If you use black and white, color the smallest region white.
10. Divide the graphics area into quadrants by coloring the upper-left and lower-right quadrants white and leaving the other two black. A star is to move clockwise through the four quadrants. When it appears in a white quadrant it should be black (and vice versa). Make sure the star is centered in each quadrant. Include a delay so that the star is easily seen. After this delay, color the star in its background color before going on to the next quadrant.
11. Allow the user to create line drawings as follows. After entering a starting point, the user should be allowed to enter L, R, U, or D (for left, right, up, or down) and a number for the length of a line segment. A segment of the chosen length and direction should be drawn from the starting point. The user should then be allowed to specify a direction and length for another

line segment that should be drawn from the endpoint of the previous segment. If instead of entering L, R, U, or D the user types A, the graphics area should be cleared and the user allowed to create another line drawing. If the user types S, program execution should terminate. Any entry other than L, R, U, D, A, or S should be ignored and a new entry requested. If the direction and length specify a line segment that will extend out of the viewing area, they should be rejected and a new entry requested.

12. Transform the 280-column by 160-row high-resolution graphics area into a Cartesian coordinate system whose origin is at the point (140,80) in the graphics area. Draw horizontal and vertical axes through this point. Display the graphs of each of the following functions. (Any point (X,Y) in the Cartesian coordinate system will have coordinates (140 + X, 80 − Y) in the graphics area. To obtain the best graphs possible, round the Y coordinates rather than allowing the Apple to truncate them.)

a. $Y = 10*SGN(X)$ $-50 \leqslant X \leqslant 50$

b. $Y = ABS(X)$ $-50 \leqslant X \leqslant 50$

c. $Y = 10*INT(X/10)$ $-50 \leqslant X \leqslant 50$

d. $Y = \dfrac{75}{X}$ $-75 \leqslant X \leqslant 75, \quad X \neq 0$

e. $Y = 5\sqrt{X + 30}$ $-30 \leqslant X \leqslant 100$

f. $Y = \dfrac{10X^2}{100 - X^2}$ $-100 \leqslant X \leqslant 100, \quad X \neq 10, \quad X \neq -10$

g. $Y = \dfrac{X(X - 10)(X + 10)}{10}$ $-20 \leqslant X \leqslant 20$

17.7 Review true-or-false quiz

1. The two programming lines `10 GR : COLOR=7` and `10 COLOR=7 : GR` are equivalent.   T   F

2. The two programming lines `20 GR : HOME` and `20 HOME : GR` are equivalent.   T   F

3. The immediate mode command `HOME : TEXT` will return you from low-resolution graphics to text mode with a clear screen.   T   F

4. The immediate mode command `COLOR=15 : PLOT 20,20` will always result in a white point at position (20,20).   T   F

5. The statements `50 HLIN 23,30 AT 15` and `50 HLIN 30,23 AT 15` result in the same display.   T   F

6. Once a point is plotted in low-resolution graphics mode, it cannot be changed in the final display.   T   F

7. The statements

```
250 HPLOT X1,Y1
260 HPLOT TO X2,Y2
```

are equivalent to the single statement `255 HPLOT X1,Y1 TO X2,Y2`.   T   F

8. In high-resolution graphics mode, the statement

```
500 HOME : PRINT "FIRST LINE"
```

will display FIRST LINE in the first line below the graphics area.   T   F

9. In high-resolution graphics mode, the statement

```
600 VTAB 1 : PRINT "FIRST LINE"
```

will display FIRST LINE in the first line below the graphics area.   T   F

Appendix A

□ □ □ □ □ □ □ □ □ □ □ □ □ □ □ □

Getting Applesoft BASIC Up and Running

Whenever your Apple is ready for you to type a command, it will display a prompt character:

]   indicates that Applesoft BASIC is operational and that the Apple will understand any Applesoft commands you type at the keyboard.

>   indicates that Integer BASIC (an alternate version of the BASIC language) is operational.

*   indicates that the Apple's Monitor program is operational. (This mode of operation is used principally by programmers using the Apple's machine language.)

In this appendix we explain how you can get Applesoft BASIC up and running for the firmware, diskette, and cassette versions of the language. We'll also show how you can recover the Applesoft prompt] without starting over from the beginning.

A.1. Firmware Applesoft BASIC

Simply turning on the Apple (the switch is on the back of the computer) may give you the desired Applesoft prompt]. If it doesn't, you will have to carry out one of these two procedures:

1. If turning on the Apple produces the Integer BASIC prompt >, type FP (for floating point) and press the RETURN key.
2. If turning on the Apple produces neither] nor >, press the RESET key. Then hold down the CTRL key and type C. This should give you one of the two prompts] and >. If > is displayed, repeat procedure 1.

If neither procedure works—and you're sure you haven't made a typing error—get help. Sometimes a simple action, such as changing the position of a switch on the back of your computer, is all that's required.

While using firmware Applesoft BASIC you may accidentally do something that produces the prompt > or * (or no prompt at all). If this happens, you can recover the Applesoft prompt as follows:

1. If > is displayed, carry out procedure 1. (If there's a program in the Apple's memory, it will be lost.)
2. In any other case, use ctrl C—that is, hold down the CTRL key while typing C.
3. If neither step gives you the prompt], try pressing the RESET key. (This should give you] or >.)
4. As a last resort, turn off the Apple and start over again.

A.2. Diskette Applesoft BASIC

To load Applesoft BASIC from a diskette, two steps are required:

1. Load the disk operating system (DOS). The easiest way to do this is to place the diskette labeled System Master in the disk unit and then turn the Apple on. (If this is your first use of a disk unit, read the detailed explanation of this step given in Section B.1 of Appendix B.)
2. Place a diskette containing the program APPLESOFT (the System Master will do) in the disk unit, type FP (for floating point), and press the RETURN key.

After you carry out these two steps, the light on the disk unit will come on for a few seconds and then the prompt] will be displayed—indicating that Applesoft BASIC is up and running. If the diskette used in step 2 does not contain the program named Applesoft, the message

```
LANGUAGE NOT AVAILABLE
```

will be displayed.

While using diskette Applesoft BASIC, you may inadvertently do something that produces the prompt > or * (or no prompt at all). If this happens, you can recover the Applesoft prompt as follows:

1. First try ctrl C—that is, hold the CTRL key down while typing C. (If this step restores], the current program will remain intact.)
2. If > or * is displayed, type FP and then press the RETURN key. (The current program will be lost.) If typing FP causes the error message

```
PROGRAM TOO LARGE
```

   you should type INT, press the RETURN key, and then repeat the FP command.
3. If * is displayed, you can type 3D0G and then press the RETURN key. (The current program will remain intact.)
4. If none of these steps works, try pressing the RESET key. If this gives you the prompt >, type FP as in step 2.
5. As a last resort, turn off the Apple and start over again.

A.3. Cassette Applesoft BASIC

To load Applesoft from cassette tape use this five-step procedure:

1. Turn on the Apple. (The Integer BASIC prompt character > and the blinking cursor will appear on the screen.)
2. Insert and rewind the Applesoft cassette tape in your cassette recorder.
3. Type LOAD, press the Play button on the recorder, and press the RETURN key on the Apple. (The blinking cursor will disappear from the screen. The Apple will signal the start and finish of reading the tape with a beep. Then the cursor will reappear on the screen.)
4. Stop the recorder and rewind the tape.
5. Type RUN and press the RETURN key.

The Applesoft prompt character] signals that the language is now available.

While using cassette Applesoft BASIC, take extra care to ensure that the Applesoft prompt is not lost accidentally—recovery may not be possible. Try the following steps if you should lose the prompt:

1. If no prompt is displayed, use the ctrl C command—that is, type C with the CTRL key held down.
2. If > is displayed, you must reload Applesoft BASIC from cassette.
3. If * is displayed, type 3D0G and then press the RETURN key. This may or may not give you the Applesoft prompt. (If * is displayed, do not use ctrl C. It will get you the prompt > and you will have to reload Applesoft BASIC.)

Appendix B

□ □ □ □ □ □ □ □ □ □ □ □ □ □

The Disk Operating System (DOS)

Apple's Disk II unit is connected by cable to its controller card, which is normally installed in slot 6 of the Apple's main circuit board. The disk operating system (DOS) includes programs that allow you to use the disk unit as an external storage device. This appendix shows how to load DOS and explains how you can use it to perform certain tasks necessary for efficient use of the disk unit. Section B.5 lists all the DOS commands used in this book and gives text references.

B.1. Booting DOS

The process of loading the disk operating system is called *booting DOS,* or *booting the disk.* To boot the disk, insert the System Master diskette into the disk unit. As shown in the illustration, the label should be up and the edge nearest the oval cutout in the diskette's cover should enter the disk unit first. Diskettes should be handled gently; they must not be bent. And be sure to touch only the cover. The portion seen through the oval cutout contains densely packed information and touching it may render the diskette useless.

Next, close the door on the disk unit and turn the Apple on. The disk unit will automatically whir as it reads DOS into the Apple's memory. After a few seconds, the Apple will display a message such as

```
DOS VERSION 3.3
APPLE II          SYSTEM MASTER
```

indicating that DOS is operational. At this point, the prompt] or > will be displayed. In either case, all of the DOS features are now available for use and you can remove the System Master from the disk unit. Before you do so, however, make sure that the IN USE light on your disk unit is off. Removing a diskette while the disk unit is in use may permanently damage the diskette.

The process just described for booting the disk requires you to insert the System Master diskette into the disk unit *before* the Apple is turned on. DOS can also be booted with the Apple turned on. To do so, insert the System Master diskette, type IN#6, and press the RETURN key. This procedure will read DOS into memory as described above. (If booting the disk leaves you with the prompt >, follow the steps described in Appendix A to get Applesoft BASIC operational.)

B.2. Initializing a diskette

Before a new diskette can be used to store information it must be **initialized.** To do this, make sure that DOS is operational and that the Applesoft prompt is displayed. Then proceed as follows:

1. Insert the diskette to be initialized into the disk unit.
2. Type the NEW command to clear any previous program from memory.
3. Type a "greeting" program such as the following:

```
1Ø REM GREETING PROGRAM
2Ø PRINT "CREATED BY PAT SHEA."
3Ø PRINT "DATE-----1 APRIL 83"
4Ø END
```

This program will be copied onto the diskette being initialized and executed each time this diskette is booted. Thus the PRINT statements you include should give useful information about the diskette.

4. Type the DOS command

```
INIT HELLO
```

When you press the RETURN key, the diskette will spin for a while (less than a minute) as the Apple copies certain information onto the diskette, including the greeting program. (Any information stored on the diskette prior to this initialization will be lost.)

5. When initialization is complete, the disk unit's IN USE light will go off and the Apple-soft prompt will appear on the screen.

The diskette is now initialized and your greeting program is named HELLO. You can use the diskette to store your programs, now or at any later time, as described in the next section. A diskette needs to be initialized only once.

During any subsequent session at the computer, you can boot DOS with your initialized diskette rather than the System Master. DOS will be read into the Apple's memory and your greeting program HELLO will be executed. For the greeting program shown, booting the disk will cause the display

```
CREATED BY PAT SHEA.
DATE-----1 APRIL 83

]
```

After initializing a diskette and booting it, you should label it. But be sure to write on the label *before* placing it on the diskette. Bearing down on the cover with a pen can damage the diskette.

If the diskette just initialized is booted and you issue the CATALOG command (described in the next section), the following display will result:

```
]CATALOG

DISK VOLUME 254

 A ØØ2 HELLO

]
```

The Apple always uses 254 unless you specify a different volume number while typing the INIT command. To specify volume number 28, you would use

```
INIT HELLO, V28
```

Volume numbers 1 to 254 are allowed. The other items in this display (A and ØØ2) are explained in the next section.

B.3. A typical session with DOS

During a session at the Apple computer you should be able to perform the following tasks: save your program for later use, retrieve and run a program that was previously saved, and modify a saved program. In this section we describe the DOS commands most commonly used while performing these three tasks: SAVE, LOAD, CATALOG, DELETE, and RENAME. To understand the action caused by these commands, you should know that information stored on a diskette is organized into units called **files.** A diskette file can contain a program or data other than a program (as described in Chapter 14). DOS always references files by name. A **file name** can be any sequence of up to 30 characters, the first of which must be a letter. The comma is the only display character that is not allowed in a file name. Thus PROG#1 and GAME A-3 are both admissible as file names but 1ST PROGRAM and FED,STATE,LOC TAXES are not.

We now describe the five DOS commands listed above and show how they are used to save, retrieve, and modify programs.

Saving your programs

To preserve a program for later use, first be sure that a properly initialized diskette is in the disk unit. Then use the command

SAVE **fn**

This command copies the program currently in the Apple's memory onto the diskette and gives it the name **fn.** (The name **fn** is added to the diskette's catalog of files.) A program copied onto a diskette will continue to exist there even after the computer is turned off.

The following printout shows how you can type two programs and save a copy of each on your diskette:

```
]NEW                              (Clears memory so that a new program can be typed.)
](Type your first program.)
        •
        •
        •
]SAVE PROG1                       (Save program on diskette under the name PROG1.)
]NEW                              (Clears memory so that a new program can be typed.)
](Type your second program.)
        •
        •
        •
]SAVE PROG2                       (Save PROG2 on diskette.)
]                                 (PROG2 also exists in Apple's memory.)
```

Caution: If a program has been previously saved on your diskette under the name **fn** and you enter the command SAVE **fn,** the copy of **fn** on your diskette will be lost and the program currently in Apple's memory will be stored on your diskette under the name **fn.** Thus, by mistakenly choosing a program name already used on your diskette, you may erase a program—one that you want to keep. (Section B.4 explains how to protect your files.)

To produce a list of all file names stored on a diskette, use the command CATALOG. This command displays the names of all files currently stored on a diskette with certain other descriptive information. If you issue the command at this point, the following display will result:

```
]CATALOG

DISK VOLUME 254

 A ØØ2 HELLO
 A ØØ2 PROG1
 A ØØ2 PROG2

 ]
```

The name HELLO was given to the greeting program when we initialized the diskette; PROG1 and PROG2 are the two programs we saved. The A in the first column indicates that these programs were written in Applesoft BASIC. Diskettes can store 496 *sectors* of information; the 002 indicates that each of these programs used two sectors.

If you issue the CATALOG command for your diskette, you may obtain file names preceded by the letters T, I, or B instead of A. (The letter T denotes a text file as described in Chapter 14; I denotes an Integer BASIC program; B denotes a binary file, which usually contains a machine-language program.) These files may be ignored. If you attempt to save an Applesoft program with the name of a T, I, or B file already on the diskette, no harm will be done. The error message

```
FILE TYPE MISMATCH
```

will be displayed and you should choose another name for your program.

Retrieving programs from a diskette

Let's assume that the programs PROG1 and PROG2 have been stored on your diskette by the SAVE command. If at a later session you wish to run these programs you may proceed as follows. (DOS must be operational—if it isn't, boot it with the diskette containing PROG1 and PROG2.)

```
]LOAD PROG1              (PROG1 is read into Apple's memory.)
]LIST
  •
  •
  •
 (PROG1 is listed.)
  •
  •
  •
]RUN
  •
  •
  •
 (PROG1 is executed.)
  •
  •
  •
]LOAD PROG2              (PROG2 is read into Apple's memory.)
]RUN
  •
  •
  •
 (PROG2 is executed.)
 ]
```

At this point the programs PROG1 and PROG2 still exist on your diskette. They can be read into the Apple's memory by using the LOAD command and, once there, can be executed or listed by using the commands RUN and LIST.

The two commands

```
LOAD fn
RUN
```

can be replaced by the single command

```
RUN fn
```

In this form, RUN is a DOS command.

Following are some key points concerning the DOS commands LOAD **fn** and RUN **fn**:

1. If **fn** is not the name of a diskette file, the message

   ```
   FILE NOT FOUND
   ```

   will be displayed. Any program currently in the Apple's memory will remain intact.
2. If **fn** is a text (T) file or binary (B) file, you'll obtain the message

   ```
   FILE TYPE MISMATCH
   ```

   (You can load only files created with the SAVE command; T and B files are created with other commands.)
3. If **fn** is preceded by the letter I in a catalog listing, the Integer BASIC program **fn** will be loaded (and executed if RUN **fn** was used). The Integer BASIC prompt > will then be displayed. To recover the Applesoft prompt, use the FP command.
4. If you type LOAD but forget to type the file name, the Apple will assume that a cassette tape file is to be loaded and it will appear as though nothing is happening. To recover the Applesoft prompt, press the RESET key.

Modifying diskette programs

Often a program is saved before it is completely debugged. Let's assume that you saved such a program with the name POWER2. To modify POWER2, you can first use the LOAD command to read it into the Apple's memory. Having done this you can modify the program just as you could when you created it. After making the necessary modifications, you may replace the old copy of POWER2 on the diskette with the modified version by typing

```
SAVE POWER2
```

The modified version is now stored on your diskette under the same name POWER2 and can be retrieved at any subsequent session. (The original version of POWER2 will be lost.) The following printout illustrates what has just been described.

```
]LOAD POWER2          (Copy of POWER2 is read into Apple's memory.)
]LIST

1ØØ   LET A = 5       (Contents of POWER2.)
11Ø   LET B = A ^ 2
12Ø   PRINT B
13Ø   END

]1ØØ LET A=6          (Change line 100.)

]LIST

1ØØ   LET A = 6       (Updated POWER2.)
11Ø   LET B = A ^ 2
12Ø   PRINT B
13Ø   END

]SAVE POWER2          (Updated version of POWER2 is saved on diskette.)
]RUN                  (Updated version of POWER2 is executed.)
36

]
```

There will be times when you want to preserve both the original and the updated version of a program. To do this, use the SAVE command but with a different file name, say POWER2A. If later you wish to *delete* the copy of the original version of POWER2 from your diskette, use the command

    DELETE **fn**

This command deletes **fn** from the diskette. (If **fn** is not in the diskette directory, the message FILE NOT FOUND is displayed.) To *change* the name of a program stored on your diskette, use the RENAME command:

    RENAME **fn1, fn2**

This command changes the name of the diskette file **fn1** to **fn2.** The following printout shows how the DELETE and RENAME commands are used:

```
]LOAD POWER2          (Copy of POWER2 is read into Apple's memory.)
]1ØØ LET A=7          (Change line 100.)

]SAVE POWER2A         (Updated version of POWER2 is saved on diskette.)
]CATALOG
```

```
          DISK VOLUME 254

          A  002 HELLO
          A  002 POWER2
          A  002 POWER2A

          ]DELETE POWER2              (POWER2 is deleted from diskette.)
          ]CATALOG

          DISK VOLUME 254

          A  002 HELLO
          A  002 POWER2A

          ]RENAME POWER2A,POWER2B     (Changes name of POWER2A to POWER2B.)
          CATALOG

          DISK VOLUME 254

          A  002 HELLO
          A  002 POWER2B

          ]
```

B.4. Protecting your files

To prevent accidental erasure of a file on your diskette, use the LOCK command. For example,

```
          LOCK POWER2
```

will prevent alteration of the name or contents of POWER2. The following printout illustrates the effect of LOCK:

```
          ]CATALOG

          DISK VOLUME 254

          A  002 HELLO
          A  002 POWER2

          ]LOCK POWER2               (POWER2 is protected.)
          ]CATALOG

          DISK VOLUME 254

          A  002 HELLO
         *A  002 POWER2              (* indicates that POWER2 is locked.)

          ]DELETE POWER2

          FILE LOCKED                (You cannot delete POWER2.)
```

```
]SAVE POWER2

FILE LOCKED                 (You cannot erase POWER2.)

]RENAME POWER2, POWER2A

FILE LOCKED                 (You cannot rename POWER2.)

]
```

To cancel the effect of LOCK on POWER2, use

```
UNLOCK POWER2
```

If you try to save a program on the System Master diskette, the Apple will respond with the message

```
WRITE PROTECTED
```

indicating that you are not allowed to write any information on this diskette. DOS allows writing only to diskettes having a small square cutout along the edge opposite the label. Your diskette will have such a cutout, whereas the System Master will not (or should not). To *write-protect* a diskette, you need only to cover the cutout with some kind of tape. Thus, to protect an individual file use the LOCK command; to protect an entire diskette, cover its cutout with tape.

B.5. Summary of DOS commands used in this text

Command	Purpose	Text reference
APPEND	To open a sequential file and position it at its end	Section 14.3
CATALOG	To print a list of files stored on diskette	Section 14.1
		Section B.3
CLOSE	To terminate communication between a program and a text file	Section 14.1
ctrl D	To inform DOS that subsequent characters are a DOS command	Section 14.1
DELETE	To delete a file from diskette	Section B.3
		Section 14.1
FP	To choose the Applesoft BASIC language	Section B.1
INIT	To initialize a diskette	Section B.2
IN#**n**	To obtain subsequent input from the device connected to slot **n**	Section B.1
LOAD	To retrieve a program from diskette	Section B.3
LOCK	To prevent alteration of name or contents of a file stored on diskette	Section B.4
MON	To monitor output to and input from text files; to monitor DOS commands used in programs	Section 14.1
NOMON	To cancel the effect of MON	Section 14.1
OPEN	To establish communication between a program and a text file	Section 14.1
		Section 14.5
PR#**n**	To direct subsequent output to the device connected to slot **n**	Section 4.7
READ	To specify a file as a READ file	Section 14.1
RENAME	To rename a file stored on diskette	Section B.3
RUN	To retrieve a program from diskette and execute it	Section B.3
SAVE	To save a program on diskette	Section B.3
UNLOCK	To cancel the effect of LOCK	Section B.4
WRITE	To specify a file as a WRITE file	Section 14.1
		Section 14.5

Appendix C

□ □ □ □ □ □ □ □ □ □ □ □ □ □

Loading and Saving Programs with Cassette Tape

C.1. Procedure for loading a program from cassette tape

1. Get Applesoft BASIC operational. (See Appendix A).
2. Insert and rewind the tape containing the program to be loaded.
3. Type LOAD, press Play on the recorder, and press the RETURN key on the Apple. (The blinking cursor and the Applesoft prompt] will disappear from the screen. The Apple will signal the start and finish of its reading of the program with beeps. Finally, the prompt character] and cursor will reappear on the screen, signaling that the program has been loaded properly into Apple's memory.)
4. Stop and rewind the tape. (The program can now be listed, run, or modified.)

C.2. Procedure for saving a program on cassette tape

1. Insert and rewind a blank tape in the recorder.
2. Type SAVE, press Record on the recorder, and press the RETURN key on the Apple. (The cursor will disappear from the screen. The apple will signal the start and finish of recording the program with beeps. Then the cursor will reappear.)
3. Stop and rewind the tape. (The program, though saved on tape, remains in the Apple's memory.)

Appendix D

□ □ □ □ □ □ □ □ □ □ □

Applesoft Reserved Words

ABS	GR	NOT	SCRN(
AND	HCOLOR=	NOTRACE	SGN
ASC	HGR	ON	SHLOAD
AT	HGR2	ONERR	SIN
ATN	HIMEM:	OR	SPC(
CALL	HLIN	PDL	SPEED=
CHR$	HOME	PEEK	SQR
CLEAR	HPLOT	PLOT	STEP
COLOR=	HTAB	POKE	STOP
CONT	IF	POP	STORE
COS	IN#	POS	STR$
DATA	INPUT	PRINT	TAB(
DEF	INT	PR#	TAN
DEL	INVERSE	READ	TEXT
DIM	LEFT$	RECALL	THEN
DRAW	LEN	REM	TO
END	LET	RESTORE	TRACE
EXP	LIST	RESUME	USR
FLASH	LOAD	RETURN	VAL
FN	LOG	RIGHT$	VLIN
FOR	LOMEM:	RND	VTAB
FRE	MID$	ROT=	WAIT
GET	NEW	RUN	XPLOT
GOSUB	NEXT	SAVE	XDRAW
GOTO	NORMAL	SCALE=	

Appendix E

□ □ □ □ □ □ □ □ □ □ □ □ □ □

Editing Features

E.1. The Repeat key REPT

The repeat key REPT allows repetitive typing of the same key. Thus pressing REPT while holding down the A key allows you to type as many A's as you wish. It is especially useful in moving the cursor quickly.

E.2. Erasing and retyping

The backspace (←) key moves the cursor one space to the left on the current line and erases any character the cursor passes over.

The retype (→) key moves the cursor one space to the right on the current line and retypes any character the cursor passes over.

E.3. Deleting lines from a program

Use CTRL X to delete the line you are typing. When CTRL X is typed, a \ appears on the screen and the entire line is deleted from the program.

Use DEL to delete a sequence of lines from a program. For example, DEL 100,500 will delete all lines numbered from 100 through 500.

E.4. Clearing the screen

Use the HOME command to clear the text screen and move the cursor to the beginning of the first line.

E.5. Listing a program

Use CTRL S to interrupt the listing of a program; if you type it again, it will continue the listing. This feature is useful while making corrections to a long program.

E.6. Edit mode: The ESC key

In edit mode you can move the cursor in any direction without affecting the characters displayed on the screen. This feature allows you to make corrections to any line of your program. The keys I, J, K, and M positioned on the keyboard as follows:

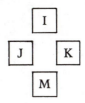

allow you to move the cursor up, left, right, and down, respectively. To make a correction using this feature, follow these steps:

1. List the line to be corrected (or the whole program if you prefer).
2. Press and release the ESC key to enter edit mode.
3. Press the I key as many times as necessary to position the cursor on the line to be corrected.
4. Press the J key until the cursor is over the *first* character on that line (the first digit in the line number).
5. Press the retype ($\rightarrow$) key until the cursor is over the first character to be corrected. (You are *retyping* the entire line, not merely changing individual characters.) Make the corrections. If the rest of the line is without error, use the retype key to the end of the line. Press the RETURN key to enter the corrected line in the Apple's memory.

Appendix F

□ □ □ □ □ □ □ □ □ □ □ □ □ □ □

Applesoft Commands

If a command is preceded by an *i*, it can only be used in immediate mode; if preceded by a *p*, it can only appear in an Applesoft program. Otherwise the following commands can be used in either mode of operation.

	Command	Purpose	Text reference
	COLOR =	To select one of 16 colors in low-resolution graphics	Section 17.1
	CONT	To resume execution (at the next instruction) of a program interrupted by STOP, END, or ctrl C	Section 5.3
i	ctrl C	To interrupt a running program or listing	Section 5.3
i	ctrl S	To interrupt and continue the listing of a program	Section E.5
i	ctrl X	To ignore the line currently being typed	Section E.3
p	DATA	To include input data as part of a program	Section 9.1
p	DEF FN	To define a function	Section 11.6
	DEL	To delete a sequence of lines from a program	Section E.3
	DIM	To specify dimensions for arrays	Sections 12.2, 12.6
	END	To terminate execution of a program	Section 3.5
	ESC	To enter edit mode	Section E.6
	FLASH	To display output on the screen alternately white on black and black on white	Section 7.5
	FOR	To initiate a FOR/NEXT loop	Sections 8.1, 8.5
	GET	To obtain a single input character from the keyboard	Section 17.2
	GOSUB	To transfer control to a subroutine	Section 15.1
	GOTO	To transfer control to a specified line	Section 5.3
	GR	To initiate low-resolution graphics	Section 17.1
	HCOLOR =	To select one of eight colors in high-resolution graphics	Section 17.5
	HGR	To initiate high-resolution graphics	Section 17.5
	HGR2	To initiate high-resolution full screen graphics	Section 17.5
	HLIN	To plot a horizontal line in low-resolution graphics	Section 17.1
	HOME	To clear the text window	Section 4.1
	HPLOT	To plot points and line segments in high-resolution graphics	Section 17.5
	HTAB	To position the cursor at a given position on the current text line	Section 7.5
	IF (as a transfer statement)	To transfer control to a specified line only if a specified condition is satisfied	Section 6.1
	IF (as a statement selector)	To execute a specified sequence of statements only if a specified condition is satisfied	Section 6.1
	INPUT	To obtain input data from the keyboard	Section 5.1
	INVERSE	To display output on the screen in black on white	

Command	Purpose	Text reference
IN#	To instruct the computer to take input from a device connected to the specified slot	Section B.1
LET	To evaluate an expression and assign its value to a variable	Section 3.5
LIST	To list an entire program or sequence of lines from a program	Section 4.2
LOAD	To read a program from cassette tape	Section C.1
NEW	To clear the current program from memory	Section 4.1
NEXT	To terminate a FOR/NEXT loop	Section 8.1
NORMAL	To cancel the effect of FLASH or INVERSE	Section 7.5
NOTRACE	To cancel the effect of TRACE	
p ON ••• GOSUB	To select one of several subroutines determined by the value of an expression	
p ON ••• GOTO	To transfer to one of several lines determined by the value of an expression	
p ONERR GOTO	To transfer to a specified line when a fatal error occurs	Section 14.1
PLOT	To plot a point in low-resolution graphics	Section 17.1
POKE	To store an integer value between 0 and 255 in a specified memory location	Section 17.2
PRINT	To transfer output to the video screen or printer	Sections 3.6, 5.3; Chapter 7
PR#	To direct output to a device connected to the specified slot	Section 4.7
READ	To obtain input data from DATA lines	Section 9.1
REM	To include comments in a program and to improve its readability	Section 3.7
RESTORE	To restore the data pointer to the first value in DATA lines	Section 9.3
RETURN	To return control from a subroutine	Section 15.1
RUN	To execute a program from the beginning or from the specified line number	Section 4.2
SAVE	To save a program on cassette tape	Section C.2
SPEED	To control the speed at which characters are sent to the screen or printer (0 is slowest; 255 is fastest)	
STOP	To terminate execution of a program	
TEXT	To return to text mode	Section 17.1
TRACE	To display the line number of each statement as it is executed (used for debugging)	
VLIN	To plot a vertical line in low-resolution graphics	Section 17.2
VTAB	To move the cursor to the specified line on the screen	Section 7.5

Appendix G

□ □ □ □ □ □ □ □ □ □ □ □ □ □

Answers to
Selected Problems

Section 1.3

1. F **2.** F **3.** T **4.** F **5.** F **6.** T
7. F **8.** F **9.** F **10.** F **11.** F

Section 2.3

1. 5% discount
2. Decide whether the discount is applicable.
3. 693.50
4. 250.00
5. 80.00 and 0, 128.00 and 0, 176.00 and 48.00, 206.00 and 78.00
6. $4
7. $6 per hour
8. Step (c) is used to determine if there is any overtime. G denotes gross pay. B denotes pay for overtime hours.
9. 21

10.
```
1     1
2     2
3     6
4    24
5   120
6   720
```
11. 55
12. 2,4,7,8,14,28,64
13. Variable names:

```
  NAME = name of an item
  COST = fixed cost for the item NAME
 PRICE = sale price for item NAME
   QTY = number of units of NAME sold
 GROSS = gross sales for item NAME
INCOME = income from item NAME
```

Algorithm:

    a. Print column headings as specified.
    b. Read NAME and values for COST, PRICE, and QTY, for one item.
    c. Assign the value of the product QTY × PRICE to GROSS.
    d. Multiply QTY times (PRICE − COST) to obtain a value for INCOME.
    e. Enter NAME and the values GROSS and INCOME under the appropriate column headings.
    f. Return to step (b) until the report is complete.

15. Variable names:

```
  CORP = corporation name
SHARES = number of shares
 PRICE = current price for one share
  EARN = earnings for one share
  EQTY = equity represented by all shares of corporation CORP
    PE = price/earnings ratio for one share
```

Algorithm:

    a. Print column headings as specified.
    b. Read CORP and values for SHARES, PRICE, and EARN.
    c. Assign the value of the product SHARES × PRICE to EQTY.
    d. Divide PRICE by EARN to obtain a value for PE.
    e. Enter CORP and the values SHARES, EARN, EQTY, and PE under the appropriate column headings.
    f. Return to step (b) until the report is complete.

17. a. Start with SUM = 0 and COUNT = 0.
    b. Add the number on the top card to SUM and add 1 to COUNT.
    c. Remove the top card and return to step (b) until all cards have been processed.
    d. Divide SUM by COUNT to obtain the average AV and proceed to step (e) with the original stack of cards in hand.
    e. If the number on the top card exceeds AV, write the letter G on the card; otherwise write the letter L.
    f. Remove the top card and return to step (e) until all cards have been examined.

18. a. Press the CLEAR key.
    b. Insert your ID card into reader as shown.
    c. Enter your four-digit code and press ENTER.
    d. Enter amount of check (2500 or 5000) and press ENTER.
    e. Place check in punch unit, blank side toward you.
    f. Remove check when READY light comes on.

Section 2.4

1. F   **2.** F   **3.** T   **4.** F   **5.** F   **6.** F   **7.** T

Section 3.4

1. a. 17   b. 33   c. −2   d. −6   e. −15   f. 9   g. 17   h. 9   i. 0.25
    j. −9   k. 64   l. −12.3   m. 12   n. 12300000   o. 0.00075   p. 4.5
    q. 3   r. 3

2. a. 3.5   b. 5   c. 0.75   d. 0.75   e. 10   f. 25   g. 4.5   h. 1.666667
    i. 10   j. 3   k. −8   l. −8

3. a. $*$ missing between $(Y + Z)$ and X.
    c. 7B is not admissible as an expression or variable name.
    e. OR is a reserved word.
    f. 2B is not admissible as an expression or variable name.
    g. 2X is not admissible as an expression or variable name.

4. a. $0.06*P$ b. $5*X+5*Y$ c. A^2+B^2 d. $6/(5*A)$
    e. $A/B+C/D$ f. $(A+B)/(C+D)$ g. $A*X^2+B*X+C$
    h. $(B^2-4*A*C)^0.5$ i. $(X^2+4*X*Y)/(X+2*Y)$

5. a. X+1+Y
   b. A^2-B^2
   c. A^3+A^2*B+A
   d. A*B/C
   e. A/B/C
   f. X^4+X^3*D+X^2*C+X*B+A
   g. P^Q^R
   h. 1/A/B/C/D

Section 3.9

1. a. 11Ø LET M=7
   b. 12Ø LET B=B+7
   c. 13Ø LET H=2*H
   d. 14Ø LET C2=(A-B)/2
   e. 15Ø LET A=(1+R)^1Ø
   f. 16Ø LET X=X-2*Y
   g. 17Ø LET C$="COST"
   h. 18Ø LET A$="DOE,JANE"
   i. 19Ø LET Q$=P$
   j. 2ØØ LET S$="*****"

2. a. 1Ø LET X=(A+B)*C
   b. correct
   c. 2Ø LET S=A+B
   d. 25 LET DEPT5=17
   e. correct
   f. 35 LET M5=2+7*M
   g. correct
   h. correct
   i. 5Ø LET Z=4*1Ø^2.5
   j. 55 LET AREA=LNGTH*WIDTH
   k. 6Ø LET SUM=SUM+NXT
   l. 65 LET D=FIRST-SECND
   m. 7Ø LET A$="SAMMY"
   n. correct
   o. correct
   p. 85 LET D$="DEPT#7"
   q. 9Ø LET M$="MONTHLY RENT"
   r. correct

3. a. 5 PRINT "SO-AND-SO"
   b. correct
   c. 15 PRINT CST$,CST
   d. 2Ø PRINT RTING
   e. correct
   f. correct
   g. 35 PRINT SCRE
   h. correct

4. a. 12
   b. AMOUNT=   1Ø8
   c. -2
   d. 5
   e. 2ØØ
      2ØØ
   f. LIST PRICE   45
      DISCOUNT   4.5
      SELLING PRICE   4Ø.5

   g. BOBBY LOVES
      MARY.

5. a.

	A	B	C
1Ø	1	2	1
2Ø	1	2	3
3Ø	4	2	3
4Ø	4	5	3
5Ø	4	20	2
6Ø	2	20	11
7Ø	2	20	11

b.

	N	Output
1Ø	1	1
2Ø	2	2
3Ø	6	6
4Ø	42	42
5Ø	42	

c.

	X	Y	Z	Output
100	0	0	0	
110	0	7	0	
120	0	7	7	
130	0	7	7	7
140	7	7	7	
150	7	343	7	
160	7	343	7	343
170	7	343	7	

6. a.

	S	A	Output
10	0	25	
20	25	25	25
30	50	25	50
40	25	25	25
50	25	25	

b.

	X	Y	Output
100	1.5	0	
110	1.5	0.6	
120	1.5	0.6	.6
130	−1.5	0.6	
140	−1.5	0.6	−1.5
150	−1.5	0.6	.6
160	−1.5	0.6	

c.

	N	C	S	G	P	Output	
10	130	0	0	0	0		
20	130	3	0	0	0		
30	130	3	3.6	0	0		
40	130	3	3.6	468	0	SALES	468
50	130	3	3.6	468	78	PROFIT	78
60	130	3	3.6	468	78		

d.

	A	P	Output		
100	0	0	NTH POWERS OF 7		
110	7	0			
120	7	7			
130	7	49			
140	7	49	FOR N = 2	49	
150	7	343			
160	7	343	FOR N = 3	343	
170	7	2401			
180	7	2401	FOR N = 4	2401	
190	7	2401			
200	7	2401			

Section 3.10

1. F   **2.** T   **3.** F   **4.** F   **5.** F   **6.** T   **7.** F   **8.** T   **9.** F
10. F   **11.** T   **12.** F   **13.** F   **14.** F   **15.** F

Section 4.9

1.
```
100 LET A = 14
110 LET B = 30
120 LET S = A + B
130 PRINT "SUM IS",S
140 END
```

Output: SUM IS   44

2.
```
100 LET X = 5
120 LET Y = 20
125 LET S = X + Y
130 PRINT "X+Y=",S
140 END
```

Output: X+Y=   25

3.
```
110 LET P = 120
120 LET D = 0.1 * P
130 LET C = P - D
140 PRINT "DISCOUNT",D
150 PRINT "COST",C
160 END
```

Output: DISCOUNT   12
        COST   108

4.
```
100 LET L$ = "AVERAGE"
110 LET A = 9
120 LET B = 7
130 LET M = (A + B) / 2
140 PRINT L$,M
150 END
```

Output: AVERAGE   8

5. Syntax: 30 LET D = 23000
Programming: 40 LET R = 0.06
Syntax: 50 LET A = R*D
Output: ANSWER IS   1380

6. Programming: 50 LET A=(N1+N2)/2
Syntax: 60 PRINT "AVERAGE IS",A
Output: AVERAGE IS   19.5

7. Programming:
20 T=5 : REM T= TAX RATE
30 P=120 : REM P=PRICE
Output: TOTAL COST: 126

8. Syntax and programming:
60 LET X= −B/A
Output:
SOLUTION IS   −6.28571

9. Programming: 165 LET T=A
                  18Ø LET B=T
   Output: A=   5
          B=   8
          A=   8
          B=   5
10. Syntax: quotes missing in lines 17Ø and 19Ø
    Programming: 185 LET T=V*R
    Output: TAX ON FIRST CAR IS   297
            TAX ON SECOND CAR IS   376.2

Section 4.10

1. T   **2.** F   **3.** F   **4.** T   **5.** T   **6.** F   **7.** T   **8.** F   **9.** T

Section 5.2

1.   12Ø LET A=1ØØ*(1.Ø6)^X   **3.**   12Ø LET A=X+Ø.Ø45*X
5.   12Ø LET A=X/19.2   **7.**   12Ø LET A=X/(52*4Ø)
9.   12Ø LET A=(4*X/3.14159)^Ø.5

Section 5.4

1. a.   Output: b.   Output: c.   Output: d.   Output:
              1   A B C   1 1   5
              1   B A C   2 2   -1
              2   C A B   3 6   4
              3   A C B   4 24   -2
              5   B C A   5 12Ø   3
              8   C B A   6 72Ø   -3
              •   •   •   •
              •   •   •   •
              •   •   •   •

2. a. 6Ø GOTO 4Ø   b. 4Ø LET D=B-A.
                                             Interchange lines 5Ø and 6Ø.
    c. 4Ø LET T=Ø.Ø8*X.   d. 5Ø LET R=N^(1/2)
       Change line number 5Ø to 25.   8Ø GOTO 5Ø

Section 5.5

1. T   **2.** F   **3.** F   **4.** T   **5.** F   **6.** F   **7.** F   **8.** T   **9.** F   **10.** T

Section 6.4

1. a. T   b. T   c. F   d. T   e. F   f. T   g. F   h. F   i. T   j. F
    k. F   l. F
2. a. $2 < Y < 4$ is not an admissible relational expression.
    b. The comma will cause a syntax error.
    c. The final letter A of ALPHA and the first letter T of THEN form the reserved word AT.
    d. If $A < B$, control is transferred to line 7Ø; infinite loop.
    e. Line 51 will be executed next whether or not $X < X - B$.
    f. Improper use of IF statement; THEN is missing.
3. a. Change line 6Ø to 6Ø IF N<=15 THEN 4Ø.
    b. Delete line 15Ø.
4. a. -1 b. 5   c. 14   d. 3   e. 52
                  1.75

5. a. 3Ø IF A>Ø THEN S=2Ø   b. 1Ø INPUT N
   Delete lines 40 and 50.   2Ø IF N>=5Ø THEN N=N/2
                                        3Ø IF N<25 THEN N=N/2
                                        4Ø PRINT N
                                        5Ø END

  c. 1Ø INPUT X,Y   d. 1Ø INPUT A,B
     2Ø IF (X<=Ø) OR (Y<=Ø) THEN 1Ø   2Ø IF A<=B THEN 6Ø
     3Ø LET S=X+Y   3Ø LET T=A
     4Ø PRINT S   4Ø LET A=B
     5Ø END   5Ø LET B=T
                                      6Ø PRINT "SMALLEST IS",A
                                    7Ø PRINT "LARGEST IS",B
                                    8Ø END

Section 6.11

1. T   **2.** T   **3.** F   **4.** F   **5.** T   **6.** T   **7.** F   **8.** T   **9.** F
10. T   **11.** T

Section 7.3

1. a. BASEBALL'S HALL OF FAME
     COOPERSTOWN, N.Y.   U.S.A.
  b. display screen:
```
Ø        5        1Ø
15       2Ø       25
3Ø       35       FINI
```

    80-column printer:
```
Ø        5        1Ø       15       2Ø
25       3Ø       35       FINI
```
  c. 5 TIMES 8 = 4Ø
  d. HAPPY
          HAPPY
                   HOLIDAY
  e. 1 3 5 7
     2 4 6 8
  f. IF A= 5 A+2= 7
     IF A= 1Ø A+2= 12
     IF A= 15 A+2= 17

2. a. 1Ø PRINT X;"/";Y;"=";X/Y   c. 3Ø PRINT "X - ";Y;" = ";-X
  e. 5Ø PRINT "DEPT.NO. ";Y+Y+X

3. a. 12Ø PRINT X;" ";   b. 12Ø PRINT 7;"A";
    145 PRINT
    15Ø PRINT X;" ";
    16Ø LET X=X+1

Section 7.6

1. a. 123456789Ø   b. 7777777
```
Ø                                      7
 -1                                    7
  -2                                   7
   -3                                  7
    -4                                 7
THAT'S ENOUGH                          7
```
  c. 123456789Ø   d. X   X^2
```
 *
  *                                    1          1
   *                                   2          4
    *                                  3          9
                                       4          16
```

2. a.   BASIC   (The first B displayed is in row 1, column 15.)
                    BASIC   BASIC
        BASIC   BASIC
   b. APPLE   (The first A displayed is in row 1, column 1.)
       APPLE
        APPLE
       APPLE
      APPLE
   c. H   H   (The first H displayed is in row 15, column 8.)
      H   H
      H   H
      HHHHH
      H   H
      H   H
      H   H
   d. The word GOOD is displayed successively 6 times on lines 10 through 15, each beginning in column 15. After all 6 GOOD's are displayed, the screen is cleared. A similar block of GRIEF's is then displayed on the same lines but beginning in column 20 and the screen is cleared again. This same sequence is repeated 500 times.

3. a. `1Ø PRINT TAB(6);"B";SPC(3);3`
   b. `2Ø PRINT X;SPC(15);2*X;SPC(15);3*X;SPC(15);4*X`
   c. `3Ø PRINT Ø;SPC(15);Ø;SPC(15);Ø;SPC(15);Ø;SPC(15);Ø;SPC(15);Ø`
   d. `4Ø PRINT TAB((8Ø-N)/2);"···name···"` where N = number of characters in *name*.

Section 7.7

1. F   **2.** F   **3.** T   **4.** F   **5.** T   **6.** T   **7.** F   **8.** T

Section 8.3

1. a. 4   b. 5   c. `TIMES THROUGH LOOP= 2`   d. +++///
      5   1   3
      6   -3
   e. `LOOP`   f. `LOOP`

2. a. Syntax error: `5Ø NEXT N`   b. Programming error: `25 LET C=Ø`
                                              Delete line 40.

   c. Programming error: d. Programming error:
      `4Ø INPUT Y`   Step S is admissible but the step value
      `5Ø LET S=S+Y`   cannot be changed within the loop.
      `65 PRINT "SUM IS",S`   `3Ø LET S=Ø`
                                           `4Ø FOR N=1 TO 5`
                                           `5Ø LET S=S+N`
                                           `6Ø PRINT S`

Section 8.5

1. a. 2   b. 13 16 11 14   c. 11111
      3   22222
      2   33333
      3
      2
      3
   d. 2   3   4   5   e. 1Ø8   f.   *
      3   4   5   ***
      4   5   *****
      5   ***
                                             *

2. a. Syntax error: interchange lines 5Ø and 6Ø
   b. Programming error: include STEP −1 in lines 2Ø and 3Ø
   c. Programming error: `2Ø FOR J=I+1 TO 4`; Delete Line 3Ø
   d. Programming error: interchange "X" and " " in lines 3Ø and 4Ø; insert 55 PRINT

Section 8.6

     1. F   **2.** T   **3.** F   **4.** T   **5.** F   **6.** T   **7.** F   **8.** T   **9.** F   **10.** T

Section 9.2

1. a. 4   b. 6   c. CATWOMAN   d. 7
    7   4   3
    1   18
                                          −5
                                          4

2. a. Change line 30 to 30 DATA 1,A.
    b. Replace ; in line 10 by ,.
    c. Replace HELLO in line 20 by "HELLO".
    d. Change line 50 to 50 DATA "DOOLEY,TOM".

3. a. 13Ø READ X   b. 13Ø READ A
       14Ø LET S=S+X   16Ø IF N<=4 THEN 13Ø
    c. 1Ø5 LET N=Ø   d. 16Ø IF X=999 THEN 19Ø
       1Ø7 LET S=Ø   17Ø LET S=S+X
       13Ø LET N=N+1   18Ø GOTO 14Ø
       15Ø GOTO 11Ø   19Ø PRINT S
                                      2ØØ GOTO 13Ø

Section 9.4

1. a. 9   b. 3   c. ROBINHEAD   d. 1Ø 2Ø 3Ø   e. ALLEN 4Ø
    3   5   1Ø 2Ø 3Ø   ALLEN 4Ø
    5   3
             5

Section 9.5

    1. T   **2.** F   **3.** F   **4.** F   **5.** T   **6.** T   **7.** F   **8.** F   **9.** T   **10.** T
11. F   **12.** T

Section 11.3

1. a. CYBER   b. Z TO A   c. CONSULTATION   d. BIOPHYSICS
2. a. 1Ø PRINT LEFT$(A$,1)
    b. 15 PRINT MID$(A$,2,1)
    c. 2Ø PRINT RIGHT$(A$,1)
    d. 25 PRINT LEFT$(A$,3)
    e. 3Ø PRINT RIGHT$(A$,3)
    f. 35 PRINT LEFT$(A$,1);RIGHT$(A$,LEN(A$))
    g. 4Ø IF LEN(A$)=LEN(B$) THEN 7Ø
    h. 45 IF LEFT$(A$,1)=RIGHT$(A$,1) THEN 95
    i. 5Ø IF LEFT$(A$,1)=MID$(A$,2,1) THEN 16Ø
    j. 55 LET T$=MID$(S$,2,1)+LEFT$(S$,1)+RIGHT$(S$,LEN(S$)-2)
    k. 6Ø LET F$=LEFT$(G$,3)+RIGHT$(H$,3)
    l. 65 IF LEFT$(A$,1)+MID$(B$,2,1)+MID$(C$,3,1)="YES" THEN 15Ø

Section 11.5

1. a. 9   b. 6   c. 18   d. 26   e. −43   f. 2.4   g. 1200   h. 4   i. 3
2. a. 4   b. 5   c. 6   d. −4   e. 2865   f. 2860   g. 2900   h. 3000
    i. 2864.714

3. a.
Ø	8
1	8
2	6
3	2
4	4

b.
1.1	1
1.21	1
1.331	1
1.4641	1

c. XX
XXXX
XX

d.
3
7
9
21

e. *
**
*****

f.
13.99	13.99
13.993	13.99
13.996	14
13.999	14

4. a. `1Ø IF ABS(A+B)=ABS(A)+ABS(B) THEN PRINT "EQUAL"`
c. `3Ø IF (INT(X)=X) AND (X>Ø) THEN 3ØØ`
e. `5Ø IF (INT(L/2)=L/2) AND (INT(L/25)=L/25) THEN PRINT`

5. b. `2Ø LET X=INT(1ØØØ*X+Ø.5)/1ØØØ`
d. `4Ø LET X=1ØØØ*INT(X/1ØØØ+Ø.5)`

Section 11.7

1. a. Programming error: `5Ø LET V=FN Z(X)`
b. Programming error: `2Ø DEF FN S(X)=X^2`
c. Syntax error: `2Ø DEF FN B(S)=2ØØ+Ø.Ø2*S` and `4Ø LET B=FN B(S)`
d. Programming error: change ADD2 to A2 and ADD5 to A5

2. a.
Ø	3
1	4
2	5
3	6

b.
5Ø
6Ø
7Ø
8Ø

3. a. `1Ø DEF FN F(C)=9/5*C+32`   b. `2Ø DEF FN C(F)=5/9*(F-32)`
c. `3Ø DEF FN M(F)=F/528Ø`   d. `4Ø DEF FN M(K)=K/1.6Ø93`
e. `5Ø DEF FN K(M)=1.6Ø93*M`   f. `6Ø DEF FN S(D)=D/T`
g. `7Ø DEF FN S(X)=X-Y/1ØØ*X`   h. `8Ø DEF FN C(X)=X/15*Y/1ØØ`
i. `9Ø DEF FN R(N)=INT(1ØØØ*N+Ø.5)/1ØØØ`
j. `1ØØ DEF FN A(R)=3.14159*R^2`   k. `11Ø DEF FN V(R)=4/3*3.14159*R^3`
l. `12Ø DEF FN S(A)=SIN(3.14159/18Ø*A)`

Section 11.8

1. F   **2.** F   **3.** T   **4.** F   **5.** T   **6.** T   **7.** T   **8.** F   **9.** F   **10.** F
11. T   **12.** F   **13.** T

Section 12.3

1. a. 5   b. 3 1 5   c. 8   d. 8   8
4   3   3

2. a. DIM statement needed.
b. Array A is redimensioned at line 3Ø after being implicitly dimensioned by line 1Ø.
c. Values of L(6) through L(10) are lost.
d. `425 LET L=A(1)`
`43Ø FOR J=2 TO N`
`44Ø IF L<A(J) THEN LET L=A(J)`

Section 12.7

1. a. 1   4   9   16   b. 246
   c. 1   1   2   d. 8   1
                          5
2. a. Interchange lines 220 and 230.
   b. 23Ø FOR J=I+1 TO 5

Section 12.8

1. T   **2.** F   **3.** F   **4.** F   **5.** F   **6.** F   **7.** T   **8.** F   **9.** F   **10.** F

Section 13.2

1. a. A   b. CAT   DOG   c. HARRY
      M   7   9   ALICE
                  BEAST   BEAST   LAST
                                             LAST

Section 13.4

1. a. ROBERT   b. ABSCAM   c. PAYCHECK,JOHN   d. SAM
      ALBERT   DENVER,JOHN   JESS
                                    JOHN,ELTON   SANDI
                                    CASH,JOHN

Section 13.6

1. a. 31+31=62
   b. E   5
   c. 7   7
   d. Ø123456789:
   e. 42 WINS AND 21 LOSSES GIVES A PERCENTAGE OF .667

Section 13.7

1. F   **2.** F   **3.** F   **4.** F   **5.** T   **6.** T   **7.** T   **8.** F

Section 14.2

1. a. SAM   b. JOAN   PASS   c. JOAN
      GREG   SAM   PASS   SAM
      MARY   GREG   FAIL   GREG
                     MARY   FAIL   MARY
                     MARK   PASS   MARK
                                            X

Section 14.7

1. F   **2.** F   **3.** F   **4.** T   **5.** T   **6.** F   **7.** F   **8.** T

Section 15.2

1. a. 4   2   16   b. 2   c. 1   d. 343
       3   −7   −5   2   3
                                    −2   6
                                    −2   1Ø

Section 15.3

1. T   2. F   3. F   4. F   5. F   6. F   7. T

Section 16.3

1. a. 20   b. 10   c. 30   d. 10
2. a. T   b. T   c. either   d. either (but most likely false)
   e. T   f. T

Section 16.6

1. a. 1Ø PRINT 4*RND(1)   b. 2Ø PRINT 6*RND(1)+5
   c. 3Ø PRINT 8*RND(1)−5   d. 4Ø PRINT INT(7*RND(1))+6
   e. 5Ø PRINT 2*INT(5*RND(1))   f. 6Ø PRINT 2*INT(5*RND(1))+1
2. a. 1, 2 (equally likely)   b. 0
   c. −2, −1, 0, 1, 2 (equally likely)   d. 2, 3, 4 (3 about half the time; 2 and 4 each
                                              about one-fourth the time)
   e. 2, 3, 4, . . ., 12 (not equally likely—simulates rolling a pair of dice)
   f. 1, 2, 3, 4, 6, 9 (not equally likely)

Section 16.10

1. T   2. F   3. T   4. F   5. F   6. F   7. F   8. F   9. T   10. F

Section 17.4

1. a. Triangle, vertices at (0,0), (0,10) and (10,10).
   b. Triangle, vertices at (10,0), (0,10) and (10,10).
   c. HI
   d. Four 4s, centered in the four quadrants.

Section 17.7

1. F   2. F   3. F   4. F   5. T   6. F   7. T   8. F   9. F

Index

To the owner of this book:

We'd like to know as much about your experiences with *BASIC: An Introduction to Computer Programming with the Apple* as you care to offer. Only through your comments and the comments of others can we learn how to make this book a better book for future readers.

1. Under what circumstances did you use this book?
   _____ As a student   _____ As an instructor
   _____ As a computer hobbyist   _____ Other

2. Approximately, how much of the book did you actually use?
   _____ 1/4 _____ 1/2 _____ 3/4 _____ All

3. What did you like most about the book?

4. What did you like least about the book?

5. Other comments:

6. Optional:

Name and address: _____

_____

_____

_____

School: _____

Date: _____

Sincerely,
Robert J. Bent
George C. Sethares

_____

FOLD HERE

CUT PAGE OUT

FOLD HERE